Testing
the
Waters

A Teen's Guide to
Career Exploration

by Alice N. Culbreath
and Saundra K. Neal

JRC Consulting, Jupiter, Florida

Testing the Waters
A Teen's Guide to Career Exploration

By Alice N. Culbreath and Saundra K. Neal

Published by:

JRC Consulting
6671 W. Indiantown Road, PMB-428
Jupiter, Florida 33458   U.S.A.

Copyright ©1999
by Alice N. Culbreath and Saundra K. Neal
First Printing 1999

Printed in the United States of America

Publisher's Cataloging-in-Publication

Culbreath, Alice N.
    Testing the waters : a teen's guide to career
exploration / by Alice N. Culbreath and Saundra K.
Neal. — 1st ed.
      p. cm.
      Includes bibliographical references and index.
      LCCN: 99-95344
      ISBN: 0-9672502-0-X

    1. Youth—Employment—Directories. 2. Summer
employment—Directories. 3. Internship programs—
Directories. 4. Voluntarism—Directories.
5. Camps—Directories.   I. Neal, Saundra K.
II. Title.

HD6270.C85 1999   331.7'02
            QBI99-1154

Table of Contents

ACKNOWLEDGEMENTS

This book would not have been possible without the help and encouragement of several key people. We would like to express our thanks to:

Bill Scheer of Resource Media Group who provided excellent advice, thoughtful critique, and invaluable encouragement during the development and writing of this book.

Our tireless editors, Jennifer Bakhshi, Sunny Roberts, Dale & Harriet Swartzmiller, Meg Wagner, Herb & Gloria Willcox, and Ollie Young. Without their attention to detail and constructive criticism, this book would not have achieved its current level of clarity and quality.

Our families without whose support this project would never have been undertaken. In particular, our husbands Garland Culbreath and Richard Neal who provided unwavering support, boundless enthusiasm, and uncompensated marketing for this book. Also, to Joseph and Wesley Culbreath and Gage and Jacob Neal, who provided the inspiration for this project — for they will one day be testing the waters themselves.

ABOUT THE AUTHORS

ALICE N. CULBREATH is the President of JRC Consulting, a grant consulting and freelance writing business. Formerly, she was the managing editor of Florida Funding Publications, publisher of *Your Guide to Florida Scholarships, The Complete Guide to Florida Foundations, A Guide to Florida State Programs,* and a monthly newsletter, *Florida Funding.* She has a degree in psychology with an emphasis in child development. Having served as the supervisor of several student interns, Ms. Culbreath knows first-hand the importance of early career preparation and exploration.

SAUNDRA K. NEAL has a degree in education and is a veteran teacher with eighteen years of experience. She has extensive experience working with students, parents, and the education system. As the parent of two grown children, Ms. Neal has real-life experience helping young adults explore career options and "test the waters."

COVER ART: The cover art was created specifically for JRC Consulting by Richard W. Neal. We thank him for his generosity and for sharing his gift.

INTRODUCTION

Youth employment in the United States is in crisis. According to *Business Week,* "While the rest of the economy picks up steam, youth job prospects are trailing badly — more than in any other recent recovery. Entry-level jobs are becoming more scarce even as the 16-24 year-old age group is increasing. The trend of company reorganization has resulted in the elimination of many jobs — an abundance of them entry-level. Furthermore, the increase in new technology is making entry-level work more skilled — requiring more highly-trained employees."

Job insecurity is becoming a defining characteristic of Generation X — the "baby busters" — youth age 15-29. This unsureness about the future is epidemic. An article in *The Economist* tells us that 75% of youth think that they will be worse off than their parents.

So what can teenagers do to prepare for the job market that they will face after graduation? According to labor secretary Robert Reich, there must be a concentration on the transition from school to work so that students can gain marketable skills. Currently, available resources overlook the 16-19 year-old age group. **Testing the Waters** is designed to help students utilize a variety of methods to gain these skills: internships, part-time work, volunteerism, entrepreneurship, educational programs, travel and adventures.

While making yourself marketable to poten-

In the past few years, many Americans have become convinced that a youth employment "crisis" is afoot. Economic recovery has done little to dissuade them. Jobs there may be, say parents and young workers alike, but not of a kind likely to lead to a stable career. Non-college graduates expect to earn little more than minimum wage. Even a college degree is no longer considered a degree of prosperity. A recent New York Times gave warning: "When college is not enough."

The Economist

"...THERE MUST BE A CONCENTRATION ON THE TRANSITION FROM SCHOOL TO WORK SO THAT STUDENTS CAN GAIN MARKETABLE SKILLS."

Former Labor Secretary
Robert Reich

tial employers is important, there is a more important goal of this book. It is always a challenge to find that special job — one that you really enjoy. Yes, it's true! Work can actually be enjoyable, but you have to find the right job for you.

Testing the Waters is designed to help you identify the ideal career now — before you need to pay the rent. Now is the safe time to explore a variety of options. You can even afford to work for free. The **most important thing to do before reading this book is to maintain an open mind**. Many of you may think you are sure of your future vocation. We urge you to try to forget any preconceived notions and contemplate areas of interest that you may never have considered previously.

One of the reasons that we wrote this book was to help you gain valuable insight into your future career path by testing the waters now. Another reason is to show you places where you can gain valuable experience to help you in achieving your career goals. As the research shows, education is not enough to secure a job or to get into the college of your choice. Employers and college recruiters want real-life experience. This book will show you how to get it.

In Chapter 1, we will explain how to use this book. We encourage you to review the chapter before proceeding on to the listings. We invite you to begin your career journey now by "testing the waters."

Alice N. Culbreath
Saundra K. Neal

TESTING THE WATERS

The teen years are an excellent time to start thinking about a potential career. It is the time to explore all of the different possibilities without pressure when there are no college majors to be chosen or mortgages to be paid. A commitment to a full-time job and lifetime career is not expected of you right now. It is possibly the best time to "test the waters."

How this Book is Organized

This book is designed to provide teenagers with five different ways of testing the waters:

- Volunteerism
- Entrepreneurship
- Educational Programs, Travel and Adventures
- Internships
- Part-time and Summer Jobs

Keep in mind that deciding which category to place a listing in is a tricky issue. What makes an unpaid internship different from a volunteer position? Is the opportunity to go to Italy, live with a family, and work on their farm while learning their language a part-time job or an educational travel and adventure opportunity? These decisions were sometimes difficult. Most of the time we relied on the organization to classify itself. If they did not provide the necessary information, an effort was made to include it in the most appropriate category. For this reason, please check out information for your field of interest in all five chapters.

Benefits of Career Exploration

In addition to providing valuable career exploration opportunities, the work and study programs included in this book provide important job-related experience. Employers want experienced personnel — even if they have a college degree. This book provides five different ways of obtaining the type of "hands-on" experience that employers and college recruiters look for in candidates.

We realize that one very important reason for teenagers to pursue job-related work prior to graduation is to earn money. This is an important consideration, but we encourage you to be open to other possibilities. There are many opportunities that may be open to you if you are willing to work for free, or for very little money, that might not be available in a paid position. Think about these types of work as an opportunity to get your foot in the door and to possibly secure a more lucrative position later on. Try to look beyond a paycheck to see what experience you will actually gain from a given work experience.

No matter what type of work you decide to pursue, use every opportunity to network with people in your field of interest. You never know when someone you have worked with in a previous position will provide a recommendation or networking opportunity for you when applying to the college of your choice, being hired full-time at a company, or attracting customers for your own business. Take every job seriously and make a good impression. Try never to burn any bridges.

How to Use This Book

We recommend that you look through the entire book and not focus immediately on their subject of interest. There are so many possibilities (over 1,200 listed here) for career exploration. We encourage you to keep an open mind and see what possibilities await them.

Once you are familiar with the book, you may wish to use the appendix to further narrow your choices. The programs listed in this book are indexed according to:

- Location
- Area of Interest
- Compensation/Cost
- Alphabetical Listing

The programs listed in this book are meant to give you a good overview of potential programs but are by no means meant to represent every possible opportunity. For this reason, each chapter will begin with information about where to go for more opportunities. Books, magazines, and websites will be included that will help you continue your search if none of the listings appeals to you.

It is our hope that "testing the waters" will be an exciting time for you. The experiences that you will have while pursuing any of these jobs, internships, volunteer positions, businesses, or educational programs will provide valuable lessons that you will take with you into whatever career you pursue. In fact, participating in any of these opportunities is something that will look good on college applications and job resumes in the years to come.

A Word of Caution

It would be impossible for us to have knowledge of the policies and practices of all of the organizations and programs listed in this guide. Before taking a position, joining an organization, or deciding to attend a program, ask your parents or a trusted adult to help you ensure the reputation of the organization.

Also, check with organizations such as the Chamber of Commerce, Better Business Bureau or your state's Division of Corporations or Department of Labor. It would also be a good idea to request information about fair business practices such as compensation, work hours, and taxes. Approach any new situation with caution and do not hesitate to seek advice and counsel from those who have experience in the workplace if any situation makes you uncomfortable.

Where to Go for More Information

In the back of this book, there are many resources listed that will help you with career exploration. You may use these resources for additional information about your particular interests. There are also organizations that you might be interested in joining or camps that you might wish to attend.

The whole idea of this book, and of the over 1,000 opportunities listed here, is to get you to consider the wide range of opportunities that are available to you. Your career is something that will impact the rest of your life. Unfortunately, there are too many people that have a job simply to pay the bills. They are not passionate about what they do. Why not have both? It is possible to find something that you love to do and to find a way to earn money doing it. It just takes creativity, diligence and a knowledge of all the options. Why not start searching now?

This book features five different ways to "test the waters", but the possibilities are endless. Here is a list of just some of the ways that you can try out different career opportunities while still in high school.

About the Data

The information in this book was collected from November 1998 through March 1999 through research and questionnaires. Although every effort has been made to ensure the accuracy of each entry, you should be aware that changes in the data may occur after the publication of the book. Please contact each of the programs directly for the most current information.

The authors and publisher do not make any claims concerning the policies or practices of any of the businesses or organizations contained in this book.

Let Us Hear From You

We would like to hear any suggestions that you might have concerning future editions of *Testing the Waters*. We are also interested in knowing about your career exploration and any advice you might have for other teenagers. You may use the Comment Form located in the back of the book or write to:

JRC Consulting
PMB-428
6671 West Indiantown Road
Jupiter, Florida 33458

"THERE MUST BE A CONCENTRATION ON THE TRANSITION FROM SCHOOL TO WORK SO THAT STUDENTS CAN GAIN MARKETABLE SKILLS."
FORMER LABOR SECRETARY
ROBERT REICH

101 WAYS TO TEST THE WATERS

1 Find a part-time job in a field that interests you.

2 Take part in an internship at a company in a field of interest.

3 Volunteer for an organization that works in an area of interest to you.

4 Start your own business and learn about entrepreneurship firsthand.

5 Take advantage of educational programs, travel and adventure opportunities.

6 Conduct informational interviews with professionals in your field of interest.

7 Read and study industry periodicals such as *Advertising Age, Nurse Practitioner, Accounting,* etc. in your field of interest.

8 Contact industry associations for information about your career choice — many offer brochures and general job information or descriptions.

9 Surf the net for websites related to your field of interest.

10 Ask your parents about their jobs.

11 Go to work with your parents to see what their workplace and jobs are really like.

12 Read want ads to get a feeling for job descriptions.

13 Observe professionals in their work environment. For instance, visit a court, classroom, or factory.

14 Purchase or borrow library books about your field of interest.

15 Observe classes at a local professional school (i.e. business, law, medicine, architecture).

16 Create a self-study program combining research, reading and other exploration with actual part-time employment in your field of interest.

17 Participate in extracurricular high school activities that provide valuable experience (i.e. Future Business Leaders of America, Junior Achievement).

18 Read a biography of a leader in your field of interest.

19 Complete a science fair project on a subject of interest to you.

20 Do a term paper on your field of interest.

21 Run for student government.

22 Work part-time (or for free) at the office of your parent, relative or family friend.

23 Attend a conference or convention in your field of interest.

24 Read the Wall Street Journal. It will provide you with valuable general business information, specific articles on your career interests, and interesting job listings.

25 Keep a journal of your career goals, wishes and information that you have collected.

26 Visit the websites of professional organizations that interest you.

27 Check your television listings for documentaries or programs related to your career of choice.

28 Rent videos or go to movies featuring characters (fictional/nonfiction) that work in your field.

29 Listen to news/talk radio for programs that relate to business or your field of interest.

30 Attend a camp focusing on your field (i.e. Spacecamp).

31 Check out the homepage of companies that you are interested in working for later.

32 Go to a chat room to participate, or listen to, discussions on topics relating to your career choice.

33 Take advantage of any travel opportunities. They widen your view and provide you with the opportunity to experience different cultures, meet diverse people, and possibly practice a second language.

34 Talk to your guidance counselor about your goals.

35 Read the newspaper daily.

36 Request catalogues and information now from colleges that interest you so that you can start working to fulfill their requirements.

37 Take any opportunity to work on your

public speaking skills.

38 Join teen organizations such as Junior Achievement (a more complete listing is included in the Appendix).

39 Take an aptitude test to see how your strengths and interests match particular careers.

40 Write a job description of the perfect job.

41 Get comfortable with using software that is utilized in your field of interest.

42 Try a "shadow day" when you "shadow" someone in your field of interest to see what they do during a typical day.

43 Participate in youth clubs and activities sponsored by organizations such as Girl/Boy Scouts, Civil Air Patrol, or 4-H.

44 Volunteer as a school assistant in areas such as the library or audio/visual center.

45 Read everything you can find relating to your field of interest.

46 Take course work at a local college or university prior to high school graduation.

47 Write a letter to a company that interests you and request an annual report.

48 Learn everything that you can about the educational requirements for your career field.

49 Visit colleges and universities before graduation.

50 Develop an alternate career plan. For instance, do not rely solely on being accepted to an Ivy League school. Develop several plans of action for achieving your goals.

51 Look at all of the different possibilities within your field of interest. For instance, just because you are interested in medicine does not mean you should necessarily become a doctor.

52 Get a book listing potential scholarships now so that you can work on meeting the requirements.

53 Learn now about money management.

54 Offer a "trade-off" by offering some service such as lawn mowing or baby-sitting in exchange for mentoring by someone in your field of interest.

55 Interview a wide-variety of people in your field of interest who hold positions at all different levels.

56 Take advantage of any leadership opportunity.

57 Open and manage your own checking account.

58 Prepare and live on a budget now.

59 Make a commitment to learning delayed gratification (i.e. making sacrifices now for your long-term happiness).

60 Make yourself a well-rounded person by becoming knowledgeable on a variety of topics.

61 Be open to changing your mind about career decisions.

62 Gain as much computer experience as possible.

63 Work on polishing your writing and communication skills.

64 Develop good listening skills.

65 Talk to your librarian and find out about other ways you can pursue information in your field.

66 Play an organized sport and learn the value of teamwork.

67 Develop selling skills — almost every job uses them in one way or another.

68 No matter what job or work you are currently doing, always take the initiative to volunteer for additional responsibilities.

69 Build your own knowledge and develop teaching skills by tutoring someone in your subject of interest.

70 Always ask questions and be curious in any situation.

71 Get in the habit now of taking control of your own life by organizing your room, managing your time wisely, and taking responsibility for your choices.

72 Develop hobbies that are related to your field of interest (i.e. build models if you are interested in engineering or architecture).

73 Organize your own volunteer group to address an issue of concern in your community.

74 Join a committee and learn about cooperation, problem solving and follow-through.

75   Take an aptitude test to identify possible areas of career interest.

76   If you are interested in history, literature, or drama, join a re-enactors group. Many cities re-enact historic events that occurred nearby.

77   If you are interested in politics and government, volunteer with your local congressman or representative.

78   Experiment with other career options to test your first choice. If you are interested in finance, take a part in the school play.

79   If your field of interest has foreign language requirements, take those languages now, consider a foreign exchange program, or plan a trip to practice your skills.

80   Do the "It Pays to Increase Your Word Power" in each month's *Reader's Digest* and build your vocabulary — an asset in any field.

81   Talk with your parents, a trusted adult, pastor, or rabbi about the ethical issues you may face in your chosen field.

82   Take the SAT's early (and often) and work to improve your score.

83   Visit museums, historic sites, and other places that will help you develop an understanding of the history of your field.

84   Use computer games or board games to test your skills and allow you to practice decision making and strategy.

85   Develop the habit of a quiet time for reflection when you think about your goals.

86   Each year, *Parade*, a publication within the Sunday newspaper gives yearly incomes for a variety of jobs. Review it to get a realistic idea of the type of income you can expect.

87   Ask a parent or other responsible adult to show you some credit card statements. Ask them to show you how to compute the interest charges and other fees. Once you are 18, everyone will offer you credit. Be careful.

88   If you plan on getting a credit card at 18, ask an adult to help you compare and choose the best one.

89   What do you dream of doing at 25, 35, 45, 55, 65 and beyond? Be realistic. Can you get there? How?

separate it from you seems impossible. If you are free-spirited, artistic, and love the outdoors, a desk job probably isn't for you.

91   Organize a club or event. Develop your leadership and organizational skills.

92   Teach someone something — how to roller blade, play a computer game, or balance equations — to see how strong your communication and teaching skills are.

93   Go to your local Chamber of Commerce to see how they can help you explore different businesses or careers.

94   If you are very interested in a particular company that does not have part-time jobs or internships, offer to work for free.

95   Consider being a foreign exchange student.

96   If your parents are open to the idea, investigate hosting a foreign exchange student.

97   If you are interested in working abroad, find a pen pal and get to know what day-to-day life in that country is really like. It's also a great way to practice foreign language skills.

98   Become a reporter or writer for your school's paper or yearbook.

99   Pick a cause and do something. Write to your congressman. Join an organization. Follow your interest in the paper. Get involved.

100   Talk to a retiree in your field of interest. They have more time available and have years of experience in your field.

101   If you can't find the kind of career exploration experience you are looking for, keep looking. Be persistent. There are endless ways to "test the waters."

NOTES

VOLUNTEERISM

Volunteerism is a great way to explore interesting careers while giving back to your community. You can volunteer close to home or almost anywhere around the world. Volunteerism is a great place to start your exploration because age is not a barrier — most organizations are open to volunteers of almost any age.

The following list contains volunteer positions available around the United States. There might be one or two in your community. This list is by no means comprehensive. It is simply meant to give you an idea of the types of opportunities out there. If something interests you, but is not in your community, consider contacting similar nonprofit organizations in your community to see about volunteering with their organization. You might want to contact:

- Organizations for seniors;
- Hospitals;
- Churches/Synagogues;
- Libraries;
- Schools;
- Shut-ins or handicapped persons;
- Other nonprofit agencies;
- Your state's volunteer agency (see the list at the end of this chapter).

Another good place to locate volunteer positions is the internet. Below are some interesting websites that you might want to visit.

- **http://www.ala.org/teenhoopla/activism.html** - Provides links to other websites regarding teen activism.
- **http://www.americaspromise.com/** - America's Promise website includes information, updates, and tips for starting your own volunteer project and participating in this nationwide volunteer movement.
- **http://www.bygpub.com** - A free on-line book, *20 Ways for Teenagers to Help Other People by Volunteering.*
- **http://www.collegeboard.org/features/home/html/involved.html** - Provides links to other websites providing teen volunteer opportunities.
- **http://www.earthsystems.org/ways/** - An online book, *54 Ways to Help the Homeless*
- **http://www.gospelcom.net/cci/ajobs/volunteer.shtml.** - This site provides information on volunteering at Christian camps and conferences.
- **http://www.idealist.org** - This is a great website that matches volunteers with 14,000 nonprofit organizations around the world. You just choose the category, country, city, state, zip, age, skills, language, gender, and when you would like to volunteer. The search then provides you with a listing of agencies that match.
- **http://www.impactonline.org/** - This is a free service that matches volunteers to organizations. You enter your zip code, how far you are willing to drive, when you can start, and the category that you are interested in, and it will provide a listing of agencies.
- **http://www.interaction.org** - This site provides information about a guide for finding volunteer work. It provides a link to the Global Work website.
- **http://www.mightymedia.com/youth/** - The Youth in Action Network is a free interactive on-line service for youth, educators, organization members and classrooms wanting to learn more about and participate in social action and service projects.
- **http://www.ngws.org/service/groups/aeowd.htm** – Amazing Environmental Organization Web Directory featuring sites from over 100 countries.
- **http://www.oprah.com/angelnet/angels6.html** - Updates and information about taking part in Oprah's nationwide volunteer initiative - the Angel Network.
- **http://www.project.org/** - The Project America site lists organizations needing volunteers, provides information on how you can organize a volunteer project in your community, and provides resources for community service.
- **http://www.talkcity.com/theinsite/** - A website providing links to other websites featuring organizations that help the environment.
- **http://www.voa.org/pubs/** - The Volunteers of America website features a variety of information on volunteerism as well as information about their two magazines, *Spirit* and *The Gazette.*.
- **http://www.volunteermatch.org** – Search thousands of volunteer opportunities by zip code, category, and dates available.
- **http://www.wilderness.org** – Environmental website with lots of information for youth about ways to get involved.
- **Http://www.ywam.org** – Website of *Youth with a Mission*. This organization publishes the *Go Manual* providing information about international mission opportunities.

Following is a list of websites for some popular and well-known nonprofit organizations. Contact them for information about volunteer opportunities in your area.

National Organization Website

- **American Cancer Society** – http://www.cancer. org
- **AmeriCorps** – http://www.americorps.org
- **American Red Cross** -http://www.redcross.org
- **Amnesty International**- http://www.amnesty. org/
- **ASPCA** - http://www.aspca.org
- **Camp Ronald McDonald**- http://www. campronald.org/
- **CityKids Foundation**- http://www.citykids.com/
- **The Conservation Fund** – http://www. conservationfund.org/ conservation/
- **Greenpeace** - http://www.greenpeace.org/
- **Habitat for Humanity**- http://www.habitat.org/
- **Homes for the Homeless**- http://www.opendoor. com/hfh/
- **The Junior State of America**- http://www.jsa. org
- **National 4-H Council**- http://www.4h-usa.org
- **Rainforest Action Network**- http://www.ran. org/ran/
- **Reading is Fundamental** – http://www.rif.edu
- **Special Olympics International** – http://www. specialolympics.org/
- **United Way** – http://www.unitedway.org
- **Youth Crime Watch** - http://www.ncpc.org

The following listing provides you with information about nonprofit organizations needing volunteers throughout the United States and worldwide. The U.S. organizations are included under the categories of

- art/history/culture
- health
- human services/education
- international
- nature/environment
- research/science
- other

All of the international opportunities, regardless of category, are listed in the international category. Each entry includes the *project location* which tells you where the volunteers actually work. It provides a *description* of the work needed. It includes a description of the *positions available*. Any *cost/compensation* associated with the project is

listed. Also, information about where you can write, call or e-mail *for more information* is included.

Enjoy exploring the exciting world of volunteerism. Remember, if you do not find what you are looking for, visit the websites listed above or contact your state volunteer agency listed at the end of the chapter.

ART/HISTORY/CULTURE

ARCHIVE OF FOLK CULTURE, AMERICAN FOLKLIFE CENTER, LIBRARY OF CONGRESS
Washington, DC
Project Location: Washington, DC
Description: National archive of folk music, ethnomusicology, and folklore.
Open to: High school seniors and graduates.
Cost/Compensation: Unpaid
For more information: Joseph C. Hickerson, Head, Archive of Folk Culture, American Folklife Center, Library of Congress, Washington, DC 20540-4610; (202)707-1725.

ASSOCIATION OF HISPANIC ARTS (AHA)
New York, New York
Project Location: New York
Description: Nonprofit organization promoting Latino artists and arts organizations.
Open to: High school students.
Positions Available: Clerical Assistants.
Cost/Compensation: Unpaid
For more information: Association of Hispanic Arts, 260 West 26 Street, New York, NY 10001; (212)727-7227; (212)727-0549 (fax); URL http://www. latinoarts.org.

CAT'S CAP – ST. CATHERINE'S CREATIVE ARTS PROGRAM
Richmond, Virginia
Project Location: Richmond, Virginia
Description: Creative arts day camp for grades 2-8. Also preschool children, ages 3½-7 years.
Open to: High school students.
Positions Available: Volunteers (14+ years), junior counselors (high school), and senior counselors (college). Six week summer camp program.
Cost/Compensation: $0-$7.00/hour.
For more information: Jan Holland, Director, Cat's CAP – St. Catherine's Creative Arts Program, 6001 Grove Avenue, Richmond, Virginia 23226; (804)288-2804 Ext. 45; E-mail jholland@st.catherines.org; URL http://www.st.catherines.org.

CULTURAL HERITAGE COUNCIL
Middletown, California

FOCUS ON...
JUSTACT

JustAct believes that young people are essential to the success of efforts to build strong, equitable, and sustainable societies worldwide. JustAct links students to organizations working for sustainable and self-reliant communities around the world.

www.justact.org

Several programs for teens are available:

- Education Program – providing support for student groups and activists on campuses around the country.
- International Opportunities Program – a clearinghouse linking students to volunteer organizations which send volunteers overseas.
- Bike-Aid Program – an annual cross-country bike ride to raise awareness of global issues and raise funding for JustAct supported programs.
- Partnerships – JustAct works with organizations around the world to provide support and develop person-to-person relationships between students and participants in JustAct programs.
- Internships – a variety of internships are available at JustAct's San Francisco office.

Project Location: Clear Lake Basin - Northern California.
Description: Archeological excavation.
Cost: Transportation cost and tuition fees.
For more information: Cultural Heritage Council, P.O. Box 808, Middletown, California 95461; (707)987-9157.

ELIZABETH DOW LTD.
New York, New York
Project Location: New York
Description: Paint and design studio.
Open to: High school students, graduates, or anyone interested in experience.
Positions Available: Product production, office management, interoffice communications, and sampling.
Cost/Compensation: Unpaid
Other Information: For more information call for an interview.
For more information: Xavier Santana, Internship Coordinator, Elizabeth Dow Ltd., 155 Avenue of the Americas, 4th Floor, New York, New York 10013; (212)463-0144; (212)463-0824 (fax).

HERE
New York, New York
Project Location: New York, New York
Description: Arts Center, theatres, puppetry, galleries, and café.
Open to: High school juniors, seniors, and graduates.
Positions Available: One-on-one apprenticeships with established theater and visual artists. Very rewarding opportunity.
Cost/Compensation: Unpaid (possible travel reimbursement).
For more information: Barbara Basackind, HERE, 145 Avenue of the Americas, New York, New York 10013; (212)647-0202 Ext. 307.

J.E. JASEN
New York, New York
Project Location: New York, New York
Description: Studio that creates enamel art objects.
Open to: High school students and graduates.
Cost/Compensation: Unpaid
For more information: June Jasen, J.E. Jasen Studio, 36 East Tenth Street, New York, New York 10003-

6219; (212)674-6113; (212)777-6371 (fax).

KANSAS ARCHEOLOGY TRAINING PROGRAM FIELD SCHOOL
Topeka, Kansas
Project Location: Kansas
Description: Archaeological excavations of prehistoric and historical sites.
Cost: All transportation, room, board and $22.00 membership fee.
For more information: Kansas Archeology Training Program Field School, 6425 SW 6th Avenue, Topeka, Kansas 66615-1099; (785)272-8681 Ext. 268; URL http://history.cc.ukans.edu/heritage/kshs/resource/katp.htm.

KTEH-TV
San Jose, California
Project Location: San Jose, California
Description: Public television station.
Open to: High school students and college students.
Positions Available: Camera, production assistant, PR assistant, and outreach assistant.
Cost/Compensation: Unpaid
For more information: Personnel Manager, KTEH-TV, 1585 Shallenberger Road, San Jose, California 95131; (408)795-5400; (408)995-5446 (fax); URL http://www.kteh.pbs.org.

MARYLAND ART PLACE
Baltimore, Maryland
Project Location: Baltimore, Maryland
Description: Nonprofit regional art center.
Open to: High school seniors and graduates interested in art.
Positions Available: Internships and volunteer opportunities.
Cost/Compensation: Unpaid
Other information: Houses the Maryland State Arts Council Artist Slide Registry.
For more information: Program Director, Maryland Art Place, 218 West Saratoga Street, Baltimore, Maryland 21201; (410)962-8565; (410)244-8017 (fax); E-mail map@charm.net; URL http://www.MDartplace.org.

NEW STAGE THEATRE
Jackson, Mississippi
Project Location: Jackson, Mississippi
Description: Professional nonprofit theater.
Open to: High school students and graduates.
Cost/Compensation: Paid and unpaid.
For more information: Education/Internship Coordinator, New Stage Theatre, 1100 Carlisle Street, Jackson, Mississippi 39202; (601)948-3533; (601)948-3538 (fax).

OPERA COMPANY OF PHILADELPHIA
Philadelphia, Pennsylvania
Project Location: Philadelphia, Pennsylvania
Description: Performing Grant Opera at the Academy of Music.
Open to: High school seniors and graduates.
Positions Available: Administrative internships – marketing, public relations, development, etc.
Cost/Compensation: Unpaid.
For more information: Tracy C. Galligher, Publicist, Opera Company of Philadelphia, 510 Walnut Street, Suite 1500, Philadelphia, Pennsylvania 19106; (215) 928-2100; (215)928-2112 (fax); E-mail galligher@operaphilly.com; URL http://www.operaphilly.com.

SOUTH STREET SEAPORT MUSEUM
New York, New York
Project Location: New York
Description: Maritime history museum.
Open to: High school students, college students, and graduate students.
Positions Available: Archeology, design, education, maritime crafts, membership, printing and stationers shop, publications/web site, tour marketing, collections management, development (fundraising), library, marketing/special events, museum store, public affairs, ship maintenance/restoration, and volunteer administration.
Cost/Compensation: Unpaid
For more information: Patricia Sands, Director of Volunteer Programs, South Street Seaport Museum, 207 Front Street, New York, New York 11771; (212)748-8727; (212)748-8610 (fax); URL http://www.southstseaport.org.

UCR/CALIFORNIA MUSEUM OF PHOTOGRAPHY
Riverside, California
Project Location: Riverside, California
Description: Nonprofit photography museum.
Open to: High school juniors and seniors.
Positions Available: Write for more information.
Cost/Compensation: Unpaid
For more information: Internship Coordinator, UCR/California Museum of Photography, 3824 Main Street, Riverside, California 92501; (909)787-4787; (909)787-4797 (fax); URL http://www.cmp.ucr.edu.

U.S. HOLOCAUST MEMORIAL MUSEUM
Washington, D.C.
Project Location: Washington, D.C.
Description: Museum dedicated to the history of the Holocaust.
Open to: High school students and graduates.
Positions Available: Internships in the areas of holocaust research and museum studies. Volunteers in the positions of museum representatives, special events

associates, and behind-the-scenes positions.

Cost/Compensation: Paid and unpaid positions available.

For more information: Jill W. Greenstein, Manager of Volunteer and Intern Services, U.S. Holocaust Memorial Museum, 100 Raoul Wallenberg Place, SW, Washington, DC 20024-2150; (202)488-0400; (202) 488-2690 (fax); URL http://www.ushmm.org.

Interested in learning more about spending the summer as an archaeologist? You might want to consult Bill McMillon's book, *The Archaeology Handbook.* It includes information about unique archaeology opportunities, each with a special mixture of education, atmosphere, and excavations. For more information, write to:

- | **The Archaeology Handbook**
Archaeologist Institute of America
15 Park Row
New York, New York 10038 |

HEALTH

AMERICAN CANCER SOCIETY
Cheshire, Connecticut
Project Location: Meriden, Cheshire, Durham, and Middlefield, Connecticut
Description: Need volunteers to help in accounting department.
For more information: American Cancer Society, 14 Village Lane, Cheshire, Connecticut 06410; (203)265-7161; E-mail wquinn@cancer.org; URL http://www.cancer.org.

ARIZONA PIONEERS' HOME VOLUNTEERS ASSOCIATION
Prescott, Arizona
Project Location: Prescott
Description: Virtual volunteers work on research for funding, media contacts, and the web site.
For more information: Jeanine Dick, Superintendent, Arizona Pioneers' Home Volunteers Association, 300 S. McCormick, Prescott, Arizona 86303; (520)445-2181; E-mail azpiom@aztec.asu.edu; URL http://aztec.asu.edu/azph.

BELLEVUE HOSPITAL CENTER
New York, New York
Project Location: New York
Description: Municipal hospital.
Open to: Students 16 years and older.
Positions Available: Emergency, nursing, clinics, and interpreters.

Other information: Interpreters needed for Spanish, Chinese, French, Polish, etc. Training will be provided.

For more information: Priscilla A. Daniels, Director of Volunteer Services, Bellevue Hospital Center, First Avenue at 27th Street, Room AG 25, New York, New York 10016; (212)562-4858.

BERKELEY COMMUNITY HEALTH PROJECT
Berkeley, California
Project Location: Berkeley
Description: Volunteer, collectively-managed free clinic.
Open to: Anyone with time to commit to the Berkeley Free Clinic.
Positions available: Volunteer opportunities (training provided) in medical, dental, peer counseling, information resource providing, HIV counseling, phlebotomy, STD screening, and lab.
Cost: None.
For more information: Kwan Chun, Volunteer, Berkeley Free Clinic, 2339 Durant Avenue, Berkeley, California 94704; (510)548-2570; (510)548-1730 (fax); E-mail bfc@lanminds.com; URL http://users.landminds.com/~bfc.

CANCER KIDS
Waxahachie, Texas
Project Location: Waxahachie
Description: Volunteers needed for web page design.
For more information: Paul O'Rear, Cancer Kids, 201 Cumberland, Waxahachie, Texas 75165; (972) 937-0937; E-mail paulorear@cancerkids.org; URL http://www.cancerkids.org.

CHRYSALIS: A CENTER FOR WOMEN
Minneapolis, Minnesota
Project Location: Minneapolis, Minnesota
Description: Multi-service center for women offering support services in mental health, chemical dependency, legal assistance, and parenting services.
Open to: Students ages 16-18 and high school graduates.
Cost/Compensation: Unpaid.
For more information: Tiffany Muller, Volunteer Coordinator, Chrysalis: A Center for Women, 2650 Nicollet Avenue South, Minneapolis, Minnesota 55408-1662; (612)871-0118; (612)870-2403 (fax); E-mail tmuller@chrysaliswomen.org; URL http://chrysaliswomen.org.

COLUMBIA PRESBYTERIAN MEDICAL CENTER IN NEW YORK CITY
New York, New York
Project Location: New York
Description: Volunteers needed in the areas of web

page design, public relations, public speaking, special events planning, tutoring and typing.

For more information: Andres Nieto, Columbia Presbyterian Medical Center, 622 West 168 Street, New York, New York 10032; (212)305-2542; E-mail nietoan@cpmc3.cis.columbia.edu; URL http://cpmcnet/dept/ph/volunteer/.

COMMUNITY HOSPICE
Crookston, Minnesota
Project Location: Crookston
Description: Assistance needed with mailings, fundraising, public relations, and patient services.
For more information: Rhonda McKay, RN, CRNH, Community Hospice, 323 S. Minnesota, Crookston, Minnesota 56716; (218)281-9449;
E-mail mckay@riverviewhealth.org.

DINNER BELL
Bakersfield, California
Project Location: Bakersfield
Description: Volunteers needed to deliver hot meals to people with AIDS.
For more information: Susan Reep, Dinner Bell, P.O. Box 2824, Bakersfield, California 93303; (805)633-1232; E-mail aids@bakersfield.org; URL http://www.bakersfield.org/aids/.

HARRIS COUNTY PUBLIC HEALTH AND ENVIRONMENTAL SERVICES
Houston, Texas
Project Location: Pasadena, Baytown, LaPorte, Humble, and Houston, Texas.
Description: Volunteers work in clinics, animal control, pollution control, mosquito control, and administration. Bilingual Spanish/English is helpful.
For more information: Ms. Lyndall Maxwell, Harris County Public Health and Environmental Services, 2223 W. Loop S., Houston, Texas 77027; (713)439-6000; E-mail lmaxwell@hd.co.harris.tx.us.

HEALTHSYSTEM MINNESOTA
St. Louis Park, Minnesota
Project Location: St. Louis Park
Description: An integrated health care network with volunteer opportunities at our hospital and clinics.
Open to: Teens 14 and older.
Positions available: Wide-variety. Contact for complete listing.
For more information: Mike Zielinski, Director, Volunteer Services, HealthSystem Minnesota, 6500 Excelsior Boulevard, St. Louis Park, Minnesota 55426; (612)993-5086; (612)993-6355 (fax);
E-mail 79740@hsmnet.com; URL http://www.healthsystemminnesota.com.

FOCUS ON...
SPECIAL OLYMPICS

> *Special Olympics provides year-round training and athletic competition for children and adults with mental retardation. One million athletes participate annually in over 15,000 competitions. More than 500,000 volunteers are needed for this program worldwide.*

"Let me win, but if I cannot win, let me be brave in the attempt."
- Olympic motto

Volunteers are needed in all 50 states, Washington DC, and four U.S. territories. To find out how you can help, visit the website at:

www.specialolympics.org

HOSPITALITY PROGRAM OF BOSTON
Boston, Massachusetts
Project Location: Boston
Description: Need volunteers for duties such as placement coordinator, grant writer, office assistant, communications intern, and fund-raising intern.
For more information: Hospitality Program of Boston, 138 Tremont Street, Boston, Massachusetts 02111; (617)482-4338; E-mail hospprog@tiac.net; URL http://www.tiac.net/users/hospprog.

JUVENILE DIABETES FOUNDATION OF CENTRAL PENNSYLVANIA
Camp Hill, Pennsylvania
Project Location: Camp Hill
Description: Volunteers perform clerical, special events planning, and typing work.
For more information: Kristine Werley, Juvenile Diabetes Foundation, 1104 Fernwood Avenue, Suite 500, Camp Hill, Pennsylvania 17011; E-mail cpajdf@pa.net; URL http://www.pa.net/jdf.

KIDS 'N BITS THERAPEUTIC RIDING PROGRAM, INC.
Teays, West Virginia
Project Location: Between Teays Valley and Winfield, WV.
Description: Provide therapeutic horseback riding to challenged children.
Open to: Students age 14 years and older.
Positions available: Leader and side walker.
Cost: None.
For more information: Leslie Perry, Secretary, Kids 'n Bits Therapeutic Riding Program, P.O. Box 213, Teays, West Virginia 25569-0213; (304)760-2356; (304)727-0112 (fax);
E-mail kidsbits@wvinter.net; URL http://www.wvinter.net/~perryle.

MONTGOMERY CITY COMMUNITY PARTNERSHIP
Rockville, Maryland
Project Location: Rockville
Description: Need volunteers in the areas of fundraising, public relations, public speaking, and special events planning.
For more information: Doug Tipperman, Montgomery County Community Partnership, 4915 Aspen Hill Road, Suite 7, Rockville, Maryland 20853-3700; (301) 929-8550;
E-mail dtipperman@aol.com; URL http://members.aol.com/MCPartners.

MONTROSE CLINIC
Houston, Texas
Project Location: Houston
Description: Volunteers needed for web page design, medical services, and public speaking.
For more information: Thad McLemore, Montrose Clinic, P.O. Box 66308, 215 Westheimer, Houston, Texas 77266; (713)520-2000;
E-mail montrose@montrose-clinic.org; URL http://www.montrose-clinic.org.

NORTH FLORIDA RACE FOR THE CURE
Jacksonville Beach, Florida
Project Location: Jacksonville Beach.
Description: Need volunteers to send letters, set up events, call volunteers, assist as kickoff event helpers, and race helpers.
For more information: Pati Merrill, Race for the Cure, 1021 Penman Road, Neptune Beach, Florida 32266; (904)241-3156; E-mail Patimer@aol.com.

RONALD MCDONALD HOUSE CHARITIES OF ROCHESTER, NY
Rochester, New York
Project Location: Rochester
Description: Volunteers clean and prepare rooms and provide emotional support for families of children receiving medical care.
For more information: Cer Niedermaier, Ronald McDonald House Charities, 333 Westmoreland Drive, Rochester, New York 14620; (716)442-5437; E-mail RochRMH@aol.com; URL http://rochester.hq.net/ronaldmcdonaldhouse.

SAN FRANCISCO CLINIC CONSORTIUM
San Francisco, California
Project Location: San Francisco
Description: Need volunteers for administrative, development, medical care, outreach, program planning, and computer processing, programming, and training.
For more information: Ruby Gin, San Francisco Clinic Consortium, 501 Second Street, Suite 120, San Francisco, California 94107; (415)243-3400 Ext. 29; E-mail rgin@sfccc.org; URL http://www.sfccc.org/index1.htm

WHITMAN-WALKER CLINIC, INC.
Washington, D.C.
Project Location: Washington, D.C.
Description: Multiple volunteer opportunities.
For more information: James R. Millner II, Whitman-Walker Clinic, Inc., 1407 S Street, NW, Washington, DC 20009; (202)797-3500; E-mail JRMillner@aol.com.

HUMAN SERVICES/ EDUCATION

ACTION (USA)
Washington, D.C.
Project Location: Nationwide

Description: Works in cooperation with the Student Community Service Program.
For more information: ACTION (USA), 1100 Vermont Avenue, NW, Washington, DC 20525.

AMERICAN RED CROSS
Washington, D.C.
Project Location: U.S., its territories, and field stations on U.S. military installations.
Description: Provides relief to victims of disasters, assists in getting ready for emergencies and helps with medical facilities.
For more information: American Red Cross, National Headquarters, 430 17th Street, NW, Washington, DC 20006; (202)737-8300.

AMERICAN LITERACY COUNCIL
New York, New York
Project Location: Throughout the U.S. (computer and tutoring programs).
Description: Organization trying to improve literacy by using computer techniques.
For more information: American Literacy Council, 454 Riverside Drive, New York, NY 10027; (212) 662-0654 or contact Literacy Center Hotline to find a literacy program near you; (800)228-8813.

AMERICANS FOR DEMOCRATIC ACTION
Washington, D.C.
Project Location: Washington, D.C.
Description: ADA does lobbying on a variety of issues at the local, state, and national levels.
Open to: All.
Cost/Compensation: Unpaid
For more information: Valerie Dulk-Jacobs, Special Assistant to the Director, Americans for Democratic Action, 1625 K Street, NW, Suite 210, Washington, DC 20006; (202)785-5980; (202)785-5969 (fax); E-mail adaction@ix.netcom.com; URL http://www.adaction.org.

AMNESTY INTERNATIONAL USA - CHICAGO
Chicago, Illinois
Project Location: Great Lakes, Illinois
Description: Group working to get prisoners of conscience released, working to get political prisoners a fair trial, no torture and no executions.
For more information: Amnesty International, Intern Coordinator, 53 W. Jackson Boulevard, Suite 1162, Chicago, Illinois 60604-3606; (312)427-2060; E-mail aivaamwro@igc.apc.org.

BIG BROTHERS/BIG SISTERS OF ROCK, WALWORTH, AND JEFFERSON COUNTIES
Beloit, Wisconsin
Project Location: Wisconsin
Description: Mentoring agency that matches adults who serve as role models to kids from single parent homes.
Open to: High school juniors or seniors and adults 18 and older.
Positions Available: Teen volunteers, secretary/office help, and intern.
Cost/Compensation: Unpaid
For more information: Nancy Mignon, Executive Director, Big Brothers/Big Sisters of Rock, Walworth, and Jefferson Counties, 1400 Huebbe Parkway, Beloit, Wisconsin 53511; (608)362-8223; (608)362-5835 (fax).

BOOK IT! PIZZA HUT, INC.
Wichita, Kansas
Project Location: Schools throughout the United States.
Description: Reading excitement program for children kindergarten through sixth grade. Teens may be able to help begin and monitor the program.
For more information: Book It! Pizza Hut, Inc., P.O. Box 2999, Wichita, Kansas 67201; (800)4-BOOK-IT.

BOYS AND GIRLS CLUB OF TAMPA BAY, INC.
Tampa, Florida
Project Location: Tampa, Florida
Description: Youth development agency.
Open to: High school students, college students, and graduates.
Positions Available: Program assistants, youth leaders, and interns.
Cost/Compensation: Varies
For more information: Lisbeth Moore, Director of Services, Boys and Girls Club of Tampa Bay, Inc., 3020 West Laurel Street, Tampa, Florida 33607; (813) 875-5771; (813)875-5483 (fax); URL http://www.bcctampa.org.

BREAKAWAY
Nashville, Tennessee
Project Location: United States and Latin America.
Description: Community projects offered as an alternative to spring break.
Cost: Travel to sites.
Other information: Provide training and assistance to high school and college students who want to start an alternative spring break program at their school. Organization does NOT set up trips for individuals during their spring break.
For more information: Rachel Tallman, Director, Breakaway, 6026 Station B, Nashville, Tennessee 37235; (615)343-0385; (615)343-3255 (fax); E-mail BREAKAWAY@ctrvax.vanderbilt.edu.

Focus On...
President's Student Service Challenge

The President's student service challenge provides an opportunity to recognize the millions of students that volunteer every day in America.

www.cns.gov/challenge

Two programs sponsored by this challenge are:

- Student Service Scholarships – High schools may select one junior or senior to receive a $1,000 scholarship for service to the community..
- Student Service Awards – Youth ages 5-25 who contribute 100 hours of service over a one-year period are eligible.

CALIFORNIA NATIONAL ORGANIZATION FOR WOMEN, INC.
Sacramento, California
Project Location: Sacramento, California
Description: Women's advocacy group working on state level.
Open to: High school students and graduates..
Cost/Compensation: Unpaid
For more information: Henry L. Horn, Project Director, California Child, Youth, and Family Coalition's California Youth Crisis Line, 2424 Castro Way, Sacramento, California 95818; (916)739-6912; E-mail henrylhorn@aol.com.

CARE
Atlanta, Georgia
Project Location: Outreach in 35 countries.
Description: Organization that was begun to serve the poor by collecting food and medical supplies.
For more information: CARE, 151 Ellis Street, Atlanta, Georgia 30303; (404)681-2552.

CENTER FOR HEALTH, ENVIRONMENT, AND JUSTICE
Falls Church, Virginia
Project Location: Falls Church, Virginia
Description: Organization providing assistance for citizen's groups fighting pollution.
Open to: High school seniors.

For more information: Barbara Sullivan, Internship Coordinator, Center for Health, Environment, and Justice, P.O. Box 6806, Falls Church, Virginia 22040; E-mail barbaras@essential.org/CCHW.

CHRISTMAS IN APRIL USA
Washington, D.C.
Project Location: Throughout the U.S.
Description: On last day in April in particular, and also on other days throughout the year, volunteers all over the country rebuild homes using donated materials.
For more information: Christmas in April USA, 1225 Eye Street, NW, Suite 601, Washington, DC 20005; (202)326-8268.

CITIZEN ACTION
Washington, D.C.
Project Location: Washington, D.C.
Description: Advocacy organization working to improve our lives through such things as better, more affordable and accessible health care.
For more information: Internship Coordinator, Citizen Action, 1730 Rhode Island Avenue, NW, Suite 403, Washington, DC 20036; (202)775-1580.

COALITION FOR APPALACHIAN MINISTRY
Richmond, Kentucky

Project Location: Alabama, Georgia, Kentucky, Maryland, North Carolina, Ohio, Pennsylvania, South Carolina, Tennessee, Virginia, and West Virginia.
Description: Work camps performing tasks such as home repair and development of small farms.
Cost: $100 to $200 per person per week.
For more information: John MacLean, Coordinator of Volunteers, Coalition for Appalachian Ministry, 111 Crutcher Pike, Richmond, Kentucky 40475-8606; (606)624-3407.

COLORADO ASSOCIATION OF NONPROFIT ORGANIZATIONS
Denver, Colorado
Project Location: Rocky Mountains, Colorado.
Description: Organization supporting the nonprofit sector through advocacy, networking, information, and group buying.
For more information: Associate Director, Colorado Association of Nonprofit Organizations, 225 E 16th Avenue, Suite 1060, Denver, Colorado 80203-1614; (303)832-5710; E-mail canpo@canpo.org; URL http://www.aclin.org/code/canpo.

CONSTITUTIONAL RIGHTS FOUNDATION (USA)
Los Angeles, California
Project Location: Nationwide
Description: Organization teaching people how to become responsible, active citizens and respond to community concerns.
For more information: Constitutional Rights Foundation, 601 South Kingsley Drive, Los Angeles, California 90005; (213)487-5590.

CYSTIC FIBROSIS FOUNDATION
San Francisco, California
Project Location: 70 field and branch offices across the country; region headquarters for Northern California and Western Nevada.
Description: Organization established to raise money for research, discover a cure, and aid those who have cystic fibrosis. To do this many special events must be organized.
Positions available: Volunteer/internship.
Cost: Unpaid.
For more information: Tania Holbrook, Special Events Coordinator, Cystic Fibrosis Foundation, 417 Montgomery Street, Suite 404, San Francisco, California 94104; (415)677-0155.

DO SOMETHING
New York, New York
Project Location: Nationwide.
Description: National nonprofit organization begun and run by young people who want to help youth community projects.
Cost: $10.00 membership fee (900) ALL OF US.

For more information: Do Something, 1 World Trade Center, 78th Floor, New York, New York 10048.
To apply for grant of up to $500 write to: Do Something! National Grants, P.O. Box 2409 JAF, New York, New York 10116.

EARLY ADOLESCENT HELPER PROGRAM (USA)
New York, New York
Project Location: New York
Description: Helps individuals locate volunteer work at after-school activities, daycare centers, and centers specializing in senior care.
For more information: The National Center for Service Learning in Early Adolescence, City University of New York, 25 West 43rd Street, Suite 612, New York, New York 10036-8099; (212)642-2946.

FUTURE EDUCATORS OF AMERICA
Bloomington, Indiana
Project Location: Future Educators of America clubs are in many middle and high schools all over the U.S.
Description: Members get to participate in teaching experiences by volunteering as a tutor.
For more information: Future Educators of America, c/o Phi Delta Kappa International, P.O. Box 789, Bloomington, Indiana 47402; (800)766-1156.

THE GLEANING NETWORK
Big Island, Virginia
Project Location: Farming areas of the U.S.: Virginia, Tennessee, North Carolina, Texas, Florida, and Mississippi.
Description: Christian hunger organization.
Open to: All ages.
Positions available: Volunteer gleaners.
Other information: Volunteers pick up the food that remains after farmers harvest their crops and they give it to the poor.
For more information: Nancy Tew, Director, The Gleaning Network/Society of St. Andrew, 3383 Sweet Hollow Road, Big Island, Virginia 24526; (800)333-4597; (804)299-5949 (fax); E-mail sosaglean@aol.com; URL http://www.endhunger.org.

GLOBAL VOLUNTEERS
St. Paul, Minnesota
Project Location: U.S. and other countries.
Description: Very similar to the Peace Corps.
Cost: Costs range from $450 to $2,395 plus transportation to site (tax deductible).
For more information: Global Volunteers, 375 East Little Canada Road, St. Paul, Minnesota 55117; (800) 487-1074; URL http://www.globalvolunteers.org.

HABITAT FOR HUMANITY
Americus, Georgia

Project Location: Throughout the U.S. and in 30 countries around the world.
Description: House building projects.
Cost: Responsible for all transportation, room, board, insurance and some contribution of a part of the cost of new house.
For more information: Habitat for Humanity, Habitat and Church Streets, Americus, Georgia 31709; (912) 924-6935.

HARVEST OF HOPE/SOCIETY OF ST. ANDREW
Big Island, Virginia
Project Location: Sites in the southeast.
Description: Christian hunger organization.
Open to: Youth through adults (senior highs-weeks; intergenerational -weekends).
Positions available: Volunteer gleaners.
Cost: $150/week; $50/weekend.
Other information: This is an educational retreat that incorporates gleaning (salvaging fresh fruits and vegetables after the harvest) for the hungry.
For more information: Julie Taylor, Harvest of Hope Director, Harvest of Hope/Society of St. Andrew, 3383 Sweet Hollow Road, Big Island, Virginia 24526; (800) 333-4597; (804)299-5949 (fax);
E-mail sosahoh@aol.com; URL http://www.endhunger.org.

HEIFER PROJECT INTERNATIONAL
Perryville, Arkansas
Project Location: Little Rock, Arkansas and throughout the world.
Description: General ranch or office work.
Cost: $500 fee per group.
For more information: International Livestock Center, Rt. 2, Perryville, Arkansas 72126; (501)889-5124.

INTERNATIONAL VOLUNTARY SERVICE (IVS)
Croset, Virginia
Project Location: Projects located throughout the world.
Description: Sponsors wide-variety of service projects around the world.
Cost: Fee of $35.00 for U.S. locations; $75-$100 for foreign locations, plus transportation to work site.
For more information: Service Civil International/ International Voluntary Service (SCI/IVS), Innisfree Village, Route 2, P.O. Box 506, Croset, Virginia 22932.

JUST SAY NO INTERNATIONAL
Oakland, California
Project Location: N/A
Description: Three projects for teens to participate in: Transitions, Peer Tutoring, and Community Service.
For more information: Just Say No International, 2101

Webster Street, Suite 1300, Oakland, California 94612; (800)258-2766.

KEY CLUB, INC.
Indianapolis, Indiana
Project Location: Nationwide.
Description: Organization sponsored by Kiwanis Clubs to help teenagers who want to help their schools and community.
For more information: Key Club, Inc., 3636 Woodview Trace, Indianapolis, Indiana 46268; (317)875-8755.

L'ARCHE MOBILE
Mobile, Alabama
Project Location: Mobile, Alabama.
Description: Communities where people with mental disability live with those who help them.
Cost: Boarding and lodging are provided.
For more information: Marty O'Malley, 152 Mobile, 151 South Ann Street, Mobile, Alabama 36604; (334)438-2094; (334)433-5835 (fax); E-mail larchmob@acan.net; URL http://www2.acan.net/~//archmob/.

LAUBACH LITERACY INTERNATIONAL
Syracuse, New York
Project Location: Nationwide.
Description: Organization training tutors to help teach reading to those with little or no English reading skills.
For more information: Laubach Literacy International, 1320 Jamesville Avenue, Syracuse, New York 13210; (315)422-9121.

LOS ALTOS FAMILY YMCA
Long Beach, California
Project Location: Long Beach, California
Description: Organization providing youth and family programming.
Open to: High school students.
Positions Available: Counselor in Training for summer day camp.
Cost/Compensation: Unpaid
For more information: Scott Christian, Program Director, Los Altos Family YMCA, 1720 Bellflower Boulevard, Long Beach, California 90815; (562)596-3394; (562)596-7911 (fax).

LUTHERAN VOLUNTEER CORPS
Washington, D.C.
Project Location: United States.
Description: Work that covers many areas such as direct service and community organizing.
For more information: Program Director, Lutheran Volunteer Corps, 1226 Vermont Avenue, NW, Wash-

ington, DC 20005; (202)387-3222.

NATIONAL COALITION FOR THE HOMELESS

Washington, D.C.

Project Location: Throughout the U.S.

Description: Aid to the homeless.

For more information: Michael Stoops, Director, Field Organizing Projects, National Coalition for the Homeless, 1012 14th Street, NW, #600, Washington, DC 20005-3406; (202)737-6444 Ext. 311; (202)737-6445 (fax); E-mail nch@ari.net; URL http://nch.ari.net.

NATIONAL CRIME PREVENTION COUNCIL

Washington, D.C.

Project Location: Nationwide.

Description: Organization enabling communities and individuals to help prevent crime and make their communities a safer place to live.

For more information: National Crime Prevention Council, National Office, 1700 K Street, NW, Suite 200, Washington, DC 20006; (202)466-6272.

NATIONAL ORGANIZATION FOR WOMEN, INC.

Washington, D.C.

Project Location: Washington, D.C.

Description: Organization that struggles to eliminate injustice and inequality faced by women daily.

Cost: All unpaid volunteer positions. They assist in finding affordable housing.

For more information: Dee Dee Anderson, Intern/Volunteer Coordinator, National Organization for Women, Inc., 1000 16th Street, NW, Suite 700, Washington, DC 20036-5705; (202)331-0066; E-mail volunteer@now.org; URL http://www.now.org/intern.

NATIONAL STUDENT CAMPAIGN AGAINST HUNGER AND HOMELESSNESS

Boston, Massachusetts

Project Location: More than 450 affiliates nationwide.

Description: Organization providing educators and students with resources to help combat hunger and homelessness.

For more information: National Student Campaign Against Hunger and Homelessness, 29 Temple Place, Boston, Massachusetts 02111; (617)292-4823.

FOCUS ON...
HABITAT FOR HUMANITY

How are you going to spend spring break? Each year high school and college students spend spring break taking the Collegiate Challenge. (Of course you may volunteer any time of the year.) Students age 16 and over work with participating Habitat for Humanity affiliate around the United States to build houses. There is no experience necessary!

"Our love should not be just words and talk, it must be true love, which shows itself in action."

- *www.habitat.org*
(1 John 3:18)

Volunteers are needed in all 50 states. To find out how you can help, visit the campus chapters and youth area at the Habitat for Humanity website at:

www.habitat.org

NATIONAL VOLUNTEER CENTER
Arlington, Virginia
Project Location: Nationwide
Description: Organization that lists organizations that are willing to find volunteer opportunities for youth.
For more information: National Volunteer Center, 111 North 19th Street, Suite 500, Arlington, Virginia 22209; (703)276-0542.

READING IS FUNDAMENTAL
Washington, D.C.
Project Location: 5,000 community-based projects nationwide.
Description: Organization helping to put books into children's homes with the hope that children will grow to love reading.
For more information: Reading is Fundamental, Smithsonian Institution, 600 Maryland Avenue, SW, Suite 600, Washington, DC 20024; (202)287-3220.

RELIGIOUS SOCIETY OF FRIENDS
Philadelphia, Pennsylvania
Project Location: Philadelphia
Description: Inner-city workcamps.
Cost: $35 per weekend work camp plus transportation.
For more information: Friends Weekend Workcamps, 1515 Cherry Street, Philadelphia, Pennsylvania 19102; (215)241-7236.

SALESIAN BOYS AND GIRLS CLUB
East Boston, Massachusetts
Project Location: East Boston, Massachusetts
Description: After-school youth care facility.
Open to: High school seniors and graduates.
Positions Available: Summer program counselors and volunteers.
Cost/Compensation: Paid – $6.50-$10.00/hour.
For more information: Fr. Michael Conway, SDB, Executive Director, Salesian Boys and Girls Club, 189 Paris Street, East Boston, Massachusetts 02128; (617) 567-0508; (617)567-0418 (fax); E-mail sbgclub@juno. com; URL http://www.eastboston.com/salesi.

SERVICE CIVIL INTERNATIONAL/INTERNATIONAL VOLUNTARY SERVICE (SCI/IVS) WORKCAMPS
Crozet, Virginia
Project Location: Sites across the United States and abroad.
Description: Workcamps consist of 8-15 volunteers working on a meaningful community problem in various sites in the U.S. or abroad.
Cost: $40 registration in U.S.; $80 registration abroad. Room, board, and health/accident insurance are provided.
For more information: Service Civil International/ International Voluntary Service (SCI/IVS), Work-camps, SCI/IVS, Route 2, Box 506, Crozet, Virginia 22932; (804)823-1826.

SOUTH BAY COMMUNITY SERVICES
Chula Vista, California
Project Location: Chula Vista, California
Description: Organization providing counseling services and community youth development.
Open to: Youth from South Bay in San Diego 14-24 years of age.
Positions Available: Peer educators, peer outreach, tutors, and mentors.
Cost/Compensation: Paid part-time positions available and volunteer opportunities.
For more information: Perla Bransburg, Associate Director, South Bay Community Services, 315 4th Avenue, Suite E, Chula Vista, California 91910; (619)420-3620.

SPANISH EDUCATION DEVELOPMENT CENTER
Washington, DC
Project Location: Washington, DC
Description: The SED Center provides educational programs for children age 3-4, their families, and adults in the Washington metropolitan area.
Open to: High school students and graduates.
Positions Available: Assistant teacher.
Cost/Compensation: Unpaid
For more information: Doris Estrada, Director, Volunteer Program, Spanish Education Development Center, 1840 Kalorama Road, NW, Washington, DC 20009; (202)462-8848; (202)462-6886 (fax); E-mail sedcen@erols.com; URL http://www.sedcenter.com.

STUDENTS AGAINST DRIVING DRUNK (SADD)
Marlboro, Massachusetts
Project Location: Chapters can be started in any school.
Description: Organization working to eliminate underage drinking, drugging and driving under the influence and other destructive decisions.
For more information: SADD, P.O. Box 800, Marlboro, Massachusetts 01752; (508)481-3568 or toll-free (877) SADD-INC.

TEENAGE REPUBLICAN (TAR)
Manassas, Virginia
Project Location: Nationwide.
Description: Organization working in the political process doing things such as working the phone bank, canvassing, making signs, and distributing information.
For more information: National TAR Headquarters, P.O. Box 1896, 10620-C Crestwood Dr., Manassas, Virginia 22110; (703)368-4214.

UNITED WAY OF WACO

Waco, Texas
Project Location: Waco, Texas
Description: Fundraising organization for member agencies.
Open to: High school students and graduates.
Cost/Compensation: Unpaid
For more information: Dorothy Wienecke, Communication Coordinator/Volunteer Center Director, United Way of Waco, 5400 Boxque Boulevard #225, Waco, Texas 76710-4459; (254)741-1980; (254)741-1984 (fax).

WOMEN'S ENTERPRISE DEVELOPMENT
Long Beach, California
Project Location: Long Beach, California
Description: Provide business management training for individuals that would like to own a business.
Open to: High school juniors, seniors, and college students.
Positions Available: Depends on projects needed.
Cost/Compensation: Unpaid
For more information: Ms. Torres Waters, Office Manager, Women's Enterprise Development, 235 E. Broadway, Suite 506, Long Beach, California 90802; (562)983-3747; (562)983-3750 (fax); E-mail WEDC1@aol.com; URL http://www.wedc.org.

WORLD HORIZONS INTERNATIONAL
Bethlehem, Connecticut
Project Location: Rural Alaska, Africa, Caribbean, Central America, and Western Samoa.
Description: Community service programs.
Cost: $3,450.
For more information: World Horizons International, P.O. Box 662, Bethlehem, Connecticut 06751; (203) 266-5874 or (800)262-5874.

YOUNG AMERICA CARES!
Alexandria, Virginia
Project Location: Nationwide.
Description: This is a part of the United Way involving volunteer opportunities for youth.
For more information: United Way of America, 701 North Fairfax Street, Alexandria, Virginia 22314; (703)836-7100 Ext. 445.

YOUNG DEMOCRATS OF AMERICA
Washington, D.C.
Project Location: Nationwide.
Description: Organization working in the political process through canvassing, answering phones, making signs, and distributing information.
For more information: Democratic National Committee, 430 S. Capitol Street, SE, Washington, DC 20003; (202)863-8000.

YOUTH ENRICHMENT SERVICES
Boston, Massachusetts
Project Location: Northeast, Massachusetts.
Description: Provides outdoor programs for low- and moderate-income Boston area youth.
For more information: Eric Pinckney, Executive Director, Youth Enrichment Services, 412 Massachusetts Avenue, Boston, Massachusetts 02118; (617)267-5877.

YOUTH SERVICE AMERICA
Washington, DC
Project Location: Washington, D.C.
Description: Publishes *National Youth Service: Answer the Call*, a publication that shows over 50 service projects and 80 community groups.
For more information: Youth Service America, 1101 15th Street, NW, Suite 200, Washington, DC 20005; (202)296-2992.

YWCA OF ST. PAUL
St. Paul, Minnesota
Project Location: St. Paul, Minnesota
Description: Organization committed to serving women and families.
Open to: High school students and graduates.
Positions Available: Teen counselors and summer positions.
Cost/Compensation: Paid – hourly wage.
For more information: Elizabeth Ellis, Volunteer Coordinator, YWCA of St. Paul, 198 Western Avenue, North, St. Paul, Minnesota 55102-1790; (651)222-3741; (651)222-6307 (fax);
E-mail eellis@ywcaofstpaul.org.

INTERNATIONAL

AMERICAN ASSOCIATION OF OVERSEAS STUDIES
London, England
Project Location: London, New York
Description: AAOS provides hands-on experience in business, law, film, medicine, government, journalism, theatre studies, and art courses.
Open to: Teenagers.
Cost: London Summer Internship Package ($3,995-$4,995). Year-round Internships in NY or London ($995).
For more information: Janet Kollek Evans, Director, American Association of Overseas Studies, 51 Drayton Gardens , Suite 4, London SW10 9RX England; (800) EDU-BRIT; 011-44-171-244-6061 (fax); E-mail aaos2000@hotmail.com; URL www.worldwide.edu/uk/aaos/.

AMERICAN FARM SCHOOL – "GREEK SUMMER"

New York, New York
Project Location: Greece
Description: Students live with a rural Greek family and work on a project while being exposed to Greek culture.
Open to: Students the summer after their sophomore, junior, or senior year in high school.
Cost: Tuition $2,600 plus $500 tax-deductible contribution. Airfare is not included.
For more information: Nicholas Apostal, Program Coordinator, American Farm School, Office of Trustees, 1133 Broadway, Suite 1625, New York, New York 10010; (212)463-8434; (212)463-8208 (fax); E-mail nyoffice@amerfarm.org; URL http://www.afs.edu.gr.

AMIGOS DE LA AMERICAS
Houston, Texas
Project Location: Throughout Latin America.
Description: Organization placing thousands of volunteers in Latin American countries.
Cost: $2,600 - $3,080 plus transportation to/from Houston.
For more information: Amigos de las Americas, 5618 Star Lane, Houston, Texas 77057; (800)231-7796 or (713)782-5290.

ARBEIA ROMAN FORT AND MUSEUM
United Kingdom
Project Location: England

Description: Archaeology and museum work.
Cost: Accommodations can be arranged at volunteer's expense. Volunteer pays cost to get to site.
For more information: Elizabeth Elliott, Arbeia Roman Fort and Museum, Baring Street, South Shields, Tyne and Wear, NE33 2BB; +44 (0)191-4544093; +44 (0)191-4276826.

ARMY CADET FORCE ASSOCIATION
London, England
Project Location: London, England.
Description: A youth group created to help 13-18 year olds develop skills to help them become responsible, contributing citizens.
Cost: N/A
For more information: E Block, Duke of York's Headquarters, London, SW3 4RR; 0171-730-9733.

ASSOCIATION LE MAT
Balazuc, France
Project Location: France
Description: Restoration, reconstruction, and farming activities.
Cost: Camp sites and some beds are available. Volunteers pay about £4 daily for food, insurance, and an association fee.
For more information: Co-ordinator, Le Viel Audon, 07120, Balazuc, France; 33-4-75-37-73-80.

ASSOCIATION POUR LA PROMOTION DE L'ARCHÉOLOGIE DE STAVELOT ET DE SA RÉGION
Stavelot, Belgium
Project Location: Belgium.
Description: Excavation of an 11th century abbey church.
Cost: Lodging, insurance, and meals are provided.
For more information: Centre Stavelotain d'Archéologie, Abbaye de Stavelot, 4970 Stavelot, Belgium; 32-80-86-41-13.

BIRMINGHAM PHAB CAMPS
Birmingham, England
Project Location: United Kingdom; Birmingham.
Description: A camping experience for the physically disabled.
Cost: Accommodations provided. Transportation to and from Birmingham is paid.
For more information: Volunteer Recruitment Officer, 39 Hounsdown Avenue, Totton, Southampton. SOLO 9FE; 01703 863445.

BIRMINGHAM YOUNG VOLUNTEERS
Birmingham, England
Project Location: Birmingham.
Description: Camping experience for disadvantaged children.
Cost: Accommodations and food are provided. Transportation to and from Birmingham is provided.
For more information: BYV Association, 4th Floor, Smithfield House, Digbeth, Birmingham B5 6BS; 0121-622-2888.

BUSCA (BRIGADA UNIVERSITARIA DE SERVICIOS COMMUNITARIOS PARA LA AUTOGESTION)
Mexico
Project Location: Mexico
Description: Volunteers are needed to join Mexicans in a 2,000 bicycle trip across Mexico to promote usage of bicycles and to raise money for community development projects.
Cost: Sponsorship of $0.50 per km. and travel to and from Mexico.
For more information: BUSCA (Brigada Universitaria de Servicios Communitarios para la Autogestion), Casa de la Cultura Raul Anguiano, Parque Ecologico Huayamilpas, Yaqui esq. Nezahuzlcoyotl s/n, Colonia Ajusco Huayamilpas, Mexico, D.F. 04390 Mexico; 525-6-66-47-71; E-mail busca@laneta.apc.org.

CAMPHILL VILLAGE TRUST
United Kingdom
Project Location: United Kingdom
Description: Villages care for learning disabled people in community settings. Volunteers aid in all aspects of operations.

Open to: Most volunteers are 18 and older.
CostCompensation: Board, lodging and pocket money is provided.
For more information: Camphill Village Trust, 19 South Road, Stourbridge, West Midlands; 01384-372122.

CANADIAN PARKS AND WILDERNESS SOCIETY
Toronto, Ontario
Project Location: Canada
Description: Citizen's conservation group.
For more information: Canadian Parks and Wilderness Society, 160 Bloor Street East, #1335, Toronto, Ontario, M4W 1B9; (416)972-8068.

CANTERBURY OAST TRUST
Kent, United Kingdom
Project Location: Kent.
Description: Commercial tourist attraction operated by adults with learning disabilities. Volunteers are needed in many areas.
Cost: Camping space is available.
For more information: Volunteers Co-ordinator, South of England Rare Breeds Centre, Highlands Farms, Woodchurch, Ashford, Kent, TIV26 3RJ; 01233-861494.

CHANTIER DE JEUNES PROVENCE CÔTE D´AZUR
Cannes la Bocca, France
Project Location: Sainte Marguerite in Cannes, France and some locations in Belgium, Italy, and Great Britain
Description: Volunteers perform work such as construction, environmental protection, and protecting historical monuments.
Open to: Volunteers from 13-17 years of age.
Cost: $200 per week.
Other information: Work in the morning for 5 hours with sports and cultural activities in the afternoon and at night.
For more information: Chantier de Jeunes, Provence Côte d´Azur, La Ferme Giaume, 7 Avenue Pierre de Coubertin, 06150 Cannes la Bocca, France; 04-33-4789-63; 04-93-48-72-01 (fax); E-mail cjpca@duh.internet.fr

CHANTIERS D'ÉTUDES MEDIEVALES
Stasbourg, France
Project Location: Chateaux d'Ottrott
Description: Restoration of historical sites and monuments and work on archeological digs.
Cost: Fr 450- Fr 500 plus transportation to sites.
For more information: Chantiers d'Études Medievales, 4 rue du Tonnelet Rouge, 67000 Strasbourg, France; (88)37-17-20.

CHILDREN'S COMMUNITY HOLIDAYS
Belfast, Northern Ireland
Project Location: Belfast.
Description: Operating youth camps and playgroups in many cities and residential weekend camps for children.
For more information: Administrator, Children's Community Holidays, P.O. Box 463, Belfast BT7 IPQ; 01232-833753.

CHRISTIAN MEDICAL/DENTAL SOCIETY - MEDICAL GROUP MISSIONS
Bristol, Tennessee
Project Location: Central America, China, Dominican Republic, Eastern Europe, Equador, Jamaica, Mexico, Philippines, and Vietnam.
Description: Families with youth 12 years old and up do medical or dental projects.
For more information: Patti Kowalchuk, Office Administrator, Christian Medical/Dental Society, P.O. Box 7500, Bristol, Tennessee 37621; (423)844-1000; (423)844-1005 (fax); E-mail gho@christian-doctors.com.

THE CHURCH'S MINISTRY AMONG JEWISH PEOPLE
United Kingdom
Project Location: Tel Aviv, Jerusalem, and Haifa, Israel
Description: CMJ evangelizes and encourages Jewish believers and educates the church on Jewish roots.
Open to: Volunteers 18-70 years of age.
Positions available: Volunteers help to run guest houses and worship centers.
Cost/Compensation: Volunteer pays travel and insurance. CMJ provides board, lodging, and pocket money.
For more information: Sheila Wright, U.K. Volunteer Coordinator, The Church's Ministry Among Jewish People, 30C Clarence Road, St. Albans, Herts AL1 4JJ; 01727-833114; 01727-848312 (fax); E-mail CMJ_STALBANS@compuserve.com.

CITY OF BRADFORD PLAYSCHEME ASSOCIATION
Bradford, United Kingdom
Project Location: Bradford.
Description: The Association plans playschemes for children, ages 6-15, during summer holidays.
Cost: A small amount is usually given to defray expenses.
For more information: c/o Community Recreation Office, Baildon Recreation Centre, Green Lane, Baildon, Bradford, W. Yorks; 01274-593234.

CLUB DU VIEUX MANOIR
Paris, France
Project Location: Guise, Argy, Pontpoint, and 12-15 other sites throughout France.

Description: Restoration of ancient sites and monuments.
Cost: Fr 90 and Fr 80 per day plus transportation to/from site.
For more information: Club du Vieux Manoir, 10 rue de la Cossonnerie, Aucienne Abbaye du Moncel, à Pontpoint, 60700 Pont Ste Maxence.

COLLEGE CEVENOL (INTERNATIONAL WORKCAMP)
Haute Loire, France
Project Location: College Cevenol International in the Massif Central (Auvergne)
Description: Work such as construction, landscaping, and maintenance.
Cost: Accommodations and food are provided. At a reduced price, volunteers may go on the discovery trip of France.
For more information: Robert Lassey, Directeur du développement, 43400 Le Chamgon-sur-Lignon, Haute Loire, France; 04-71-59-72-52; 04-71-65-87-38 (fax).

CONCORDIA
Sussex
Project Location: United Kingdom
Description: International workcamps have variety of projects including playschemes, conservation, ecology, and restoration.
Open to: USA national or residents.
Positions Available: Short-term volunteer placements.
Cost: Unpaid, but room and board are provided. Fee for registration and travel cost are paid by volunteers.
Other information: Volunteers must apply through a volunteer agency in their own country (e.g. C.I.E.E.).
For more information: Gwyn Lewis, Volunteer Project Manager, Concordia (YSU) Ltd., 20-22 Heversham House, Hove BN3 4ET United Kingdom; 01273-422218; 01273-422218 (fax).

CROSS-CULTURAL SOLUTIONS
New Rochelle, New York
Project Location: India, Ghana, and West Africa.
Description: Enables student to experience India, Ghana, or West Africa through person-to-person contact. Helps empower whole communities and foster cultural sensitivity and understanding through humanitarian volunteer action.
Open to: People of all backgrounds and skills are encouraged to participate.
Positions Available: Three-week service programs. Summer and longer programs are available.
Cost/Compensation: $1,850
For more information: Marge Rubin, Volunteer Coordinator, Cross-Cultural Solutions, 47 Potter Avenue, New Rochelle, New York 10801; (800)380-4777; (914)632-8494 (fax); E-mail

info@crossculturalsolutions.org; URL http://www.crossculturalsolutions.org.

CRUSADERS
St. Albans, United Kingdom
Project Location: Britain and abroad.
Description: Group leading Christian young people's activities emphasizing teaching the Bible, evangelism, holiday help, and expedition in Britain and abroad.
For more information: Crusaders, 2 Romeland Hill, St. Albans, Herts, AL3 4ET; 01727-855422.

DERBYSHIRE INTERNATIONAL YOUTH CAMP
Derby, United Kingdom
Project Location: Derbyshire, England
Description: Conservation and summer playground projects.
Cost: Varies.
For more information: Derbyshire County Council, Education Department, Derby Youth House, Mill Street, Derby DEI IDY United Kingdom; (01332) 345-538.

EARTHWATCH
Oxford, United Kingdom
Project Location: 40 countries and 27 states in the United States.
Description: Volunteers help scientists do research in many areas from archaeology to zoology.
For more information: Earthwatch, Belsyre Court, 57 Woodstock Road, Oxford, OX2 6HJ; 01865-311600; E-mail ewoxford@vax.oxford.ac.uk.

EIN YAEL LIVING MUSEUM
Jerusalem, Israel
Project Location: Jerusalem.
Description: Using techniques of crafts that were used at various time in history.
For more information: Eli Vaknin, Director, Ein Yael Living Museum, P.O. Box 48169, Jerusalem, 91481, Israel; 972-2-645-1866; 972-2-645-1867 (fax); E-mail einyael@internet.zahav.net..

EUROPE CONSERVATION IN ITALY
Rome, Italy
Project Location: Rome, Italy
Description: Archaeological work camps in Italy.
For more information: Europe Conservation in Italy, Via Tacito 41, 00193 Rome, Italy; 39 6-68740028.

FESTINIOG RAILWAY COMPANY
Porthmadog, United Kingdom
Project Location: The mountains of Snowdonia in Wales.
Description: Variety of work projects on working steam railway.
Cost: Responsible for transportation to project, room and board.
For more information: Volunteer Resource Manager, Festiniog Railway Company, Harbour Station, Porthmadog, Gwynedd LL49 9NF United Kingdom; (01766)512-340; URL http://www.festrail.co.uk.

FLEMISH YOUTH FEDERATION FOR THE STUDY AND CONSERVATION OF NATURE
Antwerpen, Belgium
Project Location: Belgium and Holland.
Description: Nature study and conservation.
Cost: $100 to $200 per camp.
For more information: Flemish Youth Federation for the Study and Conservation of Nature, Bervoetstraat 33, Antwerpen B-2000 Belgium; (3)231-26-04.

FOUNDATION FOR FIELD RESEARCH (FFR)
Grenada, West Indies
Project Location: Worldwide
Description: The Foundation publishes, *"Explorer News"* four times a year. This publication describes projects that need volunteers and the locations.
Cost: Varies according to the project.
For more information: Foundation for Field Research (FFR), P.O. Box 771, St. George's, Grenada, West Indies; (809)440-8854.

FRONTIER
London, United Kingdom
Project Location: Tanzania and Uganda, potentially Argentina, Brukina Faso, and Vietnam.
Description: Biological inventory and survey of natural habitats. Development of sustainable use of natural habitats.
Cost: $5,000 for ten weeks.
For more information: Society for Environmental Exploration, Studio 210, Thames House, 566 Cable Street, London E1 9HB United Kingdom; (0171)790-4424.

GLOBAL WORKS
Huntingdon, Pennsylvania
Project Location: Puerto Rico, Costa Rica, Fiji, Russia, Pacific Northwest, and Czech Republic.
Description: Projects in the past have included wildlife research, recycling programs, rebuilding habitats, and rain forest replanting.
Cost: $1,995-$2,800. Airfare not included.
For more information: Office Manager, Global Works, Inc., RD#2, Box 356B, Huntingdon, Pennsylvania 16652; (814)667-2411.

GROUPE ARCHEOLOGIQUE DU MESMONTOIS
Malain, France
Project Location: Near Dijon, France.
Description: Archaeological digs and restoration activities.

Open to: Everybody over age 17.

Cost: About FF100.00 (about $20.00) a week for food and lodging.

For more information: Roussel Louis, President, Groupe Archeologique du Mesmontois, Mairie de Malain, 21410 Pont-de-Pany, France 21410; 3380-30-05-20; 0380-5-3-48 (fax).

GWENT ASSOCIATION OF VOLUNTARY ORGANISATIONS (GAVO)

Gwent, United Kingdom

Project Location: Gwent

Description: Organization providing support for volunteers.

For more information: GAVO, 8 Pentonville, Newport, Gwent; 01633-213229.

HUNT SABOTEURS ASSOCIATION

Nottingham, United Kingdom

Project Location: Nottingham

Description: Organization working to save hunted animals.

Cost: Membership fee is £5-£8.

For more information: Hunt Saboteurs Association, P. O. Box 1, Carlton, Nottingham NG4 2JY; 0115-959037; E-mail hsa@gn.apc.org; URL http://envirollin.org/arrs/MSA/hsu.html.

IJGD (INTERNATIONALE JUGENDGEMEINSCHAFTSDIENSTE BUNDESVEREIN EV-GESELLSCHAFT FUR INTERNATIONALE UND POLITSCHE BILDNUG.

Bonn, Germany

Project Location: Germany

Description: Workcamps and workshops such as recreational activities, conservation, and educational projects.

Cost: Cost of food, accommodations, and insurance is provided.

For more information: IJGD, Kaiserstrasse 43, D-53113, Bonn, Germany; (49) 228-2280011.

INTERNATIONAL CHRISTIAN YOUTH EXCHANGE (ICYE)

Berlin, Germany

Project Location: Over 30 countries.

Description: For 6 months or one year, students have an opportunity to live with a host family and attend high school. Departure is in July.

Cost: Fee that covers travel, insurance and administrative costs.

For more information: International Office of ICYE, Georgenkirchstrasse 70, 10249 Berlin, Germany; +49-30-24063-214; E-mail icyeio@igc.apc.org.

INTERNATIONAL VOLUNTARY SERVICE (NORTHERN IRELAND)

Belfast, Ireland

Project Location: North Ireland

Description: Exchange of volunteers workcamps emphasizing such areas as study tours and conflict resolution.

Cost: Cost of own travel. On longer-term stays, pocket money is provided.

For more information: International Voluntary Service, 122 Great Victorian Street, Belfast BT2 7BG; 01232-238147; E-mail georget@ivsni.dnet.co.uk.

LES AMIS DES CHANTIERS INTERNATIONAUX DE MEKNES

Meknes, Morocco

Project Location: Meknes and exchange volunteer placement abroad.

Description: ACIM provides volunteers to work with children at summer camps.

Cost: Room, food and insurance provided.

For more information: Enclose an international reply coupon. BP 08 50001, Meknes, Morocco.

LOUIS ROUSSEL

Dijon, France

Project Location: France

Description: Volunteers work on an archeological dig: digging, sketching, photographing, restoring, or making models.

Cost: Accommodations are free in exchange for about 8 working hours a day.

For more information: M. Roussel, 52 rue des Forges, F-21000, Dijon, France.

L'OUVRE-TETE

Provence, France

Project Location: France

Description: In Provence, help is needed in various activities such as carpentry, looking after houses, and organic gardening. French lessons and group excursions are arranged for volunteers.

Cost: 100 francs daily for food and basic lodging. Travel and insurance are paid by volunteer.

For more information: Les Maurels, 04300 Pierrerue, France; +33-4-92-75-10-65.

MALTA YOUTH HOSTELS ASSOCIATION WORKCAMPS

Pawla, Malta

Project Location: Malta

Description: Repair and maintenance projects.

Cost: Transportation plus refundable $45 deposit.

For more information: Malta Youth Hostels Association Work Camps, 17 Trig Tal-Borg, Pawla PLA 06 Malta; 356-693957; E-mail myha@keyworld.mt.

NATIONAL REGISTRATION CENTER FOR STUDY ABROAD (NRSCA)

Milwaukee, Wisconsin

Project Location: Latin America, Canada, France, Switzerland, Germany, Austria, and Spain.

Description: NRCSA acts as an information and registration office for over 100 language schools in 25 countries, with about 20 that will accept students under age 18. There are four program types: Mexico Discovery, Total Immersion-Spanish, Total Immersion-French, and Total Immersion-German. Teen programs, escorted or unescorted, available in several Latin American countries as well as French speaking Canada, France, Switzerland, Austria, Germany, and Spain.

Open to: Ages 12-17 depending on program.

Cost/Compensation: Cost of $500-$1,750. Airfare is additional and can be coordinated by the NRCSA offices.

For more information: National Registration Center for Study Abroad (NRCSA), P.O. Box 1393, Milwaukee, Wisconsin 53201; (414)278-0631; (414)271-8884 (fax); E-mail teenstudy@nrcsa.com; URL http://www.nrcsa.com.

NATIONAL TRUST FOR SCOTLAND THISTLE CAMPS
Edinburgh, United Kingdom

Project Location: Throughout Scotland.

Description: Practical conservation of Trust countryside properties.

Open to: Anyone over 16 years of age.

Cost: $40 per week for food and accommodations.

For more information: National Trust for Scotland Thistle Camps, 5 Charlotte Square, Edinburgh EH2 4DU United Kingdom; (0131)226-5922; (0131)243-9501 (fax); URL http://www.nts.org.uk.

NORTH YORKSHIRE MOORS RAILWAY
North Yorkshire, United Kingdom

Project Location: North Yorkshire

Description: Helping operate and maintain an 18-mile stretch of steam railroad.

Cost: Basic accommodations are available.

For more information: Volunteer Liaison Officer, North Yorkshire Moors Railway Trust, 15 Lincoln Court, Darlington, DL1 2XN.

OCEANIC SOCIETY EXPEDITIONS
San Francisco, California

Project Location: Bahamas, Belize, Midway Atoll, California, Peruvian Amazon, and Suriname.

Description: Research projects studying whales, dolphins, primates, manatees, sea turtles, and other marine life.

Cost: $1,150-$1,990, depending on location of site and length of stay.

For more information: Oceanic Society Expeditions, Fort Mason Center, Suite E-230, San Francisco, California 94123; (415)441-1106 or (800)326-7491.

ONE WORLD WORKFORCE (OWW)
La Mesa, California

Project Location: Various beaches in Mexico and Anguilla.

Description: Hands on conservation of sea turtles, pelicans, and island and beach ecosystems.

Open to: Able-bodied people aged 10 through 75.

Positions Available: Volunteer research and conservation helpers.

Cost: Fee of $490-575 student fee covers project grant, camp fee, round transportation, all meals, and field guide.

For more information: Evelyn Hightower, Treasurer/ Field Guide, One World Workforce, P.O. Box 3188, La Mesa, California 91944-3188; (800)451-9564; (619)589-5544 (fax); E-mail 1world@infomask.com; URL http://www.1ww.org.

PENSEE ET CHANTIERS
Rabat, Morocco

Project Location: Morocco

Description: Workcamp projects such as construction, gardening, and forest maintenance.

Cost: Sleeping bags and tools are necessary. Fee of about $80 is required. Generally, room and board are provided.

For more information: Send 2 international reply coupons to Secretary General, B.P. 1423, Rabat RP, Morocco; +212-7-69-83-38.

PROFESSOR HENRY DE LUMLEY
Paris, France

Project Location: France

Description: Students help with archaeological digs. Applicants should be students in prehistory, archaeology, or the natural sciences.

For more information: Professor De Lumley, Lab. de Prehistoire, IPH, 1 rue Rene Panhard, F-75013, Paris, France.

PRO INTERNATIONAL
Marburg, Germany

Project Location: Germany

Description: International vacation workcamps are organized to promote peace through friendship.

Open to: Youth ages 16-26.

Cost: Fee of 100 DM.

For more information: Pro International, Bahnhofstrasse 26A, Marburg, Germany 35037; 06421-65277; 06421-64407 (fax); E-mail pro-international@t-online. de; URL http://www.lahn.net/pro-international.

REMPART
Paris, France

Project Location: France

Description: This association helps restore old monuments and buildings. A catalog, published yearly, lists

projects that need restoration. Rempart is a union of IUO associations in France.
Open to: All people, age 13 and over.
Cost/Compensation: 22 OFF for insurance and fees and ±4 OFF a day for food and lodging.
For more information: Sabine Guilbert, International Officer, Union REMPART, 1 rue des Guillemites, 75004 Paris; 0142719655; 0142717300 (fax).

ROYAL SOCIETY FOR THE PROTECTION OF BIRDS RESERVES MANAGEMENT
Sandy, United Kingdom
Project Location: England, Scotland, and Wales.
Description: Voluntary reserve warden.
Cost: Food and transportation to/from reserves.
For more information: Royal Society for the Protection of Birds Reserves Management, The Lodge, Sandy, Bedfordshire SG19 20L United Kingdom; (01767)680-551.

THE SAMARITANS
Slough, United Kingdom
Project Location: Worldwide
Description: 24-hour confidential and emotional support for people in crisis.
Cost: N/A
For more information: Samaritan's branch should be found in your phone book or write to The Samaritans, 10 The Grove, Slough SL1 1QP; 01753-532713.

SHARE HOLIDAY VILLAGE
Fermanagh, Northern Ireland
Project Location: Ireland
Description: A residential, outdoor activity center for the disabled offering an arts program, indoor leisure suite, outdoor activities, food, and accommodations.
Positions Available: Respite care with people with disabilities, and arts volunteers in drama, art, music, theatre, and pottery.
Cost/Compensation: Room and board plus £10 per week.
For more information: Katie Furfey, Volunteer Coordinator, Share Holiday Village, Smiths Strand, Lisnaskea, Co. Fermanagh BT92 OEQ, Northern Ireland; (+44 13657) 22122; (+44 13657) 21893 (fax); E-mail share@dnet.co.uk.

STRATHSPEY RAILWAY CO. LTD.
Aviemore, Scotland
Project Location: Aviemore and Boat of Garten
Description: Steam railway – mainly volunteer.
Open to: All subject to training and fitness for the task.
Positions Available: Various (e.g. booking clerk, trackman, and train cleaner).

Cost: Basic hotel accommodations available for about £2.50 a night.

For more information: Laurence Grant, Commercial Manager, Aviemore Station, Dalfaler Road, Aviemore, Inverness-shire PH22 1PY; 01479-810725; Laurence.grant@strathspey_railway.freeserve.co.uk.

THIRD WORLD OPPORTUNITIES
El Cajon, California

Project Location: Tecate and Las Palmas, Mexico.

Description: This is an awareness program with opportunities to become involved in community action (house-building) projects.

Open to: Students, age 15 and up, with a knowledge of Spanish.

Cost/Compensation: For six-day summer building program, $200 plus transportation.

For more information: Coordinator, Third World Opportunities, 1363 Somermont Drive, El Cajon, California 92021; (619)449-9381; E-mail pgray@ucsd.edu; URL http://www.scansd.net/two.

TIME FOR GOD
London, England

Project Location: London

Description: Help care for children, disabled, homeless, and the elderly in organizations such as the YMCA and National Children's Home.

Cost: Food and accommodations are paid. Some pocket money is provided and fares for reasonable journey in Britain.

For more information: Time for God, 2 Chester House, Pages Lane, London N10 1PR; 0181-883-1504; 0181-365-2471 (fax);
E-mail time_for_God@compuserve.com.

TURICOOP
Lisboa, Portugal

Project Location: Portugal.

Description: Construction projects helping those in need.

Cost: Esc 5,000 registration fee.

For more information: Turicoop, Rua Pascoal de Melo 15-1-DTO, 1100 Lisboa Portugal; (804) 539247.

UNIVERSITY RESEARCH EXPEDITIONS PROGRAM (UREP)
Berkeley, California

Project Location: Worldwide

Description: UREP operates programs around the world in the areas of earth sciences, natural resource conservation, environmental studies, archaeology, arts and culture.

Cost: Fees of $1,000-$2,000 including housing, meals, transportation on the ground, camping, and field gear.

For more information: University Research Expeditions Program (UREP), University of California, Berkeley, Berkeley, California 94720; (510)642-6586.

UP WITH PEOPLE
Broomfield, Colorado

Project Location: Worldwide

Description: Worldsmart™ is the Up With People Multi-Cultural leadership Program. It accelerates education and career opportunities through the unique combination of international travel, on-stage musical performance, and community service.

Open to: Students 18-25. Students can apply for up to two years in advance.

Cost: Students pay a program fee — contact UWP for current rate.

For more information: Admission Counselor, Up With People, One International Court, Broomfield, Colorado 80021; (800)596-7353; (303)438-7301 (fax); E-mail admissions@upwithpeople.org; URL http://www.upwithpeople.org.

UPPER NENE ARCHAEOLOGIC SOCIETY
Northampton, United Kingdom

Project Location: Northampton

Description: Excavation of a Romano-British villa and an underlying Iron Age settlement.

Cost: Volunteers pay a specified amount. Camp site or bed and breakfast accommodations are available at reasonable rates.

For more information: Mrs. D.E. Friendship-Taylor, Upper Nene Archaeological Society, Toad Hall, 86 Main Road, Hackleton, Northampton NN7 2AD; 01604-870312.

U.S. SERVAS
New York, New York

Project Location: Worldwide

Description: Worldwide hospitality network with a core group of international students and "Peacebuilder" families comprising a system where those traveling in pursuit of cultural education or peace work can stay in hosts' homes for two nights.

Open to: High school seniors and adults 18 and over.

Positions Available: Short-term internships lasting six weeks to three months involving general office support, outreach to other peace-education-travel groups, and possible United Nations activities. Also office volunteer positions available. Open on a rolling basis.

Cost/Compensation: Free. Reimbursement available to interns for lunch and daily commute. Some temporary housing assistance also available.

For more information: Tori Napier, Assistant Administrator, U.S. Servas, Inc., 11 John Street, Suite 407, New York, New York 10038; (212)267-0252; (212)

267-0292 (fax); E-mail usservas@servas.org; URL http://servas.org.

VOLUNTARY WORKCAMPS ASSOCIATION OF GHANA (VOLU)
Accra, Ghana
Project Location: Ghana
Description: Workcamps are in rural Guana, mainly doing manual work.
Cost: Volunteers pay their own travel costs and an inscription fee of approximately £120. Room and board are free.
For more information: Voluntary Workcamps Association of Ghana (VOLU), P.O. Box 1540, Accra, Ghana; 233-21-663486.

VOLUNTEERS FOR PEACE, INC. - INTERNATIONAL WORKCAMPS
Belmont, Vermont
Project Location: U.S. and 70 foreign countries.
Description: International workcamps.
Cost: $15.00 membership; $195 per camp plus cost of transportation to camp.
For more information: Volunteers for Peace, Inc. - International Workcamps, Tiffany Road, Belmont Vermont 05730; (802)259-2759; E-mail vfp@vfp.org; URL http://www.vfp.org.

WATERWAY RECOVERY GROUP
London, England
Project Location: Waterways in the U.K.
Description: Voluntary organization that restores canals and navigable rivers.
Open to: 17-70 year olds able to undertake manual work.
Positions Available: Volunteer on residential camps.
Cost/Compensation: £35 to cover living expenses.
For more information: Waterway Recovery Group, P. O. Box 114, Rickmansworth, WD31ZY England, 01923-711-114; 01923-897-000 (fax); E-mail wrg@waterways.org.uk; URL http://waterways.org.uk/index.htm.

WELSHPOOL AND LLANFAIR RAILWAY
Welshpool, United Kingdom
Project Location: United Kingdom
Description: Help needed to maintain, operate, and administer a narrow gauge steam railroad.
For more information: Andy Carey, Operating Manager, Welshpool & Llanfair Railway, The Station, Llanfair Caereinon, Powys, S421 OSF U.K.; 01938-810861.

VSU YOUTH IN ACTION
Kent, United Kingdom
Project Location: At VSU branches in Tunbridge Wells, Tonbridge, Sevenoaks, Dartford, and Gravesham.
Description: Youth Action Agency with charitable status.
Open to: Young people 14-25 years of age.
Positions Available: Projects and placements in the community.
For more information: Wendy Jukes, Coordinator, VSU Youth in Action, VSU Central Office, The Bradbourne School, Bradbourne Vale Road, Sevenoaks, Kent TN13 3LE; 01732-450448.

WILDLIFE TRUST WEST WALES
Haverfordwest, United Kingdom
Project Location: Skomer Island, Wales.
Description: Assistant wardening.
Cost: Transportation to project site.
For more information: Mrs Glennerster, Island Booking Offices, Wildlife Trust West Wales, 7 Market Street, Haverfordwest, Dyfed SA61 INF United Kingdom; (01437)765-462.

WILLING WORKERS ON ORGANIC FARMS (WWOOF) - AUSTRALIA
Australia
Project Location: Over 500 small organic farms around Australia.
Description: Organization offers an opportunity to learn about organic farming while giving practical help.
For more information: WWOOF (Australia), Buchan, Victoria 3885, Australia; 051-550-218.

WILLING WORKERS ON ORGANIC FARMS (WWOOF) - IRELAND
County Werfore, Ireland
Project Location: Ireland
Description: Organic gardening and farming.
Cost: Travel costs to and from host farm.
For more information: Annie Sampson, Harpoonstown, Drinaugh, County Werfore, Ireland (include 2 international postal reply coupons).

WILLING WORKERS ON ORGANIC FARMS (WWOOF) - NEW ZEALAND
Nelson, New Zealand
Project Location: New Zealand
Description: Unpaid work on organic properties.
Cost: Student pays own travel expenses. Project provides room and board.
For more information: Jane and Andrew Strange, WWOOF, P.O. Box 1172, Nelson, New Zealand; 025-345711.

WILLING WORKERS ON ORGANIC FARMS (WWOOF) - UNITED KINGDOM
Sussex, England
Project Location: Worldwide

Description: WWOOF helps volunteers find placements in farm placement service and by fix-it-yourself booklets and a bimonthly newsletter.

Open to: Students 16 and over.

Positions Available: Volunteering on organic smallholdings and farms. A wide-variety of work depending on season, climate, area, etc.

Cost: Membership fee of approximately £15. Visa requirements must be checked.

For more information: WWOOF P.O. Box 2675, Lewes, East Sussex BN7 1RB, England; 01273-476286; URL http://www.phdoc.com/sites/wwoof.

WORLD HORIZONS
Dyfed, Wales

Project Location: Britain, Europe, Middle East, Asia, Africa, Australia, and the Americas.

Description: A modern Christian missionary movement involved in short-term placement and expeditions.

Cost: Volunteers pay their own finances and cost of accommodations that are provided.

For more information: World Horizons, Centre for the Nations, North Dock, Llarelli, Wales SA15 2LF; (44)1554-750005; E-mail admin@whorizons.org.

NATURE/ENVIRONMENT

AMERICAN HIKING SOCIETY
Washington, DC

Project Location: Nationwide.

Description: National nonprofit organization dedicated to protecting trails.

Positions available: Trail crew volunteers.

Cost: $60.00 registration fee plus travel expenses.

Other information: Organizers of National Trails Day.

For more information: Shirley Hearn, Volunteer Vacations Coordinator, American Hiking Society, P.O. Box 20160, Washington, DC 20041-2160; (301)565-6704; E-mail AHSMmbrshp@aol.com; URL http://www.ahs.simplenet.com.

APPALACHIAN MOUNTAIN CLUB
Gorham, New Hampshire

Project Location: White Mountains of New Hampshire, and Massachusetts Berkshires.

Description: Outdoor environmental and educational organization.

Open to: Teens ages 16-19.

Positions available: 1-2 week volunteer trail crew opportunities.

Cost: $55-$275, travel to site, and camping gear.

Other information: Programs for adults as well!

For more information: North Country Volunteer Coordinator, Appalachian Mountain Club, P.O. Box 298, Gorham, New Hampshire 03581; (603)446-2721 Ext. 192; (603)466-2822 (fax); URL http://www.outdoors.org.

BIKES NOT BOMBS
Roxbury, Massachusetts

Project Location: Worldwide, Massachusetts.

Description: Organization helping local groups start bicycle shops and other programs in Central America, Haiti and in the United States.

For more information: Program Director, Bikes Not Bombs, 59 Amory #103A, Roxbury, Massachusetts 02119; (617)442-0004; E-mail bnbrox@igc.ape.org.

CALVIN CREST CAMP, RETREAT, AND CONFERENCE CENTER
Fremont, Nebraska

Project Location: Fremont, Nebraska

Description: Christian (Presbyterian) co-ed residential summer camp. Season from 6/1-8/25.

Open to: Must be 18-years-old.

Positions Available: Lifeguards, food service staff, housekeeping staff, group counselors, and wranglers.

Cost/Compensation: Room, board, and competitive salary.

For more information: Doug Morton, Administrator, Calvin Crest Camp, Retreat, and Conference Center, 2870 County Road 13, Fremont, Nebraska 68025; (402)628-6455; (402)628-8255 (fax); E-mail calvincrest@navix.net; URL http://members.home.net/calvincrest.

CAMP BERACHAH
Auburn, Washington

Project Location: Auburn, Washington

Description: Residential and day camps for ages 5-18.

Open to: High school students.

Positions Available: Counselors, recreation director, crafts director, lifeguards, horsemanship wrangler/instructor, safari guides, mountain bike guides, kitchen, housekeeping, and maintenance.

For more information: James Richey or Scott Rossiter, Program Director and Program Assistant, Camp Berachah, 19830 Southeast 328th Place, Auburn, Washington 98092; (253)939-0488 or (800)859-CAMP; (253)833-7027 (fax); E-mail berachah@tcmnet.com; URL http://tcmnet.com/~berachah/.

CAMP NETIMUS
Milford, Pennsylvania

Project Location: Milford, Pennsylvania

Description: Residential camp for girls, ages 6-17.

Open to: Students, age 14 and over. Counselors have to be 21+.

Positions Available: Leadership training program with a goal of counselor readiness. The four phases of this program are Major-Minor, Working Senior, Jr. Counselor In Training (JR. CIT), and Counselor in Training (CIT).

Cost/Compensation: $2,400-$2,600 for 4 weeks.

Other Information: Take part in landsports, arts, crafts, performing arts, watersports, riding, adventure, and discovery activities. Learn and gain insight into the obligations, responsibilities, rewards, and goals of a camp counselor in a fun environment.

For more information: Mark Glaser, Director, Camp Nock-A-Mixon, 16 Gum Tree Lane, Lafayette Hill, Pennsylvania 19444; (610)941-1307; E-mail mglaser851@aol.com.

CAMP WASHINGTON
Lakeside, Connecticut

Project Location: Lakeside, Connecticut

Description: Residential and day camp for children, ages 5-18.

Open to: High school students.

Positions Available: Counselors in Training (16/17), general cabin counselors, program staff, lifeguards, office, and kitchen help.

Cost/Compensation: Room and board, salary (except CIT program – fee is $200).

Other Information: Episcopal diocesan camp offering traditional program plus many specialized programs such as theater,, choir, community service, family, mini-camping skills, and wilderness tripping programs. Also offers an intensive Counselor in Training program for eight weeks of the summer season.

For more information: Elia Vecchitto, Camp Director, Camp Washington, 190 Kenyon Road, Lakeside, Connecticut 06758; (860)567-9623; (860)567-3037 (fax); E-mail eliz_v@hotmail.com.

CAPITAL CAMPS
Waynesboro, Pennsylvania

Project Location: Waynesboro, Pennsylvania

Description: Jewish residential community camp. Also sponsor leadership trip to Israel.

Open to: CITS (age 17) and staff (18+).

Positions Available: Counselors, specialists, and counselors-in-training.

Cost/Compensation: CITS ($700) and staff ($800-$1,500).

For more information: Faye Bousel, Executive Director, Capital Camps, 133 Rollins Avenue, Unit 4, Rockville, Maryland 20852; (301)468-2267; (301)468-1719 (fax); E-mail staff@capitalcamps.com; URL http://www.capitalcamps.com.

CENTER FOR MARINE CONSERVATION
Washington, D.C.
Project Location: Nationwide
Description: Group sponsoring a three-hour beach cleanup every year in September.
For more information: Center for Marine Conservation, 1725 DeSales Street, NW, Washington, DC 20036; (202)429-5609.

CITIZEN VOLUNTEER ENVIRONMENTAL MONITORING PROGRAMS
Washington, D.C.
Project Location: Various U.S. locations.
Description: This program uses volunteers to test water in rivers, streams, and lakes.
Cost: Varying costs.
For more information: Citizen Volunteer Environmental Monitoring Programs, c/o Office of Water, Environmental Protection Agency, Washington, DC 20460.

CLEAN WATER ACTION
Washington, D.C.
Project Location: Nationwide
Description: Organization using education and lobbying to aid decisions for drinkable water that is affordable.
For more information: Clean Water Action, 1320 18th Street, NW, Suite 300, Washington, DC 20036; (202)457-1286.

CLEARWATER
Poughkeepsie, New York
Project Location: Northeast; New York
Description: The sloop, *Clearwater,* is a nonprofit, environmental education program offering a traditional sailing opportunity.
Open to: Volunteers, age 12 and up (1 week at a cost of $50); Sailing apprentices (1 month) and education assistants (2 months) for ages 16 and up.
Cost/Compensation: Compensation of $25-50/week.
For more information: Captain, Clearwater, 112 Market Street, Poughkeepsie, New York 12601-4095; (914)454-7673; (914)454-7953 (fax); E-mail captain@clearwater.org; URL http://www.clearwater.org.

DELAWARE NATURE SOCIETY
Hockessin, Delaware
Project Location: Northeast and Delaware
Description: Nonprofit group dedicated to environmental education, conservation, and advocacy.
Cost: N/A
For more information: Associate Director, Education, Delaware Nature Society, P.O. Box 700, Hockessin, Delaware 19707; (302)239-2334 Ext. 14; URL http://www.dca.net/naturesociety.

EARTHWATCH
Watertown, Massachusetts
Project Location: 50 countries.
Description: Improve human understanding of our planet, diversity of its inhabitants, and the processes that affect the quality of life on Earth.
Cost: $495 to $2,200, plus expenses to sites.
For more information: Earthwatch, 680 Mount Auburn Street, Watertown, Massachusetts 02272.

FARM SANCTUARY
Watkins Glen, New York
Project Location: Work at Watkins Glen, New York; Orland, California
Description: Nonprofit organization dedicated to saving farm animals from cruelty and abuse.
Cost: Buy and prepare your own food.
For more information: Intern Program, Education Coordinator, Farm Sanctuary, P.O. Box 150, Watkins Glen, New York 14891-0150; (607)583-2225; URL http://www.farmsanctuary.org.

4H
Ottawa, Ontario
Project Location: United States and Canada.
Description: Youth are given the opportunity to contribute to conservation of energy, improvement of the environment, and better food production.
For more information:
United States: U.S.A. National 4-H Council, 7100 Connecticut Avenue, Chevy Chase, Maryland 20815-4999; (301)961-2800.
Canada: Canadian 4-H Council/Conseil de 4-H du Canada, 1690 Woodward Drive #208, Ottawa, Ontario K2C 3R8; (613)723-4444.

FRIENDS OF THE ROUGE
Detroit, Michigan
Project Location: Detroit, Michigan
Description: Organization dedicated to the restoration and protection of the Rouge River.
Open to: High school students and graduates.
Positions Available: Internships and volunteer opportunities.
Cost/Compensation: Unpaid
Other information: Teens can participate in water quality monitoring, storm drain stenciling, and office administration.
For more information: Jim Graham, Executive Director, Friends of the Rouge, 950 Michigan Building, 22586 Ann Arbor Trail, Dearborn Heights, Michigan 48127; (313)792-9900; (313)792-9628 (fax); E-mail execdirector@therouge.org; URL http://www.therouge.org.

GREEN CITY PROJECT
San Francisco, California

Project Location: San Francisco, California
Description: Environmental education organization.
Open to: High school students and graduates.
Positions Available: Administrative intern, education intern, and calendar intern.
Cost/Compensation: Unpaid
For more information: Brian Block, Programs Director, Green City Project, P.O. Box 31251, San Francisco, California 94131; (415)285-6556; (415)285-6563 (fax); E-mail planetdrum@igc.org.

GREENPEACE USA, INC.
Washington, D.C.
Project Location: N/A
Description: Nonprofit group fighting for endangered animal protection, preservation of our environment, and avoiding nuclear war.
For more information: Greenpeace USA, Inc., 1436 U Street NW, Washington, DC 20009; (202)462-1177.

IROQUOIS NATIONAL WILDLIFE REFUGE
Alabama, New York
Project Location: Alabama, New York
Description: National wildlife refuge.
Open to: High school students and graduates.
Positions Available: Volunteers
Cost/Compensation: Unpaid
For more information: Dorothy Gerhart, Outdoor Recreation Planner, Iroquois National Wildlife Refuge, 1101 Casey Road, Basam, New York 14013; (716) 948-5445.

JUSTACT: YOUTH ACTION FOR GLOBAL JUSTICE
San Francisco, California
Project Location: San Francisco, California; International (volunteer opportunities); Bike-Aid (cross-country bicycle ride).
Description: Organization working with youth to develop a life-long commitment to social and economic justice internationally. JustAct provides a network for students and graduates linking them to educational and volunteer opportunities worldwide.
Open to: High school students, college students, and graduates.
Positions Available: Office management and administration internship, communications and public relations internships, education and organizing program intern, Bike-Aid internships and volunteer opportunities, Alternative Opportunities program intern, and international volunteer opportunities.
Cost/Compensation: Varies. Contact JustAct for details.
For more information: Wendy Phillips, Internship Coordinator, JustAct: Youth ACTion for Global JUSTice, 333 Valencia Street, Suite 101, San Francisco, California 94103; (415)431-4204; (415)431-5953 (fax); E-mail info@justact.org; URL http://www.justact.org.

KEEP AMERICA BEAUTIFUL, INC.
Stamford, Connecticut
Project Location: More than 485 cities, towns and counties in 41 states.
Description: Nonprofit organization committed to improving the practices of waste handling.
For more information: Keep America Beautiful, Inc., Mill River Plaza, 9 W. Broad Street, Stamford, Connecticut 06902; (203)323-8987.

KIDS AGAINST POLLUTION (KAP)
Closter, New Jersey
Project Location: 500 chapters organized in 42 states.
Description: Organization providing information on environmental issues and ideas for action.
For more information: Kids Against Pollution, P.O. Box 775, Closter, New Jersey 07624; (201)784-0726.

LOST VALLEY EDUCATIONAL CENTER
Dexter, Oregon
Project Location: Pacific Northwest, Oregon.
Description: Education center provides hands-on experience in such things as organic gardening, herbal medicine, personal growth and sustainable living.
Cost: Tuition for 3 month program is $1,830 or $610 per month.
For more information: Julianne Ruben, Owner, Lost Valley Education Center, 81868 Lost Valley Lane, Dexter, Oregon 97431; (541)937-3351.

NATIONAL PARK SERVICE
Washington, D.C.
Project Location: Nationwide
Description: Agency administering parks, monuments, and important sites and coordinating the Wild and Scenic Rivers System and National Trail System.
For more information: National Park Service, U.S. Department of Interior, P.O. Box 37127, Washington, DC 20013; (202)208-6843.

NATIONAL WILDLIFE FEDERATION
Washington, D.C.
Project Location: Nationwide
Description: Organization helping and inspiring people to protect the earth's wildlife and environment.
For more information: National Wildlife Federation, 1400 16th Street, NW, Washington, DC 20036; (202) 797-6800.

NEW ENGLAND AQUARIUM
Boston, Massachusetts
Project Location: Boston, Massachusetts
Description: The mission of the New England Aquarium is to present, promote, and protect the world of

water to 1.2 million visitors annually.

Open to: Students age 16 and up.

Positions available: Aquarium Guide volunteers.

Cost: None. Upon completion of training and 20 hours of service, students may apply for 3 credits for Introduction to Marine Science at the local community college.

For more information: Cincy Cheney, Youth Programs Supervisor, New England Aquarium, Central Wharf, Boston, Massachusetts 02110-3399; (617) 973-0235; (617)973-6552 (fax); E-mail ccheney@neaq.org; URL http://www.neaq.org.

NORTH CAROLINA AMATEUR SPORTS

Research Triangle Park, North Carolina

Project Location: Research Triangle Park, North Carolina

Description: Organization supporting the Olympics through amateur sports programming. Host State Games of North Carolina and Cycle North Carolina.

Open to: High school students and graduates.

Positions Available: Volunteer opportunities available.

Cost/Compensation: Paid and unpaid internships available to students who have completed at least one year of college.

For more information: Linda Smith, Director of Operations, North Carolina Amateur Sports, P.O. Box 12727, Research Triangle Park, North Carolina 27709; (919)361-2559 (fax).

NORTH CAROLINA STATE PARKS AND RECREATION, RAVEN ROCK STATE PARK

Lillington, North Carolina

Project Location: Lillington, North Carolina

Description: State park.

Open to: High school students and graduates.

Positions Available: Volunteers

Cost/Compensation: Unpaid

Other information: Other North Carolina State Parks may provide housing, however, Raven Rock has no seasonal housing.

For more information: Eric Folk, Park Ranger I, Raven Rock, State Park, 3009 Raven Rock Road, Lillington, North Carolina 27546; (910)893-4888; E-mail ravenroc@fayetteville.nc.com; URL http://ils.unc.edu/parkproject/ncparks.htm.

OUTDOOR SCIENTIST

Washington, D.C.

Project Location: United States

Description: Volunteers test waters for toxic substances, evaluate fish health, catalogue litter, research acid rain, etc.

For more information: Citizen Volunteer Environmental Monitoring Programs, c/o Office of Water, Environmental Protection Agency, Washington, DC 20460.

PACIFIC WHALE FOUNDATION

Kihei, Hawaii

Project Location: Maui, Hawaii, Australia

Description: Humpback whale research.

Positions Available: Marine Debris Beach Survey, Student Naturalist, Career Shadowing with Pacific Whale Foundation, and Field Research Techniques.

Cost/Compensation: $1,395 and the cost of transportation.

For more information: Merrill Kaufman, Marine Education Specialist, Pacific Whale Foundation, 101 N. Kihei Road, Kihei, Hawaii 96753; (808)879-8811; (808)879-2615 (fax); E-mail merrill@pacificwhale.org; URL http://www.pacificwhale.org.

SAN JUAN/RIO GRANDE NATIONAL FOREST

Monte Vista, Colorado

Project Location: Monte Vista, Colorado

Description: Agency promoting multiple uses of land resources and managing Bureau of Land Management areas.

Open to: High school students and graduates.

Cost/Compensation: Most of the positions provide housing and limited subsistence (typically $16/day), but check with each project leader to verify before applying.

For more information: Dale Gomez, Partnership Coordinator, San Juan/Rio Grande National Forest, 1803 West Highway 160, Monte Vista, Colorado 81144; (719)852-5941; E-mail ls=c.keller/oul=ro2f09a@mhs-fswa.attmail.com.

SAVE THE SOUND, INC.

Stamford, Connecticut

Project Location: Stamford, Connecticut

Description: Organization committed to the preservation of Long Island Sound.

Open to: High school students and graduates depending on job.

Positions Available: Education Program Assistant, Research Assistant, Public Outreach Assistant, and Membership Assistant.

Cost/Compensation: Unpaid. Will cover costs related directly to internship/volunteer activities.

Other information: Also new Habitat Restoration Project, a nonprofit membership organization dedicated to the restoration, protection, and appreciation of Long Island Sound and its watershed.

For more information: Internship Coordinator, Save the Sound, Inc., 185 Magee Avenue, Stamford, Connecticut 06902 (submit requests here); or 50 Berry Drive, Glen Cove, New York 11842; (203)327-9786;

(203)967-2677 (fax); E-mail savethesound@snet.net; URL http://www.savethesound.org.

SERVE/MAINE

Augusta, Maine

Project Location: Maine

Description: SERVE/Maine places volunteers and interns with Maine's natural resource agencies to accomplish projects of an environmental nature.

Open to: High school age and upward.

Positions available: Environmental projects including water quality monitoring, trailbuilding, grant writing, etc.

Cost: Housing and a stipend are available for some positions.

For more information: James Lainsburgy, Coordinator, Serve/Maine, 124 State House Station, Augusta, Maine 04333-0124; (207)287-3082; (207)287-3611 (fax); E-mail corps.conservation@state.me.us.

SERVICE CIVIL INTERNATIONAL

Crozet, Virginia

Project Location: U.S. workcamps.

Description: Environmental, construction, solidarity, and social service projects.

Cost: Volunteers pay travel expenses and a small fee.

For more information: Service Civil International, c/o Innisfree Village, 5474 Walnut Level Road, Crozet, Virginia 22932; (804)823-1826.

SIERRA CLUB

San Francisco, California

Project Location: N/A

Description: Members aim to protect earth's natural resources and wilderness.

Cost: N/A

For more information: Sierra Club, 730 Polk Street, San Francisco, California 94109; (415)776-2211.

STUDENT CONSERVATION ASSOCIATION

Charlestown, New Hampshire

Project Location: National parks, forests, wilderness, and other sites throughout the U.S.

Description: Conservation projects.

Cost: $45 application fee, $5 for low-income applicants, travel expenses, and camping gear.

For more information: Student Conservation Association, High School Program, P.O. Box 550, Charlestown, New Hampshire 03603; (603)543-1700 Ext. 157; E-mail hs-program@sca-inc.org; URL http://www.sca-inc.org.

STUDENT ENVIRONMENTAL ACTION COALITION (SEAC)

Philadelphia, Pennsylvania

Project Location: Philadelphia and nationwide.

Description: SEAC is a network of high school and college environmental groups dedicated to building the capacity of students to organize for environmental justice.

Positions available: Internships in Philadelphia and volunteer and coordination opportunities nationwide.

Cost: N/A

For more information: SEAC National Office, Student Environmental Action Coalition (SEAC), National Office, P.O. Box 31909, Philadelphia, Pennsylvania 19104-0609; (215)222-4711; (215)222-2896 (fax); E-mail seac@seac.org; URL http://www.seac.org.

SURFRIDER FOUNDATION

San Clemente, California

Project Location: San Clemente, California

Description: Organization committed to the preservation of the world's oceans.

Open to: High school students, seniors, and graduates.

Cost/Compensation: Unpaid

For more information: Josh Wright, Membership Services, Surfrider Foundation, 122 South El Camino Real #67, San Clemente, California 92672; (714)495-8142; E-mail info@surfrider.org; URL http://www.surfrider.org.

U.S. ARMY CORPS OF ENGINEERS

Nashville, Tennessee

Project Location: Nationwide, Tennessee

Description: This group is the steward of land and water covering about 12 million acres. Volunteers have opportunities in natural resource management and in the recreation area.

Cost: N/A

For more information: Volunteer Clearinghouse, U.S. Army Corps of Engineers, P.O. Box 1070, Nashville, Tennessee 37202-1070; (800)865-8337.

VOLUNTEERS FOR OUTDOOR COLORADO

Denver, Colorado

Project Location: Public lands in Colorado.

Description: This organization has a list of hundreds of many opportunities for volunteers and interns around Colorado. A free catalog is available.

Cost: N/A

For more information: Jennifer Burstein, Clearinghouse Coordinator, Volunteers for Outdoor Colorado, 600 S. Marion Parkway, Denver, Colorado 80209-2597; (303)715-1010 or (800)925-2220 (303)715-1212 (fax); E-mail voc@voc.org; URL http://www.voc.org.

WENATCHEE NATIONAL FOREST

Cle Elum, Washington

Project Location: Cle Elum, Washington and the Pacific Northwest.

Description: Forest service.
Open to: Teens 18 years and older.
Positions Available: Lookout observer-interpreter and trail crew worker.
Cost/Compensation: N/A
For more information: Debbie Kelly, Information Assistant, USDA Forest Service, Wenatchee National Forest, Cle Elum Ranger District, 803 W. 2nd Street, Cle Elum, Washington 98943; (509)674-4411; (509) 674-1530 (fax); URL http://www.fs.fed.us/wnnf/welcome.htm.

YMCA CAMP SURF

Imperial Beach, California
Project Location: Imperial Beach, California
Description: Residential oceanfront camp.
Open to: High school students.
Positions Available: Camp counselors and lifeguards.
Cost/Compensation: $25-$38/day with room and board.
For more information: Mark Thompson, Camp Director, YMCA Camp Surf, 106 Carnation Avenue, Imperial Beach, California 91932; (619)423-5850; (619)423-4141 (fax); E-mail campsurf@ymca.org; URL http://www.ymca.org/camp/.

RESEARCH/SCIENCE

CARETTA RESEARCH PROJECT

Savannah, Georgia
Project Location: Wassaw Island - a barrier island off Georgia's coast.
Description: Research and conservation of loggerhead sea turtles.
Open to: Students (and everyone interested!) over 16 years of age.
Cost: $500 per week.
For more information: Kris Williams, Director, Caretta Research Project, P.O. Box 9841, Savannah, Georgia 31412-9841; (912)447-8655; (912)355-0182 (fax); E-mail WassawCRP@aol.com.

INTERCULTURAL DEVELOPMENT RESEARCH ORGANIZATION

San Antonio, Texas
Project Location: N/A
Description: This was established to aid students who are disadvantaged economically and who speak limited English.
Cost: Sometimes class credit and minimum-wage stipends are offered.
For more information: Intercultural Development Research Organization, 5835 Callaghan Road, Suite 350, San Antonio, Texas 78228; (512)684-5389.

PACIFIC WHALE FOUNDATION

Kihei, Hawaii
Project Location: Maui, Hawaii, Australia
Description: Humpback whale research.
Positions available: Marine Debris Beach Survey, Student Naturalist, Career Shadowing with Pacific Whale Foundation, and Field Research Techniques.
Cost: $1,395 and the cost of transportation.
For more information: Merrill Kaufman, Marine Education Specialist, Pacific Whale Foundation, 101 N. Kihei Road, Kihei, Hawaii 96753; (808)879-8811; (808)879-2615 (fax);
E-mail merrill@pacificwhale.org; URL http://www.pacificwhale.org.

SURFRIDER FOUNDATION

San Clemente, California
Project Location: Nationwide, California
Description: Group trying to preserve coastal waters and beaches.
For more information: Angi Guiton, Internship/Volunteer Director, Surfrider Foundation, 122 S. El Camino Real, #67, San Clemente, California 92672; (714)492-8170; E-mail surfrider0@aol.com; URL http://www.surfrider.org.

UNIVERSITY RESEARCH EXPEDITIONS PROGRAM (UREP)

Berkeley, California
Project Location: University of California, Berkeley.
Description: Students act as field assistants on research expeditions.
Cost: £350-£800 plus travel cost to get to site.
For more information: Secretary of University Research Programs, University of California, Berkeley, California 94720-7050; (510)642-6586.

STILL LOOKING FOR MORE IDEAS? CONTACT YOUR STATE'S COMMISSION ON VOLUNTEERISM. SEE THE NEXT PAGE FOR CONTACT INFORMATION.

FOCUS ON...

YOUR STATE'S COMMISSION ON VOLUNTEERISM

Many states provide assistance to those seeking a place to volunteer.. Check with your state's volunteer agency and see what information they have for teens..

ALABAMA
Patricia S. Henderson, Director, Governor's Office on National and Community Service, 401 Adams Avenue, Montgomery, Alabama 36104; (334) 242-7110; (334)242-2885 (fax); E-mail path@adeca.state.al.us.

Alabama National & Community Service State Commission, 600 Dexter Avenue, Room SB 06, Montgomery Alabama 36130; (334)242-7110.

ALASKA
Alaska State Community Service Commission, 333 W. 4th Avenue, Suite 222, Anchorage, Alaska 99501; (907)269-4611.

ARIZONA
Arizona National & Community Service State Commission, 1700 W. Washington, Street, 3rd Floor, Room 320, Phoenix, Arizona 85007; (602) 542-3461.

ARKANSAS
State of Arkansas, Arkansas Division of Volunteerism, P.O. Box 1437, Slot #1300, Little Rock, Arkansas 72203; (501)682-7540.

Arkansas Commission on National & Community Service State, 4608 McDaniel Circle, Little Rock, Arkansas 72206; (501)888-2632; (501)682-1623 (fax); E-mail Betty.Hicks@mail. state.ar.us.

CALIFORNIA
California Commission on Improving Life Through Service, 1121 L Street, Suite 600, Sacramento, California 95814; (916)323-7646.

COLORADO
Community Partnership Office, 140 E. 19th Avenue, Suite 100, Denver, Colorado 80203; (303)894-2750.

CONNECTICUT
Connecticut National & Community Service State Commission, 61 Woodland Street, Hartford, Connecticut 06105; (203)566-6154.

DELAWARE
State of Delaware Office of Volunteerism, P.O. Box 637, Dover, Delaware 19903; (302)739-4456.

Delaware National & Community Service State Commission, Carvel State Office Building, 4th Fl., 820 N. French St., Wilmington, Delaware

19801; (302)577-6650.

DISTRICT OF COLUMBIA
D.C. National & Community Service State Commission, 717 14th Street, NW, #900, Washington, DC 20005; (202)727-4970.

FLORIDA
Florida Governor's Commission on Community Service, 1101 Gulf Breeze Parkway, Box 188, Gulf Breeze, Florida 32561; (904)934-4000.

GEORGIA
Jim Marshall, Executive Director, Georgia Commission for National & Community Service, 60 Executive Park South, NE, Atlanta, Georgia 30329-2231; (404)327-6844; (404) 327-6848 (fax); E-mail jmarshal@dca.state.ga.us.

HAWAII
Hawaii State Commission on National & Community Service, 335 Merchant Street, Room 101, Honolulu, Hawaii 96813; (808)586-8675.

Statewide Volunteer Services, Office of the Governor, State Capitol, Honolulu, Hawaii 96813.

Find your state's Commission on Volunteerism

IDAHO
Kelly Houston, Executive Director, Idaho Commission for National & Community Service, P.O. Box 83720, Boise, Idaho 83720-0018; or 1299 N. Orchard, Suite 110, Boise, ID, 93706; (208)658-2000 Ext. 281; (208)327-7444 (fax); E-mail khouston@corr.state.id.us..

ILLINOIS
Lt. Governor's Advisory Council on Voluntary Action, James R. Thompson Center, 100 W. Randolph, Suite 15-200, Chicago, Illinois 60601; (312)814-5220.

INDIANA
Governor's Voluntary Action Program, 302 W. Washington, Room E220, Indianapolis, Indiana 46204; (317)232-2504.

IOWA
Governor's Office for Volunteers, State Capitol, Des Moines, Iowa 50319; (515)281-8304.

Iowa Commission for National & Community Service, 150 E. Des Moines Street, Des Moines, Iowa 50319; (515)281-9043.

KANSAS
Kansas Commission for National & Community Service, 200 SW 6th, P. O. Box 889, Topeka, Kansas 66603; (913)234-1423.

KENTUCKY
Kentucky Office of Volunteer Services, 275 E. Main Street, Frankfort, Kentucky 40621; (502)564-HELP.

Kentucky Community Service Commission, State Office Building, 501 Mero Street, Room 923, Frankfort, Kentucky 40622; (502)564-5330.

LOUISIANA
Natalie Nunley, Executive Assistant, Louisiana Serve Commission, 263 Third Street, Suite 610B, Baton Rouge, Louisiana 70801; (225)342-2038; (225)342-0106 (fax); E-mail nnunley@crt.state.la.us.

MAINE
Maine Commission on National & Community Service, State House, 184 State Street, Augusta, Maine 04333; (207)287-5313; (207)287-6489 (fax); WWW http://www.state.me.us/spo/mccs.

MARYLAND
Governor's Office on Volunteerism, 301 W. Preston Street, Suite 1501, Baltimore, Maryland 21201; (410) 225-4496.

MASSACHUSETTS
Massachusetts Commission for National & Community Service, 87 Summer Street, 4th Floor, Boston, Massachusetts 02110; (617)542-2544.

MICHIGAN
Michigan Community Service Commission, 111 S. Capitol Avenue, George W. Ronney Building, 4th Floor, Lansing, Michigan 48913; (517)335-4295.

MINNESOTA
Bonnie Esposito, Director, Minnesota Office of Citizenship and Volunteer Services, Department of Administration, 117 University Avenue, Room 300, St. Paul, Minnesota 55155-2200; (651)296-4731; (651)296-4731 (fax); E-mail admin.mocvs@state.mn.us; WWW http://mocvs.state.mn.us..

Minnesota Commission for National & Community Service, 683 Capitol Square Building, Saint Paul, Minnesota 55101; (612)296-1435.

MISSISSIPPI
Mississippi Commission for National & Community Service, 3825 Ridgewood Road, Jackson, Mississippi 39211; (601)982-6738.

MISSOURI
Krista Bailey, Program Assistant, Missouri Community Service Commission, 3225 W. Truman Boulevard, Suite 101, Jefferson City, Missouri 65109; (573)751-7488 or toll free at (877)210-7611; (573)526-0463 (fax).

MONTANA
Montana Community Services Advisory Council, State Capitol, Room 219, Helena, Montana 59601; (406) 444-5547.

NEBRASKA
Nebraska Commission on National & Community Service, State Capitol, 6th Floor, W. Side, Centennial Mall, Lincoln, Nebraska 68509; (402)471-6225.

NEVADA
Nevada Commission for National & Community Service, 1830 E. Sahara Avenue, Suite 314, Las Vegas, Nevada 89104; (702)486-7997.

NEW HAMPSHIRE
Governor's Office on Volunteerism, 25 Capitol Street, Room 431, Concord, New Hampshire 03301; (603) 271-3771.

New Hampshire Commission on National & Community Service, 64 Old Suncook Road, Concord, New Hampshire 03301; (603)228-9500.

NEW JERSEY
New Jersey Commission on National & Community Service, 240 W. Broad Street, CN 500, Trenton, New Jersey 08625; (609)633-9629.

NEW MEXICO
New Mexico Commission for National & Community Service, Teen Parent Services/AmeriCorps, 300 San Mateo Boulevard, Suite B-1, Albuquerque, New Mexico 87108; (505) 841-2967; (505)841-2769 (fax).

NEW YORK
New York Commission on National & Community Service, Executive Chamber- State Capitol, Albany, New York 12224; (518)473-8882.

NORTH CAROLINA
Traci Miller, YES Ambassador, Governor's Office on Volunteerism 116 W. Jones Street, Raleigh, North Carolina 27603; (919)733-2391.

Find your state's Commission on Volunteerism

OHIO
Community Service Council, 51 N. High Street, Suite 481, Columbus, Ohio 43215; (614)728-2916; (614) 728-2921 (fax); E-mail traci. miller@gcsc.state.oh.us; WWW http://www.state.oh.us/ohiogcsc.

OKLAHOMA
The Governor's Commission for Community Service, 1515 N. Lincoln, Oklahoma City, Oklahoma 73104; (405)235-7278.

OREGON
Oregon Community Service Commission, Portland State University, 491 Newburger, Portland, Oregon 97207; (503)725-5903.

PENNSYLVANIA
PennSERVE, The Governor's Office of Citizen Service, Dept. of Labor & Industry, 1304 Labor & Industry Building, Harrisburg, Pennsylvania 17120; (717)787-1971.

PUERTO RICO
Puerto Rico State Commission of Community Service, La Fortaleza, San Juan, PR 00901; (809)721-7877.

RHODE ISLAND
Rhode Island Commission for National & Community Service, 903 Broad St., Providence, Rhode Island 02907; (401)461-6305.

SOUTH CAROLINA
Division of Volunteer Service of the Governor's Office, 1205 Pendleton Street, Suite 405, Columbia, South Carolina 29201; (803)734-1677.

SOUTH DAKOTA
Governor's Office, Special Assistant to the Governor for Volunteerism, 500 E. Capital Avenue, Pierre, South Dakota 57501; (605)339-4357.

TENNESSEE
Tennessee Commission for National & Community Service, 302 John Sevier Building, 500 Charlotte Avenue, Nashville, Tennessee 37243; (615)532-9250.

TEXAS
Texas Commission for National & Community Service, Sam Houston Building, 201 E. 14th Street, Suite 680, Austin, Texas 78701; (512)463-1814.

UTAH
Marie Schwitzer, Executive Secretary, Utah Commission on Volunteers, 1530 N. Technology Way #D-03, Orem, Utah 84097; (801)764-0704; (801)764-9502 (fax); E-mail mschwitz@slkc.uswest.net; WWW http://www.volunteers.utah.org.

VERMONT
Jane Williams, Executive Director, Vermont Commission on Natural and Community Service, 133 State Street, Montpelier, Vermont 05633-4801; (802)828-4982; (802)828-4988 (fax); E-mail jwilliams@aot.state.vt.us.

VIRGINIA
Dee Dee Damschroder, Director, Virginia Department of Volunteerism, 730 E. Broad Street, 2nd Floor, Richmond, Virginia 23219; (804)692-1950.

WASHINGTON
Washington State Center for Voluntary Action, 9th and Columbia Building, MS-8300, Olympia, Washington 98504; (206)753-9684.

WEST VIRGINIA
Jean Ambrose, Executive Director, West Virginia Commission for National & Community Service, 900 Pennsylvania Avenue, Suite 1000, Charleston, West Virginia 25302; (304)340-3621; (304)340-3629 (fax).

WISCONSIN
Wisconsin National & Community Service Board, 101 E. Wilson St., 6th Floor, Madison, Wisconsin 53702; (608)266-8234.

WYOMING
Cathy Lymar, Exec. Director, Wyoming Commission for National & Community Service, Herschler Building 1W Room 1608, Cheyenne, Wyoming 82002; (307)777-5396; (307) 688-8967 (fax).

NOTES

ENTREPRENEURSHIP

This is the section that you should focus on if you've often dreamed of having your own business one day. It is never too early to start. The following list of potential businesses may include something that sounds interesting to you. It may spark some ideas of your own. Whatever the case may be, just let your imagination run wild. Try to find a match between something that you enjoy doing and something that people are willing to pay for.

There are several benefits to becoming an entrepreneur:

- You have control over your own destiny.
- You can make money doing what you really enjoy.
- You can work independently.

Ask anyone who works in the traditional workplace and they will probably tell you that their number one frustration is the sense that they are working "for" someone else. Many people will wistfully say, "Someday, I'd like to work for myself." Well, there's no reason to wait for someday. Start yourself on the path to owning your own business today. You can be in control of your own future — just remember that it also means that you are accepting all of the risks.

Entrepreneurship gives you the opportunity to make money doing what you really enjoy. Many home-based businesses begin simply as someone's hobby and then grow into a profitable enterprise once they realize that they can actually make money doing what they enjoy. Take an inventory of things you really enjoy. Then try to figure out who would be willing to pay money for that product or service. You'll be surprised with all of your different ideas. Just give yourself the permission to think without boundaries — the sky is the limit. Some of today's most profitable businesses started as someone's "crazy" idea.

Owning your own business allows you the opportunity to work independently. No set hours, no boss, and no rules. However, it also means no set paycheck. As an old boss of mine was fond of saying, "You eat what you kill"— meaning the only money you make is what you go out and earn yourself. This independence can be invigorating or intimidating, depending on your personality. Be honest with yourself. Does the idea of entrepreneurship appeal to you enough to live with all the risks? If your answer is yes, finish this chapter and explore some of the many types of home businesses that you can start today.

There is a lot to learn in order to run your own business. An excellent book is:

- ***The Lemonade Stand:*** *A Guide to Encouraging the Entrepreneur in Your Child* by Emanuel Modu, the Founder of the Center for Teenage Entrepreneurs.

This book will help you (and your parents, if they are helping you) start your business, develop a business plan, use basic record-keeping techniques, address legal and tax issues and avoid common mistakes.

Use Emanuel Modu's book, or a similar one, as your guide. Make sure that you have addressed all legal and tax issues before you begin. Ask your parents or a trusted adult to help you with your research. Remember that it's worth spending a little time now on planning your enterprise, in order to avoid some real headaches down the road.

If you have a computer, you may enjoy going on-line to see what other entrepreneurial youth are doing. There are a few interesting websites just for you.

- **http://www.anincomeofherown.com/** - The Independent Means Website is for women under twenty and provides information about starting a business, making, saving, and growing money, using money to make a better world, and networking with mentors. It includes an excellent resource directory and ability to order books, magazines and games.
- **http://www.aspira.org** – ASPIRA is dedicated to the education and leadership of Puerto Rican and Latino youth. Programs for youth entrepreneurship.
- **http://www.bedrock.com/tedi/tedi.htm** - This site has been helping young entrepreneurs recognize their dreams since 1991.
- **http://www.blackenterprise.com** – Entrepreneurial information for African-American youth.
- **http://www.entamerica.com** - This is a website sponsored by Entrepreneurial America. It will provide you with information on how you can order *How to Become a Teenage Entrepreneur,* a video and software package.
- **http://www.EntreWorld.org** – Extensive site providing resources for entrepreneurs.
- **http://fbla-pbl.org** - The Future Business Leaders of America site.
- **http://www.girlsinc.org/** - Girls Incorporated is dedicated to "inspiring all girls to be strong, smart, and bold."
- **http://www.ja.org/index.htma** - Junior Achievement is the world's largest nonprofit economic education program.
- **http://www.servenet.org** - Information about National Youth Service Day and the President's

Study Service Awards. Also, a volunteer match program is available.

- **http://www.yeo.org** - The Young Entrepreneurs' Organization website.
- **http://www.younginvestor.com** – Learn the fundamentals of money and investing in a comfortable, familiar, and interactive environment.

Now to the fun part! Read through the ideas in this chapter and see if any of them appeal to you. Each business idea includes a *description* of the business. The profile includes information about *start-up costs* using the scale below.

$	$0 - 49
$$	$50-99
$$$	$100 - 199
$$$$	$200+

Some *marketing ideas* are included. These are by no means all of the possibilities, but they should get you started in thinking creatively about marketing. There is a list of basic *equipment* that you will need to start-up. And finally, there are *additional resources* that you may wish to explore that will provide you with more detailed information.

The teen business ideas are organized into the following categories:

- Arts & Crafts Businesses
- Business to Business Services
- Computer Businesses
- Entertainment Services
- Food Services
- Green Businesses
- Home & Garden Businesses
- Personal Services
- Pet Services
- Special Events Services
- Sports Services

Focus On...
JUNIOR ACHIEVEMENT

Programs for high school students include:
- ***Company Program***™ - *an in-school or after-school curriculum teaching analysis and exploration of personal opportunities and responsibilities within a company.*
- ***Economics***™ - *a one-semester course focusing on micro-, macro-, and international economics.*
- ***GLOBE***™ - *a cross-culture examination of international trade.*
- ***JA Connections***™ - *a study of the knowledge, skills, and personal characteristics needed to excel in school, career, and the community.*
- ***JA BASE***™ - *teaches the economic and business knowledge required in the sports and entertainment industries.*

"To educate and inspire young people to value free enterprise, understand business and economics, and improve the quality of their lives."

-JA purpose

Opportunities are available throughout the United States. To find out more about JA and activities in your area, check out the website at:

www.ja.org

ARTS & CRAFTS BUSINESSES

ALTERATIONS

Description: Clothing repair and alterations such as hemming clothes, mending clothes, sewing on buttons, replacing zippers, etc.

Start -up Cost: $ -$$$$

Marketing Ideas: Go to the local dry cleaner and ask to post flyers. Take advantage of free advertising in church, school, and neighborhood publications. Utilize word-of-mouth advertising.

Equipment: Sewing machine and basic sewing supplies.

Additional Resources: **Fitting & Pattern Alteration: A Multi-Method Approach** by Elizabeth L. Liechty; ISBN 0870057758; softcover; $39.00; 1992.

ART INSTRUCTOR

Description: Teaching painting, sculpting, drawing, or other art forms to children or adults.

Start-up Costs: $

Marketing Ideas: This would be a good summer business. Advertise in school newspapers and on bulletin boards at libraries.

Equipment: Basic art supplies. (Have students provide own supplies.)

BADGE/BUTTON MAKING

Description: Make buttons/badges for school activities, school elections, neighborhood activities or parties.

Start-up Costs: $

Marketing Ideas: Wear your creations and have friends and family wear them, too. Anticipate special events — like the big school football game.

Equipment: Button-making kit and supplies.

CALLIGRAPHER

Description: Calligraphy for invitations, certificates, envelopes, placecards, and other special documents.

Start-up Costs: $

Marketing Ideas: Check with local bridal shops, stationers, and churches to place flyers or advertisements. Use word-of-mouth advertising. Make samples of the kind of work you can do.

Equipment: Calligraphy pens, scissors, ruler, and a selection of inks.

Additional Resources: **100 Keys to Great Calligraphy** by Judy Kastin; ISBN 0891347526; spiral bound; 64 pages; $17.00; 1996.

CARD MAKING

Description: Design your own cards.

Start-up Costs: $

Marketing Ideas: Make samples that people may order. Show these to individuals, groups, and businesses. Make sure that your display is neat, colorful, and organized. Possible ways to display might be using scrapbook formats, photo albums, or display boards.

Equipment: Plain cards with matching envelopes, paints, brushes, pens, pencils, matting, etc. as needed for your designs.

Additional Resources: **Card Crafting:** *Over 45 Ideas for Making Greeting Cards and Stationery* by Gillian Souter; ISBN 0806986832; softcover; $12.95; 1993. **Creative Greeting Cards:** *Personalized Projects for All Occasions* by Caroline Green; ISBN 089557983; softcover; 128 pages; $19.95; 1997.

CARTOON/CARICATURE ARTIST

Description: Draw cartoons or caricatures as novelty gifts. Create cartoons for newsletters, advertisements, or posters for local businesses and organizations.

Start-up Costs: $

Marketing Ideas: Create a small portfolio of your work and show it to everyone you can think of. Offer to draw caricatures for birthday parties or at craft fairs.

Equipment: Basic art supplies and an active imagination.

Additional Resources: **The Complete Book of Caricature** by Bob Staake; ISBN 0891343679; hardcover; 134 pages; $18.00; 1991. **Creating Comic Characters** by Dick Gautier; ISBN 0399523510; softcover; 128 pages; $11.95; 1997.

CRAFTS/HOLIDAY DECOR

Description: Create crafts for holiday decorating on Valentine's Day, Easter, Halloween, Thanksgiving, Hanukkah, or Christmas.

Start-up Costs: Depends on craft.

Marketing Ideas: Set up a table at local craft fairs. Sell your items at a lawn sale. Sell to your neighbors.

Equipment: Supplies needed will depend on your craft.

Additional Resources: **175 Easy-to-do Everyday Crafts** edited by Sharon Dunn Umnick; ISBN 156397441X; softcover; 64 pages; $6.95; 1995. **Better Homes & Gardens Holiday Crafts Kids Can Make**; ISBN 0696016060; softcover; $14.95; 1992. **Easy Holiday Crafts** by Laura Scott; ISBN 1882138341; softcover; $14.97; 1998.

DOLLHOUSE MAKER

Description: Create dollhouses for holiday or birthday gifts.

Start-up Costs: $$$

Marketing Ideas: Take pictures of past creations for a portfolio. Use it to pre-sell houses.

Equipment: Basic tools, dollhouse, and furnishings.

Additional Resources: **Build Your Own Inexpensive Dollhouse with One Sheet of 4X8 Plywood and**

Home Tools by Elmer John Tangerman; ISBN 0486234932; softcover; 44 pages; $3.95; 1980.
ABC's of Dollhouse Finishing: From Kit to Masterpiece by Barbara Watner and Terry Spohn; ISBN 0890241929; hardcover; 122 pages; $19.95; 1994.

ILLUSTRATOR

Description: Create illustrations for almost anything, including newsletters, advertising, posters or t-shirts.
Start-up Costs: $
Marketing Ideas: Keep a portfolio of your work to show to potential clients.
Equipment: Basic art supplies.

KNITTING

Description: Design and create knitted crafts such as sweaters, scarves, afghans, or holiday items.
Start-up Costs: $
Marketing Ideas: Make holiday or general items for sale at local craft fairs, church festivals, and garage sales. Take special orders from friends and family for gifts or special occasions.
Equipment: Knitting needles, yarn, and project guides.
Additional Resources: **Kids Knitting** by Melanie D. Falick, Kristin Nicholas, and Chris Hartlove; ISBN 1885183763; hardcover; 128 pages; $17.95; 1998.
Slip-Stitch Knitting: *Color Pattern the Easy Way* by Roxana Bartlett; ISBN 1883010322; softcover; 96 pages; $21.95; 1998.

MODEL BUILDER

Description: Purchase and build models for sale at craft fairs or for individuals. May be crafted from kits or may be of own design.
Start-up Costs: $
Marketing Ideas: Advertise by placing flyers in local craft shop, by advertising in neighborhood or church newsletters, or by word-of-mouth.
Equipment: Model kits or materials for "do-it-yourselfers."

MURALIST

Description: Design and paint murals for individuals in homes or for businesses such as daycare centers.
Start-up Costs: $$$
Marketing Ideas: Word-of-mouth will be essential. Tell everyone you know that you are creating murals. Keep a portfolio with pictures of your past projects.
Equipment: Paint, brushes, pad for sketching, drop cloths, and cleaning supplies.
Additional Resources: **Trompe L'Oeil:** *Murals and Decorative Wall Painting* by Lynette Wrigley; ISBN 0847820459; hardcover; 144 pages; $35.00; 1997.

MUSICAL INSTRUMENT INSTRUCTOR

Description: Teach another person how to play an instrument. You need to know what words, actions, or drawings would help the student to learn.
Start-up Costs: $ (assuming the customer owns his/her own instrument)
Marketing Ideas: Volunteer to play your instrument to family and friends. Make sure they know that you are available for lessons. Play for clubs, scouts, church or synagogue to make yourself known. Offer the introductory lesson as a free one.
Equipment: Instrument and other items used to help instruct.

NEEDLEPOINT INSTRUCTION/DESIGN

Description: Teach others how to needlepoint or create designs of your own.
Start-up Costs: $
Marketing Ideas: Display your work at church or school bazaars. Use word-of-mouth advertising by telling your family and friends that you are available for lessons or to create gifts. Work on your projects while waiting at dance class, the dentist's office, or anywhere else you go. It will often prompt a discussion and you can talk about your business.
Equipment: Needlepoint kits, canvas/cloth, thread/yarn/floss, needles, patterns, and lots of patience.
Additional Resources: **Complete Guide to Needlework** by Readers Digest Editors; ISBN 0895770598; hardcover; 504 pages; $28.00; 1979.

PICTURE FRAMING

Description: Mat and frame customer's pictures or have customers provide their own mat and frame.
Start-up costs: $$$$ if you provide mat and framing materials; $ if your customer provides them.
Marketing Ideas: Advertise through artists groups, school papers, and classifieds. Leave flyers with local businesses. Offer to frame the winning entry for a school art contest and display with your business card.
Equipment: Mat cutter, wood for frames, and matting materials.
Additional Resources: **Home Book of Picture Framing:** *Professional Secrets of Mounting, Matting, Framing and Displaying Artworks, Photographs, Posters, Fabrics and Collectibles* by Kenn Oberrecht; ISBN 0811727939; softcover; 272 pages; $19.95; 1998.

POSTER DESIGNER

Description: Create posters for special events.
Start-up costs: $
Marketing Ideas: Show off your artwork. Display at church bazaars, fairs, school events, and community activities. There may even be contests that you can enter.
Equipment: Paper, pens/paints, pencil, eraser, and idea books.
Additional Resources: **Poster Art** by Stephen Knapp;

FOCUS ON...
INDEPENDENT MEANS, INC.

"*Independent Means is a company that offers products and services for girls' financial independence. All IMI program activities are interactive, experiential, and encourage relationship-building between teen partners and adult entrepreneurs and mentors.*"

-*www.anincomeofherown.com*

Programs include:
- An Income of Her Own Conferences;
- National Business Plan Competition;
- Camp $tart-UP;
- School Programs;
- Free websites available for girl entrepreneurs;
- On-line newsletters;
- And much more!

Opportunities are available across the United States. You can contact IMI at:

Independent Means Inc.
126 Powers Avenue
Santa Barbara, CA 93103
(805)965-0475; (805)965-3148 (fax)

www.anincomeofherown.com

ISBN 1564962903; softcover; $14.99; 1996.

QUILTMAKING

Description: Crafting quilts for any occasion.

Start-up Costs: $$$$

Marketing: Display your work at bazaars and craft fairs. Use word-of-mouth advertising with family and friends. Take pictures of all your projects and keep in an album to show potential customers. Contact family and friends prior to special occasions or holidays and ask if they would like to give a quilt as a gift.

Equipment: Sewing machine, fabric, thread, batting, trim, and patterns.

Additional Resources: **Easy Machine Quilting: 12 Step-by-Step Lessons from the Pros Plus a Dozen Projects to Machine Quilt** edited by Jane Townswick; ISBN 0875967086; hardcover; $27.95; 1996.

SCRAPBOOK DESIGNER

Description: Use pictures and mementos of clients to create unique, personalized scrapbooks.

Scrapbooks: $$

Marketing Ideas: Because this is a very personal service, the best source of business will be family and friends. Offer to create a scrapbook for new moms or working moms with little time. Keep a scrapbook of your own and show to potential clients so they can see your work.

Equipment: Scrapbook, decorative paper, stickers, scissors, pens, and idea books.

Additional Resources: **Moments to Remember: The Art of Creating Scrapbook Memories** by Jo Packham; ISBN 0836252551; hardcover; 128 pages; $24.95; 1998.

SEWING/DRESSMAKING

Description: Sewing clothing, costumes, cloth books, doll clothes, windsocks, banners, flags, etc.

Start-up costs: $$$, less if you already have a sewing machine and if clients provide materials.

Marketing: Word-of-mouth is essential. Wear things that you make. Show people samples of cloth books, costumes, etc. Take pictures of things you make and keep in a portfolio to show people. Put flyers in businesses of people you know. Promote your business with family and friends.

Additional Resources: **The Complete Book of Sewing** by Deni Brown; ISBN 0789404192; hardcover; $39.95; 1996.

SIGN PAINTING

Description: Ask customers what should be on the sign. Draw some ideas. The customer picks something he/she likes. Then, you paint the sign.

Start-up costs: $$$, less if the client provides materials.

Marketing Ideas: Advertise in newspaper, school papers, church newsletters, and flyers in businesses. Probably word-of-mouth will be the best way to promote business, so show samples to family and friends. Make holiday signs for your lawn or door.

Additional Resources: **Signwork:** *A Craftman's Manual* by Bill Stewart: ISBN 0632033657; softcover; 288 pages; $35.00; 1993.

TOYMAKING

Description: Create handmade toys and games.

Start-up Costs: $$$$

Marketing Ideas: Sell your toys and games at yard sales, bazaars, and craft fairs. Keep track of birthdays, holidays, and special occasions, and ask family and friends if they would like you to create a gift for their child. Ask if you can place flyers on bulletin boards at your church/synagogue, childcare center, schools, etc.

Equipment: Wood, tools, paint, hardware, and patterns.

Additional Resources: **Build Your Own Wood Toys** by R.J. Decristoforo; ISBN 0806969938; softcover; 276 pages; $12.95; 1989. **Fun to Make Wooden Toys and Games** by Jeff Loader and Jennie Loader; ISBN 1861080492; softcover; 176 pages; $17.95; 1997.

T-SHIRT DESIGN

Description: Create t-shirts with designs, words, stencils, shapes or iron-ons.

Start-up costs: $

Marketing Ideas: Make samples to show customers. Take pictures of these to bring with you when the samples would be too bulky. Tell family, friends, school mates, clubs, and organizations what you can design especially for them.

Equipment: T-shirts, fabric pens and paint, glitter, iron-ons, scissors, notebook, a pen (to take orders), and an idea book with designs and graphics.

Additional Resources: **Great T-Shirt Graphics** by Stephen Knapp; ISBN 1564961982; softcover; $24.99; 1995.

WREATHMAKING

Description: Creating wreaths for holiday or year-round use.

Start-up Costs: $$

Marketing: Sell your creations at yard sales, bazaars and craft fairs. Advertise by word-of-mouth to family and friends. Take pictures of your creations and make a portfolio to show potential customers.

Equipment: Wreath forms, decorating materials, glue gun, scissors, and idea books.

Additional Resources: **The Ultimate Wreath Book:** *Hundreds of Beautiful Wreaths to Make From Natural Materials* by Ellen Spector Platt; ISBN 087596978X; softcover; 256 pages; $20.00; 1998.

BUSINESS TO BUSINESS SERVICES

ADVERTISING

Description: Provide flyers, business cards, posters, photographs, etc., for people too busy to prepare them.

Start-up Costs: $

Marketing Ideas: Make a portfolio to show your work examples. Use a ring binder or album for photos or display on a board.

Equipment: Samples of the work you can offer and your price list.

Additional Resources: **The Advertising Handbook** *Make a Big Impact with a Small Budget* by Dell Dennison; ISBN 0889087989; softcover; 328 pages; $10.95; 1994.

DELIVERY PERSON/MESSENGER

Description: Transport things between businesses such as florists, printers, or supermarkets.

Start-up Costs: $

Marketing Ideas: Approach businesses that usually do not do deliveries and convince them that it would improve their customer service to provide it as an option. Suggest to businesses that it would save valuable time to use you to run errands such as mailing packages at the post office, picking up items at the printer, or dropping things off at other businesses.

Equipment: Large shoulder bags to carry items, zippered bag to keep customer's money separate, and a bike or car for transportation would be helpful.

ENVELOPE STUFFER

Description: Stuff envelopes for businesses or non-profit organizations.

Start-up Costs: $

Marketing Ideas: Contact businesses, nonprofit organizations, political groups, or any groups that send newsletters, calendars, or direct mail advertising and offer your services.

Equipment: Transportation to pick up and deliver materials.

NEWSLETTER PUBLISHING

Description: Small publications that provide news to a particular group of readers. Examples are homeschooling and PTA newsletters.

Start-up Costs: $, if you have a computer or typewriter.

Marketing Ideas: Advertise your services to groups that may be too busy to make their own. Tell the groups your ideas. Have a sample newsletter to show your skills. You could also create your own newsletter and make money selling it or selling advertisements in it.

Equipment: Computer and printer (or typewriter), a way to make copies, notebook, and pen to make notes of customer's news.

Additional Resources: **Home-Based Newsletter Publishing:** *A Success Guide for Entrepreneurs* by William J. Bond; ISBN 007006556X; hardcover; $29.95; 1991. **Start Your Own Newsletter Publishing Business** edited by Susan Rachmeler; ISBN 0136033334; softcover; 192 pages; $13.95; 1997.

OFFICE LUNCH SERVICE

Description: Take orders, pick up, and deliver lunches to offices and businesses.

Start-up Costs: $

Marketing Ideas: Print up flyers and rolodex cards. Drop them off at offices and businesses in your neighborhood.

Equipment: Zippered bag to secure money and receipts, take-out menus from local restaurants, pencil and paper to take orders, transportation, and a box/crate to transport food in.

OFFICE SERVICES

Description: Provide copying, faxing, purchasing of supplies, and delivery services for local offices and businesses.

Start-up Costs: $

Marketing Ideas: Print flyers and rolodex cards and distribute to local offices and businesses. Offer to work for one day for free so they will see how helpful your services are. Pay special attention to busy seasons for certain types of businesses (e.g., April in tax preparation or accounting offices).

Equipment: Transportation and a willingness to learn and work hard.

RESEARCHER

Description: Research any subject for local businesses, authors, or anyone else searching for particular information.

Start-up Costs: $

Marketing Ideas: Use word-of-mouth advertising by telling family, friends, and anyone else you know that you are available for research.

Equipment: Library card and a lot of curiosity and persistence.

Additional Resources: **Find It Fast:** *How to Uncover Expert Information on Any Subject* by Robert I. Berkman; ISBN 0062734733; softcover; 352 pages; $14.00; 1997.

TRANSLATOR

Description: Translate letters, stories, documents, and other materials.

Start-up Costs: $

Marketing Ideas: Drop off flyers and rolodex cards at businesses likely to need translation services from time to time like import/export companies, small international companies, etc. Check with nonprofit agencies that provide services overseas.

Equipment: Knowledge of another language.

Additional Resources: **The Translator's Handbook** by Morry Sofer and Mordecai Schreiber; ISBN 1887563423; softcover; 450 pages; $24.95; 1998.

TYPING SERVICE

Description: Type letters, book reports, special class assignments, term papers, and stories.

Start-up Costs: $, if you have a typewriter or computer.

Marketing: Post advertisement on bulletin boards at schools, offices, and businesses. Flyers and newspapers can be used too, but they cost more.

Equipment: Typewriter or word processor.

COMPUTER BUSINESSES

COMPUTER CONSULTING

Description: You help the individual learn how to use a computer system. You might also assist with backup, designing a home page, and program installation.

Start-up Costs: $$

Marketing Ideas: Explain to your potential customers how you can make their lives easier, help them to gain needed skills to earn more money or gain access to more information. Explain plainly and slowly. Advertise in school papers. Give flyers to family and friends. Have patience! Keep instructions simple.

Equipment: Computer and equipment — although you may be using the client's own computer. Paper, pens, pencils, and highlighters.

Additional Resources: **How to be a Successful Computer Consultant** by Alan R. Simon; ISBN 0070580294; softcover; 416 pages; $21.95; 1998.

FOCUS ON...
KAUFFMAN CENTER FOR ENTREPRENEURIAL LEADERSHIP

The Kauffman Center for Entrepreneurial Leadership, funded by the Ewing Marion Kauffman Foundation, nurtures and encourages entrepreneurial leadership. The Center serves as a catalyst for understanding, supporting, and accelerating entrepreneurship in America.

www.emkf.org

The Institute for Entrepreneurship Education is dedicated to developing and creating initiatives for enhancing entrepreneurship awareness, readiness, and application experience for K-12 youth and community college students.

Programs of interest to teens include:

- Entrepreneur Invention Society
- Entreprep
- Mother and Daughter Entrepreneurs in Teams
- New Youth Entrepreneur
- YESS! Mini-Society

" We believe that the jobs of future — which are key to self-sufficiency — will come from creative entrepreneurs who build successful companies which create jobs and contribute to the community's economic vitality."

- www.emkf.org

DATA ENTRY
Description: Provide data entry services for businesses.
Start-up Costs: $, if you have a computer.
Marketing Ideas: Visit local businesses and offices to inquire about whether they have any data entry needs. Make sure you leave a flyer and rolodex card so they can get in touch with you. Ask your parents and their friends if they could use your data entry skills at work.
Equipment: Computer.

ENTERTAINMENT SERVICES

CLOWNING
Description: Providing entertainment for birthday parties, church/synagogue events, scout troops, retirement and nursing homes or camps. You could also make clown faces on other people. Perhaps you could offer your services every weekend for a store or restaurant.
Start-up Cost: $$
Marketing Ideas: Make business cards with clown faces and hand out to family, friends, and other acquaintances. Volunteer to be a clown at a special event so people will see what you do. Be a clown in a parade.
Equipment: Clown costume and makeup. You could

also use props such as magic tricks, balloons, silly sunglasses, or a hat.

Additional Resources: **The Most Excellent Book of How to Be a Clown** by Catherine Perkins and Rob Shone; ISBN 0761304991; softcover; 32 pages; $6.95; 1996.

MAGICIAN

Description: Perform as a magician at birthday parties, childcare centers, church/synagogue activities, or neighborhood gatherings.

Start-up Costs: $$

Marketing Ideas: Word-of-mouth will be the best form of advertising. You might volunteer your services for one or two performances so that people will see you in action. You might try posting flyers at local childcare centers or party stores.

Equipment: Props for magic tricks.

Additional Resources: **The Most Excellent Book of How to Be a Magician** by Peter Eldrin and Rob Shone; ISBN 0761304738; softcover; 32 pages; $6.95; 1996. **The New Magician's Manual:** *Tricks and Routines with Instructions for Expert Performance by the Amateur* by Walter Brown Gibson; ISBN 0486231135; softcover; 142 pages; $8.95; 1976.

MIME

Description: Create routines to perform at birthday parties, festivals, neighborhood gatherings, and church/synagogue activities.

Start-up Cost: $$

Marketing Ideas: Getting people to see your act should be your primary form of advertising. Volunteer to perform for free at a couple of events to get yourself known.

Equipment: Costume and makeup.

Additional Resources: **Mime Time:** *45 Complete Routines for Everyone* by Happy Jack Feder and Marc Vargas; ISBN 0916260739; softcover; 208 pages; $12.95; 1992.

PUPPETEER

Description: Buy or make your own puppets. Write skits or simple plays. Help children make their own puppets to take home. You could entertain at parties, nursing homes, churches, and synagogues.

Start-up Costs: $

Marketing Ideas: Word-of-mouth, business cards that you create, family, friends, businesses, schools, scouts, churches, and synagogues.

Equipment: Puppets, props, and skits.

Additional Resources: **The Most Excellent Book of How to Be a Puppeteer** by Roger Lade and Rob Shone; ISBN 0916260739; softcover; 32 pages; $5.95; 1996.

SINGER

Description: Perform at special occasions such as parties, weddings, church/synagogue activities, and other community functions.

Start-up Costs: $

Marketing Ideas: Perform as much as possible so that people become familiar with your work. Participate in the choir and tell the director that you are available as a soloist. Contact your church/synagogue and offer your services for weddings. Word-of-mouth will be your basic form of marketing.

Equipment: Excellent vocal skills, comfort performing in front of audiences, sheet music, and accompaniment tracks if necessary.

STORYTELLER

Description: Tell stories to groups in a vibrant and interesting way.

Start-up Costs: $

Marketing Ideas: Offer to show your skills to libraries, childcare centers or nursing homes. Organize neighborhood storytime for children. Read stories onto tapes for sight-impaired persons. Put up flyers in daycare centers, churches, and synagogues.

Equipment: Books and lots of personality.

For more information: The National Association for the Preservation and Perpetuation of Storytelling, P. O. Box 112, Siemons House, Fox Street, Jonesborough, Tennessee 37659; (615) 753-2171.

Additional Resources: **The Storytellers Guide:** *Storytellers Share Advice for the Classroom, Boardroom, Showroom, Podium, Pulpit and Central Stage* by William Mooney and edited by David Holt; ISBN 0874834821; softcover; $23.95; 1996. **The Storyteller's Start-Up Book:** *Finding, Learning, Performing, and Using Folktales: Including Twelve Tellable Tales* by Margaret Read MacDonald; ISBN 0874833051; softcover; 215 pages; $14.95; 1993.

FOOD SERVICES

CAKE DECORATING

Description: Create beautiful cakes for birthday parties, weddings, anniversaries, and other special occasions.

Start-up Costs: $$$

Marketing Ideas: Most of your customers will be friends or relatives. Start out by showing off your skills by preparing a cake for a special gathering. Take pictures of your creations and make a book to show potential customers.

Equipment: Baking materials, decorating materials, boxes or trays for transporting, and idea books.

Additional Resources: **Colette's Cakes:** *The Art of Cake Decorating* by Colette Peters; ISBN

0316702056; hardcover; 163 pages; $27.50; 1991.
How to Make Money in Cake Decorating: Owning and Operating a Successful Business in Your Home by Del Carnes; ISBN 0686301927; softcover; $9.95; 1990.

LEMONADE/DRINK STAND

Description: Making lemonade to sell. Perhaps a health-conscious plan would be to use only fresh lemons and bottled water, and make a sugar-free option.

Start-up Costs: $

Marketing Ideas: If you decide to provide a health-conscious option, advertise it. Make signs and posters. Pick a good, safe location and stick with it so that people get used to seeing you there. Flyers, signs on posts, and word-of-mouth all work well. Perhaps you could open a stand at a sporting event like Little League, the neighborhood pool, or playground.

Equipment: Table, signs, ingredients for lemonade, container, spoon, measuring cup, and spoons.

GREEN BUSINESSES

COMPOST SALES

Description: If you are already composting, you could sell compost to others for gardening.

Start-up Costs: N/A

Marketing Ideas: Word-of-mouth to family and friends is the best way of marketing. You might contact local gardening clubs and tell them you have compost available for sale.

Equipment: Composting equipment, bags or containers, wheelbarrow, gloves, and transportation for delivery.

Additional Resources: **The Rodale Book of Composting** by Deborah L. Martin (editor) and Grace Gershuny; ISBN 0878579915; softcover; 278 pages; $14.95; 1992.

HOME & GARDEN BUSINESSES

CARWASHING/DETAILING

Description: People today want their high-priced cars to be pampered. So, emphasize your careful attention to making the inside and outside of the car spotless. Offer waxing and detailing at additional prices.

Start-up Costs: $

Marketing Ideas: If you live near an office building, school or shopping area, give a flyer to employees saying "car wash express." Get some friends and develop the ability to team wash a car in 15 minutes. Then set appointments and guarantee to do it in 15 minutes or it's free.

Equipment: A water source, hose, buckets, clean cloths, car washing detergent, items to clean tires, and dry cloths to dry car.

CLEANING

Description: Many families have all of the adults working outside the home, so there is a need for many kinds of cleaning. You could do complete house/apartment cleaning, or you could offer specifics such as window washing.

Start-up Costs: $, if customer provides own cleaning equipment.

Marketing Ideas: Word-of-mouth will be your primary form of marketing. Make business cards and hand out to family and friends. Provide free, one-time cleaning for new mothers; many will want to keep you permanently.

Equipment: A well-rested, healthy strong body, an attention to detail and the willingness to work hard.

Additional Resources: **All-New Hints from Heloise** by Heloise; ISBN 0399515100; softcover; 416 pages; $13.00; 1989.

GARAGE SALE PREPARATION

Description: Help busy people sell their household goods and clothing. You will help assemble things in advance and arrange the pre-sale advertising.

Start-up Costs: $

Marketing Ideas: The customer should pay for advertising in the classifieds. If flyers are used, you could help hand them out or post them. If you design the flyers, put "garage sale preparation by" and your name and phone number at the bottom. Word-of-mouth is your best form of advertising. Hand out business cards or flyers you make to family and friends.

Equipment: Pens, tags, tape, calculator, and bags.

Additional Resources: **Backyard Money Machine: How to Organize and Operate a Successful Garage Sale** by Les R. Schmeltz; ISBN 0963532103; softcover; $9.95; 1993.

HANDYPERSON

Description: Provide basic repair and do-it-yourself maintenance.

Start-up Costs: $$$$

Marketing Ideas: Word-of-mouth will be your best form of advertising. When you do work for a customer, make sure to leave a rolodex card or refrigerator magnet with your name and number so they can contact you easily.

Equipment: Tools and transportation.

Additional Information: **The Family Handyman Helpful Hints:** *Quick and Easy Solutions, Timesaving Tips, and Tricks of the Trade* by Readers Digest; ISBN 0895776170; hardcover; $30.00; 1995.

"GO-FER" DELIVERIES

Description: You "go-fer" things when busy people don't have time to "go-fer" their own stuff.

Start-up Costs: $

Marketing Ideas: Your most regular clients will be working parents, older people, handicapped people, or small shops or offices near your house. Make flyers, business cards, and a rolodex card (so they can call you easily) and give them to these people.

Equipment: Car or bike may be needed, paper and pen for writing lists, and a zippered bag to carry customer's money and collect receipts.

HOUSE PAINTER

Description: Outdoor painting is a good way to learn how to paint without too much risk. You could offer to paint outdoor furniture, fences, decks, porches, or sheds. Once you become more advanced, try interior painting or special techniques such as rag or sponge painting.

Start-up Costs: $$

Marketing Ideas: Walk around your neighborhood and see jobs you might be able to do. Print flyers about your painting service. Take flyers to neighbors and make an offer of your painting service. Agree on what needs doing, the price, timetable, and who supplies the paint and equipment.

Equipment: Paint, brushes, rollers, tape, rags, paint scraper, and drop cloths or newspaper as needed.

Additional Resources: **The Complete Painters Handbook:** *How to Paint Your House Inside and Out — The Right Way* by Gregg E. Sandreuter; ISBN 0878577564; softcover; 150 pages; $14.95; 1988.

HOUSEHOLD INVENTORY

Description: Take photographs or videotape of homes and their belongings to be used for insurance purposes.

Start-up Costs: $, if you have a camera or video recorder.

Marketing Ideas: Because this is a highly personal service, your market will be family and friends. Make sure that they know your services are available. Place a sticker with your name and phone number on the album or video that you provide so they can contact you or make referrals.

Equipment: Camera/video recorder and film.

HOUSESITTING

Description: Stay in or keep an eye on houses while people are away. Collect newspapers and mail for the owners. Maybe water plants or care for pets.

Start-up Costs: $

Marketing Ideas: Your customers will be people that you know well. Rely on word-of-mouth advertising. The best way to build a regular clientele is to be extremely conscientious in your work.

Equipment: Maturity and trustworthiness.

LAUNDRY/IRONING

Description: Ironing is a chore most busy people cannot take time to do. You will mostly iron men's shirts. Stick to basic cotton or cotton blends. Check with customer about fabrics, creasing needs, and use of sizing or starch.

Start-up Cost: $

Marketing Ideas: Tell family, friends, and neighbors about your service. Use flyers if necessary. Three or four customers a week would probably be enough. When you return your work, ask about next week's batch of items. Offer pick-up and delivery service. Offer express service for an additional cost.

Equipment: Ironing board, iron, starch, and sizing sprays.

LAWN MAINTENANCE

Description: Mowing, fertilizing, and maintaining lawns and landscaping.

Start-up Costs: $$$$

Marketing Ideas: Use word-of-mouth advertising with family and friends. Advertise in your neighborhood newsletter. Place flyers on bulletin boards in your community.

Equipment: Lawnmower, edger, trimmer, weedeater, gloves, trash bags, clippers and other lawn maintenance equipment. You may be able to reduce equipment costs significantly by using your client's equipment.

Additional Resources: **Lawn Care and Gardening:** *A Down-to-Earth Guide to the Business* by Kevin Rossi and Lee Weisman (illustrator); ISBN 0963937197; softcover; 220 pages; $26.00; 1994.

LEAF RAKING

Description: Carefully rake leaves and ask the customer what he/she would like done with the piles (e.g., bagged or composted).

Start-up Cost: $$

Marketing Ideas: Tell family, friends, teachers, and other adults what you can do to help them. Make flyers and business cards if you need them.

Equipment: Rake, plastic bags, and wheelbarrow.

ORGANIZER

Description: If you are a person who likes to have your room and possessions neat, you could use this talent to organize people's rooms, closets, children's toys, garages, etc.

Start-up Costs: $

Marketing Ideas: Most people's homes and possessions are very personal and private. Your best customers will be people you know. Word will get around and bring you more customers. Some people may re-schedule you.

Equipment: Do a consultation first where you identify items needed. Then have the customer pay for the necessary hangers, boxes, paper labels, and garbage bags or purchase them themselves.

Additional Resources: **Organize Yourself** by Ronni Eisenberg and Kate Kelly; ISBN 0028615077; softcover; 320 pages; $9.95; 1997.

PLANT CARE

Description: You maintain business', institutions' or households' plants and keep them looking healthy. Take charge of watering, pruning, feeding, rooting, and replacing them as necessary.

Start-up Costs: $$

Marketing Ideas: Use word-of-mouth for family, friends, and businesses. Flyers on bulletin boards and business cards may be helpful.

Equipment: Gloves, lawn bags, pruner, scissors, watering devices, step ladder, and fertilizer. (Customer may supply some of these items)

Additional Resources: **The Plant Care Manual:** *The Essential Guide to Caring for and Rejuvenating Over 300 Garden Plants* by Stefan T. Buczacki; ISBN 0517592835; hardcover; $26.00; 1993.

WALLPAPERING

Description: Hang wallpaper in homes or offices. If you do not already know how to do this yourself, you need to be taught the process. Some hardware stores offer classes.

Start-up Costs: $, if the customer provides the paper and equipment needed.

Marketing: Encourage word-of-mouth referrals from satisfied customers. Hand out flyers and business cards.

Equipment: Ladder, assorted paint brushes and rollers, papering brushes, knives, razor blades, and drop cloths.

Additional Resources: **The Complete Guide to Wallpapering** by David M. Groff; ISBN 1880029243; softcover; 135 pages; $12.95; 1993.

WINDOW WASHING

Description: Cleaning windows for homes or businesses.

Start-up Costs: $

Marketing Ideas: Visit local businesses and homes in your neighborhood. Drop off flyers, rolodex cards or magnets with your name, business name, and phone number so they can contact you. Advertise in neighborhood or church directories or newsletters. Print up a t-shirt with your name and phone number on back so people will see it while you are working.

Equipment: Bucket, water source, cleaning solution, rags, and squeegee.

PERSONAL SERVICES

BEENIE BABY CONSULTANT

Description: Locate individual Beenie Babies for collectors.

Start-up Cost: $

Marketing Ideas: Word-of-mouth advertising is the best idea. Tell all your friends who are interested in collecting that you will find whatever Beenie Baby they need for their collection.

Equipment: Tranportation to stores, paper and pencil to write down Beenie Babies you are trying to locate.

CARPOOL SERVICE

Description: Pick-up and drop off children, the elderly or homebound at classes, clubs, stores, or other activities.

Start-up Cost: $

Marketing Ideas: Talk to people in your neighborhood to find out who might be interested. Call your church/synagogue and explain what you are doing. Ask if there is anyone who could use your service.

Equipment: Transportation.

CHESS INSTRUCTOR

Description: Teach children or adults how to play chess.

Start-up Cost: $

Marketing Ideas: Advertise your services in the school newspaper. Contact the chess club and tell them you are available for lessons. Contact your local community center, scout troops, or other youth associations and tell them you are available — you might be able to start a class.

Equipment: Chess board, good communications skills, and the ability to work with students patiently.

Additional Resources: **The ABC's of Chess:** *Invaluable, Detailed Lessons for Players at All Levels* by Bruce Pandolfini; ISBN 0671619829; softcover; 222 pages; $11.00; 1986.

CHILDCARE

Description: Babysitting or being a mother's helper has always been an excellent way for teens to make money.

Start-up Cost: $

Marketing Ideas: Take a Babysitting/CPR class. This will make you more marketable. Use word-of-mouth advertising with family, friends, and people in your neighborhood. You might want to print up rolodex cards or refrigerator magnets with your name and number so customers can contact you easily. You might earn some extra money by compiling a *Babysitter Directory* with your name and those of your friends. You could then sell it for a small fee to people in your neighborhood.

ENVELOPE ADDRESSING
Description: Offer your services to address envelopes for Christmas or Hanukkah cards, wedding invitations, baby announcements, or change of address cards.
Start-up Cost: $
Marketing Ideas: Make flyers showing the possible types of work you do and demonstrating your handwriting abilities.
Equipment: Neat handwriting, envelopes, pens, and flyers.

FAMILY HISTORIAN
Description: Tracing family trees (genealogy) has become very popular. However, few people have the time to put in all the hours of research necessary to complete a family history. That is what you will do.
Start-up Cost: $, if you have a computer.
Marketing Ideas: You might complete a history of your own family and then show it to all your family and friends. Let them know that you are available to do this for their family.

Equipment: Library card, paper, pencils, and type-writer/computer for compiling the final report.
Additional Resources: **How to Interview a Sleeping Man** by Milli Brown; ISBN 0964388596; softcover; 109 pages; $14.95; 1997.

SCHOLARSHIP FINDER
Description: Research and create a report listing available scholarships for particular students.
Start-up Cost: $
Marketing Ideas: Contact your high school newspaper to see if you can advertise or have them write an article about your service. Advertise in your church/synagogue and neighborhood newsletter.
Equipment: Library card, paper, and pencil.
Additional Resources: **The Complete Scholarship Book:** *The Biggest, Easiest-to-Use Guide for Getting the Most Money for College*; ISBN 15707113901; softcover; 664 pages; $22.95; 1998.

FOCUS ON...
NATIONAL FFA ORGANIZATION

The FFA is dedicated to making a positive difference in the lives of young people by developing their potential for premier leadership, personal growth, and career success through agricultural education.

-FFA mission statement

Opportunities for:
- Leadership development;
- U.S. or international travel;
- Career development training;
- Community service;
- Competition and awards;
- Scholarships;
- And fun.

Opportunities are available in all 50 states. You can contact FFA at:

The National FFA Organization
6060 FFA Drive
P.O. Box 68960
Indianapolis, IN 46268-0960
(317)802-6060; (317)802-6061 (fax)
E-mail webmaster@ffa.org
Website http://www.ffa.org

SHOPPING SERVICE

Description: Shop for people who do not have time such as the elderly, new moms, or shut-ins.
Start-up Costs: $
Marketing Ideas: Word-of-mouth advertising will work best. Telling people that you know well will work the best because it is a personal service and involves handling money.
Equipment: Transportation.

TUTOR

Description: If you are an excellent student in math, science, English, history, or any foreign language, you could help tutor children or adults.
Start-up Cost: $
Marketing Ideas: Tell all your friends at school that you are available for tutoring. Post flyers on bulletin board. You might talk to your teacher and ask him/her if anyone might be interested in tutoring. Word-of-mouth will be your best source of business. Place an advertisement in your church, synagogue, or neighborhood newsletter.
Equipment: Books on your subject, paper, pencils, good communications skills, and patience.
Additional Resources: **How to Tutor** by Samuel L. Blumenfeld; ISBN 0941995011; softcover; 304 pages; $24.95; 1991.

PET SERVICES

ANIMAL SITTING/TRAINING

Description: If you love pets, make money caring for them while their owners are away or training them if you are skilled in that area.
Start-up Costs: $
Marketing Ideas: Word-of-mouth advertising will be an excellent way to get customers. Advertise in your church, synagogue, or neighborhood newsletter.
Equipment: Transportation.
Additional Resources: **Opportunities in Animal and Pet Care Careers** by Mary Price Lee and Richard S. Lee; ISBN 0844240796; hardcover; $14.95; 1993.

AQUARIUM DESIGNER

Description: Design and maintain aquariums for busy people.
Start-up Cost: $; the customer will pay for the aquarium supplies.
Marketing Ideas: Tell all your family and friends that you are in business. Post flyers at local pet supply stores. Advertise in your church, synagogue, or neighborhood newsletter.
Equipment: Pencil and paper to write down customer's likes/dislikes and budget.
Additional Resources: **ABC's of Marine Aquariums**

by Warren Burgess; ISBN 0866227644; hardcover; $12.95; 1987.

DOG WALKER

Description: Walk dogs for busy people.
Start-up Cost: $
Marketing Ideas: Word-of-mouth advertising will work best. If you live in an apartment building, post a flyer on the bulletin board. Make a t-shirt with your company name and phone number on the back so people who see you walking dogs will know whom to call.
Equipment: Good pair of walking shoes.

PET GROOMER

Description: Offer to wash animals, clean cages, or freshen aquariums.
Start -up Costs: $
Marketing Ideas: Talk to people you know and learn about/get to know their pet. Learn about the pet you are grooming so you sound knowledgeable and people will trust you with their pets.
Equipment: Rubber gloves and towels. The customer will provide the products they would like you to use.

SPECIAL EVENTS SERVICES

BALLOON DECORATING

Description: Provide balloons to decorate homes, schools, or offices for special occasions such as birthdays, anniversaries, graduation, birth of baby, etc.
Start-up Costs: $$$
Marketing Ideas: Advertise in newspaper, on bulletin boards, with business cards, on signs, or by word-of-mouth. Put together a scrapbook of ideas to show customers.
Equipment: Balloons, scissors, string or ribbon, and a helium tank.
Additional Resources: **The Big Book of Balloons: Create Almost Anything for Every Party and Holiday** by Captain Visual; ISBN 0806519207; spiral binding; 144 pages; $15.95; 1998.

CHILDREN'S BIRTHDAY PARTY PLANNER

Description: If you enjoy and are good with children, this could be a good idea for you. Be original with ideas. You could plan character parties, magic parties, craft parties, clown or puppet parties, etc. Offer to stay and help clean up after the party.
Start-up Costs: $, if customer pays for necessary items.
Marketing Ideas: Word-of-mouth to family and friends is best. Present your ideas for how you think the decorating should look, games and handouts. If you are artistic, draw pictures of your proposals. Put flyers and/or business cards on bulletin boards at schools, churches/synagogues, day cares, etc. Perhaps you

could also offer to do holiday parties.

Equipment: Party supplies, props such as games, and costumes if you are dressing up to entertain.

Additional Resources: **Birthday Parties: Best Party Tips and Ideas** by Vicki Lansky and Jack Lindstrom (illustrator); ISBN 0916773361; softcover; 160 pages; $8.95; 1995.

GIFT BASKET PREPARATION

Description: Fill baskets with an assortment of specialty foods and gifts that can be tailored for occasions such as birthdays, births, anniversaries, and house-warmings.

Start-up Costs: $$, depending on the costs of items you put in the basket.

Marketing Ideas: Draw and/or describe what baskets would look like. Put out flyers, but use word-of-mouth advertising with family and friends. Make a basket, perhaps for your parent's birthday, and take a picture of it to show potential customers.

Equipment: Baskets, ribbon, straw-like filler, and basket items.

Additional Resources: **How to Start a Home-Based Gift Basket Business** by Shirley George Frazier; ISBN 0762701447; softcover; 288 pages; $17.95; 1998.

GIFT BUYING/WRAPPING

Description: Very busy people may want to pay someone to buy, wrap, and mail a gift for them to give someone for a birthday, anniversary, birth, etc.

Start-up Costs: $, customer should provide for the costs of gift, wrapping, and card.

Marketing Ideas: Send flyers and business cards to family, friends and businesses who would not mind telling employees or co-workers how you can help them. Keep a record of dates and occasions of past clients. Contact them next year prior to these dates to see if they would like to use your services again.

Equipment: Willingness to shop carefully for what the customer needs you to find.

Additional Resources: **The Complete Guide to Creative Gift-Giving** by Cynthia G. Yates; ISBN 089283997X; softcover; 235 pages; $10.99; 1997.

GIFT REMINDER SERVICE

Description: Your job is to remind clients of important dates for special days - birthdays, anniversaries, graduations, etc.

Start-up Costs: $

Marketing Ideas: Referrals from family and friends. Offer to do it for someone so they can see how helpful it is. Then ask them to tell others. Flyers and business cards given to family and friends could be helpful.

Equipment: Pen, notebook, and calendar.

HOLIDAY DECORATING/UNDECORATING

Description: People love to hang lights on their homes, put up wreaths and assemble lawn decorations, but many do not have the time. You provide the service for them.

Start-up Costs: $

Marketing Ideas: Tell all of your family and friends about your business. Advertise in your church, synagogue, or neighborhood newsletter. Give rolodex card or magnets to your customers so they can call you next year and refer other customers. Ask if you can attach a label to the boxes in which they store their decorations indicating how you can be reached.

Equipment: Transportation.

PARTY CLEAN-UP

Description: After a big party or gathering, you provide the clean-up.

Start-up Cost: $, if you use the customer's cleaning supplies.

Marketing Ideas: Most of your business will come from family and friends. Be sure to tell them about your business. Also, if you become aware of a large party, let them know you are available for clean-up. Many hosts/hostesses will be relieved not to have to worry about cleaning up.

Equipment: Transportation.

PARTY PLANNING

Description: A party planner may organize the entire event or a part of it. Responsibilities might include buying party items, writing invitations, decorating, or clean-up.

Start-up Costs: $

Marketing Ideas: Encourage word-of-mouth referrals. Use flyers and business cards, if you find them useful.

Equipment: Pen, pencil, notebook, scissors, tape, and party items.

Additional Resources: **Absolutely Unforgettable Parties:** *Great Ideas for Party People* by Janet Litherland and Lafe Locke; ISBN 0916260631; softcover; 192 pages; $9.95; 1990. **The Best Party Book:** *1001 Creative Ideas for Fun Parties* by Penny Warner and Kathy Rogers (illustrator); ISBN 0671780492; softcover; 210 pages; $8.00; 1992.

PHOTOGRAPHER/VIDEOGRAPHER

Description: There are business opportunities open to photographers and videographers of pets, newborns, family portraits, sports events, parties, weddings, holidays, etc.

Start-up Costs: $, if you have a camera/video recorder.

Marketing Ideas: Take pictures and be ready to show potential customers the ideas you have and what you could offer them. Offer videos of special events and also to tape what is in their home for insurance needs.

Equipment: Camera/videorecorder, film, pen, and notebook.

Additional Resources: **The Basic Book of Photography** by Tom Grimm and Michele Grimm; ISBN 0452278252; softcover; 528 pages; $19.95; 1997. **Guide to Basic Videography** by On Assignment Photo; ISBN 6301062930; VHS; video edition; $29.99; 1996.

REUNION PLANNING

Description: Reunion planners arrange get-togethers for schools, families, and clubs. Reunions are usually held every year, or every 5 or 10 years.

Start-up Costs: $

Marketing Ideas: Pass out flyers to family, friends, clubs, businesses, churches, and synagogues. Word-of-mouth will help the most as you begin this service.

Equipment: Notebook and pen.

Additional Resources: **Family Reunion Handbook: A Guide for Reunion Planners** by Barbara E. Brown and Thomas Ninkovich; ISBN 0961047038; softcover; $14.95; 1993.

SPORTS SERVICES

ATHLETIC EQUIPMENT MAINTENANCE & REPAIR

Description: Are you an avid mountain biker, surfer, or snowboarder? If you know a lot about the maintenance and repair of athletic equipment, you can help others take care of their equipment.

Start-up Costs: Varies

Marketing: Where do people interested in your sport go? What clubs are they members of? Wherever they are, that is where you will want to advertise. Word-of-mouth will be an excellent source of business.

Equipment: This will vary depending on the sport you specialize in.

BICYCLE REPAIR

Description: You will make basic repairs on road bikes or mountain bikes.

Start-up Cost: N/A

Marketing Ideas: Contact local bike clubs and let them know your services are available. Advertise in your high school paper. Advertise in your church, synagogue, or neighborhood newsletter. Put up flyers at your local recreation center or anywhere else that bicyclists go.

Equipment: N/A

Additional Resources: **Bicycling Magazine's Complete Guide to Bicycle Maintenance and Repair: Including Road Bikes and Mountain Bikes;** ISBN 0875962076; softcover; 324 pages; $16.95; 1994.

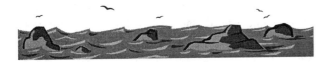

EDUCATIONAL PROGRAMS, TRAVEL AND ADVENTURE

This chapter is filled with all sorts of interesting career exploration opportunities that do not fit into the previous categories. There are educational programs, travel opportunities and adventures of every kind.

Many of the programs listed are summer or short-term educational programs. If you do not find a program that interests you, you might want to try contacting the following sources to ask about educational programs they might offer:

- Colleges and universities;
- Local, state and federal government agencies;
- Nonprofit organizations;
- Camps and student organizations.

STUDY ABROAD

Almost any travel experience can provide learning opportunities. The possibilities are endless. Some ideas are listed here. Another idea for combining education and travel is to spend a semester or year studying abroad. There are several resources that will provide you with information about these opportunities:

- **http://www.his.com/~council/howto2.html** - The Council of American Ambassadors provides a link to websites for student exchanges.
- **http://www.afs.org** - The AFS site allows students to search for student exchange programs in the country of their choice.
- **www.yfu.org/** - The Youth for Understanding website allows students to search for student exchange programs worldwide.
- **www.csum.edu** - Provides information about the High School Foreign Exchange and Language Study Program.
- *Peterson's Study Abroad 1998: Over 1,600 Semester and Year Abroad Academic Programs* by Ellen Beal. www.petersons.com.
- *The Student's Guide to the Best Study Abroad Programs* (1996 edition) by Greg Tannen & Charley Winkler.
- *The Exchange Student Survival Kit* by Bettina Hansel.

ADVENTURE

If adventure is what you have in mind, then visit some of the sites listed below.

- **http://www.aave.com** - AAVE Teen Adventures provide summer wilderness travel for teens in Hawaii, Alaska, and Europe.
- **http://www.apadventures.com/** - Adventure Pursuits provides wilderness adventure programs for young adults in the Western U.S., Canada, and Alaska.
- **http://www.bctravel.net/adv-experts/calendar.htm** - Kootenay Adventure Experts provides adventures for teens in British Columbia.
- **http://www.fieldstudies.org/** - Environmental problem-solving summer programs for teens located around the world.
- **http://www.gmu.edu/departments/hemlock/summercamp/ta.htm** - Teen Adventure is for teens, ages 14-17, and combines outdoor adventure with activities in conservation education in the Blue Ridge Mountains of Virginia.
- **http://www.gorp.com/gorp/trips/spi_YUT.htm** - Provides links to other websites featuring teen adventures.
- **http://www.gorp.com/arkansasriver** - Arkansas River Tours provide whitewater adventures and teen whitewater camps.
- **http://www.gorp.com/broadreach/** - Broadreach provides summer adventure programs for teens in the Caribbean, Costa Rica, Ecuador, Amazon, Galapagos, Egypt, Red Sea, and Israel.
- **http://www.gorp.com/cobs/** - Colorado Outward Bound provides wilderness-based schools for teens in Colorado, Utah, Arizona, New Mexico, Alaska, Nepal, and Baja, California.
- **http://www.gorp.com/dragons/** - Dragons provides small-group teen travel to China, Thailand, Vietnam, India, Mongolia, the Himalayas, Nepal, Tibet, and Pakistan.
- **http://www.inmex.com/inmex/programs.html** - Listing of summer, semester or full-year programs for teens.
- **http://www.natrails.com** - North American Trails site includes information for students, ages 13-16.
- **http://www.sni.net/trips** - Adventure Tour Directory

Educational programs, travel and adventure are divided into the following categories:

- Archeology/History
- Arts/Culture
- Communication

- Foreign Language
- Health
- Human Services/Education
- International Exchange
- Math/Science/Engineering
- Nature/Environment
- Tours

Each listing will include the *project location*. A detailed *description* will provide you with information about the organization and its activities. The listing will indicate what students the program is *open to* (e.g., grade level, age, minority, women, etc.). Any *cost* associated with the program is given as well as amenities provided. An address, phone number, e-mail address and website are given for you to use to request *more information*.

ARCHAEOLOGY/HISTORY

BIG HORN BASIN FOUNDATION/WYOMING DINOSAUR CENTER
Thermopolis, Wyoming
Project Location: Thermopolis, Wyoming
Description: One and a half-day event of digging, preparing, and casting dinosaur bones.
Open to: Ages 13-15.
Cost: $50. Enrollment limited to 20 per event.
For more information: Shawna L. Creamer, Director, Big Horn Basin Foundation/Wyoming Dinosaur Center, P.O. Box 71, Thermopolis, Wyoming, 82443; (307)864-2259; (307)864-5762 (fax); E-mail BHBF@Thermopwy.net; URL http://www.wyodino.org.

CROW CANYON ARCHAEOLOGICAL CENTER
Cortez, Colorado
Project Location: Southwest Colorado near Mesa Verde National Park.
Description: Become an active member in the Research Team through field excavation and lab analysis.
Open to: High school students.
Cost: Four-week *High School Field School* – $3,500; one-week *High School Excavation Program* – $725.
For more information: Crow Canyon Archaeological Center, 23390 County Road K, Cortez, Colorado 81321; (970)565-8975 or (800)422-8975 Ext. 130; URL http://www.crowcanyon.org.

HANDS-ON ARCHAEOLOGICAL EXPERIENCE
St. Johns, Arizona
Project Location: St. Johns, Arizona
Description: White Mountain is an archaeological field school. Its purpose is to protect, preserve, and research prehistoric southwest Indian sites. Participants work with professional archaeologists.
Open to: All ages - families, groups, clubs, etc.
Cost: $24.00 to age 17; $42.00 age 18 and up. Overnight rates range from $44-$66 and include housing, meals, and program.
For more information: A Hands-On Archaeological Experience, White Mountain Archaeological Center, HC 30, St. Johns, Arizona 85936; (602)333-5857.

LOST WORLD TRADING COMPANY
Oakdale, California
Project Location: Worldwide and California
Description: Work for those interested in becoming a scientist, archaeologist, or marine biologist.
Open to: Students, age 16 and up.
Cost: N/A
For more information: Program Director, Lost World Trading Company, P.O. Box 365, Oakdale, California 95361; (209)847-5393.

OREGON MUSEUM OF SCIENCE AND INDUSTRY SCIENCE CAMPS
Portland, Oregon
Project Location: Oregon Coast and Oregon high Desert.
Description: One, two, or three week programs in astronomy, paleontology, arid lands or marine biology research, or rafting, backpacking, and travel programs from San Juan Islands, WA to Redwoods, CA to Yellowstone National Park.
Open to: Students entering grades 9-12.
Cost: $350 one week, $500 two week, and $600 three week program. Housing in cabins or at field sites. Meals are provided.
For more information: OMSI Camp Registrars, 1945 SE Water Avenue, Portland, Oregon 97214; (503)797-4547.

ARTS/CULTURE

ART WEEKEND WORKSHOPS
Savannah, Georgia
Project Location: Savannah, Georgia
Description: Visual arts workshops and interesting activities are offered on Saturdays in October and May.
Open to: High school students entering 11-12 grade.
Cost: $25 registration fee in fall. $35 registration fee in spring. Housing is available at special rates. Some meals are provided.
For more information: Director of Special Events, Art Weekend Workshops, Savannah College of Art and Design, 342 Bull Street, P.O. Box 3146, Savannah, Georgia 31402-3146; (800)869-7223.

COLUMBIA COLLEGE HIGH SCHOOL SUMMER INSTITUTE
Chicago, Illinois
Project Location: Columbia College, Chicago, Illinois
Description: Classes offered for students interested in communication arts, fine arts, media arts, and performing arts.
Open to: High school sophomores, juniors, and seniors.
Cost: $125 per college credit hour and housing if needed.
For more information: Bonnie Lennon, Director, Columbia College High School Summer Institute, Columbia College Chicago, 600 South Michigan Avenue, Chicago, Illinois 60605-1996; (312)344-7130; (312) 344-8024 (fax); E-mail blennon@popmail.colum.edu; URL http://www.colum.edu/affiliatedprograms.

DORA STRATOU DANCE THEATER
Athens, Greece
Project Location: Greece
Description: There are daily classes in Ancient Greek dance, Greek folk dance, and folk culture. These take place on Philopappou Hill, opposite the Acropolis.
Open to: Minimum age of 16.
Cost: Approximately $85 per week. School will help student arrange accommodations.
For more information: Dora Stratou Dance Theater, 8 Scholiou Street, 10558 Athens, Plaka, Greece; (30)1-3244395.

EASTERN CAROLINA SUMMER THEATER APPRENTICE PROGRAM
Greenville, North Carolina
Project Location: East Carolina University, Greenville, North Carolina
Description: This is an opportunity to be a part of a production apprentice program and to observe professionals at work.
Open to: Students, 16-years and up.
Cost: Participants live in university dorms and are responsible for their own meals.
For more information: Jay Herzog, East Carolina Summer Theater Program, East Carolina University, Department of Theater Arts, Greenville, North Carolina 27858; (919)757-6390.

GALLAUDET YOUNG SCHOLARS PROGRAM
Washington, DC
Project Location: Washington, DC
Description: Students study the performing arts, focusing on a particular culture.
Open to: Students entering 9-12 grade who are deaf or hard-of-hearing.
Cost: $1,800. Students live in dormitories and eat in dining halls. Four-week program.

For more information: Gallaudet Young Scholars Program, Gallaudet University, HMB E111, 800 Florida Avenue, N.E., Washington, DC 20002-3695; (202)651-5755; (202)651-5065 (fax); URL http://www.gallaudet.edu.

HERE
New York, New York
Project Location: New York, New York
Description: Arts, center, theatres, puppetry, galleries, and café.
Open to: High school juniors, seniors, and graduates.
Positions Available: One-on-one apprenticeships with established theatre and visual artists. Very rewarding opportunity.
Cost/Compensation: Unpaid (possible travel reimbursements).
For more information: Barbara Busackind, HERE, 145 Avenue of the Americas, New York, New York 10013; (212)647-0202 Ext. 307.

IRISH SCHOOL OF LANDSCAPE PAINTING
Dublin, Ireland
Project Location: Ireland
Description: Amateur and advanced painters are welcome. There are one-week and three-day courses.
Open to: Students, age 14 and over.
Cost: One-week course approximately $36-$243. Three-day course approximately $159. Hostel rooms with breakfast and dinner are available at special rates.
For more information: Irish School of Landscape Painting, The Blue Door Studio, 16 Prince of Wales Terrace, Ballsbridge, Dublin 4 Ireland; (353) 1-685548.

LEARN WHILE YOU VACATION
Chautaugua, New York
Location: Chautaugua, New York
Description: Learning vacations are organized by colleges, universities, and educational organizations such as this one with an interest in concerts, seminars, workshops, and culture vacations.
Open to: Any age.
Cost: Approximately $500/week. Some package deals include lodging, etc.
For more information: Learn While You Vacation, Chautaugua Institution, Chautaugua, New York 14722.

LOWER ASTON HOUSE POTTERY AND PAINTING SUMMER SCHOOL
Worcestershire, England
Project Location: England
Description: There are week-long and weekend courses organized to have maximum teacher-student interaction.

Open to: Students, age 14 and over.

Cost: Approximately $441 for a weeklong stay and $190 for a weekend stay, which includes instruction, room and board.

For more information: Organizer, Lower Aston House Pottery and Painting Summer School, Aston Bank, Knighton-on-Teme, Tenbury Wells, Worcestershire WR15 8LW England; 01584-781-404.

NATIONAL ENDOWMENT FOR THE HUMANITIES YOUNGER SCHOLARS AWARDS
Washington, D.C.

Project Location: Various sites.

Description: Scholars have the means and help to pursue independent research and write research papers.

Open to: High school students.

Cost: $2,100 provided for student to cover expenses. $500 of this is for the student's advisor.

For more information: The National Endowment for the Humanities (NEH), Division of Fellowships and Seminars, Room 316, 1100 Pennsylvania Avenue, NW, Washington, DC 20506.

NEW STAGE THEATRE
Jackson, Mississippi

Project Location: Jackson, Mississippi

Description: Professional nonprofit theater.

Open to: High school students and graduates.

Cost/Compensation: Paid and unpaid.

For more information: Education/Internship Coordinator, New Stage Theatre, 1100 Carlisle Street, Jackson, Mississippi 39202; (601)948-3533; (601)948-3538 (fax).

OXFORD SCHOOL OF DRAMA
Oxford, England

Project Location: England

Description: This school offers teenagers the chance to study and perform drama.

Open to: Students, ages 14-18.

Cost: Tuition is approximately $847 for two weeks and $1,540 for four weeks, including housing, breakfast, dinner, theater tickets, and travel during the course.

For more information: Administrator, Oxford School of Drama, Sansomes Farm Studios, Woodstock, Oxford OX20 1ER, Britain; (44) 1993-812883; (44) 1993-811220 (fax); E-mail info@oxford.drama.ac.uk; URL http://www.oxford.drama.ac.uk/.

PARSONS SCHOOL OF DESIGN
New York, New York

Project Location: France

Description: During four weeks in July, famous museums and art communities are used to advantage in art and design classes.

Open to: Minimum 16 years.

Cost: $150 orientation fee; $2,418 tuition; $40 health insurance; and $800 housing and meals.

For more information: Office of Admissions, Parsons School of Design, 66 5th Avenue, New York, New York 10011; (212) 229-8910.

PENNSYLVANIA GOVERNOR'S SCHOOL FOR THE ARTS
Erie, Pennsylvania

Project Location: Erie, Pennsylvania

Description: This program is for talented students who are interested in music, dance, arts (including photography), theater, and creative writing.

Open to: Students entering grades 11-12.

Cost: Students stay in dormitories and eat in dining halls.

For more information: Pennsylvania Governor's School for the Arts, Mercyhurst College, Erie, Pennsylvania; (717)524-5244.

SALZBURG INTERNATIONAL SUMMER ACADEMY OF FINE ARTS
Salzburg, Austria

Project Location: Salzburg, Austria

Description: During five weeks, students have opportunity to draw and paint alongside artists who are well-known in the areas of modeling, sculpture, graphic arts, architecture, stage design, photography, goldsmithing, video and stone sculpture.

Open to: Students, age 17 and over.

Cost: Approximately $800. Housing, food insurance, and transportation are the student's responsibility.

For more information: Dr. Barbara Wally, Director, International Summer Academy of Fine Arts, Kapitelgasse 5 RGB., Postvach 18, A-5010, Salzburg, Austria 5010; ++43-662-842113, 843727; ++43-662-849638 (fax); E-mail SoAk.Salzburg@magnet.at; URL http://www.land-sbg.gv.at/sommerakademie.

SNAKE RIVER INSTITUTE
Jackson, Wyoming

Project Location: Jackson, Wyoming

Description: Classes are offered in photography, sculpture, and art history.

Open to: Anyone interested.

Cost: $65-$700. Lodging is included with some courses; meals are not.

For more information: Snake River Institute, P.O. Box 7724, Jackson, Wyoming 83001.

STUDIO ART CENTERS INTERNATIONAL (SACI)
New York, New York

Project Location: Italy

Description: Using the rich resources of Florence, excellent studio art and art history courses are taught.

Open to: Seniors at least 17 years of age.

FOCUS ON...
JUNIOR STATE OF AMERICA

"Since its inception in 1934, more than 300,000 student members have become active, informed citizens through the Junior State. Students organize every aspect of JSA. Student leaders, elected by their fellow JSA members, plan and execute all of the conventions, conferences, and political awareness events put on by the Junior State."

-www.jsa.org

Junior Statesman Summer School

For 57 years, this rigorous program has been available for outstanding high school students. Students attend month-long sessions at colleges and universities throughout the U.S. The curriculum includes an introduction to American government and politics, exciting speakers, and student debates on current issues. Participants generally receive high school credit.

Opportunities are available across the United States. You can contact JSA at:

Junior State of America
60 East Third Avenue, Suite 320
San Mateo, California 94401
(800)334-5353; (650)347-7200 (fax)
E-mail jsa@jsa.org
Website http://www.jsa.org

Cost: Academic year costs $6,500. Monthly cost is $2,435. Included are: tuition, library use, field trips, lectures, and seminars.
For more information: Institute of International Education (IIE), SACI Coordinator, 809 United Nations Plaza, New York, New York 10017-3580; (212)984-5548; (800)344-9186.

SUMMER ART EXPERIENCE
San Francisco, California
Project Location: San Francisco, California
Description: Professional-level art training is available to students who want to pursue interest in the visual arts.
Open to: High school students entering grades 9-12.
Cost: $35.00 application fee. Students pay for transportation, supplies and fees. Out-of-town students are housed in dormitories or off-campus apartments and pay for own meals.
For more information: Summer Art Experience, Academy of Art College, 79 New Montgomery Street, San Francisco, California 94105; (800)544-ARTS.

COMMUNICATION

ARVON FOUNDATION
Devon, England
Project Location: England
Description: At Arvon, each course lasts five days. Students investigate and practice creative writing with the help of two professionals.
Open to: Students, age 16 or over.
Cost: Approximately £320 for five days; includes board and tuition.
For more information: Senior Administrator, Arvon Foundation, Totleigh Barton, Sheepwash, Devon EX215NS, England; (44)409-23-338.

HIGH SCHOOL JOURNALISM WORKSHOP
Athens, Ohio
Project Location: Athens, Ohio

Description: Hands-on workshop experiences for high school journalism students who hold important positions beginning the next school year.
Open to: N/A
Cost: $130.00 covers housing and meals.
For more information: High School Journalism Workshop, Ohio University, Haning Hall, Athens, Ohio 45701-2979.

KEMPA SUMMER JOURNALISM WORKSHOP
Whitewater, Wisconsin
Project Location: University of Wisconsin
Description: Courses offered in three types of journalism: photojournalism, newspaper/yearbook, and desktop publishing.
Open to: High school students.
Cost: A residence hall and its dining room provide housing and meals. Yearbook or newspaper workshops ($200); Photojournalism workshops ($220); and desktop publishing workshops ($230).
For more information: Kempa Summer Journalism Workshop, University of Wisconsin, Whitewater, Continuing Education Services, 2005 Roseman, Whitewater, Wisconsin 53190; (414)472-3165.

OPPORTUNITIES TO MINGLE WITH PUBLISHERS, AUTHORS, AND AGENTS
Project Location: Nationwide
Description: Conferences and workshops mix students with professionals in the field of creative writing.
Open to: Students, age 15 and up.
Cost: $25-$80 per lecture. Housing in dormitories, bed and breakfasts, inns, and motels. Food sometimes provided.
For more information: If interested check listing in the magazines *Writer's Digest* and *Writer* or consult the *Literary Market Place (LMP)* at your library.

YOUNG SCHOLARS PROGRAM IN COMPUTING
Greenville, South Carolina
Project Location: Greenville, South Carolina
Description: Students in research teams explore a project in virtual reality simulations, internet usage, image processing, neural networks, multimedia computing, and sound processing.
Open to: Students entering grades 11-12.
Cost: Housing in dormitories and meals in dining halls.
For more information: Young Scholars Program in Computing, Furman University, Department of Computer Science, Greenville, South Carolina 29613; (803)294-2097.

YOUTH VOICE COLLABORATIVE/YWCA BOSTON
Boston, Massachusetts
Project Location: Boston
Description: Media literacy and technology program.
Open to: Teens ages 13-18.
Cost: N/A
For more information: Ann Manubay, Program Coordinator, Youth Voice Collaborative/YWCA Boston, 140 Clarendon Street, Boston, Massachusetts, 02116; (617)351-7644; (617)351-7615 (fax); URL http://www.yvc.org.

FOREIGN LANGUAGE

AMERICAN LANGUAGE CENTER
Fez, Morocco
Project Location: Morocco
Description: ALI/Fez offers an intense three-week course in survival Moroccan Arabic. There are also intermediate and specialized courses available.
Open to: People of all ages.
Cost: Costs vary. Students pay costs of housing, meals, and travel.
For more information: The Arabic Language Institute of Fez, BP 2136, Fez, Morocco.

AMERISPAN UNLIMITED
Philadelphia, Pennsylvania
Project Location: Costa Rica, Guatemala, and Mexico.
Description: Programs vary according to country. These are some offerings: language instruction, homestay housing and meals, dance classes, lectures, discussions, and excursions.
Open to: Varies with countries. Age 14 and up.
Cost: Cost varies.
For more information: AmeriSpan Unlimited, P.O. Box 40513, Philadelphia, Pennsylvania 19106; (800) 879-6640.

ANGLO-GERMAN INSTITUTE
Stuttgart, Germany
Project Location: Stuttgart
Description: German language courses offered for year program. Summer courses offer 20 lessons.
Open to: Students age 16 and up.
Cost: Summer courses approximately $957/two weeks. Four-week courses approximately $1,342. Tuition, housing with families, breakfast and dinner, and some materials are included.
For more information: Anglo-German Institute (AGI), Christophstrasse 4, D-70178, Stuttgart, Germany; (49) 711-603858.

ATHENS CENTRE
Athens, Greece
Project Location: Greece
Description: The Centre offers modern Greek throughout the year for all levels of ability. Travel programs

are also available during the summer.

Open to: Students, at least 16 years of age, entering the 12th grade.

Cost: Language courses are approximately $260. Tours are $1,800-$2,500 and include accommodations, breakfast, field trips, and travel within Greece.

For more information: Program Director, Athens Centre, 48 Archimidous Street, 11636 Athens, Greece; (30)1-701-2268.

BABEL
Nice, France

Project Location: France

Description: French language courses.

Open to: Young adults, age 16 and up.

Cost: Two-week course approximately FF 2600. Accommodations and excursions are extra.

For more information: Director of Studies, 22 ter, rue de France, Nice, France 06000; +33-493822744; +33-493882130 (fax); E-mail 101755.2404@compuserve.com.

THE BRITISH INSTITUTE OF FLORENCE
Firenze, Italy

Project Location: Italy

Description: There are various offerings: Italian language, history, drawing, opera, Italian cooking, photography, and excursions.

Open to: Minimum age of 16.

Cost: $350-$600 depending on language level and length of stay. Host homes and small hotels are available.

For more information: The British Institute of Florence, Lungarno Guicciardini, 9, 50125 Firenze, Italy; (39)552-84031.

CENTRAL AMERICAN INSTITUTE FOR INTERNATIONAL AFFAIRS (ICAI)
San Jose, Costa Rica

Project Location: Costa Rica

Description: Students have four hours of language instruction daily and live with Costa Rican host families.

Open to: Minimum age of 15.

Cost: $575-$740 includes housing and two meals daily.

For more information: Language Studies Enrollment Center, P.O. Box 5095, Anaheim, California 92814; (714)527-2918 or Central American Institute for International Affairs (ICAI), P.O. Box 10302-1000, San Jose, Costa Rica; (506)338571.

CENTRO DE ESTUDIOS DE CASTELLANO
Málaga, Spain

Project Location: Spain

Description: Spanish courses are taught at all levels, beginner to advanced.

Open to: Minimum age of 16.

Cost: Varies depending on program.

For more information: F. Marin Fernández, Director, Centro de Estudios de Castellano, Avda. Juan Sebastian Elcano, 120, Malaga, Spain 29017; (34)95-2290-551; (34)95-2290-551 (fax); E-mail ryoga@arrakis.es; URL http://wwwarrakis.es~ryoga..

CENTRO DE IDIOMAS
Mazatlán, Mexico

Project Location: Mexico

Description: Courses are offered at all levels. At least 2 months are suggested.

Open to: Individuals ages 16-20.

Cost: $1,113 for one month of study, two activities weekly, and shared room and board with local family.

Other information: Conversational Spanish for serious students - emphasis is on speaking abilities and listening.

For more information: Dixie Davis, Director, Centro de Idiomas, Belisario Dominguez No. 1908, Mazatlán Sinaloa, Mexico 82000; 52(69)82-2053; 52(69)82-2053 (fax); E-mail 74174.1340@compuserve.com.

CENTRO LINGUISTICO ITALIANO DANTE ALIGHIERI
Florence, Italy

Project Location: Italy

Description: The program offers language and culture courses. It also offers tours, dinners, and parties to encourage more language learning.

Open to: Minimum age 15.

Cost: 16-hour course ($150); 20-hour course ($185); 100-hour course ($650); 100-hour individual study ($6,460). Students pay own housing, meals, and travel.

For more information: Centro Linguistico Italiano Dante Alighieri, Via Dei Bardi, 12, Florence 50125 Italy; (39)55-2342984.

CIAL-CENTRO DE LINGUAS
Lisbon, Portugal

Project Location: Portugal

Description: Language programs are offered for individuals and groups. Also offered are excursions and other activities.

Open to: Minimum age 16.

Cost: Costs vary according to hours, weeks, groups, and individuals ($240-$1,560). Family host accommodations ($126-$385).

For more information: Director of Studies, Cial-Centro de Linguas, Av. da Republica, 41-8", 1000 Lisbon, Portugal; (351)1-7940448.

DEUTSCH IN GRAZ (DIG)
Graz, Austria

Project Location: Austria

Description: As well as language courses, this program offers sports activities and extensive leisure time.

Open to: Ages 15-17.

Cost: Three-week program approximately $700.

For more information: Deutsch in Graz (DIG), Zinzendorfgasse 30, A-8010 Graz Austria; (43)316-383747.

EL INSTITUTO ALLERIDE

San Miguel de Allende, Mexico

Project Location: Mexico

Description: In the charming village of San Miguel de Allende, daily lectures are given by excellent teachers, and impromptu conversation in Spanish is continually encouraged.

Open to: People of all ages.

Cost: Cost varies. Students pay costs of housing, meals, and travel.

For more information: El Instituto, San Miguel de Allende, Mexico.

FRENCH AMERICAN STUDY CENTER (FASC)

Lisieux, France

Project Location: France

Description: Students live with host families and speak only French.

Open to: Students, at least 14 years of age.

Cost: $580-$780/week includes tuition, room, and board.

For more information: Director, French American Study Center (FASC), Boite Postale 176, 14014 Lisieux, France; (33)31312201.

GRAN CANARIA SCHOOL OF LANGUAGES

Las Palmas, Spain

Project Location: Spain

Description: Various class times and duration are offered for language study, excursions, and social events.

Open to: Minimum age 16.

Cost: Tuition and activities ($70/week). Private instruction ($410/week). Lodging ($100/week).

For more information: Gran Canaria School of Languages, Ruiz de Alda 12-3, E-35007 Las Palmas, Spain; (34)28-267971.

IFK GERMAN COURSES SALZBURG

Salzburg, Austria

Project Location: Austria

Description: Nine-day to three-week courses in German and related social science and culture courses.

Open to: Children to adults.

Cost: ATS 700-ATS 18,000, depending on the program.

For more information: IFK Deutschkurse Salzburg, (IFK), und Collegium Austriacum, Postfach 120, A-5010 Salzburg, Austria; +43-662-84-96-11; E-mail Office@ifk-ca.ac.at; URL http://www.ifk-ca.ac.at/ifk-ca/

INSTITUTE OF CHINA STUDIES

Lincolnwood, Illinois

Project Location: Fudan University, Illinois

Description: There are four- to six-week courses offered and extracurricular activities.

Open to: Minimum age 16.

Cost: $2,500 for the four-week program includes tuition, room and board, and international flights from the West Coast.

For more information: Institute of China Studies, 7341 North Kolmar, Lincolnwood, Illinois 60646; (708)677-0982.

INSTITUTE OF SPANISH STUDIES

San Francisco, California

Project Location: Spain

Description: Two five or six-week sessions are offered with three programs available: independent study with study-travel; study then travel; and study only.

Open to: Minimum age 15.

Cost: $989 (tuition) - $4,278 depending on airfare and session chosen.

For more information: Registrar, Institute of Spanish Studies, 3410 Geary Boulevard, San Francisco, California 94118-3357; (415)586-0180 or (415)387-6817.

LANGUAGE STUDIES ABROAD

Solana Beach, California

Project Location: Costa Rica, Mexico, Ecuador, Spain, Italy, France, Germany, and French Canada.

Description: Programs are offered year-round. Four hours of class daily or more with cultural activities and small classes.

Open to: Anyone 16 or older.

Cost: Two-week programs start at $600. Includes language studies with homestays and some meals.

For more information: Charlene Biddulph, Director, Language Studies Abroad, 249 South Highway 101, Suite 226, Solana Beach, California 92075; (800)424-5522; (760)943-1201 (fax); E-mail Cbiddulph@aol.com; URL http://www.dnai.com/~bid/language/.

NATIONAL REGISTRATION CENTER FOR STUDY ABROAD (NRCSA)

Milwaukee, Wisconsin

Project Location: Latin America, Canada, France, Switzerland, Germany, Austria, and Spain.

Description: NRCSA acts as an information and registration office for over 100 language schools in 25 countries, with about 20 that will accept students under age 18. There are four program types: Mexico Discovery, Total Immersion-Spanish, Total Immersion-French, and Total Immersion-German. Teen pro-

grams, escorted or unescorted, available in several Latin American countries as well as French speaking Canada, France, Switzerland, Austria, Germany, and Spain.
Open to: Ages 12-17, depending on program.
Cost: $500-$1,750. Airfare is additional and can be coordinated by the NRCSA offices.
For more information: National Registration Center for Study Abroad (NRCSA), P.O. Box 1393, Milwaukee, Wisconsin 53201; (414)278-0631; (414)271-8884 (fax); E-mail teenstudy@nrcsa.com; URL http://www. nrcsa.com.

OIDEAS GAEL
Donegal, Ireland
Project Location: Donegal, Ireland
Description: Organization promoting Ireland's language and culture.
Open to: Students interested in Irish studies. Minimum age 16.
Cost: $130-$160/week, housing and meals (approximately $50/week).
Other information: Cultural activity holidays also available.
For more information: Director, Oideas Gael, Gleann Cholm Gille, County Donegal, Ireland; 073-30248; 073-30348 (fax); E-mail oidsgael@iol.le; URL www. oeideas-gael.com.

THE SCHOOL FOR INTERNATIONAL TRAINING
Brattleboro, Vermont
Project Location: Worldwide
Description: Summer immersion courses with social and cultural experiences allowing further involvement in a foreign language.
Open to: People of all ages.
Cost: Costs vary. Students provide own housing, meals, and travel.
For more information: School for International Training, Kipling Road, Brattleboro, Vermont 05302.

TORRE DI BABELE - LANGUAGE STUDY LINK
Rome, Italy
Project Location: Italy
Description: Study Italian in Rome. Language choices go from beginning to advanced with various choices on means of instruction and time allocated.
Open to: Minimum age 16.
Cost: Two-week group intensive course is approximately $300. Room and board are extra.
For more information: Torre Di Babele- Language Study Link, Via Bixio, 74, Rome 00185 Italy; (39)06-7008434; (39)06-70497150 (fax); E-mail info@torredibabele.it; URL http://www.torredibabele. it.

VIENNA INTERNATIONAL UNIVERSITY COURSES
Vienna, Austria
Project Location: Austria
Description: The school teaches German from beginning level up to a "perfectionist course."
Open to: Minimum age 16.
Cost: Summer course, accommodations, and meals (student needs to make own arrangements) approximately $935.
For more information: Vienna International University Courses, Universität, A-1010 Vienna, Austria; (43)1-421254.

HEALTH

APACHE RESCUE TEAM
Springville, Arizona
Project Location: South, Midwest, and Arizona
Description: Organization teaches youth rescue teams emphasizing medical and technical training.
Open to: N/A
Cost: N/A
For more information: Outdoor Program Coordinator, Apache Rescue Team, P.O. Box 2012, Springville, Arizona 85938; (520)333-5867.

INSTITUTE FOR PRE-COLLEGE ENRICHMENT: SCOPE SCIENCE CAREERS OPPORTUNITY ENRICHMENT
Prairie View, Texas
Project Location: Prairie View, Texas
Description: While getting a taste of college life, students learn about what careers in health sciences are about.
Open to: Students entering grades 10-12 and in the top 1/3 of their class.
Cost: $50, housing in dormitories and meals in dining halls.
For more information: Institute for Pre-College Enrichment: SCOPE, Prairie View A&M University, P. O. Box 66, Prairie View, Texas 77446-0066; (800) 622-9643.

NURSE CAMP
Madison, Wisconsin
Project Location: Madison, Wisconsin
Description: Students see nursing being practiced in hospitals, hospices, clinics, home health agencies, and nursing homes while learning nursing skills such as CPR and first aid.
Open to: Students, ages 13-18.
Cost: Housing in dormitories and meals in dining hall.
For more information: Nurse Camp, University of Wisconsin, Madison, 600 Highland Avenue, Madi-

son, Wisconsin 53792; (608)263-5183.

REGIONAL CENTER FOR MATHEMATICS AND SCIENCE: HEALTH SCIENCES EMPHASIS

Green Bay, Wisconsin

Project Location: Green Bay, Wisconsin

Description: This is an opportunity for students to explore opportunities in health sciences while experiencing college life.

Open to: Students entering the 11th grade who reside in Wisconsin, Ohio, Illinois, Indiana, Michigan, or Minnesota; have a GPA of 2.3 and up; and come from a home where the parents' income meets the income criteria defined by the U.S. Dept. of Ed., OR where neither parent has completed a four-year college degree.

Cost: The program is free— including housing in dormitories and meals in a dining hall, as well as round-trip transportation from your home.

For more information: Michael Casbourne, Director, Regional Center for Mathematics and Science, UW-Green Bay, SS 1929, 2420 Nicolet Drive, SS 1929, Green Bay, Wisconsin 54311-7001; (920)465-2671; (920)465-2954 (fax); E-mail RCMS@UWGB.EDU; URL http://www.uwgb.edu/~rcms.

HUMAN SERVICES/ EDUCATION

COUNSELOR PROGRAM

Rhinebeck, New York

Project Location: Rhinebeck, New York

Description: Counselors live in cabins with children identified as emotionally disturbed and learning-impaired.

Open to: Students entering 12th grade.

Cost: No cost.

For more information: Counselor Program, Ramapo Anchorage Camp, P.O. Box 266, Rhinebeck, New York 12572; (914)876-8403.

DYNAMY-EDUCATION IN ACTION

Worcester, Massachusetts

Project Location: Northeast, Massachusetts

Description: The beginning of the program is with an outdoor experience at an Outward Bound school in Maine. Then the program changes to learning during a series of 3-9 week internships in your career field. During the week, there are workshops and meetings.

Open to: N/A

Cost: Tuition is $9,950 and housing is $3,500. Some financial aid is available.

For more information: Admissions Director, Dynamy-Education in Action, 27 Sever Street, Worcester, Massachusetts 01609-2129; (508)755-2571;

E-mail dynamy@nesc.org; URL http://www.nesc.org/~dynamy.

MISSOURI COMMUNITY SERVICE COMMISSION

Jefferson City, Missouri

Project Location: Missouri

Description: State government agency.

Open to: Anyone 17 or over.

Positions Available: Part-time or full-time Americorps member positions.

Cost: Living stipend plus $4,725. (Full-time education award).

Other information: Opportunities for individuals to provide community service in return for a living allowance, education award, and the satisfaction of "getting things done."

For more information: Krista Bailey, Program Assistant, Missouri Community Service Commission, 3225 W. Truman Boulevard, Suite 101, Jefferson City, Missouri 65109; (573)751-7488 or toll-free (877)210-7611; (573)526-0463 (fax).

PENNSYLVANIA GOVERNOR'S SCHOOL FOR TEACHING

Millersville, Pennsylvania

Project Location: Millersville, Pennsylvania

Description: The program is designed to give students the opportunity to research and design a lesson plan and present it to elementary students. Also, students are exposed to the latest educational ideas in varied workshop experiences.

Open to: Students entering grades 11-12 who are interested in teaching as a profession. Students must be residents of Pennsylvania and complete a highly competitive application process.

Cost: Students have housing in dormitories and meals in a cafeteria.

For more information: Pennsylvania Governor's School for Teaching, Millersville University, Millersville, Pennsylvania 17551-0302; (717)871-2026 or (717)524-5244.

INTERNATIONAL

ACADEMIC STUDY ASSOCIATES

Armonk, New York

Project Location: France, Spain, and England.

Description: Study programs are offered in Oxford, England; Royan and Nice, France; and Andalusia, Spain.

Open to: Students, ages 13-18, 9th through 12th grade. One year in a foreign language.

Cost: $4,495-$3,895 including meals and housing in homes or Residential Language Center.

For more information: Academic Study Associates,

355 Main Street, P.O. Box 38, Armonk, New York 10504; (914)273-2250; URL http://www.asaprograms. com.

ACCENT
San Francisco, California
Project Location: Florence, Italy and Paris, France.
Description: Summer and semester studies. There are academic programs planned along with U.S. universities and colleges.
Open to: Students, age 17, having completed 11th grade.
Cost: $2,100-$2,600 for summer programs; $3,600-$4,900 for semester program. Fee includes housing, partial meals, orientation, and excursions.
For more information: Accent, 425 Market Street, 2nd Floor, San Francisco, California 94105; (415)904-7756.

AFS INTERCULTURAL PROGRAMS
New York, New York
Project Location: More than 50 countries.
Description: Programs include these possibilities: semester programs, mission teams, year programs, summer programs, summer stay with a family, stay with family and study their language, study the environment (Brazil), and outdoor education while living with a family.
Open to: Students, age 15-18, who have not yet graduated. Grade point average at least 2.7.
Cost: $2,395-$6,875.
For more information: AFS Intercultural Programs, 220 East 42nd Street, Third Floor, New York, New York 10017; (212)949-4242 or (800)AFS-INFO.

ALEXANDER MUSS HIGH SCHOOL IN ISRAEL (AM/HSI)
Miami, Florida
Project Location: Israel
Description: Using historical sites, history is taught from ancient to modern times. Classes are taught in mathematics, foreign language, and science.
Open to: Students in grades 11-12 with a 2.5 GPA and school recommendation.
Cost: $3,625-$4,700, including housing, meals, and transportation.
For more information: Alexander Muss High School in Israel (AM/HSI), Admission Department, 3950 Biscayne Boulevard, Miami, Florida 33137; (305)576-3286 or (800)327-5980.

ALLIANCES ABROAD
San Francisco, California
Project Location: Spain, Africa, England, Australia, Mexico, Ecuador, Germany, Italy, and France.
Description: The thrust is to immerse students into the life and culture of the chosen country. You live with a host family.
Open to: N/A
Cost: Student pays tuition, airfare, and individual expenses.
For more information: Program Director, Alliances Abroad, 2830 Alameda, San Francisco, California 94103; (415)487-0691 or (800)266-8047; E-mail AlliancesA@aol.com; URL http://www. studyabroad.com/alliances.

AMERICAN ASSOCIATION OF OVERSEAS STUDIES
London, England
Project Location: London and New York.
Description: AAOS provides hands-on experience in business, law, film, medicine, government, journalism, theatre studies, and art courses.
Open to: Teenagers.
Cost: London Summer Internship Package ($3,995-$4,995). Year-round Internships in New York or London ($995).
For more information: Janet Kollek Evans, Director, American Association of Overseas Studies, 51 Drayton Gardens, Suite 4, London SW10 9RX England; (800)EDU-BRIT; 011-44-171-244-6061 (fax); E-mail aaos2000@hotmail.com; URL http://www.worldwide. edu/uk/aaos/.

AMERICAN ASSOCIATION OF TEACHERS OF GERMAN
Cherry Hill, New Jersey
Project Location: Germany
Description: Four-week travel/study program.
Open to: 15-year-olds with at least two years of German and recommendation from German teacher.
Cost: $2,200-$2,450 includes housing and meals, transportation, classes, excursions, and insurance.
For more information: American Association of Teachers of German (AATG), 112 Haddontown Court 104, Cherry Hill, New Jersey 08034; (609)795-5553; E-mail AATG@bellatlantic.net.

AMERICAN COLLEGE OF SWITZERLAND
Leysin, Switzerland
Project Location: Switzerland
Description: This program is planned for high school students who desire to do their senior year in a university setting.
Open to: Students, age 16 and older, entering 12th grade.
Cost: Approximately $18,000, including housing and meals.
For more information: Administrative Director, American College of Switzerland, 1854 Leysin, Switzerland; (41)25-342223.

AMERICAN FARM SCHOOL – "GREEK SUMMER"
New York, New York
Project Location: Greece
Description: Students live with a rural Greek family and work on a project while being exposed to Greek culture.
Open to: Students the summer after their sophomore, junior, or senior year in high school.
Cost: $2,600 plus $500 tax-deductible contribution. Airfare is not included.
For more information: Nicholas Apostal, Program Coordinator, American Farm School, Office of Trustees, 1133 Broadway, Suite 1625, New York, New York 10010; (212)463-8434; (212)463-8208 (fax); E-mail nyoffice@amerfarm.org; URL http://www.afs.edu.gr.

AMERICAN INSTITUTE FOR FOREIGN STUDY FOUNDATION/ACADEMIC YEAR ABROAD
Greenwich, Connecticut
Project Location: Germany, Netherlands, France, Spain, Brazil, Austria, and Chile.
Description: Programs vary depending upon location. Study in an overseas high school for a semester or full year, play soccer in Brazil for a summer, attend summer camp in Spain, counsel at an English camp in Brazil, explore the arts in Austria, and more!
Open to: Students, ages 15-18, with at least a C average. Language requirements vary by country and program.
Cost: $2,500-$7,000.
For more information: Terri L. Williams, Director, AIFS Foundation, Academic Year in America/ Academic Year Abroad, Greenwich Office Park #1, 52 Weaver Street, Greenwich, Connecticut 06831-5119; (800)322-4678(HOST); (203)625-5450 (fax); E-mail twilliams@aifs.org; URL http://www.aifs.org..

AMERICAN INTERNATIONAL YOUTH STUDENT EXCHANGE PROGRAM
Tiburon, California
Project Location: Australia, Switzerland, Austria, Sweden, Belgium, Spain, Canada, Netherlands, Denmark, New Zealand, England, Japan, France, Italy, Ireland, and Germany.
Description: This program offers year-long, semester, and summer studies.
Open to: Students, ages 15-18, with three years of language for those in non-English speaking countries.
Cost: $1,800-$4,800 includes housing, meals, insurance fees, and travel.
For more information: American International Youth Student Exchange Program, 200 Round Hill Road, Tiburon, California 94920; (800)847-7575.

AMIGOS DE LAS AMERICAS
Houston, Texas
Project Location: Latin America and Texas
Description: Work in teams in houses, health clinics, and schools. Training is provided before students go.
Open to: Students 16-years and older.
Cost: $3,000-$3,100 includes airfare, training sessions, room and board, supplies, transportation, and staff support.
For more information: Field Program Director, Amigos de las Americas, 5618 Star Lane, Houston, Texas 77057; (713)782-5290 or (800)231-7796; E-mail info@amigoslink.org; URL http://www.amigoslink.org.

ASSE INTERNATIONAL STUDENT EXCHANGE PROGRAMS
Laguna Beach, California
Project Location: Australia, Canada, Denmark, Czech Republic, Great Britain, Finland, Germany, France, Malta, Iceland, Japan, Italy, New Zealand, Mexico, Netherlands, Portugal, Norway, Poland, Switzerland, Slorakia, and Spain.
Description: Three options are open to U.S. students: a year attending school, a summer program, and a 28-day language adventure. Choice of options determines which countries are available.
Open to: Students, ages 15-18, with a B average (C+ average for summer program).
Cost: $2,950-$6,500 includes airfare (except to Canada and Mexico), insurance, accommodations, supervision, and placement. Summer option: $2,200-$2,600.
For more information: President, ASSE International Student Exchange Programs, 228 North Coast Highway, Laguna Beach, California 92651; (800)333-3802.

BICYCLE AFRICA TOURS
Seattle, Washington
Project Location: Africa; Washington
Description: Promotes pride in the environment and varied cultures.
Open to: N/A
Cost: $900-$1,290
For more information: Director, Bicycle Africa Tours, 4887 Columbia Drive, South, Seattle, Washington, 98108-1919; (206)767-0848; E-mail ibike@ibike.org; URL http://www.ibike.org/bikeafrica.

CENTER FOR CULTURAL INTERCHANGE
St. Charles, Illinois
Project Location: Spain
Description: The exchange provides summer and academic year programs.
Open to: Students, ages 15-18, in grades 10-12. Two years of Spanish is helpful.
Cost: $2,650 includes housing with families, insurance, orientation, and supervision.
For more information: Center for Cultural Inter-

change, 42W273 Retreat Court, Dept. CS, St. Charles, Illinois 60175; (708)377-2272.

CENTER FOR GLOBAL EDUCATION
Minneapolis, Minnesota
Project Location: Worldwide; Minnesota
Description: One to three-week travel/educational seminar trips.
Open to: Students, 16 years and older.
Cost: $1,295-$3,795
For more information: Travel Counselor, Center for Global Education, Augsburg College, 2211 Riverside Avenue, Box 307, Minneapolis, Minnesota 55454; (612)330-1159 or (800)299-8889; E-mail globaled@augsburg.edu; URL http://www.augsburg.edu/global.

COUNCIL ON INTERNATIONAL EDUCATION EXCHANGE
New York, New York
Project Location: Worldwide
Description: The Exchange works together with educational institutions in Europe coordinating classes and accommodations for students who want to study during their vacation.
Open to: Students, ages 16-23.
Cost: Cost varies. Room and board generally provided. Student pays travel costs.
For more information: Council on International Education Exchange, 205 East 42nd Street, New York, New York 10017.

CROSS-CULTURAL SOLUTIONS
New Rochelle, New York
Project Location: India, Ghana, and West Africa.
Description: Enables student to experience India and Africa in a meaningful way by working on substantial volunteer projects.
Open to: Everybody. No prior experience is necessary; the only prerequisite is an open mind and a desire to help others.
Cost: Program is $1,850 and includes food, lodging, in-country transportation, professional support, and other in-country costs. Airfare is not included, however, the airfare and program fee are tax deductible for U.S. residents.
For more information: Cross-Cultural Solutions, 47 Potter Avenue, New Rochelle, New York 10801; (800)380-4777; E-mail info@crossculturalsolutions.org; URL www.crossculturalsolutions.org.

EF FOUNDATION
Cambridge, Massachusetts
Project Location: New Zealand, Australia, France,

England, and Germany.

Description: Students live with families and attend local schools. A one-month program is offered in Spain, France, and Austria.

Open to: Students, ages 14-18, with a GPA of at least 2.7. In France, two years of language is required.

Cost: $4,500 for European countries; $5,200 for Australia or New Zealand; $4,200 for a semester in Europe; $4,900 for a semester in Australia or New Zealand; $2,000-$2,500 for a one-month program. Housing in homes, transportation and fees included.

For more information: EF Foundation, 1 Memorial Drive, Cambridge, Massachusetts 02142; (800)447-4273.

EUROPEAN STUDIES ASSOCIATION

San Francisco, California

Project Location: Paris, France

Description: Summer study includes French language instruction, civilization courses, conversation courses, and trips around Paris.

Open to: Students, 16-years-old and a junior in high school.

Cost: $2,400 includes lodging, breakfast, tuition, program, and activities.

For more information: Director, European Studies Association, 424 Dorado Terrace, San Francisco, California 94112-1753; (415)334-4222.

EXPERIENCE LIFE ON AN ISRAELI KIBBUTZ

Israel

Project Location: Israel

Description: Some special youth programs are available in the summer for youth, including "work camp vacation" and laboring in the fields.

Open to: Students, ages 15 and up. There is no need to be Jewish, but you will need a certain amount of spirituality to fit in on a kibbutz.

Cost: Fee of $65/week plus airfare; meals provided; housing with kibbutz family.

For more information: American Zionist Youth Foundation, 110 East 59th Street, 3rd Floor, New York, New York 10022.

EXPERIMENT IN INTERNATIONAL LIVING/WORLD LEARNING

Brattleboro, Vermont

Project Location: 19 countries worldwide.

Description: Students can choose from extraordinarily diverse programs. Some programs provide intense immersion in the language and culture of a single place and people; some engage students in a culture through community service; and others develop the global perspective necessary to tackle international ecological problems.

Open to: High school students and recent high school grads.

Cost: $1,800-$4,975.

For more information: Chris Frantz, Outreach Manager, Experiment in International Living/World Learning, P.O. Box 676, Kipling Road, Brattleboro, Vermont 05302-0676; (802)258-3446; (800)345-2929; (802)258-3428 (fax); E-mail eil@worldlearning.org; URL http://www.worldlearning.org.

IBEROAMERICAN CULTURAL EXCHANGE PROGRAM (ICEP)

Kirkland, Washington

Project Location: Bolivia, Costa Rica, Guatemala, and Mexico

Description: This organization was designed to enhance foreign language usage, have important study programs, and improve intercultural and international understanding.

Open to: Students, ages 15-18, with two years or equivalent of Spanish and recommendation of Spanish teacher.

Cost: $725 for six weeks; $2,500 for a full year; ground transportation, orientation, and arrangements with a host family are included. Airfare is not included.

For more information: Iberoamerican Cultural Exchange Program (ICEP), 13920 93rd Avenue, NE, Kirkland, Washington 98034; (206)821-1463.

INSTITUTO ALLENDE

San Miguel de Allende, Gto., Mexico

Project Location: Mexico

Description: Art and Spanish classes in the charming village of San Miguel de Allende, Gt. Also offer a Masters of Fine Arts and Bachelors in Visual Arts. Also offer field trips to different nearby areas such as Guanajuanto, Querètaro, Mexico City, Michoacàn, etc.

Open to: People of all ages (minimum age of 16).

Cost: $20 registration; $15/month insurance; $210 program. 6 hrs. Intensive Spanish $465 for four-weeks. Housing is available with Mexican families and the price is $18 per person/per day in a private room with three meals included and the student is responsible for payment.

For more information: Instituto Allende, Ancha de San Antonio 20, San Miguel de Allende, Gto.; (415)2-01-90 or 2-02-26; (415)2-45-38 (fax); E-mail iallende@instituto-allende.edu.mx; URL http://www.instituto-allende.edu.mx.

INTERNATIONAL COUNCIL FOR CULTURAL EXCHANGE

Rockville, Maryland

Project Location: French Riviera, Costa del Sol, and Riviera della Versilia.

Description: Two, three, four, or more weeks are offered for these programs: Spanish Language and Culture, Italian Language and Culture with painting option, or French Language and Culture.

Open to: Ages 16 and up.

Cost: $2,499-$2,999 (one-month program), housing, meals, airfare, tuition, registration, excursions, and use of University facilities.

For more information: International Council for Cultural Exchange, 1559 Rockville Pike, Rockville, Maryland 20852; (301)983-9479.

INTERNATIONAL STUDENT EXCHANGE
Fort Jones, California

Project Location: Italy, Spain, Mexico, and Germany.

Description: The purpose is for students to learn about the culture through language usage and living with a host family.

Open to: Ages 14-18, with some language experience preferred.

Cost: Fees vary; range of $3,000-$4,400.

For more information: International Student Exchange, P.O. Box 840, Fort Jones, California 96032; (916)468-2264.

INTERNATIONAL VOLUNTEER EXPEDITIONS
Sacramento, California

Project Location: Worldwide and California

Description: Short-term work projects in Latin America, California, Caribbean, and Africa.

Open to: High school students.

Cost: $395-$1,070 excluding airfare.

For more information: Executive Director, International Volunteer Expeditions, 2001 Vallejo Way, Sacramento, California 95818-3486; (916)444-6856; E-mail oakland2@ix.netcom.com.

IRISH AMERICAN CULTURAL INSTITUTE
Morristown, New Jersey

Project Location: Ireland

Description: This is an opportunity to learn Irish culture for five weeks during the summer.

Open to: Students in grades 9-12.

Cost: $2,150, housing and meals in dormitories, with host families and in hotels. Airfare is not included.

For more information: Irish Way, Irish American Cultural Institute, 3 Elm Street, Suite 204, Morristown, New Jersey 07960; (201)605-1991.

JUSTACT: YOUTH ACTION FOR GLOBAL JUSTICE
San Francisco, California

Project Location: San Francisco, California; International (volunteer opportunities); and United States (Bike-Aid cross-country bicycle ride).

Description: Organization working with youth to develop a life-long commitment to social and economic justice internationally. JustAct provides a network for students and graduates linking them to educational and volunteer opportunities worldwide.

Open to: High school students, college students, and graduates.

Positions Available: Office management and administration internship; communications and public relations internships; education and organizing program intern; Bike-Aid internships and volunteer opportunities; Alternative Opportunities program intern; and international volunteer opportunities.

Cost/Compensation: Varies. Contact JustAct for details.

For more information: Wendy Phillips, Internship Coordinator, JustAct, 333 Valencia Street, Suite 101, San Francisco, California 94103; (415)431-4204; (415)431-5953 (fax); E-mail info@justact.org; URL http://www.justact.org.

KW INTERNATIONAL
Atlanta, Georgia

Project Location: India

Description: This organization supports a year-long high school year in India (SAGE), at either The Woodstock School or the Kodaikanal International School. Two well-known international high schools.

Open to: High school students in grades 10-12.

Cost: $11,000 two semester tuition, housing and meals, and travel. Airfare not included.

For more information: Executive Director, KW International, 159 Ralph McGill Boulevard, NE, Room 408, Atlanta, Georgia 30308; (404)524-0988; E-mail kwi@mindspring.com.

NORTH CAROLINA STATE UNIVERSITY STUDY ABROAD
Raleigh, North Carolina

Project Location: London, Moscow, and Vienna.

Description: There are three summer experience programs available stressing education, culture, language, interaction, and experiencing the arts.

Open to: Students at least 17 years of age entering their senior year in high school. For Vienna, prior experience with German.

Cost: $2,100 for London program (room, some meals, theater tickets, trips); $1,850 for Vienna program (tuition, housing, meals, excursions); and $1,499 for Moscow (housing, meals, and excursions.)

For more information: Study Abroad Office, North Carolina State University Study Abroad, 2118 Pullen Hall, Box 7344, Raleigh, North Carolina 27695; (919)515-2087.

OVERSEAS DEVELOPMENT NETWORK
San Francisco, California

Project Location: Pacific Northwest; California

Description: This is a national student-based group for young students to address worldwide issues like injustice, poverty, or hunger.

Open to: High school students.

Cost: No compensation.

For more information: Program Coordinator, Overseas Development Network, 333 Valencia Street, Suite 330, San Francisco, California 94103; (415) 431-4204;

E-mail odn@igc.org; URL http://www.igc.apc.org/odn.

OXBRIDGE ACADEMIC PROGRAMS

New York, New York

Project Location: Oxford University and Cambridge University in England and Paris, France.

Description: Intensive academic/cultural enrichment programs in Oxford University, Cambridge University, and Paris. Superb faculties; wide range of courses covering humanities, creative arts, sciences, and more; many field trips and activities.

Open to: Ages 14-15 in grades 8-9 (Cambridge); ages 15-18 in grades 10-12 (Oxford, Cambridge, and Paris).

Cost: $4,295-$4,595 depending on the program.

For more information: Dr. Steven Farrelly-Jackson, Executive Director, Oxbridge Academic Programs, 601 Cathedral Parkway, Suite 7R, New York, New York 10025-2186; (800)828-8349; (212)663-8169 (fax); E-mail oxbridge@interport.net; URL http://www.oxbridgeprograms.com.

PARTNERSHIP INTERNATIONAL E.V.

Vienna, Virginia

Project Location: Germany

Description: Academic year programs are for individuals and summers are for student groups. For the full-year program, full scholarships are offered to special high school students that are selected.

Open to: Age 14-18.

Cost: Costs vary.

For more information: The Parrish Foundation, 109 Oakmont Court, NE, Vienna, Virginia 22180.

ROTARY INTERNATIONAL

Project Location: Worldwide

Description: Rotary offers full academic and short-term programs.

Open to: Ages 15-19. Applicants chosen by local club. Parents do not need to be Rotarians.

Cost: Cost varies. Room and board with host families.

For more information: Contact your local Rotary Club for information.

SCHOOL YEAR ABROAD

Andover, Massachusetts

Project Location: Spain, France, and China.

Description: Student participates fully in the life and community of the host family. Classes are taught in English and language of the country. School trips are also organized.

Open to: Students entering 11th or 12th grades with good grades and two years of language.

Cost: In 1994-95, the costs were: $18,100 for France and Spain; $9,000 for China. Students pay airfare.

For more information: Executive Director, School Year Abroad, Phillips Academy, Andover, Massachusetts 01810; (508)749-4420.

SEVEN CONTINENTS' EXCHANGE PROGRAMS

Paramus, New Jersey

Project Location: Spain

Description: The program has 80 hours of Spanish civilization, culture, and language courses offered at the University of Granada. Field trips are conducted in Granada, Cordoba, and Sevilla.

Open to: Age 17 and up.

Cost: $2,000-$2,200/month depending on housing choice - private apartment or host family.

For more information: Director, Seven Continents' Exchange Programs, P.O. Box 8163, Paramus, New Jersey 07653-8163; (201)444-8689.

STUYVESANT CENTER FOR INTERNATIONAL EDUCATION

New York, New York

Project Location: Australia, Russia, and China.

Description: Three-week summer programs with courses in history, foreign language, culture, and research. Various excursions are included.

Open to: Age 14-18 in grades 8-12.

Cost: $1,995 for Russia, $2,695 for Australia and China programs. All expenses paid including airfare and housing with university families.

For more information: Stuyvesant Center for International Education, P.O. Box 843, Bowling Green Station, New York, New York 10274; (212)747-1755 or (800)292-4452.

SUMMER DISCOVERY PRE-COLLEGE ENRICHMENT PROGRAMS

Roslyn, New York

Project Location: UCLA, UC San Diego, University of Vermont, University of Michigan, Georgetown University, and Cambridge University.

Description: High school students can prepare for the challenges of college by earning college credit, take SAT preparation with Princeton Review, take Drivers Education, athletic enrichment, community service, as well as enjoy excursions and workshops. Three to six-week programs.

Open to: Students completing grades 9-12.

Cost: $2,800-$5,400, includes full academic program, university housing, 3 meals daily, activities, trips, and excursions.

For more information: Summer Discovery Pre-College Enrichment Programs, 1326 Old Northern Boulevard, Roslyn, New York 11576; (888)8SUMMER or (516) 621-3939 (in NY); (516)625-3438; E-mail musiker@summerfun.com; URL http://www.summerfun.com.

THIRD WORLD OPPORTUNITIES
El Cajon, California

Project Location: Tecate and Las Palmas, Mexico.

Description: This is an awareness program with opportunities to become involved in community action (house-building) projects.

Open to: Students, age 15 and up, with a knowledge of Spanish.

Cost: For 6-day summer building program, $200 plus transportation.

For more information: Coordinator, Third World Opportunities, 1363 Somermont Drive, El Cajon, California 92021; (619)449-9381; E-mail pgray@ucsd.edu; URL http://www.scansd.net/two.

UP WITH PEOPLE
Broomfield, Colorado

Project Location: Worldwide

Description: Worldsmart™ is the Up With People Multi-Cultural Leadership Program. It accelerates education and career opportunities through the unique combination of international travel, on-stage musical performance, and community service.

Open to: Students, age 18-25. Students can apply for up to two years in advance.

Cost: Students pay a program fee — contact UWP for current rate.

For more information: Admission Counselor, Up With People, One International Court, Broomfield, Colorado 80021; (800)596-7353; (303)438-7301 (fax); E-mail admissions@upwithpeople.org; URL http://www.upwithpeople.org.

U.S. SERVAS
New York, New York

Project Location: Worldwide

Description: Worldwide hospitality network with a core group of international students and "Peacebuilder" families comprising a system where those traveling in pursuit of cultural education or peace work can stay in hosts' homes for two nights.

Open to: High school seniors and adults 18 and over.

Positions Available: Short-term internships lasting six weeks to three months involving general office support, outreach to other peace-education-travel groups, and possible United Nations activities. Also, office volunteer positions available. Open on a rolling basis.

Cost: Free. Reimbursement available to interns for lunch and daily commute. Some temporary housing assistance also available.

For more information: Tori Napier, Assistant Administrator, U.S. Servas, Inc., 11 John Street, Suite 407, New York, New York 10038; (212)267-0252; (212) 267-0292 (fax); E-mail usservas@servas.org; URL http://www.servas.org.

WO INTERNATIONAL CENTER
Honolulu, Hawaii

Project Location: China, France, Japan, and Spain.

Description: China, France, and Japan have a four-week program of language/culture studies and activities. Spain's program is five weeks.

Open to: Ages 15-18 in grades 9-12.

Cost: $4,250-4,500 for housing, meals, tuition, excursions, and airfare from Hawaii.

For more information: Judy Kunita, Program Coordinator, WO International Center, Punahou School, 1601 Punahou Street, Honolulu, Hawaii 96822; (808) 944-5871; (808)944-5712 (fax); E-mail judyk@punahou.edu; URL http://www.punahou.edu/wo.html.

YOUTH EXCHANGE SERVICES (YES)
Newport Beach, California

Project Location: Countries in Asia, Europe, or Latin America.

Description: Students participate in a homestay exchange program for the academic year or second semester.

Open to: Students, ages 15-18.

Cost: $4,000 for academic year; $3,100 for second semester. Transportation is not included.

For more information: Youth Exchange Service (YES), 4675 MacArthur Court, Suite 830, Newport Beach, California 92660; (714)955-2030 or (800) 848-2121.

YOUTH FOR UNDERSTANDING (YFU) INTERNATIONAL EXCHANGE
Washington, D.C.

Project Location: Argentina, Australia, Belarus, Belgium, Brazil, Chile, Czech/Slovak Republics, Denmark, Ecuador, Estonia, Finland, France, Germany, Hungary, Italy, Japan, Latvia, Mexico, Netherlands, New Zealand, Norway, Paraguay, Philippines, Russia, South Africa, Spain, Sweden, Switzerland, Ukraine, United Kingdom, Uruguay, Venezuela, Greece, and Poland.

Description: YFU offers full-year, semester, summer, or month programs. For full-year or semester programs, students live with families and attend school. For summer program, students live with families and participate in sponsored activities.

Open to: Ages 15-18. Language requirement in some programs and some countries.

Cost: $5,775-$6,575 for full-year; $5,272-$5,975 for

semester; $2,775-$4,675 for summer. Live with families. International airfare to host family from U.S. gateway included in tuition.

For more information: Youth for Understanding (YFU) International Exchange, 3501 Newark Street, NW, Washington, DC 20016; (202)966-6800 or (800)833-6243(TEENAGE).

MATH/SCIENCE/ ENGINEERING

ACADEMICALLY INTERESTED MINORITIES (AIM)
Flint, Michigan
Project Location: Flint, Michigan
Description: To make the high school to college move easier, students are in college level classes in computer science, chemistry, communications, math, and humanities. Tutors are available.
Open to: Students entering 12th grade. Available to minorities with 3.0 average in math, English, chemistry (with lab), algebra 1 and 2, and geometry.
Cost: Housing and meals provided.
For more information: Academically Interested Minorities, GMI Engineering and Management Institute, 1700 W. 3rd Avenue, Flint, Michigan 48504-4898; (313)762-9825 or (800)955-4464 ext. 9825.

AMERICAN INDIAN RESEARCH OPPORTUNITIES
Bozeman, Montana
Project Location: Bozeman, Montana
Description: Summer enrichment programs designed to increase interest in engineering, math, and science career fields.
Open to: American Indian students entering grades 9-12.
Cost: No cost for most programs. Housing and meals in dormitories and cafeterias.
For more information: American Indian Research Opportunities (AIRO) Programs, Montana State University, 309 Culbertson Hall, Bozeman, Montana 59717; (406)994-5569.

AMERICAN INDIAN SCIENCE AND ENGINEERING SOCIETY SCIENCE CAMP (AISES); CLARKSON MATHEMATICS PROGRAM
Boulder, Colorado
Project Location: Potsdam, New York
Description: The program is designed to have students experience creative approaches in science, mathematics, and engineering and enjoy interaction with American Indian role models.
Open to: American Indian students entering 11th grade and in the top half of their class.
Cost: Housing in dormitory and meals in cafeteria.
For more information: Mathematics Program for Native Americans, AISES, 1630 30th Street, Suite 301, Boulder, Colorado 80301; (303)939-0023.

ARCOSANTI
Mayer, Arizona
Project Location: South/Midwest; Arizona
Description: This is a prototype for a town that uses energy efficiently. Workshops are 1-4 weeks of hands-on learning.
Open to: N/A
Cost: For five-week construction workshop ($800). Silt, clay and bronze workshop ($385). Housing and meals are provided.
For more information: Workshops Registrar, Arcosanti, HC74, Box 4136, Mayer, Arizona 86333; (520) 632-7135; E-mail Terigrin@getnet.com; URL http://www.arcosanti.org.

CARNEGIE MELLON UNIVERSITY PRE-COLLEGE PROGRAM
Pittsburgh, Pennsylvania
Project Location: Pittsburgh, Pennsylvania
Description: The Carnegie Mellon Pre-College Program is a six-week residential program for academically and artistically motivated students. The following programs are available: Advanced Placement/Early Admission (APEA), which offers college credit for courses in engineering, science, computer science, and humanities; or one of five Fine Arts programs: Architecture, Art, Design, Drama, and Music, all of which expose students to a college-level, professional training program.
Open to: Rising high school juniors or seniors.
Cost: Students live in residence halls, eat on campus, and participate in a wide variety of events and activities.
For more information: Office of Admission, Pre-College Programs, Carnegie Mellon University, 5000 Forbes Avenue, Pittsburgh, Pennsylvania 15213; (412) 268-2082; URL http://www.cmu.edu/enrollment/admission/.

CENTER FOR EXCELLENCE IN EDUCATION
McLean, Virginia
Project Location: Metropolitan Washington, DC; Los Angeles, CA; and Chicago, IL
Description: Exposure to careers in science, technology, and business with college preparatory activities.
Open to: Second semester high school juniors from populations traditionally underrepresented in math and sciences.
Cost: N/A
For more information: Monica Ortiz, RMLP National Coordinator, Center for Excellence in Education, 7710 Old Springhouse Road, Suite 100, McLean, Virginia 22102; (703)448-9062; (703)442-9513 (fax); E-mail

monica@cee.org; URL http://www.cee.org.

ENGINEERING CAREER ORIENTATION (ECO)
Amherst, Massachusetts

Project Location: Amherst, Massachusetts

Description: This program introduces students to the many careers in science and engineering.

Open to: Students entering grades 9-12. Available to minority students.

Cost: Fees approximately $700. Housing in residence halls and meals in dining rooms.

For more information: Engineering Career Orientation, University of Massachusetts, Minority Engineering Program, 128 Marston Hall, Amherst, Massachusetts 01003; (413)545-2030.

FOCUS PROGRAMS IN MATHEMATICS AND SCIENCE
Carlisle, Pennsylvania

Project Location: Carlisle, Pennsylvania

Description: This is a three-summer program designed to encourage multicultural students to pursue careers in mathematics and science.

Open to: Students apply while in 9th grade, attend the programs during the summers before 10th and 11th grades, and may be invited to the 3rd summer program. Open to African-Americans, Asian-Americans, Native Americans, and Hispanic-Americans.

Cost: Students live in dormitories and eat in dining halls.

For more information: Focus Program in Mathematics and Science, Dickinson College, Office of Admissions, Carlisle, Pennsylvania 17013; (717)245-1231.

GALLAUDET SUMMER SCIENCE PROGRAM
Washington, D.C.

Project Location: Washington, D.C.

Description: Students work in research teams to do experiments in physics, chemistry, and biology.

Open to: Students entering grades 9-11 who are deaf or hard-of-hearing.

Cost: $1,800. Students live in dormitories and eat in dining halls. Four-week program.

For more information: Gallaudet Summer Science Program, Gallaudet University, HMB E111, 800 Florida Avenue, NE, Washington, DC 20002-3695; (202) 651-5755; (202)651-5065 (fax); URL http://www.gallaudet.edu.

HONORS SUMMER MATH CAMP: SOUTHWEST TEXAS STATE UNIVERSITY
San Marcos, Texas

Project Location: San Marcos, Texas

Description: A six-week residential program for academically talented students. This is a cooperative program in which the students work together exploring new ideas and share in the excitement of finding the simple mathematical ideas which underlie and explain seemingly complex problems.

Open to: Rising 10th-12th graders.

Cost: $1,500 which covers room, board, books, supplies, and activities. Scholarships are available based on need.

Other information: Student application form including personal essay; teacher recommendation; SAT; PSAT; GPA; and transcript.

For more information: Professor Max Warshauer, SWT Honors Summer Math Camp, Southwest Texas State University, San Marcos, Texas 78666; (512) 245-3439; (512)245-1469 (fax); E-mail mw07@swt.edu; URL http://www.math.swt.edu/mity/mathcamp/.

INSTITUTE FOR PRE-COLLEGE ENRICHMENT: MITE MINORITY INTRODUCTION TO ENGINEERING
Prairie View, Texas

Project Location: Prairie View, Texas

Description: This program is designed to stimulate interest in architecture and engineering careers.

Open to: Minority high school students entering grades 11-12 and in the top 1/3 of their class.

Cost: $50 registration and activity fee. Housing in dormitories and meals in dining hall.

For more information: Institute for Pre-College Enrichment, Prairie View A&M University, P.O. Box 66, Prairie View, Texas 77446-0066; (800)622-9643 or (409)857-2055.

JACKLING MINERAL INDUSTRIES SUMMER CAREERS INSTITUTE AND JACKLING-2
Rolla, Missouri

Project Location: Rolla, Missouri

Description: This institute introduces students to the career opportunities in ceramic, petroleum, metallurgical, geological, mining, nuclear engineering, geology, and geophysics.

Open to: Students entering 12th grade.

Cost: Introductory program ($125). Housing in dormitories and meals in dining hall.

For more information: Jackling Mineral Industries Summer Careers Institute, University of Missouri-Rolla, School of Mines and Metallurgy, 305 McNutt Hall, Rolla, Missouri 65401; (314)341-4734.

MINORITIES IN ENGINEERING PROGRAM
Houghton, Michigan

Project Location: Houghton, Michigan

Description: Students explore careers in space science, engineering technology, biotechnology, bioengineering, and electrical, geological, mechanical, chemical, and mining engineering.

Open to: Minority and economically disadvantaged students entering grades 10-12.

Cost: Small registration fee. Housing in residence halls and meals in dining hall.

For more information: Minorities in Engineering Program, Michigan Technological University, Youth Programs Office, 1400 Townsend Drive, Houghton, Michigan 49931-1295; (906)487-2219; E-mail yp@mtu.edu; URL http://www.yth.mtu.edu/syp.

MENTORING ENRICHMENT SEMINAR IN ENGINEERING TRAINING (MESET)
Houston, Texas
Project Location: Houston, Texas
Description: This program is designed to give gifted minority students the chance to become acquainted with the field of engineering in a college setting.
Open to: Students entering 12th grade. Minority students are encouraged to apply.
Cost: Housing is in dormitories and meals in dining hall (except weekends - meals are the responsibility of students).
For more information: Dr. G.F. Paskusz, Director, Mentoring Enrichment Seminar in Engineering Training, Engineering/PROMES, University of Houston, 4800 Calhoun Road, Houston, Texas 77204-4790; (713)743-4222; (713)743-4228 (fax); E-mail Paskusz@uh.edu.

MINORITY INTRODUCTION TO ENGINEERING (MITE): ILLINOIS
Urbana, Illinois
Project Location: Champaign, Illinois
Description: Students are able to learn about engineering as a profession and experience college-level work.
Open to: Minority students entering grade 12.
Cost: $25. Housing and meals in residence halls.
For more information: Minority Introduction to Engineering, University of Illinois, Urbana-Champaign, College of Engineering, 1308 West Green Street, Room 207, Urbana, Illinois 61801-2982; (217)244-4974 or (800)843-5410.

MINORITY INTRODUCTION TO ENGINEERING (MITE): UNITED STATES COAST GUARD ACADEMY
New London, Connecticut
Project Location: New London, Connecticut
Description: Students are familiarized with various fields of engineering and exposed to life at the Academy.
Open to: Students entering grade 11 with A or B average and test scores of at least: PSAT 95, SAT 950, or ACT 40.
Cost: Housing in dormitories and meals in dining hall.
For more information: Minority Introduction to Engineering, c/o Director of Admissions, 31 Mohegan Avenue, New London, Connecticut 06320; (850)444-8500; (800)883-8924; E-mail admissions@cga.uscg.mil; URL http://www.cga.edu/admiss/mite.

MINORITY SCHOLARS IN COMPUTER SCIENCE AND ENGINEERING
College Park, Maryland
Project Location: College Park, Maryland
Description: This six-week program allows the student to explore educational and career opportunities in the fields of engineering and computer science.
Open to: Students entering 12th grade.
Cost: Housing in dormitories and meals in dining halls. Student pays for meals.
For more information: Minority Scholars in Computer Science and Engineering, University of Maryland, Center for Minorities in Science and Engineering, College Park, Maryland 20742; (301)405-3878.

NASA – LEWIS RESEARCH CENTER
Cleveland, Ohio
Project Location: Cleveland, Ohio
Description: Offer four programs for teens: National Engineer's Week, Shadowing Program, Explorers Program, and Lewis' Educational and Research Collaborative Internship Program.
Open to: Students, ages 14-20.
For more information: NASA Research Center, Office of Educational Programs, M.S. 7-4, 21000 Brookpark Road, Cleveland, Ohio 44135; (216)433-2957; (216)433-3344 (fax); URL http://www.lerc.nasa.gov/WWW/OEP.

THE NATIONAL SCIENCE FOUNDATION'S (NSF) YOUNG SCHOLARS PROGRAM
Arlington, Virginia
Project Location: On campuses throughout the United States.
Description: Students can experience intensive study in the field they wish to pursue, using state-of-the-art equipment, labs, and computers.
Open to: High school students.
Cost: Most programs provide housing and meals at minimal or no cost.
For more information: The National Science Foundation's Young Scholars Foundation, National Science Foundation, 4201 Wilson Boulevard, Room 885, Arlington, Virginia 22230; (703)306-1616.

PREFACE PROGRAM
Troy, New York
Project Location: Troy, New York
Description: Two-week residential summer program. Participants take a realistic look at a future in engineering.
Open to: Students entering the 12th grade. Open to academically-talented women and minority students.
Cost: Housing in dormitories and meals in dining hall. Transportation to and from site is provided.
For more information: Mark Smith, Associate Dean/

Focus On...
National Aeronautics and Space Administration (NASA)

The National Aeronautics and Space Administration (NASA) has a wide-variety of programs for teenagers including educational programs, internships, and part-time jobs.

Opportunities include:
- EarthSense;
- Explorer Scouts;
- Moonbuggy Competition;
- Job Shadowing Days;
- Student Internships;
- National Engineers Week;
- And many more!

Opportunities are available at NASA facilities and throughout the United States. For more information, visit the NASA website at:

www.hq.nasa.gov/ education

Director, OMSA, Preface Program, Rensselaer Polytechnic Institute, Office of Minority Student Affairs, Troy Building, Troy, New York 12180-3590; (518) 276-6272; (518)276-4034 (fax); E-mail smithm@rpi.edu..

PROJECT SEE (SUMMER EDUCATION EXPERIENCE)
Morris, Minnesota
Project Location: Morris, Minnesota
Description: This project introduces students to college classwork in various scientific areas.
Open to: Students entering the 12th grade. Some math and science prerequisites. Women, physically/economically challenged, or minority students are encouraged to participate as part of SEE.
Cost: Housing provided and cash to cover meals.
For more information: Project SEE, University of Minnesota, Morris, 231 Community Services Building, Morris, Minnesota 56267; (612)589-6450.

RESEARCH SCIENCE INSTITUTE
McLean, Virginia
Project Location: Massachusetts Institute of Technology (MIT)
Description: Six-week summer program at MIT combining classroom lectures and tutoring with off-campus internships in scientific research.
Open to: Open to students who have completed the equivalent of three years of high school. Admission is based on high school academic record, recommendations, PSAT scores (approximately 135), and personal essays. The application deadline is February 1.
Cost: No cost except transportation to and from the Research Science Institute.
For more information: Please send a self-addressed envelope with .55 postage to: Ms. Maite Ballestero, Director of Programs, Center for Excellence in Education, 7710 Old Springhouse Road, Suite 100, McLean, Virginia 22102; (703)448-9062.

ROLE MODELS & LEADERS PROJECT (RMLP)

McLean, Virginia

Project Location: Washington, DC; Chicago; Los Angeles

Description: Program encouraging minority students to pursue careers in science and industry.

Open to: High school students.

Cost: Free of charge

For more information: The Center for Excellence in Education, 7710 Old Springhouse Road, Suite 100, McLean, Virginia 22102-3406; (703)448-9062; URL http://www.rsi.cee.org.

SCIENTIFIC DISCOVERY PROGRAM

St. Cloud, Minnesota

Project Location: St. Cloud, Minnesota

Description: This is an opportunity for students to work together in research projects that benefit their community socially and environmentally.

Open to: Students entering grades 9-11.

Cost: Housing in dormitories and meals in dining hall.

For more information: Scientific Discovery Program, St. Cloud State University, EB B 120A, 720 4th Avenue, South, St. Cloud, Minnesota 56301-4498; (612) 255-4928.

SUMMER SCIENTIFIC SEMINAR

Colorado Springs, Colorado

Project Location: USAF Academy

Description: Students have the opportunity to observe life at the Air Force Academy, attend seminars, tour labs, and explore careers in science.

Open to: Students entering grade 12 with good grades and test scores.

Cost: $225 and transportation to and from site. Housing in cadet dormitory and meals in dining hall.

For more information: Summer Scientific Seminar, United States Air Force Academy, HQ USAFA/RRPX, 2304 Cadet Drive, Suite 211, USAF Academy, Colorado 80840-5025; (719)333-2236.

WOMEN IN ENGINEERING

Houghton, Michigan

Project Location: Houghton, Michigan

Description: This workshop helps young women explore various engineering fields such as: bioengineering, space science, biotechnology/forestry, chemical, geological, mining, civil, and mechanical.

Open to: Students entering grades 10-12. Two years of math and 1 year of chemistry are required.

Cost: $25 registration. Housing in residence hall and meals in dining hall.

For more information: Women in Engineering Program, Michigan Technological University, Youth Programs Office, 1400 Towsend Drive, Houghton, Michigan 49931; (906)487-2219; E-mail yp@mtu. edu; URL http://www.yth.mtu.edu/syp.

YOUNG SCHOLARS PROGRAM: INTRODUCTION TO ENGINEERING

Cookeville, Tennessee

Project Location: Cookeville, Tennessee

Description: The goals of the workshop are to show the career options in engineering and to promote problem-solving abilities.

Open to: Students entering grades 11-12 and ranked in top 20% of class in math and science.

Cost: $750. Scholarships available. Please inquire about applying. Housing in dormitories and meals at University Center.

For more information: Tony D. Marable, Director/Minority Engineering Program, Young Scholars Program: Introduction to Engineering, Tennessee Technological University, P.O. Box 5005, Cookeville, Tennessee 38505; (931)372-3172; (931)372-6172 (fax); E-mail tmarable@tntech.edu; URL http://www.tntech. edu..

NATURE/ENVIRONMENT

ACTIONQUEST

Sarasota, Florida

Project Location: Caribbean, Mediterranean, Galapagos, Australia, Tahiti, and Fiji.

Description: Worldwide, teen, live-aboard sailing and scuba certification programs. Includes marine biology. No experience necessary.

Open to: Teens ages 13-19.

Cost: $2,885-$4,285, excluding airfare.

Other information: Also available: ARGO Academy (nine-month high school afloat) and Sea-mester Programs (live-aboard college-level semester voyages).

For more information: James Stoll, Director, ActionQuest, P.O. Box 5507, Sarasota, Florida 34277; (941) 924-6789; (800)317-6789; (941)924-6075 (fax); E-mail actionquest@msn.com; URL http://www. actionquest.com.

ADVENTURE CONNECTION, INC.

Coloma, California

Project Location: Pacific Northwest; California

Description: This group leads river trips.

Open to: N/A

Cost: $800.00 cost of white-water rafting class offered each spring.

For more information: Adventure Connection, Inc., P. O. Box 475, Coloma, California 95613; (530)626-7385 or (800)556-6060.

ARTS AND ENVIRONMENTAL EDUCATION WORKSHOPS
Dingmans Ferry, Pennsylvania

Project Location: Dingmans Ferry, Pennsylvania

Description: The National Park Service and the Pocono Environmental Education Center (PEEC) offer varieties of weekend activities throughout the year to promote an understanding of and appreciation for our natural environment.

Open to: Some programs are designed for teens.

Cost: $84-114. Housing in cabins and meals in dining hall.

For more information: Arts and Environmental Education Workshops, Pocono Environmental Education Center, RR2 Box 1010, Dingmans Ferry, Pennsylvania 18328; (717)828-2319.

BARU ADVENTURES
Washington, D.C.

Project Location: Costa Rica.

Description: Their aim is to immerse students in another culture, provide activities that are ecologically-oriented, and give students some adventures.

Open to: Students between ages 14-18.

Cost: $1,150-$2,880 includes room and board. During school year, airfare is included; in summer, it is not.

For more information: President and Program Director, Baru Adventures, 1718 M Street, NW #187, Washington, DC 20036-4503; (800)297-2278.

THE BIKING EXPEDITION
Henniker, New Hampshire

Project Location: Canada

Description: This is a commercial organization that plans summer biking trips for youth.

Open to: Ages 13-18.

Cost: $1,300-$4,000 including airfare, food, and housing.

For more information: The Biking Expedition, P.O. Box 547, Henniker, New Hampshire 03242; (603)428-7500 or (800)245-4649.

BSES EXPEDITIONS
London, England

Project Location: Greenland, Norway, Iceland, Russia, North America, South Africa, Himalayas, South Pacific, India, North Africa, Kyrghyzstan, Antarctica, and Australia

Description: This society provides opportunities to go on expedition to "remote and harsh environments."

Open to: Ages 16.5-20.

Cost: £2,600-£3,000 ($4,160-$4,800) depending on the location and program. This is a contribution toward expedition costs.

For more information: Executive Director, BSES Expeditions, at the Royal Geographical Society, 1 Kensington Gore, London SW7 2AR England; +44(0)171-591-3141; +44(0)591-3140 (fax); E-mail bses@rgs.org; URL http://www.bses.org.uk.

CAMP ENCORE-CODA
Sweden, Maine

Project Location: Sweden, Maine

Description: Music and sports camp for campers, ages 8-17.

Open to: High school graduates by June. CIT program after 10th grade.

Positions Available: Junior counselor. Certified waterfront staff needed (boating, swimming, sailing, etc.). Counselor in Training (CIT) program after 10th grade.

Cost/Compensation: $650 for the season.

Other: Camper cost of $2,800 for ½ season or $4,900 for full season.

For more information: Ellen Donahue-Saltman, Director, Camp Encore-Coda, 32 Grassmere Road, Brookline, Massachusetts 02467; (617)325-1541; (617)325-7278 (fax); E-mail ellen@encore-coda.com; URL http://www.encore-coda.

CAMP NOCK-A-MIXON
Kintnersville, Pennsylvania

Project Location: Kintnersville, Pennsylvania

Description: Residential camp for boys and girls.

Open to: High school students.

Positions Available: Counselors, swimming instructors, tennis counselors, drama directors, crafts director, kitchen staff, maintenance workers, athletic directors, and adventure course instructor.

For more information: Mark Glaser, Director, Camp Nock-A-Mixon, 16 Gum Tree Lane, Lafayette Hill, Pennsylvania 19444; (610)941-1307; E-mail mglaser851@aol.com.

CANOE QUEBEC KAPITACHOUANE
Washington, Connecticut

Project Location: Canada

Description: The camp teaches the fundamentals of camping and canoeing. The canoe trips along lakes, rivers, and portages follow routes where the Algonquin and Cree Indians traveled for centuries.

Open to: Good swimmers between ages 14-18 and in ninth to twelfth grades.

Cost: $600 for the two-week trip includes all but the cost of train from Montreal to the camp.

For more information: Canoe Quebec Kapitachouane, 67 East Street, Washington, Connecticut 06793; (203)868-7898.

CAPITAL CAMPS
Waynesboro, Pennsylvania

Project Location: Waynesboro, Pennsylvania

Description: Jewish residential community camp.

Also sponsor leadership trip to Israel.
Open to: CITS (age 17); staff (18+).
Positions Available: Counselors, specialists, and counselors-in-training.
Cost/Compensation: CITS ($700); staff ($800-$1,500).
For more information: Faye Bousel, Executive Director, Capital Camps, 133 Rollins Avenue, Unit 4, Rockville, Maryland 20852; (301)468-2267; (301) 468-1719 (fax); E-mail staff@capitalcamps.com; URL http://www.capitalcamps.com.

CARETTA RESEARCH PROJECT
Savannah, Georgia
Project Location: Wassaw Island – a barrier island off Georgia's coast.
Description: Research and conservation of loggerhead sea turtles.
Open to: Students (and everyone interested!) over 16 years of age.
Cost: $500 per week.
For more information: Kris Williams, Director, Caretta Research Project, P.O. Box 9841, Savannah, Georgia 31412-9841; (912)447-8655; (912)355-0182 (fax); E-mail WassawCRP@aol.com.

CENTRALE DES AUBERGES DE JEUNESSE LUXEMBOURGEOISES
Luxembourg
Project Location: Luxembourg
Description: This organization is the youth association of Luxembourg and is affiliated with Hostelling International. In addition to operating 13 youth hostels, they also offer do-it-yourself tours: Cycling Tour of Luxembourg, Hiking Tour of Luxembourg, Stopover, and Multisport in Luxembourg.
Open to: Students at least 16 years of age. Some programs require 18 years of age.
Cost: Approximately $80-$568.
For more information: Centrale des Augerges de Jeunesse Luxembourgeoises, 2 rue du Fort Olisy, L2261 Luxembourg; (352)22-55-88; (352)46-39-87 (fax); E-mail information @youthhostels.lu; URL http://www.youthhostels.lu..

CLEARWATER
Poughkeepsie, New York
Project Location: Northeast; New York
Description: The sloop, *Clearwater*, is a nonprofit, environmental education program offering a traditional sailing opportunity.
Open to: Volunteers, age 12 and up (1 week at a cost of $50); Sailing apprentices (1 month) and education assistants (2 months) for ages 16 and up.
Compensation: $25-50/week.
For more information: Captain, Clearwater, 112 Market Street, Poughkeepsie, New York 12601-4095; (914)454-7673; (914)454-7953 (fax); E-mail captain@clearwater.org; URL http://www.clearwater.org.

COLORADO MOUNTAIN SCHOOL
Estes Park, Colorado
Project Location: Worldwide; Colorado
Description: Organization works with beginners, intermediate, and advanced climbers with rock courses and expeditions to major peaks: Mt. McKinley, Mexican volcanoes, Kilimanjaro, Huascaran, and Aconcagua.
Open to: N/A
Cost: $1,495
For more information: Program Director, Colorado Mountain School, P.O. Box 2062, Estes Park, Colorado 80517; (970)586-5758 or (800)444-0730; URL http://www.sni.net/homepage/cms.

DEPARTMENT OF ENERGY HIGH SCHOOL HONORS PROGRAM IN ENVIRONMENTAL SCIENCE
Washington, D.C.
Project Location: Oak Ridge, Tennessee
Description: The program allows students to work together at an environmental research laboratory that is the largest in the world, focusing on aquatic and terrestrial ecosystems.
Open to: Students entering the 12th grade with superior academic achievement and specified courses completed.
Cost: Housing, meals, and transportation to and from the site are paid.
For more information: DOE High School Honors Program in Environmental Science, Oak Ridge National Laboratory, ER-80, United States Department of Energy, Washington, DC 20585; (202)586-8949.

DICK PHILLIPS
England
Project Location: Ireland
Description: Dick Phillips has tours encompassing hiking, motor coach, photography, cycling, sailing, and ocean liner tours.
Open to: Ages 16 and up.
Cost: Approximately $643-$1,767, depending upon the program and housing. Housing is mostly in simple mountain huts.
For more information: Dick Phillips, Director, Whitehall House, Nenthead, Alston, Cumbria CA9 3PS England; (44)434-381440.

EXUM MOUNTAIN GUIDES
Moose, Wyoming
Project Location: Rocky Mountains; Wyoming
Description: Exum offers customized training programs from this most-experienced, versatile service.
Open to: N/A
Cost: N/A

For more information: Program Director, Exum Mountain Guides, Grand Teton National Park, Box 56, Moose, Wyoming 83012; (307)773-2297.

EYE OF THE WHALE
Kapa'au, Hawaii
Project Location: Pacific Northwest; Hawaii
Description: Through such activities as sailing, snorkeling, and hiking, professionals will teach you the history of Hawaii, emphasizing its plant life, coral reefs, and marine mammals.
Open to: N/A
Cost: $950 per person/week
For more information: Eye of the Whale, Hawaiian Outdoor Adventures, P.O. Box 1269, Kapa'au, Hawaii 96755; (808)889-0227 or (800)659-3544; E-mail e-whale@aloha.net; URL http://www.gorp.com/ewhale.

INTERACTION ADVENTURES
Danville, California
Project Location: Pacific Northwest; California
Description: Three-week summer program. First week - observation and data recording of something in nature. Second week - exploration into Sierra Nevada's wilderness. Third week - community service activity.
Open to: Students, ages 14-17.
Cost: $950 fee.
For more information: Summer Programs Director, InterAction Adventure, Athenian School, 2100 Mt. Diablo Boulevard, Danville, California 94526; (510) 837-5375.

JACKSON HOLE MOUNTAIN GUIDES
Jackson, Wyoming
Project Location: Rocky Mountains; Wyoming
Description: A year-round climbing service with small classes and experienced guides.
Open to: N/A
Cost: N/A
For more information: Program Director, Jackson Hole Mountain Guides, 165 N. Glenwood, P.O. Box 7477, Jackson, Wyoming 83001; (307)733-4979.

JUGI TOURS
Zurich, Switzerland
Project Location: Switzerland
Description: Jugi Tours plans cycling, walking, and mountaineering experiences around the Swiss mountains and valleys.
Open to: Minimum age of 16.
Cost: Approximately $210-$588 for seven days includes housing, meals, and local transportation.
For more information: Jugi Tours, Belpstr.49, CH-3000, Bern 14; Zurich, Switzerland; ++41-31-380-68-

68; ++41-31-380-68-69 (fax)..

MARINE SCIENCES UNDER SAILS
Hollywood, Florida
Project Location: Southeast; Florida
Description: Short study cruises examining the role of sea and coast and ways to protect these resources.
Open to: N/A
Cost: N/A
For more information: Program Director, Marine Sciences Under Sails, P.O. Box 3994, Hollywood, Florida 33023; (954)983-7015.

NATIONAL OCEAN ACCESS PROCESS
Annapolis, Maryland
Project Location: Northeast; Maryland
Description: Week-long sailing program in the Bahamas. This ship is designed to be accessible to people with disabilities.
Open to: Students, age 16 and up.
Cost: N/A
For more information: Program Director, National Ocean Access Process, Annapolis City Marina, Suite 306, 410 Severn Avenue, Annapolis, Maryland 21403.

NATIONAL OUTDOOR LEADERSHIP SCHOOL
Lander, Wyoming
Project Location: Southwest, Pacific Northwest, Rocky Mountains, Alaska, British Columbia, Kenya, Chile, and Mexico
Description: NOLS trains its graduates to appreciate environmental ethics and to operate with overall competence.
Open to: N/A
Cost: $750-$8,300, depending upon location, the types and length of courses taken.
For more information: Admissions Department, National Outdoor Leadership School, 288 Main Street, Lander, Wyoming 82520; (307)332-6973; E-mail admissions@nols.edu; URL http://www.nols.edu.

NORTHERN LIGHTS ALPINE RECREATION (NLAR)
British Columbia, Canada
Project Location: British Columbia
Description: Trips for up to 4 participants tailored to their goals and experience. Trips may entail a summer hike, a tour on skis or snowshoes, climbing striking peaks on icefields, or more advanced mountaineering.
Open to: Minimum age of 14.
Cost: Fees vary depending on choice of programs. A course of eight day duration can cost $570.
For more information: Katie Mauthner, Director, Northern Lights Alpine Recreation (NLAR), Box 399, Invermere, BC VOA 1KO Canada; (250)342-

6042; (250)342-6042 (fax); E-mail mauthner@rockies.net.

OFFSHORE SAILING SCHOOL
Fort Myers, Florida
Project Location: Southeast; Florida
Description: When you complete this sailing class, you will be ready to daysail a boat of up to 30 feet in size.
Open to: High school students.
Cost: $100-$200 per day. Housing usually on ship and meals provided.
For more information: Director, Off-Shore Sailing School, 16731 McGregor Boulevard, Fort Myers, Florida 33908; (941)454-1700 or (800)221-4326; E-mail offshore@coco.net.

ONE WORLD WORKFORCE (OWW)
La Mesa, California
Project Location: Various beaches in Mexico and Anguilla.
Description: Hands on conservation of sea turtles, pelicans, and island and beach ecosystems.
Open to: Able-bodied people age 10 through 75.
Cost: Fee of $490-$575 covers project grant, camp fee, ground transportation, all meals, and field guide.
For more information: Evelyn Hightower, Treasurer/Field Guide, One World Workforce, P.O. Box 3188, La Mesa, California 91944-3188; (800)451-9564; (619)589-5544 (fax); E-mail 1world@infomask.com; URL http://www.1ww.org.

OUTWARD BOUND (OB)
Greenwich, Connecticut
Project Location: Various locations.
Description: Survival programs and instruction in various adventures such as white water rafting, sailing, backpacking, and rappelling.
Open to: Minimum age of 14.
Cost: $395-$6,695. Most housing in tents.
For more information: Outward Bound National Office, 384 Field Point Road, Greenwich, Connecticut 06830.

OVERSEAS ADVENTURE TRAVEL
Cambridge, Massachusetts
Project Location: Worldwide
Description: This group grades trips by degree of difficulty from day hikes to climbing expeditions.
Open to: Ages 16-23.
Cost: Cost varies. Room and board generally provided. You pay cost of travel.
For more information: Overseas Adventure Travel, 349 Broadway, Cambridge, Massachusetts 02139.

PACIFIC CREST TRAIL ASSOCIATION
Sacramento, California

Project Location: Pacific Northwest; California
Description: This organization promotes volunteer trail maintenance activities.
Open to: N/A
Cost: N/A
For more information: Program Coordinator, Pacific Crest Trail Association, 5325 Elkhorn Boulevard, Box 256, Sacramento, California 95842-2526; (916)349-2109 or (888)728-7245;
E-mail 71204.1015@compuserve.com; URL http://www.gorp.com/pcta.

PACIFIC WHALE FOUNDATION
Kihei, Hawaii
Project Location: Maui, Hawaii, and Australia
Description: Humpback whale research.
Positions Available: Marine Debris Beach Survey, Student Naturalist, Career Shadowing with Pacific Whale Foundation, and Field Research Techniques.
Cost: $1,395 and the cost of transportation.
For more information: Merrill Kaufman, marine Education Specialist, Pacific Whale Foundation, 101 N. Kihei Road, Kihei, Hawaii 96753; (808)879-8811; (808)879-2615 (fax); E-mail merrill@pacificwhale.org; URL http://www.pacificwhale.org.

POULTER COLORADO CAMPS
Steamboat Springs, Colorado
Project Location: Steamboat Springs, Colorado
Description: Co-ed residential camp and wilderness adventures for youth, ages 8-18.
Open to: Age 16+ for counselors in training. Age 17+ for all others.
Positions Available: Wranglers, cooks, arts and crafts counselors, CITs and assistant counselors.
Cost/Compensation: Varies
For more information: Lisa Nutkin, Director, Poulter Colorado Camps, P.O. Box 772947-T, Steamboat Springs, Colorado 80477; (888)879-4816; (970)879-1307 (fax); E-mail poulter@poultercamps.com.

RHIWIAU RIDING CENTRE
Gwynedd, Wales
Project Location: Wales
Description: Rhiwiau is a horseback riding center with instruction in jumping, rides in woods, and stable management training.
Open to: N/A
Cost: The fee for youth under 16 is $308; over 16 is $338. This includes room, food, riding, activities, and field trips.
For more information: Rhiwiau Riding Centre, Llanfairfechan, Gwynedd LL330 EH Wales; (44)248-680094.

ROCK LEA ACTIVITY CENTRE

Derbyshire, England

Project Location: Activity choices are caving, rock climbing, mountain biking, sailing, windsurfing, canoeing, orienting, bog trotting, gorge walking, and a tour of mystery.

Open to: Minimum age of 16.

Cost: From £500+/week, depending on the activities of choice and time of year.

For more information: Dr. Iain Jennings, Managing Director, Peak Activities Ltd., Rock Lea Activity Centre, Station Road, Hathersage, Hope Valley, Peak National Park S32 1DD United Kingdom; +44-1433-650345; +44-1433-650342 (fax); E-mail testwater@iain.co.uk; URL http://www.iain.co.uk.

SAIL CARIBBEAN

Northport, New York

Project Location: British Virgin Islands and Leeward Islands.

Description: 50-foot yachts sail through the islands for two to six weeks. With the guidance of a skipper, participants learn sailing skills and take responsibility for cleaning and maintenance of the yacht. Scuba, marine biology, and oceanography instruction are also available.

Open to: 13-19-year-olds in grades 7-12.

Cost: $1,500-$5,500 including housing, meals, equipment rentals, and instruction.

For more information: Michael Liese, Owner/Director, Sail Caribbean, 79-B Church Street, Northport, New York 11768; (516)754-2202.

SONS OF NORWAY

Minneapolis, Minnesota

Project Location: Skogn, Norway

Description: The camp offers language courses, discussions, field trips, and cultural and sports activities. College and high school credits can be earned.

Open to: Minimum age is 16 with a B average or more in school.

Cost: $2,650 includes travel in Norway, room and board, instruction, activities, and field trips. Scholarships available.

For more information: Sons of Norway, 1455 West Lake Street, Minneapolis, Minnesota 55408; (800)945-8851 or (612)827-3611.

SOUTH SHORE YMCA CAMPS

Sandwich, Massachusetts

Project Location: Cape Cod, Massachusetts

Description: Summer residential camp, adventure trips, and travel.

Open to: Open to 15, 16, and 17 year olds.

Positions Available: Counselor in Training (CIT), Junior Counselor (JC), and campers.

Cost/Compensation: CIT cost $900, JC pays $90/week, and trips cost $900.

For more information: Carol Sharman, Camp Director, South Shore YMCA Camps, 75 Stowe Road, Sandwich, Massachusetts 02563; (508)428-2571; (508)420-3545 (fax); E-mail ssymca@capecod.net; URL http://www.oncapecod.net/ssymca.

SUMMER PROGRAM IN MARINE SCIENCE

Morgantown, West Virginia

Project Location: Wallops Island, Virginia

Description: Hearing-impaired students enjoy hands-on experiences in marine science studies.

Open to: Students entering grades 9-12.

Cost: Housing (students, faculty, and counselors) in dormitories and meals in cafeteria.

For more information: Summer Program in Marine Science, Marine Science Consortium - West Virginia University, Department of Biology, P.O. Box 6057, Morgantown, West Virginia 26506-6057; (304)293-5201.

T.M. INTERNATIONAL SCHOOL OF HORSEMANSHIP

Cornwall, England

Project Location: Southwest England

Description: The Riding Centre is a residential riding school with instruction at all levels. It is a British Horse Society approved training center.

Open to: All persons 16 years or older.

Cost: Working pupils – $112 per week, includes accommodations, meals, lessons in riding, and lectures about stable management and horse care. For "holidays," the cost starts at approximately $280 a week.

Other information: Three, six, and nine-month courses leading to B.H.S. qualifications.

For more information: Captain Ted Moore, Principal, T.M. International School of Horsemanship, Sunrising Riding Centre, Liskeard, Cornwall PL14 5BP England; (01579) 362895.

U.S. ARMY CORPS OF ENGINEERS

Nashville, Tennessee

Project Location: Nationwide; Tennessee

Description: This group is the steward of land and water covering about 12 million acres. Volunteers have opportunities in national resource management and in the recreation area.

For more information: Volunteer Clearinghouse, U.S. Army Corps of Engineers, P.O. Box 1070, Nashville, Tennessee 37202-1070; (800)865-8337.

YOUNG SCHOLARS PROGRAM IN COASTAL EROSION AND PRESERVATION

Lake Charles, Louisiana

Project Location: Lake Charles, Louisiana

Description: Students explore ways to use technology

to stop coastline erosion.

Open to: Students entering grades 10-12.

Cost: Housing in dormitories and meals in cafeteria. $10/day for food when off campus.

For more information: Young Scholars Program in Coastal Erosion and Preservation, McNeese State University, P.O. Box 90215, Lake Charles, Louisiana 70609; (318)475-5123.

YOUNG SCHOLARS RESEARCH PARTICIPATION IN AQUATIC ECOLOGY

Portland, Oregon

Project Location: Portland, Oregon

Description: Research into the relationship between forest and aquatic resource management is conducted at a field site at Mt. Hood National Forest.

Open to: High school students in grades 10-12 or ages 15-18.

Cost: Students live in cabins and eat in dining hall.

For more information: Young Scholars Research Participation Programs in Aquatic Ecology, Oregon Museum of Science and Industry (OMSI), 1945 SE Water Avenue, Portland, Oregon 97214; (503)797-4571.

TOURS

AMERICAN ZIONIST YOUTH FOUNDATION (AZYF)

New York, New York

Description: AZYF provides Israel-related educational programs and activities.

Open to: Ages 12-35.

Cost: $650-$5,000

For more information: Israel Program Center, American Zionist Youth Foundation (AZYF), 110 East 59th Street, New York, New York 10022; (212)339-6916 or (800)274-7723.

CET

Washington, D.C.

Project Location: China

Description: CET specializes in academic programs and provides educational tours of China.

Open to: Minimum age of 13.

Cost: $3,165 includes airfare from New York, tuition, visa fees, housing, activities, and texts.

For more information: CET, 3210 Grace Street, NW, Washington, DC 20007; (800)225-4262 or (202)333-7873.

HABONIM DROR NORTH AMERICA

New York, New York

Project Location: Israel

Description: HDNA arranges summer programs to Israel for 16 year of age.

Open to: Must be 16 years of age.

Cost: $3,600 plus a $225 registration fee.

For more information: Programs Coordinator, 27 West 20th Street, New York, New York 10011; (212)255-1796.

LEARNING ADVENTURE PROGRAMS, INC.

Concord, Massachusetts

Project Location: Great Britain

Description: This is designed for high school students who want to experience and learn about the world through travel, study, and recreation.

Open to: Age 15 and older completing 10-12 grades.

Cost: $5,950 includes airfare, housing, meals, ground transportation, fees, events, and entertainment.

For more information: Learning Adventure Programs, Inc., 11 Davis Court, Concord, Massachusetts 01742; (508)462-3345.

MUSIKER STUDENT TOURS

Roslyn, New York

Project Location: Five-week tour of England, France, Belgium, Italy, and Switzerland.

Description: Tours emphasize sight-seeing, cultural activities, and recreational experiences.

Open to: Between age 14-18 years.

Cost: Tour costs $5,500, including meals, activities, admissions, excursions, and recreation. Student pays airfare.

For more information: Musiker Student Tours, 1326 Old Northern Boulevard, Roslyn, New York 11576; (516)621-0718 or (800)645-6611.

PHENIX INTERNATIONAL CAMPUSES

Castle Rock, Colorado

Project Location: France, Germany, Spain, and Mexico.

Description: Summer programs include three-week German adventures, three-week "España en su Casa," three-week tours of Spain, adventures in France, modern and historic Mexico, and today's Russia.

Open to: Between ages of 13-19, with one year language study.

Cost: $1,189-$2,789 includes airfare from Denver, travel, excursions, room, and board.

For more information: Manager, Phenix International Campuses, 7651 North Carolyn Drive, Castle Rock, Colorado 80104; (303)688-9397.

SCOTTISH YOUTH HOSTELS ASSOCIATION (SYHA)

Scotland

Project Location: Scotland

Description: SYHA offers budget accommodations for young people traveling throughout Scotland.

Open to: Students 14 and older.

Cost: Approximately $75 a week includes accommodations, some meals, and activity fees.

For more information: Scottish Youth Hostels Association (SYHA), 7 Glebe Crescent, Stirling FK8 2JA Scotland; (44)786-51181.

WESTCOAST CONNECTION TRAVEL
Mamaroneck, New York
Project Location: Western U.S., Canada, Quebec, Europe, and Israel.
Description: Active teen tours and outdoor adventures.

Open to: Ages 13-17 and 17-19.
Cost: $2,599 and up.
For more information: Mark Segal, Director, Westcoast Connection Travel, 154 East Boston Post Road, Mamaroneck, New York 10543; (914)835-0699; (914)835-0798 (fax); E-mail USA@westcoastconnect.com; URL http://www.westcoastconnection.com.

FOCUS ON...

UNITY: UNITED NATIONAL INDIAN TRIBAL YOUTH

UNITY (United National Indian Tribal Youth) is a national network organization promoting personal development, citizenship and leadership among Native American Youth.

Opportunities include:
- Community service;
- Youth councils;
- Promotion of tribal identity;
- Training and national conferences;
- Athletic activities;
- And much more!

Opportunities are available throughout the United States:

UNITY
P.O. Box 25042
Oklahoma City, OK 73125
(405)236-2800; (405)971-1071 (fax)
www.unityinc.org

NOTES

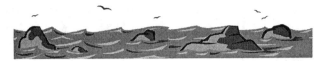

INTERNSHIPS

Internships are a great way to test out a potential career. They are also an excellent way to make yourself more competitive in the job market after graduation from high school or college. According to a 1997 Michigan State University survey of employers, internships are the most important factor in landing a first job — even more important than GPA, leadership qualities, attitude and technical skills.

Internships give you the opportunity to really see how the company works. Often the tasks are dull or may seem menial (filing, data entry, answering the phones, etc.), but there is often a mentoring aspect, too. You are often in a position to talk with and watch those in company management. You may be encouraged to attend meetings or seminars. The idea is for you to really get a feel for the industry and the particular company.

Because they are so vital to future employment, internships tend to be very competitive. Therefore, you want to contact the company you are interested in and apply early: many have deadlines in the spring. The companies are looking at several factors including grades, job experience, extracurricular activities and other interests. The key to winning an internship is your attitude. You must be willing to be a team player; to work hard and contribute to the project or company.

There are several steps that you will need to take in order to apply for and win an internship. You should prepare a resume and cover letter. If the company is interested, you will be asked to interview. If you win the internship, you may want to set up a learning contract outlining your duties and what learning experiences the company will provide. There are many excellent sources of information that will help you with each of these steps. Refer to the resource listing in the back of this book for further information.

Remember, once you have an internship, some of the work may be dull or menial. Keep a good attitude and pay attention to the overall organization, not just your individual tasks. Show initiative. Volunteer for more responsibility. Once you have proven yourself, you will often be given additional and more interesting tasks.

If you are interested in finding an internship, there are several places that you might try looking:

- State Governor's Office
- Office of your local Senator or Representative;
- Local government agencies;
- Chamber of Commerce;
- Social service agencies;
- Local firms or businesses;
- Local political campaigns;
- Offices of family and friends.

Contact these organizations, or any other business or agency that you might be interest in working for. Inquire about any internship opportunities available. If they do not have a program, offer to work for free. It's an offer that is hard to refuse.

There are also some very interesting web sites that you might want to visit:

- **http://www.aaja.org** – Asian-American Journalists Association website provides scholarship and internship information.
- **http://www.cie.uci.edu/** - A listing of internships overseas.
- **http://www.collegeboard.org/features/home/html/involved.html** - Links to several internship sites.
- **http://www.fbla-pbl.org** - The Future Business Leaders of America links to internship sites.
- **http://www.feminist.org/911/internship/internship.html** - The Feminist Foundation Majority Internships Director provides a listing of internships for young women.
- **http://www.rsinternships.com** - Rising Star Internships site.
- **http://www.tripod.com/explore/jobs_career/** - The Lifelong-Learning Internships site.
- **http://www.vicon.net/~internnet** - Inter-Net site
- **http://www.worldwide.edu/** - The World Wide Classroom has a directory of over 10,000 schools with international programs worldwide — some of these programs are internships..

This chapter lists some of the internships available throughout the country. Although care was taken in compiling the list, there are undoubtedly internships available that are not included in this listing. Also, although extreme care was taken to ensure accuracy, the nature and availability — sometimes even the contact name or address — may have changed since the publication of this book. If you find an error, please see the back of the book for information on how you can contact us so that it will be changed for the next edition.

The internships located in this chapter are organized by the field of interest. The following list includes the major categories, as well as specific topics which may be found within each one.

- **BUSINESS AND TECHNOLOGY**
Accounting, Banking , Computers, Construction, Electronics, Engineering, Finance, General Business, Insurance, Law, Manufacturing, Real Estate, Retail, Utilities

- **COMMUNICATIONS**
Advertising/Public Relations, Film/Audio/Video, Magazine/Publishing, Newspaper/Journalism, Radio, Television

- **CREATIVE, PERFORMING & FINE ARTS**
Architecture, Art, Dance, Entertainment, Interior Design, Museums, Music, Photography, Theater

- **HISTORY**
Archaeology, Historical Preservation

- **HUMAN SERVICES**
Disabled, Education, Health Services, Human/Civil Rights, Medicine, Philanthropy, Social Services

- **INTERNATIONAL**
Foreign Affairs

- **NATURE/RECREATION**
Environmental, Nature, Parks, Recreation, Wildlife Management

- **PUBLIC AFFAIRS**
Corrections, Government/Public Administration, Law/Criminal Justice, Libraries, Public Interest, Public Service, Tourism, Urban Planning

- **SCIENCE/RESEARCH**
Aerospace, Agriculture, Aquariums, Chemicals, Geography, Marine Studies, Oceanography, Physics

- **INTERNSHIP REFERRAL & PLACEMENT**

Each listing includes a *description* of the company or organization providing the internship. Information is given concerning whether the internship is *open to* high school juniors, seniors, students or graduates. *Positions available* lists what positions are filled by interns. The *cost/compensation* information indicates whether the internship is paid or unpaid. Details are given about where to go *for more information*.

*NOTE: When only a fax number is given, the business or organization prefers that contact be made in writing or via fax. <u>No telephone calls, please.</u>

BUSINESS & TECHNOLOGY

AETNA LIFE & CASUALTY
Hartford, Connecticut
Description: Health care benefits company and global insurance and financial services organization.
Open to: High school students.
Type: Paid
For more information: College Relations, Attn: RSAA, Aetna Life & Casualty, 151 Farmington Avenue, Hartford, Connecticut 06156; (800)722-9860.

AMERICAN MANAGEMENT ASSOCIATION
New York, New York
Description: Nonprofit organization providing training and services for management and business.
Open to: High school students.
Type: Paid
For more information: Charlene Venturio, Senior Employment Representative or Jennifer Spillane, Senior Human Resources Coordinator, American Management Association, 1601 Broadway, New York, New York 10019; (212)903-8021; URL http://www.amanet.org.

ASSOCIATION OF TRIAL LAWYERS OF AMERICA
Washington, DC
Description: Association of lawyers focusing on personal injury law.
Open to: High school seniors.
Type: Paid
For more information: Internship Coordinator, Association of Trial Lawyers of America, 1050 31st Street, NW, Washington, D.C. 20007; (800)424-2725.

BENETTON USA CORPORATION
New York, New York
Description: Apparel company.
Open to: High school students and graduates.
Type: Unpaid
For more information: Internship Coordinator, Benetton USA Corporation, 597 Fifth Avenue, New York, New York 10017; (212)593-0290.

CAROLYN RAY
Yonkers, New York
Description: Manufacturer of fabric and wallcoverings.
Open to: High school students, seniors and graduates.
Type: Unpaid
For more information: Noelle Mills, Internship Coordinator, Carolyn Ray, 578 Nepperhan Avenue, Yonkers, New York 10701; (914)476-0619; E-mail carolyn-ray@msn.com.

DONNA MAIONE
New York, New York
Description: Women's clothing company.
Open to: High school students 17 years and older.
Type: Unpaid
For more information: Internship Coordinator, Donna Maione, 525 Seventh Avenue, 19th Floor, New York, New York 10019; (212)730-6701.

F.A.O. SCHWARZ
Boston, Massachusetts
Chicago, Illinois
San Francisco, California
Description: Toy store chain.
Open to: High school students.
Type: Paid
For more information:
Boston: Store Manager, F.A.O. Schwarz, 440 Boylston Street, Boston, Massachusetts 02116; (617)262-5900.
Chicago: Store Manager, F.A.O. Schwarz, 840 North Michigan Avenue, Chicago, Illinois 60611; (312)587-5000.
San Francisco: Store Manager, F.A.O. Schwarz, 48 Stockton Street, San Francisco, California 94108; (415)394-8700.

FEDERAL RESERVE BANK OF NEW YORK
New York, New York
Description: One of twelve branches in the Federal Reserve System.
Open to: High school students from the New York area.
Type: Paid
For more information: Internship Coordinator, Federal Reserve Bank of New York, 33 Liberty Street, New York, New York 10045; (212)720-6557.

FEDERAL RESERVE BOARD
Washington, D.C.
Description: Independent agency governing US monetary policy.
Open to: High school students.
Type: Paid
For more information: Board of Governors of the Federal Reserve System, 20th and Constitution NW, Stop #129, Washington, DC 20551; (800)448-4894.

GRUBB AND ELLIS
San Francisco, California
Description: Real estate company.
Open to: High school students.
Type: Unpaid
For more information: Human Resources, Grubb and Ellis, One Montgomery Street, Telesis Tower, 9th Floor, San Francisco, California 94104; (415)956-1990.

HALT
Washington, D.C.
Description: Organization dedicated to legal reform.
Open to: High school juniors and seniors.
Type: Paid
For more information: Internship Coordinator, HALT, 1319 F Street, NW, Suite 300, Washington, DC 20004; (202)347-9600.

INROADS, INC.
St. Louis, Missouri
Description: Trains minorities for management positions.
Open to: Minority high school students.
Type: Paid
For more information: INROADS, Inc., 10 South Broadway, Suite 700, St. Louis, Missouri 63102; (314)241-7488; URL http://www.inroadsinc.org.

IOWA STATE UNIVERSITY PROGRAM FOR WOMEN IN SCIENCE & ENGINEERING
Ames, Iowa
Description: Iowa State University program providing internships for women. Interns conduct research, write science reports, and attend group seminars.
Open to: High school juniors.
Type: Paid
For more information: Iowa State University, 210 Lab of Mechanics, Amex, Iowa 50011-2131; (515) 294-0966; E-mail pwse@iastate.edu.

MONROE COUNTY FEDERATION OF SOCIAL WORKERS
Rochester, New York
Description: Labor union.
Open to: High school seniors.
Type: Unpaid
For more information: Trudy Humphrey, President, Monroe County Federation of Social Workers, 167 Flanders Street, Rochester, New York 14619; (716) 328-7170; E-mail fedsw381@mail.netacc.net.

OAK RIDGE INSTITUTE FOR SCIENCE AND EDUCATION, SAVANNAH RIVER SITE
Oak Ridge, Tennessee
Description: Research and development facility that studies national defense issues, conducts work related to nuclear fuel, and operates nuclear reactors.
Open to: High school seniors.
Type: Paid
For more information: Kathy Ketner, Program Manager or Cheryl Terry, Program Specialist, Oak Ridge Institute for Science & Education, ENR-ETD-36 P.O. Box 117, Oak Ridge, Tennessee 37831-0117; (423) 576-3427; E-mail ketnerk@orau.gov.

PREMIER INSURANCE COMPANY OF MASSACHU-SETTS
Worcester, Massachusetts
Description: Insurance company.
Open to: High school students, seniors and graduates.
Type: Paid
For more information: Joyce Kimball, Human Resource Manager, Premier Insurance Company of Massachusetts, 10 Chestnut Street, Suite 300-HR, Worcester, Massachusetts 01608; (508)751-4237 (fax).

PROGRAM FOR WOMEN IN SCIENCE AND ENGINEERING
Ames, Iowa
Description: Program encouraging women in the science and engineering fields.
Open to: High school juniors.
Type: Paid
For more information: Dr. Krishna Athreya, Coordinator, Program for Women in Science and Engineering, 210 Lab of Mechanics, Iowa State University, Ames, Iowa 50011; (515)294-0966; E-mail ksathrey@isuadp2.adp.iastate.edu; URL http://www.public.iastate.edu/!pwse_info/homepage/html.

SILICON GRAPHICS
Mountain View, California
Description: Supplier of interactive computer systems.
Open to: High school students.
Type: N/A
For more information: Intern Program Cruise Director, Silicon Graphics, 2011 North Shoreline Boulevard, MS. 742, Mountain View, California 95125; (415)932-0916 (fax); E-mail benton@corp.sgi.com; URL http://www.sgi.com.

THE SOUTHWESTERN COMPANY
Nashville, Tennessee
Description: Summer work program for college students.
Open to: High school seniors and graduates.
Type: Paid
For more information: Melanie Yappen, Corporate Recruiting Manager, The Southwestern Company, P. O. Box 305140; Nashville, Tennessee 37230; (800) 424-6205; E-mail sw@southwestern.com; URL http://www.southwestern.com/~sw.

TEXAS INSTRUMENTS
Dallas, Texas
Description: Electronics manufacturer.
Open to: High school seniors.
Type: Paid
For more information: Internship Coordinator, Texas Instruments, P.O. Box 655012 M/S 70, Dallas, Texas 75265.

3M
St. Paul, Minnesota
Description: Manufacturer of diversified products.
Open to: High school students.
Type: Paid
For more information: M. Webb, Student Programs Representative, 3M, 224-1W-02, 3M Center, St. Paul, Minnesota 55144-1000; (612)733-0687; URL http://www.mmm.com.

ZANY BRAINY
Wynnewood, Pennsylvania
Description: Educational tools store chain.
Open to: High school juniors and seniors.
Type: Paid
For more information: Zany Brainy, 308 East Lancaster Avenue, Wynnewood, Pennsylvania 19096; (610) 896-1500 Ext. 1141.

COMMUNICATIONS

ACKERMAN MCQUEEN
Fairfax, Virginia
Irving, Texas
Oklahoma City, Oklahoma
Tulsa, Oklahoma
Description: Advertising agency.
Open to: High school students and graduates.
Type: Unpaid
For more information: Write to Internship Coordinator, Ackerman McQueen
Fairfax: 11250 Waples Mill Road, Suite 350, Fairfax, Virginia 22030; (703)352-6400.
Irving: 600 Commerce Tower, 545 East John Carpenter Freeway, Irving, Texas 75062; (214)444-9000.
Oklahoma City: 1100 Equity Tower, Oklahoma City, Oklahoma 73118; (405)843-7777.
Tulsa: 320 South Boston, Suite 1200, Tulsa, Oklahoma 74103; (918)582-6200.

AMERICAN VISIONS MAGAZINE
Washington, D.C.
Description: Magazine about African-American history and culture.
Open to: High school students and graduates.
Type: Unpaid
For more information: Joanne Harris, Editor, American Visions Magazine, 1156 15th Street, NW, Suite 615, Washington, DC 20005; No telephone calls; E-mail 72662.2631@compuserve.com; URL http://www.americanvisions.com.

ASIAN AMERICAN JOURNALISTS ASSOCIATION
San Francisco, California
Description: Professional organization for Asian-American journalists.
Open to: High school students and college students.
Type: Dependent on situation, largely unpaid.
Other Information: Provide listings of interships and jobs available, mentoring program, and scholarships.
For more information: Karen Jaw, Program Coordinator, Asian American Journalists Association, 1765 Sutter Street, San Francisco, California 94115; (415)346-2051; (415)346-6343 (fax);
E-mail national@aaja.org; URL http://www.aaja.org.

BAYWATCH PRODUCTION COMPANY
Los Angeles, California
Description: Company producing hit show, *Baywatch.*
Open to: High school seniors and graduates.
Type: Unpaid
For more information: Internship Coordinator, Baywatch Production Company, Berk, Schwartz, Bonann Productions, 5433 Beethoven Street, Los Angeles, California 90066; (310)302-9199 (fax).

BLACK ENTERTAINMENT TELEVISION
Washington, D.C.
Description: Cable network channel, 2 magazines, a pay-per-view channel, and other communication venues.
Open to: High school students.
Type: Unpaid
For more information: Derrick Harris, Human Resource Assistant, Black Entertainment Television, 1900 West Place, NE, Washington, D.C. 20018; (202) 608-2081; URL http://www.msbet.com.

BUZZCO ASSOCIATES, INC.
New York, New York
Description: Animation company.
Open to: High school seniors and graduates.
Type: Unpaid
For more information: Candy Kugel, Director/Producer, Buzzco Associates, Inc., 33 Bleecker Street, New York, New York 10012; (212)473-8800;
E-mail info@buzzzco.com.

CABLEVISION 6/CABLEVISION OF RAFITAN VALLEY
Piscataway, New Jersey
Description: Television production facility.
Open to: Students enrolled in school designated intern program.
Type: Unpaid. Receive school credit.
Other information: Transportation needed.
For more information: David Garb, Internship Coordinator, Cablevision 6/
Cablevision of Rafitan Valley, 275 Centennial, CN 6805, Piscataway, New Jersey 08855-6805; (732)457-0131 Ext. 6005; (732)457-0209 (fax).

CENTER FOR INVESTIGATIVE REPORTING, INC.
San Francisco, California
Description: Nonprofit organization that creates television and print media reports on a variety of national and international issues.
Open to: High school students and graduates.
Type: Paid
For more information: Communications Director, Center for Investigative Reporting, Inc., 500 Howard Street, Suite 206, San Francisco, California 94105; (415)543-1200; E-mail cir@igc.apc.org.

CONCRETE MARKETING
New York, New York
Description: Marketing firm that works with rock bands.
Open to: High school students.
Type: Paid
For more information: Internship Coordinator, Concrete Marketing, 1133 Broadway, Suite 1220, New York, New York 10010; (212)645-1360; E-mail concrete6@aol.com

EDUCATIONAL COMMUNICATIONS, INC.: ECONEWS TELEVISION, ENVIRONMENTAL DIRECTIONS RADIO, ECOLOGY CENTER OF SOUTHERN CALIFORNIA, PROJECT ECOTOURISM
Los Angeles, California
Description: Environmental broadcasting and conservation association.
Open to: High school students.
Type: Unpaid
For more information: Leslie Lewis, Internship Coordinator, Educational Communications, Inc., P.O. Box 351419, Los Angeles, California 90035; (310)559-9160; E-mail ecnp@aol.com; URL http://home.earthlink.net/~dragonflight/ecoprojects.htm.

EMI RECORDS
New York, New York
Description: Record company.
Open to: High school seniors.
Type: Unpaid
For more information: EMI Records Group North America, Human Resources, 1290 Avenue of the Americas, 35th Floor, New York, NY 10104; (212) 492-1700.

EMPIRE STATE WEEKLIES
Webster, New York
Description: Weekly community newspapers.
Open to: High school seniors and graduates.
Type: Unpaid
For more information: Jenifer Calus, Managing Editor, Empire State Weeklies, 2010 Empire Boulevard,

Webster, New York 14580; (716)671-3554.

ENTERTAINMENT DESIGN AND LIGHTING DIMENSIONS MAGAZINE

New York, New York

Description: Trade publisher for entertainment designers.

Open to: High school and college students.

Positions available: Editorial and marketing interns.

Type: Paid - minimum wage.

Other information: Summer only.

For more information: Greg Havas, Office Manager, Entertainment Design and Lighting Dimensions Magazine, 32 West 18th Street, 11th Floor, New York, New York 10011-4612; (212)229-2965; (212) 229-2084 (fax); E-mail ed/loc.intertec.com; URL http://www.etecnyc.net.

FOLLIS ADVERTISING

New York, New York

Description: Advertising agency.

Open to: High school seniors.

Type: Unpaid

For more information: John Follis, Follis Advertising, 280 Madison Avenue, #304, New York, New York 10016; (212)889-9443.

FORTY ACRES AND A MULE FILMWORKS

Brooklyn, New York

Description: Film company.

Open to: High school students.

Type: Unpaid

For more information: Forty Acres and a Mule Filmworks, Inc., Internship Program, 124 Dekalb Avenue, Brooklyn, New York 11217.

GREATER DAYTON PUBLIC TELEVISION, WPTD-TV/WPTO-TV

Dayton, Ohio

Description: Two public television stations.

Open to: High school students.

Type: N/A

For more information: Brenda Bathgate, Office/ Personnel Manager, Greater Dayton Public Television, WPTD-TV/WPTO-TV, 110 South Jefferson St., Dayton, Ohio 45402-2415; (513)220-1642 (fax).

GREY DIRECT

New York, New York

Description: Direct response advertising agency.

Open to: High school seniors and graduates.

Type: Paid

For more information: Emilie Schaum, Vice President/Human Resource Director, Grey Direct, 875 Third Avenue, New York, New York 10022; (212) 303-6708 (fax).

INTERNATIONAL VIDEO SERVICES

New York, New York

Description: Video duplication and editing facility.

Open to: High school students and graduates.

Type: Unpaid

For more information: Jim Maher, International Video Services, 1501 Broadway, Suite 515, New York, New York 10036; (212)730-1411; E-mail ivs212@aol.com.

IOWA FILM OFFICE

Des Moines, Iowa

Description: Coordinates the filming of motion pictures and commercials in Iowa.

Open to: High school students and graduates.

Type: Unpaid

For more information: Internship Coordinator, Iowa Film Office, 200 East Grand Avenue, Des Moines, Iowa 50309; (515)242-4726.

JONES COMMUNICATIONS, INC.

Reston, Virginia

Description: Television studio.

Open to: High school students and graduates.

Type: Unpaid

For more information: Thomas F. Bartelt, Community Program Manager, Jones Communications, Inc, 12345G Sunrise Valley Drive, Reston, Virginia 22091; (703)758-8099.

KIDSNET

Washington, D.C.

Description: National resource for children's television, audio, video, and radio programs.

Open to: High school seniors and graduates.

Type: Unpaid

For more information: Research Manager, Kidsnet, 6856 Eastern Avenue, NW, Suite 208, Washington, D. C. 20012; (202)291-1400; E-mail kidsnet@aol.com; URL http://www.kidsnet.org.

KRCB

Rohnert Park, California

Description: Public television station.

Open to: High school students and graduates.

Type: Unpaid

For more information: Internship Coordinator, KRCB, 5850 LaBath Avenue, Rohnert Park, California 94928; (707)585-8522.

KTEH-TV

San Jose, California

Description: Public television station.

Open to: High school students and college students.

Positions Available: Camera; production assistant; PR assistant; and outreach assistant.

Type: Unpaid

For more information: Personnel Manager, KTEH-

TV, 1585 Shallenberger Road, San Jose, California 95131; (408)795-5400; (408)995-5446 (fax); URL http://www.kteh.pbs.org.

LEVINE COMMUNICATIONS OFFICE
Los Angeles, California
Description: Public relations firm.
Open to: High school seniors.
Type: Unpaid
For more information: Internship Coordinator, Levine/ Schneider Public Relations, 873 Sunset Boulevard, 6th Floor, Los Angeles, California 90069; (310)659-6400 Ext. 228.

LOVETT PRODUCTIONS, INC.
New York, New York
Description: Independent production company.
Open to: High school seniors and graduates.
Type: Unpaid
For more information: Office Manager, Lovett Productions, Inc., 155 Sixth Avenue, 10th Floor, New York, New York 10013; (212)242-8999; E-mail lovett@interport.com.

MARINA MAHER COMMUNICATIONS
New York, New York
Descriptions: Public relations firm.
Open to: High school seniors and graduates.
Type: Paid
For more information: Internship Coordinator, Marina Maher Communications, 400 Park Avenue, 4th Floor, New York, New York 10022; (212)759-7543.

MERIP INTERNSHIP
Washington, D.C.
Description: Publisher of *Middle East Report.*
Open to: High school students and graduates.
For more information: MERIP Internship, 1500 Massachusetts Avenue NW, Suite 119, Washington, DC 20005; (202)223-3677; E-mail merip@igc.org.

MTV: MUSIC TELEVISION
New York, New York
Description: Cable television channel.
Open to: High school students.
Type: Unpaid
For more information: MTV Networks Internship Program, Human Resources, 1515 Broadway, 22nd Floor, New York, New York 11036; (212)248-8000.

NATIONAL ASSOCIATION OF COLLEGE BROADCASTERS
Providence, Rhode Island
Description: Association for students studying broadcast media.
Open to: High school students and graduates.
Type: Unpaid

For more information: Kelley Cunningham, Internship Coordinator, National Association of College Broadcasters, 71 George Street, Providence, Rhode Island 02912-1824; (401)863-2225; E-mail nacb@brown.edu; URL http://www.hofstra.edu/nacb.

NEW HAVEN ADVOCATE
New Haven, Connecticut
Description: Weekly alternative newspaper.
Open to: High school students and graduates.
Type: Unpaid
For more information: Karen Unger, Listings Editor, New Haven Advocate, One Long Wharf Drive, New Haven, Connecticut 06511; (203)787-1418 (fax); E-mail listings @newhavenadvocate.com; URL http://www.newhavenadvocate.com.

NORTHWEST FILM CENTER
Portland, Oregon
Description: Regional media arts center.
Open to: High school students and graduates.
Type: Unpaid
For more information: Internship Coordinator, Northwest Film Center, 1219 Southwest Park Avenue, Portland, Oregon 97205; (503)221-1156.

OVERLAND ENTERTAINMENT
New York, New York
Description: Produces events for corporate clients.
Open to: High school seniors.
Type: Unpaid
For more information: Internship Coordinator, Overland Entertainment, 257 West 52nd Street, New York, New York 10019; (212)262-1270.

PARTOS COMPANY
Los Angeles, California
Description: Talent and literary agency.
Open to: High school students and graduates.
Type: Unpaid
For more information: Elena Gerli, Internship Coordinator, Partos Company, 6363 Wilshire Boulevard, Suite 227, Los Angeles, California 90048; (213)876-5500.

PENOBSCOT BAY PRESS
Stonington, Maine
Description: Publisher of books, computer graphics and weekly newspapers.
Open to: High school seniors and graduates.
Type: Paid
For more information: Nat Barrows, Publisher, Penobscot Bay Press, P.O. Box 36, Stonington, Maine 04681; (207)367-2200.

RESNICK COMMUNICATIONS
Philadelphia, Pennsylvania

Description: Communications firm.
Open to: High school students, seniors, and graduates.
Type: Unpaid
For more information: Internship Coordinator, Resnick Communications, 1528 Walnut Street, Philadephia, Pennsylvania 19102; (215)893-0204; (214) 893-0311 (fax); E-mail prres@aol.com.

RUSH LIMBAUGH SHOW
New York, New York
Description: Conservative radio show.
Open to: High school seniors.
Type: Unpaid
For more information: Internship Coordinator, The Rush Limbaugh Show, Excellence in Broadcasting Network-WABC Radio, 2 Penn Plaza, 17th Floor, New York, New York 10121.

SALLY FISCHER PUBLIC RELATIONS
New York, New York
Description: Public relations firm.
Open to: High school students and graduates.
Type: Unpaid
For more information: Sally Fischer, Sally Fischer Public Relations, 315 West 57th Street, Suite 407, New York, New York 10019; (212)246-2977; E-mail SallyFPR@aol.com.

SAN FRANCISCO BAY GUARDIAN
San Francisco, California
Description: Independent, alternative weekly newspaper.
Open to: High school students.
Type: Unpaid
For more information: Internship Coordinator, San Francisco Bay Guardian, 520 Hampshire Street, San Francisco, California 94110; E-mail mandy@fbayguardian.com.

SCOTT RUDIN PRODUCTIONS
Hollywood, California
New York, New York
Description: Independent film and theater producer.
Open to: High school students.
Type: Unpaid
For more information: Internship Coordinator, Scott Rudin Productions
Hollywood: Demille 200, 5555 Melrose Avenue, Hollywood, California 90038; (213)956-4600.
New York: 15 Columbus Circle, 23rd Floor, New York, New York 10023; (212)373-0262.

SEVENTEEN MAGAZINE
New York, New York
Description: Teen magazine.
Open to: High school and college students.
Positions available: Editorial internships.
Type: Unpaid for high school; paid for college students in summer only.
Other information: Spring, summer, and fall positions available.
For more information: Lori Mollo, Internship Coordinator, Seventeen Magazine, 850 Third Avenue, 9th Floor, New York, New York 10022; (212)407-9745; (212)407-9899 (fax); URL http://www.seventeen.com.

THE SOURCE
New York, New York
Description: Monthly magazine featuring hip hop music, culture, and politics.
Open to: High school students.
Type: Unpaid
For more information: Internship Coordinator, The Source, 594 Broadway, Suite 510, New York, New York 10012; (212)274-0464.

SPIN MAGAZINE
New York, New York
Description: Music magazine.
Open to: High school seniors.
Type: Unpaid
For more information: Patricia Charles, Advertising Assistant/Internship Coordinator, SPIN Magazine, 205 Lexington Avenue, New York, New York 10016; (212)231-7400; (212)231-7300 (fax); E-mail PCharles@spinmag.com

TCI CABLE OF WESTCHESTER
Mamaroneck, New York
Description: Provides local programming for cable.
Open to: High school students and graduates.
Type: Unpaid
For more information: Myles Rich, Production Manager, TCI Cable of Westchester, 609 Center Avenue, Mamaroneck, New York 10543; (914)777-3900 Ext. 342.

TEXAS MONTHLY
Austin, Texas
Description: Monthly magazine.
Open to: High school students.
Type: Unpaid
For more information: Internship Coordinator, Texas Monthly, P.O. Box 1569, Austin, Texas 78767.

UNIVERSITY DIRECTORIES
Chapel Hill, North Carolina
Description: Publisher of college and university telephone directories.
Open to: High school students.
Type: Paid
For more information: Advertiser Services Manager, University Directories, 88 McClamroch Circle, Chapel Hill, North Carolina 27514; (919)968-0225.

THE VILLAGE VOICE
New York, New York
Description: Weekly newspaper.
Open to: High school students and graduates.
Type: Unpaid
For more information: Intern Coordinator, The Village Voice, 36 Cooper Square, New York, New York 10003; (212)475-3300 Ext. 2300.

VIRGIN RECORDS
London, England
Description: Record company.
Open to: High school students 16 years and up.
Type: Unpaid
For more information: Personnel Administrator, Virgin Records, 553-570 Harrow Road, London, W10 4RH; 44-181-964-6000.

WALK FM/AM
Patchoque, New York
Description: FM/AM radio station.
Open to: High school seniors and graduates.
Type: Unpaid
For more information: Donna Vaughan, News Director or Priscilla Lee, Promotion Director, WALK FM/AM, 66 Colonial Drive, Patchoque, New York 11722; (516)475-5200; E-mail walkfm@aol.com.

WBCC-TV
Cocoa, Florida
Description: Educational television station.
Open to: High school students and graduates.
Type: Unpaid
For more information: Michael Pope, Promotions Director, WBCC-TV, 1519 Clearlake Road, Cocoa, Florida 32922, (407)634-3724 (fax);
E-mail pope.m@al.brevard.cc.fl.us; URL http://www.brevard.cc.fl.us

WBUX RADIO
Doylestown, Pennsylvania
Description: Radio station.
Open to: High school students and graduates.
Type: Unpaid
For more information: Nanci Harris, Office Manager, WBUX Radio, P.O. Box 2187, Doylestown, Pennsylvania 18901; (215)345-1570;
E-mail nanci1570@aol.com.

WILM NEWS RADIO
Wilmington, Delaware
Description: AM news radio station.
Open to: High school students.
Type: Unpaid
For more information: Allan Loudell, Program Director or Fred Hosier, News Director, WILM News Radio, 1215 French Street, Wilmington, Delaware 19801; (302)656-9800.

WIRED
San Francisco, California
Description: Magazine focusing on the computer age.
Open to: High school students and graduates.
Type: Paid
For more information: Internship Coordinator, Wired, 520 3rd Street, 4th Floor, San Francisco, California 94107; (415)276-5000; E-mail hotjobs@hotwired.com.

WOMEN MAKE MOVIES, INC.
New York, New York
Description: National women's media organization.
Open to: High school students and graduates.
Type: Unpaid
For more information: Krista Anderson, Office Manager, Women Make Movies, Inc., 462 Broadway, 5th Floor, New York, New York 10013; (212)925-2052 (fax); E-mail kanderson@wmm.com.

WPRI-TV/WNAC-TV
East Providence, Rhode Island
Description: CBS affiliate broadcast television station.
Open to: High school seniors.
Type: Unpaid.
Positions available: Production, news, promotion, and engineering internships.
For more information: Richard Lynch, Internship Coordinator, WPRI-TV/WNAC-TV, 25 Catamore Boulevard, East Providence, Rhode Island 02914; (401)438-7200 Ext. 1711; (401)434-3761 (fax).

WRSC-AM/WQWK-FM/WQKK-FM/WIKN-FM
State College, Pennsylvania
Description: Diverse format radio stations.
Open to: High school seniors and graduates.
Type: Unpaid
For more information: Pat Urban, Operations and Program Director, WRSC-AM/WQWK-FM/WQKK-FM/WIKN-FM, 160 Clearview Avenue, State College, Pennsylvania 16803; (814)238-5085.

CREATIVE, PERFORMING & FINE ARTS

ABRAMS ARTISTS AGENCY
Los Angeles, California
New York, New York
Description: Talent agency.
Open to: High school juniors, seniors, and graduates.
Type: Unpaid
For more information: Internships Coordinator,

Abrams Artists Agency
Los Angeles: 9200 Sunset Boulevard, 11th Floor, Los Angeles, California 90069; (310)859-0625.
New York: 420 Madison Avenue, Suite #1400, New York, New York 10017; (212)935-8980.

ACTORS THEATRE OF LOUISVILLE
Louisville, Kentucky
Description: Regional theater.
Open to: High school students and graduates.
Type: Unpaid
For more information: Apprentice/Intern Office, Actors Theatre of Louisville, 316 West Main Street, Louisville, Kentucky 40202-4218; (502)584-1265.

THE AMERICAN PLACE THEATRE
New York, New York
Description: Nonprofit off-Broadway theatre that produces new works by American authors and playwrights.
Open to: Incoming high school juniors/seniors and graduates.
Positions available: Administrative, artistic, technical, and education interns.
Type: Unpaid.
For more information: Paul Michael Fontana, Director of Education, The American Place Theatre, 111 West 46th Street, New York, New York 10036-8502; (212)840-2960 Ext. 16; (212)391-4019; E-mail PMFontana@aol.com.

AMERICAN REPERTORY THEATRE
Cambridge, Massachusetts
Description: Harvard University's resident theater company.
Open to: High school students and graduates.
Type: Unpaid
For more information: Coordinator of Internship Programs, Loeb Drama Center, American Repertory Theatre, 64 Brattle Street, Cambridge, Massachusetts 02138; (617)495-2668; E-mail dehetre@husc.harvard.edu.

THE ANDY WARHOL MUSEUM
Pittsburgh, Pennsylvania
Description: Art museum.
Open to: High school students.
Type: Unpaid
For more information: Administrative Assistant, The Andy Warhol Museum, 117 Sandusky Street, Pittsburgh, Pennsylvania 15212; (412)237-8300; URL http://www.warhol.org/warhol.

ANNE SCHWAB'S MODEL STORE
Washington, D.C.
Description: Modeling and casting agency.
Open to: High school students and graduates.
Type: Unpaid
For more information: Anne Schwab, President, Anne Schwab's Model Store, 1529 Wisconsin Avenue, NW, Washington, DC 20007; (202)333-3560.

ANNIE LIEBOVITZ STUDIO
New York, New York
Description: Photography studio of one of world's top photographers.
Open to: High school students.
Type: Unpaid
For more information: Studio Manager, Annie Liebovitz Studio, 55 VanDam Street, 14th Floor, New York, New York 10013; (212)807-0220.

ARCADY MUSIC SOCIETY
Bar Harbor, Maine
Description: Presenter of chamber music.
Open to: High school students and graduates.
Type: Paid
For more information: Melba C. Wilson, Executive Director, Arcady Music Society, P.O. Box 780, Bar Harbor, Maine 04609; (207)288-3151.

ARDEN THEATRE COMPANY
Philadelphia, Pennsylvania
Description: Theatre company dedicated to performing the works of the greatest storytellers.
Open to: High school students.
Type: Paid
For more information: Amy Murphy, Managing Director, Arden Theatre Company, 40 North Second Street, Philadelphia, Pennsylvania 19106; (215)922-1122 (fax); E-mail arden@libertynet.org; URL http://www.libertynet.org/~arden.

ASIAN AMERICAN ARTS CENTRE
New York, New York
Description: Community-based visual and contemporary Asian-American art organization.
Open to: High school students.
Positions Available: Gallery Assistant.
Type: N/A
Other Information: Interns' responsibility includes: filing managing, bulletin board, annual exhibition, and archives and library. Intern will work closely with director learning overall management of a gallery.
For more information: Robert Lee, Director, Asian American Arts Centre, 26 Bowery Street, 3rd Floor, New York, New York 10013; (212)233-2154; (212) 766-1287 (fax); E-mail AAAtrsctr@aol.com.

ATLANTA BALLET
Atlanta, Georgia
Description: Ballet company.
Open to: High school seniors and graduates.
Type: Unpaid

For more information: Christine Mentzer, Development Associate, Atlanta Ballet, 1400 West Peachtree Street, Atlanta, Georgia 30309; (404)873-5811.

BATTERY DANCE COMPANY
New York, New York
Description: Dance and touring company.
Open to: High school students and graduates.
Type: Unpaid
For more information: Claire Pannell, Company Manager, Battery Dance Company, 380 Broadway, 5th Floor, New York, New York 10013-3518; (212)219-3910.

BERKSHIRE PUBLIC THEATRE
Pittsfield, Massachusetts
Description: Theater company.
Open to: High school students and graduates.
Type: Unpaid
For more information: Internship Coordinator, Berkshire Public Theatre, P.O. Box 860, 30 Union Street, Pittsfield, Massachusetts 01202-0860.

BROOKLYN ACADEMY OF MUSIC
Brooklyn, New York
Description: Organization promoting innovative approaches to dance, opera, music, and theater.
Open to: High school seniors and graduates.
Type: Paid
For more information: Liz Sharp, Personnel Director, Brooklyn Academy of Music, 30 Lafayette Avenue, Brooklyn, New York 11217-1486; (718)636-4179.

CAROLYN RAY
Yonkers, New York
Description: Fabric designer for interior design industry.
Open to: High school juniors and seniors.
Type: N/A
For more information: Internship Coordinator, Carolyn Ray, 578 Napperhan Avenue, Yonkers, New York 10701; (914)476-0619.

CHAMBER MUSIC AMERICA
New York, New York
Description: Organization for chamber music ensembles and presenters.
Open to: High school seniors and graduates.
Type: Unpaid
For more information: Dean K. Stein, Executive Director, Chamber Music America, 305 Seventh Avenue, 5th Floor, New York, New York 10001-6008; (212)242-2022.

CHEN AND DANCERS
New York, New York
Description: Dance company.
Open to: High school students and graduates.
Type: Unpaid
For more information: Dian Dong, Associate Director, Chen and Dancers, 70 Mulberry Street, 2nd Floor, New York, New York 10013; (212)349-0494 (fax).

CHILD'S PLAY TOURING THEATRE
Chicago, Illinois
Description: Professional touring children's theater.
Open to: High school students and graduates.
Type: Unpaid
For more information: June Podagrosi, Executive Director, Child's Play Touring Theatre, 2518 West Armitage Street, Chicago, Illinois 60647; (773)235-8911; E-mail CPTTI@sprynet.com.

CLASSIC STAGE COMPANY
New York, New York
Description: Nonprofit theater promoting revival of the classics.
Open to: High school students.
Type: Unpaid
For more information: Jason Loewith, General Manager, Classic Stage Company, 136 East 13th Street, New York, New York 10003; (212)677-4210.

COLLEGE LIGHT OPERA COMPANY
Falmouth, Massachusetts
Description: Summer stock music theater - 31st season.
Open to: High school seniors and graduates.
Type: Room and board with stipend (varies with position).
Positions available: Stage and costume staff, box office, orchestra, and vocal company.
For more information: Robert A. Haslun, Producer, 162 South Cedar Street, Oberlin, Ohio 44074; (440) 774-8485; (440)775-8642 (fax);
E-mail bob.haslun@oberlin.edu; URL http://www.capecod.net/cloc.

CORTLAND REPERTORY THEATRE, INC.
Cortland, New Jersey
Description: Professional summer stock theater.
Open to: High school students and graduates.
Type: Paid
For more information: William V. Morris, Producing Director, P.O. Box 783, Cortland, New York 13045; (607)753-6161; E-mail crt@clarityconnect.com.

DETROIT INSTITUTE OF ARTS
Detroit, Michigan
Description: Art museum.
Open to: High school seniors.
Positions available: Volunteer work and internships.
Type: Unpaid

For more information: Gina Alexander Granger, Assistant Educator, Detroit Institute of Arts, 5200 Woodward Avenue, Detroit, Michigan 48202; (313) 833-1858; (313)833-7355 (fax);
E-mail granger@diapo.ci.detroit.mi.us; URL http://www.dia.org.

DRAMA LEAGUE
New York, New York
Description: Organization that promotes the growth of artists and audiences.
Open to: High school students and graduates.
Positions available: Internships in development, arts management and marketing.
Type: Paid and unpaid
For more information: Intern Coordinator, Drama League, 165 West 46th Street, Suite 601, New York, New York 10036; (212)302-2254 (fax);
E-mail dlny@echonyc.com; URL http://www.echonyc.com/~dlny.

ELIZABETH DOW LTD.
New York, New York
Description: Paint and design studio.
Open to: High school students, graduates, or anyone interested in experience.
Positions available: Product production, office management, interoffice communications, and sampling.
Type: Unpaid
Other information: For more information call for an interview.
For more information: Xavier Santana, Internship Coordinator, Elizabeth Dow Ltd., 155 Avenue of the Americas, 4th Floor, New York, New York 10013; (212)463-0144; (212)463-0824 (fax).

FARGO-MOORHEAD COMMUNITY THEATRE
Fargo, North Dakota
Description: Regional theater.
Open to: High school students and graduates.
Type: Unpaid
For more information: Bruce Tinker, Managing Artistic Director; Fargo-Moorhead Community Theatre, P.O. Box 644, Fargo, North Dakota 58107; (701)235-2685 (fax); E-mail fmct@pol.org; URL http://www.fargoweb.com/fmet.

FOOLS COMPANY, INC.
New York, New York
Description: Nonprofit cultural and educational organization.
Open to: High school students and graduates.
Type: Unpaid
For more information: Martin Russell, Artistic Director, Fools Company, Inc., 356 West 44th Street, New York, New York 10036-6413; (212)307-6000.

FRANKLIN FURNACE ARCHIVE, INC.
New York, New York
Description: Nonprofit arts organization presenting performance art on the world wide web.
Open to: All.
Positions available: Internships include web site design, working with artists, fundraising, and general administration.
Type: Unpaid
Other information: This is a rare opportunity to work closely with the staff of a vital avant-garde organization.
For more information: Harley Spiller, Administrator, Franklin Furnace Archive, Inc., 45 John Street #611, New York, New York 10038-3706; (212)766-2606; (212)766-2740 (fax);
E-mail info@franklinfurnace.org; URL http://www.franklinfurnace.org.

GEORGE STREET PLAYHOUSE
New Brunswick, New Jersey
Description: Theater company.
Open to: High school students.
Type: Unpaid
For more information: Mr. Cree Ranklin, Intern Coordinator, George Street Playhouse, 9 Livingston Avenue, New Brunswick, New Jersey 08901; (908)846-2895 Ext. 115.

GO MANAGEMENT
New York, New York
Description: Artist management company.
Open to: High school students and graduates.
Type: Unpaid
For more information: Paul Goldberg, President, Go Management, 1725 York Avenue, Apt. 27B, New York, New York 10128-7813; (212)586-6700; E-mail info@gomangement.com; URL http://www.gomangement.com.

GOWANUS ARTS EXCHANGE
Brooklyn, New York
Description: Community arts organization.
Open to: High school seniors and graduates.
Type: Paid and unpaid positions available.
For more information: Marya Warshaw, Executive Director, Gowanus Arts Exchange, 295 Douglass Street, Brooklyn, New York 11217; (718)896-5250; E-mail gowarts@aol.com.

HERE
New York, New York
Description: Arts center, theatres, puppetry, galleries, and cafe.
Open to: High school juniors, seniors, and graduates.
Positions Available: One-on-one apprenticeships with established theatre and visual artists. Very rewarding

FOCUS ON...
YOUTH ALIVE!

YouthALIVE! programs at science centers and children's museums around the country provide youth, ages 10 to 17, with positive experiences that integrate work and education.

A recent search of this site identified the following internships:

- Audubon Institute – *New Orleans,*
- *Louisiana*
- Bay Area Discovery Museum – *Sausalito, California*
- Brooklyn Children's Museum -
- *Brooklyn, New York*
- Miami Museum of Science, Inc. –
- *Miami, Florida*

URL http://www.astc.org/info/youth

---

opportunity.
Type: Unpaid (possible travel reimbursements).
For more information: Barbara Busackind, HERE, 145 Avenue of the Americas, New York, New York 10013; (212)647-0202 Ext. 307.

HIGH MUSEUM OF ART
Atlanta, Georgia
Description: Art museum.
Open to: High school seniors and graduates.
Type: Unpaid
For more information: Internship Coordinator, High Museum of Art, 1280 Peachtree Street, NE, Atlanta, Georgia 30300; (404)733-4506.

THE HUDSON RIVER MUSEUM OF WESTCHESTER
Yonkers, New York
Description: Community museum.
Open to: High school students and graduates.
Type: Unpaid

For more information: Suzanne Smith, Volunteer Coordinator, The Hudson River Museum of Westchester, 511 Warburton Avenue, Yonkers, New York 10701; (914)963-4550; E-mail hrm@hrm.org; URL http://www.hrm.org.

INSTITUTE FOR UNPOPULAR CULTURE
San Francisco, California
Description: Nonprofit organization dedicated to supporting alternative artists and fighting censorship.
Open to: High school students.
Type: Unpaid
For more information: Internship Coordinator, The Institute for Unpopular Culture, 1850 Union Street, Suite 1523, San Francisco, California 94123; (415) 986-4382.

INTERIOR DESIGN COLLECTIONS
New York, New York
Description: Interior design product sales.

Open to: High school seniors.
Type: Unpaid
For more information: Internship Coordinator, Interior Design Collections, 39 East 12th Street, Suite 205, New York, New York 10003; (212)995-9154.

ISLIP ART MUSEUM
East Islip, New York
Description: Art museum featuring contemporary and avant-garde works.
Open to: High school seniors.
Type: Unpaid
For more information: Mary Lou Cohalan, Director, Islip Art Museum, 50 Irish Lane, East Islip, New York 11730; (516)224-5412.

J.E. JASEN STUDIO
New York, New York
Description: Studio that creates enamel art objects.
Open to: High school students and graduates.
Type: Unpaid
For more information: June Jasen, J.E. Jasen Studio, 36 East Tenth Street, New York, New York 10003-6219; (212)674-6113; (212)777-6371 (fax).

JOSEPH PAPP PUBLIC THEATER/NEW YORK SHAKESPEARE FESTIVAL
New York, New York
Description: Nonprofit theatrical producer.
Open to: All.
Positions available: Internships in theatrical production and administration.
Type: Paid - $50/week stipend for 3-6 months.
Other information: Candidate must submit resume and cover letter indicating area of interest. Also, should note available dates.
For more information: Alison Harper, Director of Special Services, Joseph Papp Public Theater, New York Shakespeare Festival, 425 Lafayette Street, New York, New York 10003; (212)539-8659; (212)539-8505 (fax); URL http://www.publictheater.org.

LOWER MANHATTAN CULTURAL COUNCIL
New York, New York
Description: Arts council.
Open to: High school students and graduates.
Type: Unpaid
For more information: Christopher R. Gillespie, Program Director, Lower Manhattan Cultural Council, 5 World Trade Center, Suite 9235, New York, New York 10048; (212)432-0900; E-mail lmccdix@artswire.org.

MAINE STATE MUSIC THEATRE
Brunswick, Maine
Description: Professional music theater.
Open to: High school students and graduates, 18 years and older.
Type: Paid
For more information: Rachel Clarke, Company Manager, Maine State Music Theatre, 14 Maine Street, Suite 109, Brunswick, Maine 04011; (207)725-8769; E-mail msmtjobs@blaznetme.net; URL http://www.msmt.org.

MARYLAND ART PLACE
Baltimore, Maryland
Description: Nonprofit regional art center.
Open to: High school seniors and graduates interested in art.
Positions available: Internships and volunteer opportunities.
Type: Unpaid
Other information: Houses the Maryland State Arts Council Artist Slide Registry.
For more information: Program Director, Maryland Art Place, 218 West Saratoga Street, Baltimore, Maryland 21201; (410)962-8565; (410)244-8017 (fax); E-mail map@charm.net; URL http://www.MDartplace.org.

MERCE CUNNINGHAM STUDIO
New York, New York
Description: Modern dance studio.
Open to: High school seniors and graduates.
Type: Unpaid. Free dance classes.
Other information: Cunningham Technique/College Accredited School.
For more information: Sutton Brown, Studio Administrator, Merce Cunningham Studio, 55 Bethune Street, New York, New York 10014; (212)691-9751 Ext. 30; (212)633-2453 (fax); E-mail sutton@merce.org; URL http://www.merce.org.

MERRIMACK REPERTORY THEATRE
Lowell, Massachusetts
Description: Professional theater.
Open to: High school seniors and graduates.
Type: Paid and unpaid internships available.
For more information: Harriet Sheets, General Manager, Merrimack Repertory Theatre, 50 East Merrimack Street, Lowell, Massachusetts 01852; (978)454-6324; (978)934-0166; E-mail mrtlowell@aol.com; URL http://www.mrtlowell.com.

THE MUSEUM OF TELEVISION AND RADIO
New York, New York
Description: The museum of television and radio is an archive of television and radio recording housing over 100,000 programs.
Open to: High school seniors and graduates.
Positions Available: Education Intern.
Type: Unpaid
For more information: Carla Fantozzi, Education

Manager, The Museum of Television and Radio, 465 N. Beverly Drive, Beverly Hills, California 90210; (310)786-1034; (310)786-1086 (fax); E-mail cfantozzi@mtr.org; URL http://www.mtr.org.

MUSICAL THEATRE WORKS
New York, New York
Description: Professional theater organization.
Open to: High school seniors and graduates.
Type: Unpaid
For more information: Jacqueline Siegel, Managing Director, Musical Theatre Works, 440 Lafayette Street, 4th Floor, New York, New York 10003; (212)667-0040.

NATIONAL GALLERY OF ART, MUSIC DEPARTMENT
Washington, D.C.
Description: Program of free weekly concerts.
Open to: High school seniors.
Type: Unpaid
For more information: George Manos, Music Director, National Gallery of Art, Music Department, 6th and Constitution Avenue, NW, Washington, D.C. 20565; (202)842-6075.

NEW DRAMATISTS
New York, New York
Description: Service organization for playwrights.
Open to: Everyone.
Positions available: Internships in stage management, literary, development, artistic, and administration.
Type: Paid - $25/week for full-time interns.
For more information: Stephen Haff, Internship Coordinator, New Dramatists, 424 West 44th Street, New York, New York 10036; (212)757-6960; (212)265-4738 (fax).

NEW FEDERAL THEATRE WORKS
New York, New York
Description: Theater group performing minority drama.
Open to: High school seniors and graduates.
Type: Unpaid
For more information: Pat White, Company Manager, New Federal Theatre, Inc., 292 Henry Street, New York, New York 10002; (212)353-1176.

NEW JERSEY SHAKESPEARE FESTIVAL
Madison, New Jersey
Description: Theater producing Shakespeare and other classic works.
Open to: High school seniors and graduates.
Type: Unpaid
For more information: Joe Discher, Artistic Associate, New Jersey Shakespeare Festival, 36 Madison Avenue, Madison, New Jersey 07940; (201)408-3278; E-mail njsf@njshakespeare.org; URL http://www.njshakespeare.org.

NEW STAGE THEATRE
Jackson, Mississippi
Description: Professional nonprofit theater.
Open to: High school students and graduates.
Type: Paid and unpaid.
For more information: Education/Internship Coordinator, New Stage Theatre, 1100 Carlisle Street, Jackson, Mississippi 39202; (601) 948-3533; (601)948-3538 (fax).

NEW YORK CITY PERCENT FOR ART PROGRAM
New York, New York
Description: Organization that commissions art for city-owned property.
Open to: High school seniors and graduates.
Type: Unpaid
For more information: NYC Department of Cultural Affairs, New York City Percent for Art Program, 330 West 42nd Street, 14th Floor, New York, New York 10036; (212)643-7770.

NEW YORK STATE THEATRE INSTITUTE
Troy, New York
Description: Professional theater and arts education program.
Open to: High school seniors and graduates.
Type: Unpaid
For more information: Arlene Leff, Intern Program Administrator, New York State Theatre Institute, Russell Sage Campus, 155 River Street, Troy, New York 12180; (518)274-3573; E-mail nysti@crisny.org.

NEW YORK YOUTH THEATER
New York, New York
Description: Children's theater.
Open to: High school seniors.
Type: Unpaid
For more information: Lawrence Axsmith, Artistic Director, New York Youth Theater, P.O. Box 2153, Times Square Station, New York, New York 10108; (212)315-1737.

OMAHA MAGIC THEATRE
Omaha, Nebraska
Description: Professional theater and touring group.
Open to: High school students and graduates.
Type: Unpaid
For more information: Jo Ann Schmidman, Artistic Director, Omaha Magic Theatre, 325 South 16th Street, Omaha, Nebraska 68102.

OPERA COMPANY OF PHILADELPHIA
Philadelphia, Pennsylvania
Description: Performing Grant Opera at the Academy of Music.

Open to: High school seniors and graduates.
Positions available: Administrative internships - marketing, public relations, development, etc.
Type: Unpaid
For more information: Tracy C. Galligher, Publicist, Opera Company of Philadelphia, 510 Walnut Street, Suite 1500, Philadelphia, Pennsylvania 19106; (215) 928-2100; (215)928-2112 (fax);
E-mail galligher@operaphilly.com; URL http://www.operaphilly.com.

PACT, INC.

Clearwater, Florida
Description: Performing arts presenter.
Open to: High school students and graduates.
Type: Unpaid
For more information: Susan Crockett, Business Analyst, PACT, Inc., 1111 McMullen Booth Road, Clearwater, Florida 34619; (813)791-7060 Ext. 361; URL http://zipmall.com/reh/.

PHILADELPHIA INSTITUTE OF CONTEMPORARY ART

Philadelphia, Pennsylvania
Description: Art museum.
Open to: High school seniors and graduates.
Type: Unpaid
For more information: Rilice Lefton, Director of Volunteers, Philadelphia Institute of Contemporary Art, 118 South 36th Street, Philadelphia, Pennsylvania 19104; (215)
898-7108; URL http://www.upenn.edu.ka.

PIONEER PLAYHOUSE

Danville, Kentucky
Description: Summer stock theater.
Open to: High school students and graduates.
Type: Unpaid. Cost of $900 for approximately 10 weeks covers room and board.
Other information: Interns try out for parts and are involved in every aspect of theatre.
For more information: Eben Henson, Producer, Pioneer Playhouse, 840 Stanford Road, Danville, Kentucky 40422; (606)236-2747; (606)236-2341 (fax).

PREGONES THEATRE COMPANY

Bronx, New York
Description: Puerto Rican theater company.
Open to: High school seniors and graduates.
Type: Unpaid
For more information: Judith Rivera, Associate Director, Pregones Theatre Company, 700 Grand Concourse, Bronx, New York 10451; (718)585-1202.

PRIMARY STAGES

New York, New York
Description: Produces new American plays.

Open to: High school seniors and graduates.
Type: Unpaid
For more information: Seth Gordon, Associate Producer, Primary Stages, 584 Ninth Avenue, New York, New York 10036; (212)333-2025 (fax); E-mail primaryeix.netcom.com.

QUEENS THEATER IN THE PARK

Flushing, New York
Description: Performing arts center.
Open to: High school students and graduates.
Type: Unpaid
For more information: Lois Newhart, General Manager, Queens Theater in the Park, P.O. Box 520069, Flushing, New York 11352; (718)760-1972; E-mail qtiplois@aol.com.

REPERTORIO ESPAÑOL

New York, New York
Description: Spanish language theater company.
Open to: High school seniors and graduates.
Type: N/A
For more information: Angelica Aquino Gonzalez, Repertorio Español, 138 East 27th Street, New York, New York 10016; (212)889-2850.

ROCKPORT CHAMBER MUSIC FESTIVAL

Rockport, Massachusetts
Description: Chamber music festival.
Open to: High school seniors and graduates.
Type: Paid
For more information: Kathleen Pomfret, Administrator, Rockport Chamber Music Festival, P.O. Box 312, Rockport, Massachusetts 01966; (508)546-7391.

765-ARTS

New York, New York
Description: Nonprofit organization providing cultural event information.
Open to: High school seniors.
Type: Unpaid
For more information: Internship Coordinator, 765-ARTS (Big Apple Arts and Festivals Information Project), 225 West 57th Street, 8th Floor, New York, New York 10019-2194; (212)315-4186.

SHADOW BOX THEATRE

New York, New York
Description: Children's theater.
Open to: High school students and graduates.
Type: Paid and unpaid internships available.
For more information: Marlyn Baum, Managing Director, Shadow Box Theatre, 325 West End Avenue, 12B, New York, New York 10023; (212)724-0677.

SIGNATURE THEATRE COMPANY

New York, New York

Description: Theater devoted to a single playwright's works each year.
Open to: High school students.
Type: Unpaid
For more information: Elliot Fox, Associate Director, Signature Theatre Company, 424 West 42nd Street, 2nd Floor, New York, New York 10036; (212)967-1913.

OFFICE OF EXHIBITS CENTRAL, SMITHSONIAN INSTITUTION
Washington, D.C.
Description: Office that provides support for museums and bureaus throughout the Smithsonian.
Open to: High school seniors and graduates.
Type: N/A
For more information: Timothy Smith, Intern Coordinator, Office of Exhibits Central, Smithsonian Institution, MRC 808, 111 North Capitol Street, Washington, D.C. 20560; (202)357-2526;
E-mail tsmith@ic.si.ed.

SOURCE THEATRE COMPANY
Washington, D.C.
Description: Theater producing new and contemporary works.
Open to: High school students and graduates.
Type: Unpaid
For more information: Intern Coordinator, Source Theatre Company, 1835 14th Street, NW, Washington, DC 20009; (202)462-1073; E-mail sourceth@shirenet.com.

STATEN ISLAND INSTITUTE OF ARTS AND SCIENCES
Staten Island, New York
Description: Organization focusing on Staten Island and its people.
Open to: High school seniors and graduates.
Type: N/A
For more information: Peggy Hammerle, Vice President of Collections, Staten Island Institute of Arts and Sciences, 75 Stuvesant Place, Staten Island, New York 10301-1998; (718)727-1135.

STUDIO MUSEUM IN HARLEM
New York, New York
Description: Art museum featuring the works of Black America and the Africa Diaspora.
Open to: High school seniors and graduates.
Type: Paid and unpaid internships available.
For more information: Internship Program/Education, Studio Museum in Harlem, 144 West 125th Street, New York, New York 10027; (212)864-4500 Ext. 215.

THEATRE DE LA JEUNE LUNE
Minneapolis, Minnesota
Description: Innovative, interactive theater company.
Open to: High school seniors and graduates.
Type: Unpaid
For more information: Luverne Seifert or Joel Spence, Theatre de la Jeune Lune, 105 First Street North, Minneapolis, Minnesota 55401; (612)332-3968.

THEATRE FOR THE NEW CITY FOUNDATION, INC.
New York, New York
Description: Nonprofit off-Broadway theater.
Open to: High school students and graduates.
Type: Unpaid
For more information: Jerry Jaffe, Administrator, Theatre for the New City Foundation, Inc., 155 First Avenue, New York, New York 10003; (212)254-1109; E-mail thetheater@aol.com.

THE THEATRE-STUDIO, INC.
New York, New York
Description: Studio theatre committed to growth of the theater arts in the community.
Open to: High school students and graduates.
Type: Unpaid
For more information: A.M. Raychel, Artistic Director/Producer, The Theatre-Studio, Inc., 750 Eighth Avenue, Suite 200, New York, New York 10036; (212)719-0500.

THIRTEENTH STREET REPERTORY COMPANY
New York, New York
Description: Nonprofit off-Broadway theater.
Open to: High school students and graduates.
Type: Unpaid
For more information: Edith O'Hara, Artistic Director, Thirteenth Street Repertory Company, 50 West 13th Street, New York, New York 10011; (212)675-6677.

THREAD WAXING SPACE
New York, New York
Description: Nonprofit visual and performing arts organization.
Open to: High school juniors and seniors.
Type: Unpaid
For more information: Internship Coordinator, Thread Waxing Space, 476 Broadway, 2nd Floor, New York, New York 10013; (212)966-9520.

TOMMY BOY MUSIC
New York, New York
Description: Record label.
Open to: High school seniors and college students.
Type: Unpaid
For more information: Karen Tumelty, Quality of Life, Tommy Boy Music, 902 Broadway, 13th Floor, New York, New York 10010; (212)388-8300; E-mail karen.tumelty@tommyboy.com.

TRURO CENTER FOR THE ARTS AT CASTLE HILL
Truro, Massachusetts
Description: Art school.
Open to: High school students and graduates.
Type: Unpaid
For more information: Mary Stackhouse, Director, Truro Center for the Arts at Castle Hill, P.O. Box 756, Truro, Massachusetts 02666; (508)349-7511.

TUSCON CHILDREN'S MUSEUM
Tuscon, Arizona
Description: Children's museum.
Open to: High school students and graduates.
Type: Unpaid
For more information: Paula Yingst, Education Director, Tuscon Children's Museum, P.O. Box 2609, Tuscon, Arizona 86702-2609; (520)792-9985 Ext. 103.

UCR/CALIFORNIA MUSEUM OF PHOTOGRAPHY
Riverside, California
Description: Nonprofit photography museum.
Open to: High school juniors and seniors.
Type: Unpaid
Positions available: Write for more information.
For more information: Internship Coordinator, UCR/California Museum of Photography, 3824 Main Street, Riverside, California 92501; (909)787-4787; (909)787-4797 (fax); URL http://www.cmp.ucr.edu.

U.S. SERVAS
New York, New York
Description: Worldwide hospitality network with a core group of international students and "Peacebuilder" families comprising a system where those traveling in pursuit of cultural education or peace work can stay in hosts' homes for two nights.
Open to: High school seniors and adults, 18 and over.
Positions available: Short-term internships lasting six weeks to three months involving general office support, outreach to other peace-education-travel groups, and possible United Nations activities. Also office volunteer positions available. Open on a rolling basis.
Type: Free. Reimbursement available to interns for lunch and daily commute. Some temporary housing assistance also available.
For more information: Tori Napier, Assistant Administrator, U.S. Servas, Inc., 11 John Street, Suite 407, New York, New York 10038; (212)267-0252; (212)267-0292 (fax); E-mail usservas@servas.org; URL http://servas.org.

VINEYARD THEATER
New York, New York
Description: Theater featuring new dramatic and musical works.
Open to: High school students and graduates.
Type: Unpaid
For more information: Laura Ma, General Manager, Vineyard Theater, 108 East 15th Street, New York, New York 10003-9689; (212)353-3803.

THE WESTERN STAGE
Salinas, California
Description: Theater featuring emerging artists and new works.
Open to: High school seniors and graduates.
Type: Paid
For more information: Melissa Chin, Associate Artistic Director, The Western Stage, 156 Homestead Avenue, Salinas, California 93901; (408)759-6037.

WILHEMINA MODELS
New York, New York
Beverly Hills, California
Description: Modeling agency.
Open to: High school students and high school grads.
Type: Unpaid
For more information: Internship Coordinator, Men's Division or Women's Division, Wilhemina Models
New York: 300 Park Avenue South, New York, New York 10010; (212)473-0700.
Beverly Hills: 8383 Wilshire Boulevard, Suite 650, Beverly Hills, California 90211; (213)655-0909.

WILLIAMSTOWN THEATRE FESTIVAL
Williamstown, Massachusetts
Description: Summer theater.
Open to: High school students and graduates.
Type: Unpaid
For more information: Internships, Williamstown Theatre Festival, 100 East 17th Street, 3rd Floor, New York, New York 10003; (212)228-2286; E-mail wtfcm@aol.com.

WORCESTER FOOTHILLS THEATRE COMPANY
Worcester, Massachusetts
Description: Nonprofit professional theater.
Open to: High school students.
Type: Unpaid
For more information: Kristin Langord, Associate Producer, Worcester Foothills Theatre Company, Worcester Commons Fashion Outlets, 100 Front Street, Suite 137, Worcester, Massachusetts 01608; (508)754-3314.

HISTORY

ARCHIVE OF FOLK CULTURE, AMERICAN FOLKLIFE CENTER, LIBRARY OF CONGRESS
Washington, D.C.

Description: National archive of folk music, ethnomusicology and folklore.

Open to: High school seniors and graduates.

Type: Unpaid

For more information: Joseph C. Hickerson, Head, Archive of Folk Culture, American Folklife Center, Library of Congress, Washington, DC 20540-4610; (202)707-1725.

BOOKER T. WASHINGTON NATIONAL MONUMENT

Hardy, Virginia

Description: National Park Service site where Booker T. Washington was born.

Open to: High school students and graduates.

Type: Unpaid

For more information: Alice Hanawalt, Volunteers-In-Parks Coordinator, Booker T. Washington National Monument, 12130 Booker T. Washington Highway, Hardy, Virginia 24101; (540)721-2094; E-mail alice_hanawalt@nps.gov.

CALIFORNIA DEPARTMENT OF PARKS AND RECREATION, OLD TOWN SAN DIEGO STATE HISTORIC PARK

San Diego, California

Description: Historic park that offers a variety of educational activities.

Open to: High school students.

Type: Unpaid

For more information: Joe Vasquez, State Park Ranger, California Department of Parks and Recreation, Old Town San Diego State Historic Parks, 4002 Wallace Street, San Diego, California 92110; (619) 220-5422.

CENTER FOR FOLKLIFE PROGRAMS & CULTURAL STUDIES - SMITHSONIAN INSTITUTION

Washington, D.C.

Description: Center for cultural conservation.

Open to: High school students and graduates.

Type: Unpaid

For more information: Arlene Reiniger, Program Specialist/Intern Coordinator, Center for Folklife Programs & Cultural Studies, 955 L'Enfant Plaza, Suite 2600, Washington, D.C. 20560; (202)287-3259; E-mail cfps.arlene@folklife.si.edu.

FLORIDA PARK SERVICE, KORESHAN STATE HISTORIC SITE

Estero, Florida

Description: Facility offering programs of cultural interest.

Open to: High school students and graduates.

Type: Unpaid

For more information: Ezell Givens, Florida Park Service, Koreshan State Historic Site, P.O. Box 7, Estero, Florida 33928; (941)992-0311.

KANSAS STATE HISTORICAL SOCIETY

Topeka, Kansas

Description: Historical society dedicated to preserving Kansas history.

Open to: High school students and graduates.

Type: Unpaid

For more information: Dr. David Haury, Assistant Director, Kansas State Historical Society, 6425 Southwest Sixth Avenue, Topeka, Kansas 66615-1099; (785)272-8681; E-mail dhaury@hspo.wpo.state.ks.us; URL http://www.kshs.org.

NATIONAL MUSEUM OF AMERICAN HISTORY

Washington, DC

Description: Museum dedicated to the history of the United States of America.

Open to: High school seniors and graduates.

Positions Available: Varies. Contact office for updated list of projects.

Type: Unpaid

Other Information: Application required. Contact office for details.

For more information: Allison Wickens, Internship Coordinator, National Museum of American History, Office of Internships and Fellowships, Room 1040, MRC 605, Smithsonian Institution, Washington, DC 20560-0605; (202)357-1606; (202)786-2851 (fax); E-mail Intern@nmah.si.edu; URL http://www.si.edu/nmah/interns.

NATIONAL PARK SERVICE, CASA GRANDE RUINS NATIONAL MONUMENT

Coolidge, Arizona

Description: Prehistoric Hohokam Indian ruins.

Open to: High school students and graduates.

Type: Unpaid

For more information: Volunteer-In-Park Coordinator, National Park Service, Casa Grande Ruins National Monument, 1100 Ruins Drive, Coolidge, Arizona 85228; (520)723-3172.

OLD POST OFFICE TOWER, NATIONAL PARK SERVICE

Washington, DC

Description: Historical building located near Congress.

Open to: High school students.

Type: Unpaid

For more information: Park Ranger Michael Laws, Education Coordinator, Old Post Office Tower, National Park Service, 900 Ohio Drive, SW, Washington, DC 20024-2000; (202)606-8691; E-mail michael~laws@nps.gov; URL http://www.nps.gov/opot.

SOUTH STREET SEAPORT MUSEUM

New York, New York

Description: Maritime history museum.

Open to: High school students, college students, and graduate students.

Positions available: Archaeology, design, education, maritime crafts, membership, printing and stationers shop, publications/web site, tour marketing, collections management, development (fundraising), library, marketing/special events, museum store, public affairs, ship maintenance/restoration, and volunteer administration.

Type: Unpaid

For more information: Patricia Sands, Director of Volunteer Programs, South Street Seaport Museum, 207 Front Street, New York, New York 11771; (212) 748-8727; (212)748-8610;
URL http://www.southstseaport.org.

U.S. HOLOCAUST MEMORIAL MUSEUM
Washington, D.C.

Description: Museum dedicated to the history of the Holocaust.

Open to: High school students and graduates.

Positions Available: Internships in the areas of holocaust research and museum studies. Volunteers the positions of museum representatives, special events associates, and behind-the-scenes volunteers.

Type: Paid and unpaid positions available.

For more information: Jill W. Greenstein, Manager of Volunteer & Intern Services, U.S. Holocaust Memorial Museum, 100 Raoul Wallenberg Place, SW, Washington, DC 20024-2150; (202)488-0400; (202) 488-2690 (fax); URL http://www.ushmm.org.

HUMAN SERVICES

ACCURACY IN ACADEMIA
Washington, D.C.

Description: Nonprofit organization promoting traditional academics in colleges and universities.

Open to: High school seniors and graduates.

Type: Paid

For more information: Brendan Slattery, Managing Editor, Accuracy in Academia, 4455 Connecticut Avenue, NW, Suite 330, Washington, D.C. 20008; (800)787-0429; E-mail cr@aim.org; URL http://www.aim.org.

AIM FOR THE HANDICAPPED
Dayton, Ohio

Description: Nonprofit agency providing recreational and rehabilitative services.

Open to: High school students and graduates.

Type: Unpaid

For more information: Education Department, AIM, 945 Danbury Road, Dayton, Ohio 45420; (937)294-4611.

AMERICAN ANOREXIA/BULIMIA ASSOCIATION, INC.
New York, New York

Description: Organization providing services to individuals with eating disorders and their friends and family.

Open to: High school and college students.

Positions available: Volunteer positions. Internships available to college level students.

Type: Unpaid

For more information: Claire Mysko, Administrative Director, American Anorexia/Bulimia Association, Inc., 165 West 46 Street, Suite 1108, New York, New York 10036; (212)575-6200; (212)278-0698 (fax); URL http://www.aaba.inc.org.

AMERICAN FRIENDS SERVICE COMMITTEE
Philadelphia, Pennsylvania

Description: Religious, international social service organization.

Open to: Anyone 15 years of age or older.

Type: Unpaid

For more information: Personnel Department-Helene Pollock, American Friends Service Committee, 1501 Cherry Street, Philadelphia, Pennsylvania 19102; (215) 251-7295; E-mail hpollack@afsc.org.

ANXIETY DISORDERS ASSOCIATION OF AMERICA
Rockville, Maryland

Description: Nonprofit organization promoting the prevention, treatment and cure of anxiety disorders.

Open to: High school seniors and graduates.

Type: Unpaid

For more information: Carrie Plowden, Intern Coordinator, Anxiety Disorders of America, 11900 Parklawn Drive, Rockville, Maryland 20852-2624; (301)231-9159.

ASSOCIATION FOR EXPERIENTIAL EDUCATION
Boulder, Colorado

Description: Nonprofit association dedicated to the promotion of experiential learning.

Open to: High school students and graduates.

Type: Unpaid

For more information: Sharon Heinlen, Executive Director, Association for Experiential Education, 2305 Canyon Boulevard, Suite 100, Boulder, Colorado 80302; (303)440-9334; E-mail sharon@aee.org; URL http://www.princeton.edu/~rcurtis/aee.html.

BIG BROTHERS/BIG SISTERS OF OTERO COUNTY
Almogordo, New Mexico

Description: Organization that pairs children with responsible adult role models.

Open to: High school students and graduates.

Type: Unpaid

For more information: Leroy Copeland, Executive Director, Big Brothers/Big Sisters of Otero County, 821

Alaska Avenue, Alamogordo, New Mexico 88310; (505)434-3652.

BIG BROTHERS/BIG SISTERS OF ROCK, WALWORTH, AND JEFFERSON COUNTIES
Beloit, Wisconsin
Description: Mentoring agency that matches adults who serve as role models to kids from single parent homes.
Open to: High school junior or seniors and adults, 18 and older.
Positions available: Teen volunteers, secretary/office help, and intern.
Type: Unpaid
For more information: Nancy Mignon, Executive Director, Big Brothers/Big Sisters of Rock, Walworth and Jefferson Counties, 1400 Huebbe Parkway, Beloit, Wisconsin 53511; (608)362-8223; (608)362-5835 (fax).

BOSTON YMCA
Boston, Massachusetts
Description: Organization promoting health, economic security and child care.
Open to: High school students and graduates.
Type: Unpaid
For more information: Eileen Smart, Membership and Volunteer Coordinator, Boston YWCA, 140 Claredon Street, Boston, Massachusetts 02116; (617)351-7600.

BOYS AND GIRLS CLUB
Scottsdale, Arizona
Description: Organization promoting youth development.
Open to: High school students and graduates.
Type: Paid
For more information: Steven Davidson, Director of Operations, Boys and Girls Club, 7502 East Osborn Road, Scottsdale, Arizona 85251; (602)947-6331.

BOYS AND GIRLS CLUB OF ALBANY
Albany, New York
Description: Organization providing educational, social and vocational programming for youth.
Open to: High school seniors and graduates.
Type: Unpaid
For more information: Lena Thomas, Executive Director, Boys and Girls Club of Albany, 21 Delaware Avenue, Albany, New York 12210; (518)462-5540 (fax).

BOYS AND GIRLS CLUB OF PLYMOUTH, INC.
Plymouth, Massachusetts
Description: Organization providing youth activities.
Open to: High school students and graduates.
Type: Unpaid
For more information: Ron Randall, Executive Director, Boys and Girls Club of Plymouth, Inc., P.O. Box 3479, Plymouth, Massachusetts 02361; (508)746-6070.

BOYS AND GIRLS CLUB OF TAMPA BAY, INC.
Tampa, Florida
Description: Youth development agency.
Open to: High school students, college students, and graduates.
Positions available: Program assistants, youth leaders, and interns.
Type: Varies.
For more information: Lisbeth Moore, Director of Services, Boys and Girls Club of Tampa Bay, Inc., 3020 West Laurel Street, Tampa, Florida 33607; (813)875-5771; (813)875-5483 (fax); URL http://www.bcctampa.org.

BOYS AND GIRLS CLUB OF WORCESTER
Worcester, Massachusetts
Description: Organization providing educational and recreational activities to youth.
Open to: High school students and graduates.
Type: Paid and unpaid internships available.
For more information: Jim McEachern, Unit Director, Boys and Girls Club of Worcester, 2 Ionic, Worcester, Massachusetts 01608; (508)753-3377; (508)754-2686 (fax).

BOYS AND GIRLS CLUB OF ZIONSVILLE
Zionsville, Indiana
Description: Organization providing educational, recreational, and cultural programming for youth.
Open to: High school seniors and graduates.
Type: Paid and unpaid internships available.
For more information: Ms. Cary Bowman, Program Director, Boys and Girls Club of Zionville, 1575 Mulberry Street, Zionsville, Indiana 46077; (317) 873-6670.

BOYS/GIRLS CLUBS OF GREATER MARLBOROUGH, INC.
Marlborough, Massachusetts
Description: Organization providing educational, recreational and cultural programming for youth.
Open to: High school seniors and graduates.
Type: Unpaid
For more information: Ms. Chris Duane, Program Coordinator, Boys/Girls Clubs of Greater Marlborough, Inc., 169 Pleasant Street, Marlborough, Massachusetts 01752; (508)485-4912.

CALIFORNIA CHILD YOUTH AND FAMILY COALITION'S CALIFORNIA YOUTH CRISIS LINE
Sacramento, California
Description: Nonprofit organization providing support to the underprivileged.

Open to: High school students and graduates.

Type: Unpaid

For more information: Henry L. Horn, Project Director, California Child Youth and Family Coalition's California Youth Crisis Line, 2424 Castro Way, Sacramento, California 95818; (916)739-6912; E-mail henrylhorn@aol.com.

CALIFORNIA NATIONAL ORGANIZATION FOR WOMEN, INC.

Sacramento, California

Description: Women's advocacy group working on state level.

Open to: All.

Positions available: Internships open year-round.

Type: Unpaid.

For more information: Elena Perez, Executive Assistant, California National Organization for Women, Inc., 926 J Street, Suite 820, Sacramento, California 95814; (916)442-3414; (916)442-6942 (fax); E-mail canow@canow.org; URL http://www.canow.org.

CAMP FIRE BOYS AND GIRLS, NORTH GARLAND COUNCIL

Ashburn Hills, Michigan

Description: Organization providing informal educational programming.

Open to: High school students and graduates.

Type: Paid and unpaid internships available.

For more information: Dana Garwood, Program Director, Camp Fire Boys and Girls, North Garland Council, 1267 Doris Road, Auburn Hills, Michigan 48326; (810)377-2888.

CENTRAL FAMILY BRANCH, YMCA CENTER

Portland, Oregon

Description: Athletic and aquatic facility.

Open to: High school seniors.

Type: Unpaid

For more information: Karen Erskine, Program Director, Central Family Branch, YMCA Center, 6036 SE Foster Road, Portland, Oregon 97206; (503)774-3311.

CENTRO PARA LOS ADOLESCENTES DE SAN MIGUEL DE ALLENDE

Guanajuato, Mexico

Description: Nonprofit health and social service organization.

Open to: High school students and graduates.

Type: Unpaid

For more information: Clerkship Program, Centro para los Adolescentes de San Miguel de Allende, Umaran 62, San Miguel de Allende, Guanajuato, Mexico 37700; 52-415-2-26-88.

CHRYSALIS: A CENTER FOR WOMEN

Minneapolis, Minnesota

Description: Multi-service center for women offering support services in mental health, chemical dependency, legal assistance, and parenting services.

Open to: Students ages 16-18 and high school graduates.

Type: Unpaid

For more information: Tiffany Muller, Volunteer Coordinator, Chrysalis: A Center for Women, 2650 Nicollet Avenue South, Minneapolis, Minnesota 55408-1662; (612) 871-0118; (612)870-2403 (fax); E-mail tmuller@chrysaliswomen.org; URL http://chrysaliswomen.org.

CLINICAL DIRECTORS NETWORK OF REGION II

New York, New York

Description: Network of doctors, dentists and nurses providing services for the poor and disadvantaged.

Open to: High school seniors.

Type: Unpaid

For more information: Internship Coordinator, Clinical Directors Network of Region II, 54 West 39th Street, 11th Floor, New York, New York 10018; (212) 382-0699; (212)382-0669 (fax); URL http://www.CDNEtwork.org.

COMMUNITY BOARD PROGRAM

San Francisco, California

Description: Organization providing conflict resolution.

Open to: High school students and graduates.

Type: Unpaid

For more information: Terry Amsler, Executive Director, Community Board Program, 1540 Market Street, Suite 490, San Francisco, California 94102; (415)552-1250.

COMMUNITY HARVEST FOOD BANK

Fort Wayne, Indiana

Description: Organization that collects and distributes food.

Open to: High school students and graduates.

Type: Unpaid

For more information: Mike Eling, Program Coordinator, Community Harvest Food Bank, P.O. Box 10967, Fort Wayne, Indiana 46855; (219)447-3696.

CYSTIC FIBROSIS FOUNDATION

San Francisco, California

Project Location: 70 field and branch offices across the country; region headquarters for Northern California and Western Nevada.

Description: Organization established to raise money for research, discover a cure, and aid those who have cystic fibrosis. To do this, many special events must be organized.

Positions Available: Volunteer and internship.

Cost/Compensation: Unpaid.

For more information: Tania Holbrook, Special Events Coordinator, Cystic Fibrosis Foundation, 417 Montgomery Street, Suite 404, San Francisco, California 94104; (415)677-0155.

DOWNTOWN ATLANTA YMCA
Atlanta, Georgia
Description: Nonprofit organization providing athletic facilities, activities, child care and community services.
Open to: High school students and graduates.
Type: Unpaid
For more information: Heather Etzler, Fitness Coordinator, Downtown Atlanta YMCA, 260 Peachtree Street, 2nd Floor, Atlanta, Georgia 30303; (404)527-7682 (fax).

ELIZABETH GLASER PEDIATRIC AIDS FOUNDATION
Santa Monica, California
Description: Foundation raising funds for AIDS research.
Open to: High school seniors, college, graduate, and medical school students.
Positions available: Internships should be oriented towards basic medical research, clinical research (including epidemiological), or psychosocial research.
Type: Paid - $2,000 for 320 hours of work.
Other information: Application required. Students must apply through a sponsor who has expertise in pediatric HIV/AIDS. It is the responsibility of students to find their sponsor.
For more information: Chris Hudnall, Elizabeth Glaser Pediatric AIDS Foundation, 2950 31st Street, Suite 125, Santa Monica, California 90405; (310)314-1459; (310)314-1469 (fax); E-mail research@pedaids.org; URL http://www.pedAIDS.org.

ELIZABETH STONE HOUSE
Jamaica Plain, Massachusetts
Description: Shelter for battered women and their children.
Open to: High school seniors and graduates.
Type: Unpaid
For more information: Sandra Newson, Outreach and Education Coordinator, Elizabeth Stone House, P.O. Box 59, Jamaica Plain, Massachusetts 02130; (617) 522-3417; E-mail stonehse@aol.com.

FAMILY PEACE CENTER
Honolulu, Hawaii
Description: Center providing assistance to victims of domestic violence.
Open to: High school seniors and graduates.
Type: Unpaid
For more information: Lorrie Alfonsi, Program Director, Family Peace Center, 938 Austin Lane, Honolulu, Hawaii 96817; (808)845-1445.

FAMILY Y CENTER (YMCA) OF BATTLE CREEK
Battle Creek, Michigan
Description: Facility providing athletic and social activities.
Open to: High school seniors and graduates.
Type: Paid and unpaid internships available.
For more information: Dan Fullenkamp, Director of Programming, Family Y Center of Battle Creek, 182 Capital Avenue, NE, Battle Creek, Michigan 49017; (616)962-7551.

GIRLS INCORPORATED OF BLOUNT COUNTY
Maryville, Tennessee
Description: Organization providing all day summer camp.
Open to: High school students.
Type: Unpaid
For more information: Janet T. Bosman, Executive Director, Girls Incorporated of Blount County, 715 West Broadway, Maryville, Tennessee 37801-4715; (423)983-7616.

GIRLS INCORPORATED OF HAMBLEN COUNTY
Morristown, Tennessee
Description: Facility providing programming for girls.
Open to: High school seniors and graduates.
Type: Paid and unpaid internships available.
For more information: Tish Osbourne, Executive Director, Girls Incorporated of Hamblen County, P.O. Box 3058, Morristown, Tennessee 37815; (423)581-4430; E-mail girlsinc@kidsurf.net.

GIRLS INCORPORATED OF METROPOLITAN DALLAS
Dallas, Texas
Description: Nonprofit organization providing assistance for disadvantaged girls.
Open to: High school students and graduates.
Type: Unpaid
For more information: Brenda Snitzer, Director of Development, Girls Incorporated of Metropolitan Dallas, 2040 Empire Central Drive, Dallas, Texas 75235; (214)654-4536.

HABITAT FOR HUMANITY
Americus, Georgia
Description: Organization providing housing for families in need.
Open to: High school seniors and graduates.
Type: Paid
For more information: Director of Human Resources, Habitat for Humanity International, 121 Habitat Street, Americus, Georgia 31709-3498; (912)924-6935 Ext. 124.

HARDEE COUNTY FAMILY YMCA
Wauchula, Florida
Description: Organization dedicated to strengthening families.
Open to: High school seniors and graduates.
Type: Unpaid
For more information: Cassandra White, Executive Director, Hardee County Family YMCA, 119 South Florida Avenue, Wauchula, Florida 33873; (941)773-3411.

H.O.M.E.
Orland, Maine
Description: Nonprofit cooperative community.
Open to: High school students.
Type: Unpaid
For more information: Volunteer Coordinator, H.O.M.E., P.O. Box 10, Orland, Maine 04472; (207)469-7961.

HUMAN SERVICE ALLIANCE
Winston-Salem, North Carolina
Description: Nonprofit organization providing free housing for the terminally ill and services for families with developmentally disabled children.
Open to: High school students.
Type: Unpaid
For more information: Coordinator of Internships, Human Service Alliance, 3983 Old Greensboro Road, Winston-Salem, North Carolina 27101; (910)761-8745.

INTERNATIONAL PLANNED PARENTHOOD FEDERATION
New York, New York
Description: Reproductive health care agencies located throughout the United States and worldwide.
Open to: High school students and graduates.
Type: Unpaid
For more information: Volunteer Coordinator, Planned Parenthood, Federation of America, 810 Seventh Avenue, New York, New York 10019; (800) 473-7732.

KIPS BAY BOYS AND GIRLS CLUB
Bronx, New York
Description: Organization providing athletic and social programming for boys and girls.
Open to: High school seniors and graduates.
Type: Unpaid
For more information: Dale B. Drakeford, Associate Executive Director, Kips Bay Boys and Girls Club, 1930 Randall Avenue, Bronx, New York 10473; (718)893-8254.

L'ARCHE MOBILE
Mobile, Alabama
Project Location: Mobile, Alabama
Description: Communities where people with mental disability live with those who help them.
Cost/Compensation: Boarding and lodging are provided.
For more information: Marty O'Malley, 152 Mobile, 151 South Ann Street, Mobile, Alabama 36604; (334) 438-2094; (334)433-5835 (fax); E-mail larchmob@acan.net; URL http://www2.acan.net/~//archmob/.

LAWRENCE GIRLS CLUB
Lawrence, Massachusetts
Description: After-school program for girls.
Open to: High school students and graduates.
Type: Unpaid
For more information: Jull Nelson, Unit Director, Lawrence Girls Club, 136 Water Street, Lawrence, Massachusetts 01840; (508)683-2747.

MULTIFAITH AIDS PROJECT OF SEATTLE
Seattle, Washington
Description: Organization providing housing to low-income and homeless individuals with AIDS.
Open to: High school students.
Type: Unpaid
For more information: Debbie Cuddihy, Volunteer Program Director, Multifaith AIDS Project of Seattle, 1729 Harvard Avenue, Seattle, Washington 98122; (206)324-2216.

NATIONAL STUDENT CAMPAIGN AGAINST HUNGER AND HOMELESSNESS
Los Angeles, California
Description: Organization committed to fighting hunger and homelessness.
Open to: High school students and graduates.
Type: Unpaid
For more information: Julie Miles, Executive Director, National Student Campaign Against Hunger and Homelessness, 11965 Venice Boulevard, Suite 408, Los Angeles, California 90066; (800)664-8647 Ext. 324; E-mail NSCAH@aol.com.

THE NEW YORK HOSPITAL - CORNELL MEDICAL CENTER
White Plains, New York
Description: Psychiatric facility.
Open to: High school seniors.
Type: Unpaid
For more information: Diane A. Clark, MA, Director of Volunteers, The New York Hospital - Cornell Medical Center, Westchester Division, 21 Bloomingdale Road, White Plains, New York 10605; (914)997-5780.

FOCUS ON...
THE SMITHSONIAN

For more information, visit the website or write to:

**Intern Services
Center for Museum Studies
900 Jefferson Drive, SW
Room 2235-MRC 427
Smithsonian Institution
Washington, DC 20560
(202)357-3102**

*Interns must be at least 16-years-old.

The Smithsonian is the world's largest museum complex — incorporating 16 museums and galleries plus the National Zoo. With over 600 internships offered each year, it is quite possibly the largest museum internship program in the world.

URL http://www.si.edu/cms/ intern.htm

OXFAM AMERICA
Boston, Massachusetts
Description: International organization that provides development and disaster relief assistance.
Open to: High school students and graduates.
Type: Unpaid
For more information: Diana Hughes, Volunteer Coordinator, Oxfam America, 26 West Street, Boston, Massachusetts 02111-1206; (617)728-2561; E-mail diana@igc.abc.org.

PENN LAUREL GIRL SCOUT COUNCIL
York, Pennsylvania
Description: Girls organization.
Open to: High school seniors and graduates.
Type: Paid
For more information: Anne Marie Wells, Camp Administrator, Penn Laurel Girl Scout Council, 1600 Mount Zion Road, York, Pennsylvania 17402; (717) 757-3561.

SAN DIEGUITO BOYS AND GIRLS CLUBS
Solana Beach, California
Description: Agency providing programming and support for youth.
Open to: High school students and graduates.
Type: Unpaid
For more information: Duncan Smith, Director of Program, San Dieguito Boys and Girls Clubs, P.O. Box 615, Solana Beach, California 92075; (619)755-9371.

SARAH HEINZ HOUSE
Pittsburgh, Pennsylvania
Description: Recreation center for youth.
Open to: High school seniors and graduates.
Type: Paid
For more information: Sherri L. Kotwica, Program Director, Sarah Heinz House, East Ohio and Heinz Streets, Pittsburgh, Pennsylvania 15212; (412)231-2377.

SCOTT COUNTY FAMILY YMCA

Davenport, Iowa

Description: Agency providing athletic and developmental programming.

Open to: High school seniors and graduates.

Type: Unpaid

For more information: Bridget Cullen, Senior Program Director, Scott County Family YMCA, 606 West Second Street, Davenport Iowa 52801; (319) 322-7171.

SPANISH EDUCATION DEVELOPMENT CENTER

Washington, D.C.

Description: The SED Center provides educational programs for children age 3-4, their families, and adults in the Washington, metropolitan area.

Open to: High school students and graduates.

Positions available: Assistant teacher.

Type: Unpaid

For more information: Doris Estrada, Director, Volunteer Program, Spanish Education Development (SED) Center, 1840 Kalorama Road, NW, Washington, DC 20009; (202)462-8848; (202)462-6886 (fax); E-mail sedcen@erols.com; URL http://www. sedcenter.com.

SUMMERBRIDGE NATIONAL

San Francisco, California

Description: Educational enrichment program.

Open to: High school students, seniors and graduates.

Type: Unpaid

For more information: Teneh Cleveland, Faculty Development Coordinator, 1902 Van Ness Avenue, San Francisco, California 94109; (415)749-2037; E-mail sbnation@aol.com.

TEXAS ALLIANCE FOR HUMAN NEEDS

Austin, Texas

Description: Statewide alliance dedicated to serving the needs of low- and moderate-income families.

Open to: High school students and graduates.

Type: Paid and unpaid internships available.

For more information: Ms. Jude Filler, Executive Director, Texas Alliance for Human Needs, 1016 East 12th Street, Austin, Texas 78702-1056; (512)474-5019; (512)474-5058 (fax); E-mail hn0796@handsnet.org.

UNITED WAY OF HOWARD COUNTY

Kokomo, Indiana

Description: Fundraising and service agency dedicated to meeting community needs.

Open to: High school students and graduates.

Type: Unpaid

For more information: Lori Tate, Vice President of Operations, United Way of Howard County, 210 West Walnut, Kokomo, Indiana 46901; (317)457-6691.

UNITED WAY OF WACO

Waco, Texas

Description: Fundraising organization for member agencies.

Open to: High school students and graduates.

Type: Unpaid

For more information: Dorothy Wienecke, Communication Coordinator/Volunteer Center Director, United Way of Waco, 5400 Boxque Boulevard #225, Waco, Texas 76710-4459; (254)741-1980; (254)741-1984 (fax).

VALLEY OF THE MOON BOYS AND GIRLS CLUB

Sonoma, California

Description: Organization providing youth development activities.

Open to: High school students and graduates.

Type: Unpaid

For more information: Sharon Somogyi, Program Director, Valley of the Moon Boys and Girls Club, P.O. Box 780, Sonoma, California 95476; (707)938-8544.

WASHINGTON D.C. RAPE CRISIS CENTER

Washington, D.C.

Description: Organization providing counseling and assistance and community education programming.

Open to: Juniors and seniors in high school, college students, and college graduates.

Type: Unpaid

For more information: Genevieve Villamora, Internship Coordinator, Washington, D.C., Rape Crisis Center, P.O. Box 34125, Washington, DC 20043; (202) 387-0789; (202)387-3812 (fax); E-mail dcrcc@erols.com; URL http://www.dcrcc.org.

WEST ROXBURY/ROSLINDALE YMCA

West Roxbury, Massachusetts

Description: Organization providing recreational, social, and developmental programming.

Open to: High school students and graduates.

Type: Unpaid

For more information: Arthur Leger, Youth and Family Director, West Roxbury/Roslindale YMCA, 15 Bellevue Street, West Roxbury, Masschusetts 02132; (617)323-3200.

WINANT-CLAYTON VOLUNTEERS

New York, New York

Description: Agency dedicated to community service projects in Britain.

Open to: High school seniors and graduates.

Type: Paid

For more information: Nanette Rousseau, Coordinator of Volunteers, Winant-Clayton Volunteers, 109 East

50th Street, New York, New York 10022; (212)751-1616.

YMCA Camp Potawotami
South Milford, Indiana
Description: Residential camp.
Open to: High school students and graduates.
Type: Paid
For more information: David Steele, Executive Director, YMCA Camp Potawotami, P.O. Box 38, South Milford, Indiana 46786; (219)351-2525;
E-mail ymcacamp@kuntry.com; URL http://www.camp-potawotami.org.

YMCA of Greater Buffalo-Delaware Branch
Buffalo, New York
Description: Organization providing recreational and developmental programming.
Open to: High school students and graduates.
Type: Unpaid
For more information: Bill Jedlicka, Executive Director, YMCA of Greater Buffalo-Delaware Branch, 2564 Delaware Avenue, Buffalo, New York 14216; (716) 875-1283.

Youth for Understanding International Exchange
Washington, D.C.
Description: Agency that offers high school student exchange programs around the world. Internships available in offices throughout the U.S.
Open to: High school juniors, seniors, and graduates.
Type: Unpaid
For more information: Internship Coordinator, Youth for Understanding International Exchange, 3501 Neward Street, NW, Washington, DC 20016; (800)424-3691 Ext. 116.

Youth Opportunities Upheld
Worcester, Massachusetts
Description: Association assisting troubled youth and their families.
Open to: High school students and graduates.
Type: Unpaid
For more information: Nathan Peterson, Program Coordinator, Court Volunteers, Youth Opportunities Upheld, 81 Plantation Street, Worcester, Massachusetts 01604; (508)849-5600 Ext. 337.

YWCA of St. Paul
St. Paul, Minnesota
Description: Organization committed to serving women and families.
Open to: High school students and graduates.
Positions available: Teen counselors and summer positions.
Type: Paid - hourly wage.

For more information: Elizabeth Ellis, Volunteer Coordinator, YWCA of St. Paul, 198 Western Avenue, North, St. Paul, Minnesota 55102-1790; (651)222-3741; (651)222-6307 (fax);
E-mail eellis@ywcaofstpaul.org.

YWCA of Warren
Warren, Ohio
Description: Organization committed to serving women and families.
Open to: High school seniors and graduates.
Type: Paid
For more information: Debbie Budd, Program Director, YWCA of Warren, 375 North Park Avenue, Warren, Ohio 44481; (330)393-6483 (fax).

INTERNATIONAL

Africa Fund - American Committee on Africa
New York, New York
Description: Nonprofit organization dedicated to encouraging development and democracy in Africa.
Open to: High school students and graduates.
Type: Unpaid
For more information: Annie King, Office Manager, Africa Fund - American Committee on Africa, 50 Broad Street, Suite 711 New York, New York 10004; (212)785-1024; (212)785-1078 (fax); E-mail africa-fund@igc.apc.org; URL http://www.prairienet.org/acas/afund.html.

Amnesty International, Midwest Region
Chicago, Illinois
Description: International human rights organization.
Open to: High school students and graduates.
Type: Unpaid
For more information: Audrey Randall, Office Administrator, Amnesty International, Midwest Region, 53 West Jackson, Suite 1162, Chicago, Illinois 60604-3606; (312)427-2060;
E-mail olrandall@aivsa.usa.com; URL http://www.amnesty-usa.org.

Arms Control Association
Washington, D.C.
Description: Organization committed to promoting arms control and its relationship to national security. Publisher of *Arms Control Today*.
Open to: High school students.
Type: Paid
For more information: Internship Coordinator, The Arms Control Association, 1726 M Street, NW, Suite 201, Washington, DC 20036; (202)463-8270.

CAMP COUNSELORS, USA
Sausalito, California
Description: Coordinates exchange programs for summer camps around the world.
Open to: High school seniors and graduates.
Type: Unpaid
For more information: Emily E. Casperson, Outbound Program Director, Camp Counselors, USA, Marina Office Plaza, 2330 Marinshipway, Suite 250, Sausalito, California 94965; (800)999-2267; E-mail 102642.3531@compuserve.com.

COUNCIL ON HEMISPHERIC AFFAIRS
Washington, D.C.
Description: Information gathering and research organization studying Latin-American/U.S. relations.
Open to: High school students and graduates.
Type: Unpaid
For more information: Secretary for Internships, Council on Hemispheric Affairs, 724 Ninth Street, NW, Suite 401, Washington, DC 20001; (202)393-3322; E-mail coha@the-hermes.net; URL http://www.the_hermes.net/~coha.

FOREIGN POLICY RESEARCH INSTITUTE
Philadelphia, Pennsylvania
Description: Institute conducting research and educational programming relating to foreign affairs.
Open to: High school seniors.
Type: Unpaid
For more information: Internship Coordinator, Foreign Policy Research Institute, 1528 Walnut Street, Suite 610, Philadelphia, PA 19102; (215)732-3774.

GLOBAL VOLUNTEERS
St. Paul, Minnesota
Description: Coordinates volunteers with organizations that need their help around the world.
Open to: High school students, seniors, and graduates.
Type: Cost of $450-$2,395.
Other information: Volunteers under 18 must be accompanied by a guardian.
For more information: Volunteer Coordinator, Global Volunteers, 375 East Little Canada Road, St. Paul, Minnesota 55117; (800)487-1074; URL http://www.globalvolunteers.org.

INTERNATIONAL TRADE COMMISSION
Washington, D.C.
Description: Organization assisting businesses in trading overseas. Also regulates foreign trade policy.
Open to: High school seniors.
Type: Paid and unpaid internships available.
For more information: Michelle Johnson, International Trade Administration, 14th Street and Constitution Avenue, NW, Room 4809, Washington, DC 20230; (202)482-3301.

INTERSPEAK LTD.
Chester, England
Description: Provides youth with European work opportunities.
Open to: High school students over 16 years old with relevant language ability.
Positions Available: Office-based: law, banking, media, retail, manufacturing, marketing, computer, word processing, or hotel work, shops, childcare, tourism, and leisure.
Type: $495 placement fee and approximately $260 per week for accommodations. Housing is in homes and most meals are provided.
Other information: Family-based accommodations are available for those students wishing to learn a language but not interested in a placement or internship.
For more information: Irene Radclyffe, Interspeak Ltd., The Pages, Whitchurch road, Handley, Chester, CH39OT England; +441829-770101; +4441829-770255 (fax).

JAPAN-AMERICA SOCIETY OF WASHINGTON
Washington, D.C.
Description: Nonprofit group promoting understanding between the U.S. and Japan.
Open to: High school students.
Type: Unpaid
For more information: Internship Coordinator, Japan-America Society of Washington, 1020 19th Street LL#40, Washington, DC 20036; (202)833-2210.

JUSTACT: YOUTH ACTION FOR GLOBAL JUSTICE
San Francisco, California
Location: San Francisco, CA, International (volunteer opportunities), Bike-Aid (cross-country bicycle ride).
Positions Available: Office management and administration internship, communications and public relations internships, education and organizing program intern, Bike-Aid internships and volunteer opportunities, Alternative Opportunities program intern, and international volunteer opportunities.
Description: Organization working with youth to develop a life-long commitment to social and economic justice internationally. JustAct provides a network for students and graduates linking them to educational and volunteer opportunities worldwide.
Open to: High school students, college students and graduates.
Type: Varies. Contact JustAct for details.
For more information: Wendy Phillips, Internship Coordinator, JustAct: Youth ACTion for Global JUSTice, 333 Valencia Street, Suite 101, San Francisco, California 94103; (415)431-4204; (415)431-5953 (fax); E-mail info@justact.org; URL http://www.justact.org.

NATIONAL REGISTRATION CENTER FOR STUDY ABROAD (NRCSA)
Milwaukee, Wisconsin
Description: NRCSA acts as an information and registration office for over 100 language schools in 25 countries, with about 20 that will accept students under age 18. There are four program types: Mexico Discovery, Total Immersion – Spanish; Total Immersion – French; and Total Immersion – German. Teen programs, escorted or unescorted, available in several Latin American countries as well as French speaking Canada, France, Switzerland, Austria, Germany, and Spain.
Open to: Ages 12-17, depending on program.
Cost/Compensation: $500-$1,750. Airfare is additional and can be coordinated by the NRCSA offices.
For more information: National Registration Center for Study Abroad (NRCSA), P. O. Box 1393, Milwaukee, Wisconsin 53201; (414)278-0631; (414)271-8884 (fax); E-mail teenstudy@nrcsa.com; URL http://www.nrcsa.com.

UNITED STATES AGENCY FOR INTERNATIONAL DEVELOPMENT
Washington, D.C.
Description: Primary organization providing U.S. foreign aid.
Open to: High school juniors and seniors.
Type: Paid
For more information: Student Programs Coordinator, U.S. Agency for International Development, 2401 E Street, NW, Room 1026, Washington, DC 20523-0116; (202)663-3340.

VOLUNTEERS FOR ISRAEL
New York, New York
Description: Organization providing assistance to Israel through volunteer work.
Open to: High school seniors and graduates.
Type: Cost - transportation to Israel.
For more information: Volunteer Coordinator, Volunteers for Israel, 330 West 42nd Street, Suite 1618, New York, NY 10036-6029; (212)643-4848; E-mail vol4israel@aol.com.

WOMEN'S INTERNATIONAL LEAGUE FOR PEACE AND FREEDOM
New York, New York
Philadelphia, Pennsylvania
Geneva, Switzerland
Description: Organization promoting political rather than military solutions to international conflict.
Open to: Female high school students.
Type: Paid and unpaid internships available.
For more information:
New York: Director, WILPF Office at the United Nations, 777 United Nations Plaza, 6th Floor, New York,

New York 10017; (212)682-1265.
Philadelphia: Internship Coordinator, WILPF National Office, 1213 Race Street, Philadelphia, Pennsylvania 19107; (215)563-7110; E-mail wilpfnatl@igc.org.
Geneva: SILPF International Secretariat, 1, rue de Varembe, CP 28, CH-1211, Geneva 20, Switzerland; 41-22-733-615.

NATURE/RECREATION

ARANSAS NATIONAL WILDLIFE REFUGE
Austwell, Texas
Description: Wildlife refuge.
Open to: High school students and graduates.
Type: Unpaid
For more information: Bernice Jackson, Outdoor Recreation Planner/Volunteer Coordinator, Aransas National Wildlife Refuge, P.O. Box 100, Austwell, Texas 77950; (512)286-3559.

BIKE-AID
San Francisco, California
Description: Bicycle expedition dedicated to increasing awareness of environmental and development issues.
Open to: High school students and graduates.
Type: Unpaid
For more information: Internship Coordinator, Overseas Development Network/Bike-Aid, 333 Valencia Street, Suite 330, San Francisco, California 94103-3547; (800) RIDE-808; E-mail odn@igc.apc.org.

BROOKLYN BOTANIC GARDEN
Brooklyn, New York
Description: Botanical garden.
Open to: High school juniors and seniors.
Type: Paid
For more information: Internship Coordinator, Brooklyn Botanic Garden, 1000 Washington Avenue, Brooklyn, New York 11225-099; (718)622-4433 Ext. 216.

CALVIN CREST CAMP, RETREAT AND CONFERENCE CENTER
Fremont, Nebraska
Description: Christian (Presbyterian) co-ed residential summer camp. Season from 6/1-8/25.
Open to: Must be 18-years-old.
Positions Available: Lifeguards, food service staff, housekeeping staff, group counselors, and wranglers.
Cost/Compensation: Room, board, and competitive salary.
For more information: Doug Morton, Administrator, Calvin Crest Camp, Conference and Retreat Center,

2870 County Road 13, Fremont, Nebraska 68025; (402)628-6455; (402)628-8255 (fax); E-mail calvincrest@navix.net; URL http://members.home.net/calvincrest.

CAMP BERACHAH
Auburn, Washington
Description: Residential and day camps for ages 5-18.
Open to: High school students. Approximately 15 positions available.
Positions Available: Counselors, recreation director, crafts director, lifeguards, horsemanship wrangler/instructor, safari guides, mountain bike guides, kitchen, housekeeping, and maintenance.
For more information: James Richey or Scott Rossiter, Program Director and Program Assistant, Camp Berachah, 19830 Southeast 328th Place, Auburn, Washington 98092; (253)939-0488 or (800)859-CAMP; (253)833-7027 (fax); E-mail berachah@tcmnet.com; URL http://tcmnet.com/~berachah/.

CAMP NETIMUS FOR GIRLS
Milford, Pennsylvania
Description: Residential summer girls camp with 2-, 4-, or 8-week programs.
Open to: Students age 14 and over. Counselors have to be 21+.
Positions Available: Counselors, specialists, and counselors-in-training (CIT).
Cost/Compensation: $2,400-$2,600 for 4 weeks.
Other information: Take part in land sports, arts, crafts, performing arts, water sports, riding, adventure, and discovery activities. Learn and gain insight into the obligations, responsibilities, rewards, and goals of a camp counselor in a fun environment.
For more information: Widge Hazell, Assistant Director, Camp Netimus, 708 Raymondskill Road, Milford, Pennsylvania 18337; (570)296-6131; (717)296-6128 (fax); E-mail netimus@warwick.net; URL http://www.netimus.com.

CAMP WASHINGTON
Lakeside, Connecticut
Description: Residential and day camp for children ages 5-18.
Open to: High school students. Approximately 12 positions available.
Positions Available: Counselors in Training (16/17), general cabin counselors, program staff, lifeguards, office help, and kitchen help.
Cost/Compensation: Room and board, salary (except CIT program – fee is $200).
Other information: Episcopal diocesan camp offering traditional program plus many specialized programs such as theater, choir, community service, family, mini-camping skills, and wilderness tripping programs. Also offers an intensive Counselor in Training program for eight weeks of the summer season.
For more information: Elia Vecchitto, Camp Director, Camp Washington, 190 Kenyon Road, Lakeside, Connecticut 06758; (860)567-9623; (860)567-3037 (fax); E-mail elia_v@hotmail.com.

CAPITAL CAMPS
Waynesboro, Pennsylvania
Description: Jewish residential community camp. Sponsor leadership trip to Israel.
Open to: CITS (age 17); staff (18+)
Positions available: Counselors, specialists, and counselors-in-training.
Cost/Compensation: CITS ($700); staff ($800-$1,500).
For more information: Faye Bousel, Executive Director, Capital Camps, 133 Rollins Avenue, Unit 4, Rockville, Maryland 20852; (301)468-2267; (301)468-1719 (fax); E-mail staff@capitalcamps.com; URL http://www.capitalcamps.com.

CENTER FOR HEALTH, ENVIRONMENT, AND JUSTICE
Falls Church, Virginia
Description: Organization providing assistance for citizen's groups fighting pollution.
Open to: High school seniors.
Type: N/A
For more information: Barbara Sullivan, Internship Coordinator, Center for Health, Environment, and Justice, P.O. Box 6806, Falls Church, Virginia 22040; E-mail barbaras@essential.org; URL http://www.essential.org/CCHW.

CITY OF NEW YORK PARKS & RECREATION
New York, New York
Description: Organization overseeing the management of New York's parks and recreation activities.
Open to: High school students.
Type: Unpaid
For more information: Internship Coordinator, City of New York Parks & Recreation, 830 Fifth Avenue, New York, New York 10021; (212)360-1349.

CLEARWATER
Poughkeepsie, New York
Description: The sloop, *Clearwater*, is a classroom offering programs on environment, biology, and history. There are opportunities to become a sailing apprentice or an education assistant.
Open to: Students age 16 and up.
Cost/Compensation: Apprentices and education assistants get room and board on the sloop, plus $25-50/week. Crews receive $140-$300/week. Food and lodging are rustic.
For more information: Captain, Clearwater, 112 Mar-

ket Street, Poughkeepsie, New York 12601-4095; (914)454-7673 or (800 677-5667; URL http://www. clearwater.org.

EDUCATIONAL COMMUNICATIONS, INC.: ECONEWS TELEVISION, ENVIRONMENTAL DIRECTIONS RADIO, ECOLOGY CENTER OF SOUTHERN CALIFORNIA, PROJECT ECOTOURISM

Los Angeles, California
Description: Environmental broadcasting and conservation association.
Open to: High school students.
Type: Unpaid
For more information: Leslie Lewis, Internship Coordinator, Educational Communications, Inc., P.O. Box 351419, Los Angeles, California 90035; (310)559-9160; E-mail ecnp@aol.com; URL http://home. earthlink.net/~dragonflight/ecoprojects.htm.

EL MALPAIS NATIONAL CONSERVATION AREA AND NATIONAL MONUMENT

Grants, New Mexico
Description: Conservation area surrounding Grant's Lava Flows.
Open to: High school students and graduates.
Type: Unpaid
For more information: Peg Sorensen, Volunteer Coordinator/Park Ranger, El Malpais National Conservation Area and National Monument, 2001 East Santa Fe Avenue, Grants, New Mexico 87020; (505)287-7911; E-mail psorense@nmo151wp.nmso.nm.blm.gov.

ENVIRONMENTAL RESOURCE CENTER

Ketchum, Idaho
Description: Environmental organization providing resources and educational programming.
Open to: High school students and graduates.
Type: Unpaid
For more information: Anita Smith, Executive Director, Environmental Resource Center, P.O. 819, 411 East Sixth Street, Ketchum, Idaho 83340; (208)726-4333; E-mail anitasb@sunvalley.net.

ERIE NATIONAL WILDLIFE REFUGE

Guys Mills, Pennsylvania
Description: Wildlife refuge.
Open to: High school students and graduates.
Type: Unpaid
For more information: Janet A. Marvin, Volunteer Coordinator, Erie National Wildlife Refuge, 11296 Wood Duck Lane, Guys Mills, Pennsylvania 16327; (814)789-3585; E-mail r5rw_ernwr@mail.fws.gov.

FLORIDA PARK SERVICE

Tallahassee, Florida
Description: Agency overseeing the management of 145 state parks.

Open to: High school seniors and graduates.
Type: Unpaid
For more information: Phillip A. Werndli, Volunteer Coordinator, Florida Park Service, 300 Commonwealth Boulevard, MS 535, Tallahassee, Florida 32399; (904)488-8243; E-mail werndli@ngw.dep. state.fl.us.

FRIENDS OF THE ROUGE

Detroit, Michigan
Description: Organization dedicated to the restoration and protection of the Rouge River.
Open to: High school students and graduates.
Positions Available: Internships and volunteer opportunities.
Type: Unpaid
Other Information: Teens can participate in water quality monitoring, storm drain stenciling, and office administration.
For more information: Jim Graham, Executive Director, Friends of the Rouge, 950 Michigan Building, 22586 Ann Arbor Trail, Dearborn Heights, Michigan 48127; (313)792-9900; (313)792-9628 (fax); E-mail execdirector@therouge.org; URL http://www. therouge.org.

GREEN CITY PROJECT

San Francisco, California
Description: Environmental education organization.
Open to: High school students and graduates.
Positions Available: Administrative intern, education intern, and calendar intern.
Type: Unpaid
For more information: Brian Block, Programs Director, Green City Project, P.O. Box 31251, San Francisco, California 94131; (415)285-6556; (415)285-6563 (fax); E-mail planetdrum@igc.org.

THE MARITIME AQUARIUM

Norwalk, Connecticut
Description: An aquarium featuring over 200 species of Long Island Sound.
Open to: High school seniors and college students.
Positions available: Intern position and part-time marine educator.
Type: Paid and unpaid.
Other information: Interns rotate through 3 departments: education/programs, the aquarium, and volunteers where they learn all facets of running an aquarium.
For more information: Lauren Sikorski, Sound Science Coordinator/Internship Coordinator, The Maritime Aquarium, 10 North Water Street, Norwalk, Connecticut 06854; (203)852-0700 Ext. 269; (203) 855-0829 (fax); E-mail interncoor@aol.com.

NORTH BEACH OUTFITTERS, INC.
Duck, North Carolina
Description: Provide adventure-travel, clothes, gear, and kayaks.
Open to: Must be 18 or older.
Positions available: Sales associate. Opportunity to learn business practices, marketing techniques, and display. Must be people-oriented and show initiative in work behavior.
Cost/Compensation: $5.50/hour until trained, then $6.00/hour. Bonus for staying until end of contract. Staff housing available; rent taken from paycheck. Store is located on the sound side and beach is two blocks away.
For more information: Sandra or George Keefe, Owners, North Beach Outfitters, Inc., 1240 Duck Road, Suite 10, Duck, North Carolina 27949; (252) 261-6262; (252)261-7012 (fax); E-mail nboduck@pinn.net.

NORTH CAROLINA AMATEUR SPORTS
Research Triangle Park, North Carolina
Description: Organization supporting the Olympics through amateur sports programming. Host State Games of North Carolina and Cycle North Carolina.
Open to: High school students and graduates.
Type: Volunteer opportunities available. Paid and unpaid internships available to students who have completed at least one year of college.
For more information: Linda Smith, Director of Operations, North Carolina Amateur Sports, P.O. Box 12727, Research Triangle Park, North Carolina 27709; (919)361-2559 (fax).

NORTH CAROLINA STATE PARKS AND RECREATION, MOUNT MITCHELL STATE PARK
Burnsville, North Carolina
Description: State park.
Open to: High school students eligible for park attendant or refreshment stand clerk position. Prefer graduate with experience for refreshment stand manager and naturalist positions.
Positions available: Park attendant, refreshment stand manager, refreshment stand clerk, and naturalist.
Type: Park attendant and refreshment stand clerk ($6.00/hr); refreshment stand manager and naturalist ($7.25/hr.)
For more information: Jonathan Griffith, Park Ranger, Mount Mitchell State Park, Route 5, Box 700, Burnsville, North Carolina 28714; (828)675-4611; (828)675-9655 (fax); E-mail momi@yancy.main.nc.us.

NUCLEAR INFORMATION AND RESOURCE SERVICE
Washington, D.C.
Description: Organization encouraging alternatives to nuclear energy.
Open to: High school students and graduates.
Type: Unpaid
For more information: Administrative Coordinator, Nuclear Information and Resource Service, 1424 16th Street, NW, Suite 404, Washington, DC 20036; (202) 328-0002;
E-mail nirsnet@igc.org; URL http://www.nirs.org.

PACIFIC WHALE FOUNDATION
Kihei, Hawaii
Project Location: Maui, Hawaii, and Australia
Description: Humpback whale research.
Positions Available: Marine Debris Beach Survey, Student Naturalist, Career Shadowing with Pacific Whale Foundation, and Field Research Techniques.
Cost/Compensation: $1,395 and the cost of transportation.
For more information: Merrill Kaufman, Marine Education Specialist, Pacific Whale Foundation, 101 N. Kihei Road, Kihei, Hawaii 96753; (808)879-8811; (808)879-2615 (fax); E-mail merrill@pacificwhale.org; URL http://www.pacificwhale.org.

PALMER GULCH RESORT/MT. RUSHMORE KOA
Hill City, South Dakota
Description: Full-service resort providing camping, cabin, and motel accommodations.
Open to: U.S. students, 16 years or older. Approximately 25-26 positions available.
Positions available: Registration, retail sales, maintenance, housekeeping, and waterslide.
Cost/Compensation: 1997 – $5.30/hr. plus season end bonus.
For more information: Sharon Nilson, Assistant Manager, Palmer Gulch Resort/Mt. Rushmore KOA, Box 295, Hill City, South Dakota 57745; (605)574-2525; (605)574-2574 (fax); E-mail palmerkoa@aol.com.

PENN LAUREL GIRL SCOUT COUNCIL
York, PA and Denver, PA
Description: Girls organization.
Open to: High school students.
Positions Available: Counselors, lifeguards, riding instructors, and sailing instructors.
Cost/Compensation: Paid
For more information: Vicky Miley, Camp Administrator, Penn Laurel Girl Scout Council, Inc., 1600 Mt. Zion Road, P.O. Box 20159, York, Pennsylvania 17402-0140; (717)757-3561; (717)755-1550 (fax); E-mail gsinfo@pennlaurel.org; URL http://www.pennlaurel.org.

PERA CLUB
Phoenix, Arizona
Description: Private country club for employees of the Salt River Project, a water and power utility.
Open to: High school seniors.

Type: Paid

For more information: Internship Coordinator, PERA Club, PER 200, P.O. Box 52025, Phoenix, Arizona 85072-2025; (602)236-5782.

SAM HOUSTON NATIONAL FOREST

New Waverly, Texas

Description: National forest.

Open to: High school students and graduates.

Type: Unpaid

For more information: Dawn Carrie, Wildlife Biologist (botany & wildlife internships) or Chip Ernst, Resources Forester (recreation internships), Sam Houston National Forest, P.O. Drawer 1000, New Waverly, Texas 77358; (409)344-6205.

SAN JUAN/RIO GRANDE NATIONAL FOREST

Monte Vista, Colorado

Description: Agency promoting multiple uses of land resources and managing Bureau of Land Management areas.

Open to: High school students and graduates.

Type: Most of the positions provide housing and limited subsistence (typically $16/day), but check with each project leader to verify before applying.

For more information: Dale Gomez, Partnership Coordinator, San Juan/Rio Grande National Forest, 1803 West Highway 160, Monte Vista, Colorado 81144; (719)852-5941; E-mail ls=c.keller/oul=ro2f09a@mhs-fswa.attmail.com.

SAVE THE SOUND, INC.

Stamford, Connecticut

Description: Organization committed to the preservation of Long Island Sound.

Open to: High school students and graduates depending on jobs.

Positions available: Education Program Assistant, Research Assistant, Public Outreach Assistant, and Membership Assistant.

Type: Unpaid. Will cover costs related directly to internship/volunteer activities.

Other information: Also new Habitat Restoration Project a nonprofit membership organization dedicated to the restoration, protection, and appreciation of Long Island Sound and its watershed.

For more information: Internship Coordinator, Save the Sound, Inc., 185 Magee Avenue, Stamford, Connecticut 06902 (submit requests here); or 50 Berry Drive, Glen Cove, New York 11842; (203)327-9786; (203)967-2677 (fax); E-mail savethesound@snet.net; URL http://www.savethesound.org.

SERVE/MAINE

August, Maine

Project Location: Maine

Description: SERVE/Maine places volunteers and interns with Maine's natural resource agencies to accomplish projects of an environmental nature.

Open to: High school age and upward.

Positions available: Environmental projects including water quality monitoring, trail building, grant writing, etc.

Cost/Compensation: Housing and stipend are available for some positions.

For more information: James Lainsburgy, Coordinator, SERVE/Maine, 124 State House Station, Augusta, Maine 04333-0124; (207)287-3082; (207) 287-3611 (fax); E-mail corps.conservation@state.me.us.

SIX FLAGS – ST. LOUIS

Eureka, Missouri

Description: Theme park.

Open to: Anyone 15 or over.

Positions available: Food service, operations, admissions, merchandise, retail, security, entertainment, and cash control staff.

For more information: Karen Wood, Human Resources Recruiting Supervisor, Six Flags-St. Louis, P. O. Box 60, Eureka, Missouri 63025; (314)938-5300; (314)938-4964 (fax); E-mail kwood@sftp.com; URL http://www.sixflags.com.

SOUTHFACE ENERGY INSTITUTE

Atlanta, Georgia

Description: Organization encouraging energy conservation and the use of renewable energy technologies.

Open to: High school students.

Type: Paid

For more information: Internship Coordinator, Southface Energy Institute, 241 Pine Street, NE, Atlanta, Georgia 30308-3424; (404)525-7657.

STUDENT CONSERVATION ASSOCIATION

Charlestown, New Hampshire

Description: Student organization promoting environmental preservation.

Open to: High school students.

Type: Unpaid

For more information: Student Conservation Association, P.O. Box 550, Charlestown, New Hampshire 03603-0550; (603)543-1700 Ext. 157; E-mail hs-program@sca-inc.org; URL http://www.sca-inc.org.

STUDENT ENVIRONMENTAL ACTION COALITION

Philadelphia, Pennsylvania

Project Location: Philadelphia and nationwide.

Description: SEAC is a network of high school and college environmental groups dedicated to building the capacity of students to organize for environmental justice.

Positions available: Internships in Philadelphia and

volunteer and coordination opportunities nationwide.
For more information: SEAC National Office, Student Environmental Action Coalition (SEAC), P.O. Box 31909, Philadelphia, Pennsylvania 19104-0609; (215)222-4711; (215)222-2896 (fax); E-mail seac@seac.org; URL http://www.seac.org.

SURFRIDER FOUNDATION
San Clemente, California
Description: Organization committed to the preservation of the world's oceans.
Open to: High school students, seniors, and graduates.
Type: Unpaid
For more information: Josh Wright, Membership Services, Surfrider Foundation, 122 South El Camino Real #67, San Clemente, California 92672; (714)495-8142; E-mail info@surfrider.org; URL http://www.surfrider.org.

U.S. FOREST SERVICE, NATIONAL FORESTS IN NORTH CAROLINA
Asheville, North Carolina
Description: Agency dedicated to preserving and improving public lands.
Open to: High school students and graduates.
Type: Unpaid
For more information: Fred Foster, Human Resource Programs Staff Officer, U.S. Forest Service, P.O. Box 2750, Asheville, North Carolina 28802; (704)257-4262.

UTAH STATE PARKS AND RECREATION, CORAL PINK SAND DUNES STATE PARK
Kanab, Utah
Description: State park.
Open to: High school seniors and graduates.
Type: Unpaid
For more information: Rob Quist, Park Manager, Utah State Parks and Recreation, Coral Pink Sand Dunes State Park, P.O. Box 95, Kanab, Utah 84741; (801)648-2800.

VOLUNTEERS FOR OUTDOOR COLORADO
Denver, Colorado
Project Location: Public lands in Colorado.
Description: This organization has a list of hundreds of opportunities for volunteers and interns around Colorado. A free catalog is available.
For more information: Jennifer Burstein, Clearinghouse Coordinator, Volunteers for Outdoor Colorado, 600 S. Marion Parkway, Denver, Colorado 80209-2597; (303)715-1010 or (800)925-2220; (303)715-1212 (fax); E-mail voc@voc.org; URL http://www.voc.org.

WORLDS OF FUN/OCEANS OF FUN
Kansas City, Missouri
Description: Amusement park.
Open to: High school students. Approximately 2,100 positions available.
Positions available: Food operations staff, ride operations staff, merchandise staff, games staff, lifeguards, ticket sellers, and grounds personnel. Internships available.
For more information: Human Resources Department, Worlds of Fun/Oceans of Fun, 4545 WOF Avenue, Kansas City, Missouri 64161; (816)454-4545.

YMCA CAMP SURF
Imperial Beach, California
Description: Residential oceanfront camp.
Open to: High school students.
Positions available: Camp counselors and lifeguards.
Cost/Compensation: $25-$38/day with room and board.
For more information: Mark Thompson, Camp Director, YMCA Camp Surf, 106 Carnation Avenue, Imperial Beach, California 91932; (619)423-5850; (619)423-4141 (fax); E-mail campsurf@ymca.org; URL http://www.ymca.org/camp/.

PUBLIC AFFAIRS

ACADEMY FOR ADVANCED AND STRATEGIC STUDIES
Washington, D.C.
Description: Think tank investigating issues pertinent to social and personal progress.
Open to: High school students and graduates.
Type: Paid
For more information: Internship Coordinator, The Academy for Advanced and Strategic Studies, 1647 Lamont Street, NW, Washington, DC 20010-2796.

ACCURACY IN MEDIA
Washington, D.C.
Description: Conservative, nonpartisan organization promoting accuracy in news reporting.
Open to: High school students and seniors.
Type: Paid
For more information: Internship Coordinator, Accuracy in Media, 4455 Connecticut Avenue, NW, Suite 330, Washington, DC 20008; (202)364-4401.

AMERICAN CORRECTIONAL ASSOCIATION
Laurel, Maryland
Description: Professional organization for those in the corrections field.
Open to: High school students and graduates.
Type: Unpaid
For more information: Internship Coordinator, Ameri-

can Correctional Association, 8025, Laurel Lakes Court, Laurel, Maryland 20707-5075.

AMERICAN WOMEN'S ECONOMIC DEVELOPMENT CORP.
New York, New York
Description: Organization providing training and counseling to women who own or would like to own a business.
Open to: High school seniors.
Type: Unpaid
For more information: Internship Coordinator, American Women's Economic Development Corp.
New York: 71 Vanderbilt Avenue, Suite 320, New York, New York 10169; (212)692-9100.

AMERICANS FOR DEMOCRATIC ACTION
Washington, D.C.
Description: ADA does lobbying on a variety of issues at the local, state, and national levels.
Open to: All.
Positions available: Legislative and media internships.
Type: Unpaid
For more information: Valerie Dulk-Jacobs, Special Assistant to the Director, Americans for Democratic Action, 1625 K Street, NW, Suite 210, Washington, DC 20006; (202)785-5980; (202)785-5969 (fax); E-mail adaction@ix.netcom.com; URL http://www.adaction.org.

BOSTON MOBILIZATION FOR SURVIVAL
Cambridge, Massachusetts
Description: Organization promoting peace and justice encouraging health care reform, campaign finance reform and reducing the military budget.
Open to: High school seniors and graduates.
Type: Unpaid
For more information: Mr. Wells Wilkinson, Internship Coordinator, Boston Mobilization for Survival, 11 Garden Street, Cambridge, Massachusetts 02138; (617)354-0008; E-mail bostonmobe@igc.apc.org.

CENTER FOR THE STUDY OF CONFLICT, INC.
Baltimore, Maryland
Description: Organization conducting studies on conflict resolution.
Open to: High school seniors and graduates.
Type: Unpaid
For more information: Dr. Richard Wendell Fogg, Director, Center for the Study of Conflict, Inc., 5846 Bellona Avenue, Baltimore, Maryland 21212; (410)323-7656.

CITIZENS FOR PARTICIPATION IN POLITICAL ACTION (CPPAX)
Boston, Massachusetts
Description: Multi-issue political group currently focusing on economic democracy.
Open to: High school students and graduates.
Type: Unpaid
For more information: Sara Lewis, Administrative Coordinator, CPPAX, 25 West Street, 4th Floor, Boston, Massachusetts 02111; (617)426-3040; E-mail cppax@xensei.com.

CITY OF NEW YORK/ PARKS & RECREATION
New York, New York
Description: Agency responsible for overseeing New York's parks and cultural activities.
Open to: High school students and graduates.
Type: Paid and unpaid internships available.
For more information: Internship Coordinator, City of New York/Parks & Recreation, 830 Fifth Avenue, New York, New York 10021; (212)360-1395.

COMMON CAUSE
Washington, D.C.
Description: Nonprofit organization lobbying for finance reform.
Open to: High school seniors and graduates.
Type: Unpaid
For more information: Volunteer Coordinator, Common Cause, 1250 Connecticut Avenue, NW, Washington, DC 20036; (202)833-1200; E-mail adraheim@commoncause.org; URL http://www.commoncause.org.

THE CONSERVATIVE CAUCUS, INC.
Vienna, Virginia
Description: Organization lobbying for conservative politics.
Open to: High school students and graduates.
Type: Unpaid
For more information: Charles Orndorff, Administrative Vice Chairman, The Conservative Caucus, Inc., 450 Maple Avenue East, Suite 309, Vienna, Virginia 22180; (703)938-9626; E-mail corndorf@cais.com

COUNCIL ON ECONOMIC PRIORITIES
New York, New York
Description: Organization researching the practices of U.S. companies and issues impacting national security.
Open to: High school seniors and graduates.
Type: Paid and unpaid internships available.
For more information: Internship Coordinator, Council on Economic Priorities, 30 Irving Place, New York, New York 10003-2386; (800)729-4237.

DEMOCRATIC CONGRESSIONAL CAMPAIGN COMMITTEE
Washington, D.C.
Description: Committee dedicated to getting Democrats elected to the House of Representatives.

Open to: High school seniors and graduates.
Type: Unpaid
For more information: Jacqui Vaughn, Intern Coordinator, Democratic Congressional Campaign Committee, 430 South Capitol Street, 2nd Floor, Washington, DC 20003; (202)485-3413; E-mail vaughn@dccc.org; URL http://www.dccc.org.

DEMOCRATIC NATIONAL COMMITTEE
Washington, D.C.
Description: Committee responsible for planning the national convention and assisting with state and local elections.
Open to: High school seniors and graduates.
Type: Unpaid
For more information: Intern Coordinator, Democratic National Committee, 430 South Capital Street, SE, Washington, DC 20003; (202)863-7173; URL http://www.democrats.org.

FEDERAL BUREAU OF PRISONS
Washington, D.C.
Description: Responsible for operating federal correctional facilities across the U.S.
Open to: High school students, 16 years and older.
Type: Unpaid
For more information: Internship Coordinator, Federal Bureau of Prisons, National Office of Citizen Participation, 320 First Street, NW, Washington, DC 20003; (202)307-3998.

GOVERNMENT PRINTING OFFICE
Washington, D.C.
Description: Prints and distributes government publications.
Open to: High school students.
Type: Paid and unpaid internships available.
For more information: Charles Kirkpatrick, Supervisory Personnel Staffing Specialist, Government Printing Office, 732 North Capital Street, NW, Washington, DC 20401; (202)512-1137.

LEARNING ALLIANCE
New York, New York
Description: Organization committed to a wide-range of educational and social issues.
Open to: High school students and graduates.
Type: Unpaid
For more information: Dianne Williams, Program Director, Learning Alliance, 14 Wooster Street #5, New York, New York 10013-2227; (212)226-7171; E-mail lalliance@igc.apc.org.

METRO JUSTICE OF ROCHESTER
Rochester, New York
Description: Community organization focusing on a wide-range of social and political issues.

Open to: High school students and graduates.
Type: Unpaid
For more information: William Appel, Organizer, Metro Justice of Rochester, 36 St. Paul Street, Room 112, Rochester, New York 14604; (716)325-2560; URL http://www.ggw.org/freenet/m/MetroJustice.

MICHIGAN FEDERATION OF PRIVATE CHILD AND FAMILY AGENCIES
Lansing, Michigan
Description: Group of nonprofit agencies that lobby Michigan government about human service issues.
Open to: High school students and graduates.
Type: Unpaid
For more information: Melissa Soule, Communications Coordinator, Michigan Federation of Private Child and Family Agencies, 230 North Washington Square, Suite 300, Lansing, Michigan 48933-1312; (517)485-8552; E-mail missoule@aol.com; URL http://www.michfed.org.

NASSAU COUNTY DEPARTMENT OF COMMERCE AND INDUSTRY- OFFICE OF CINEMA/TV PROMOTION
Mineola, New York
Description: Department created to attract film and commercial production to Nassau County.
Open to: High school students and graduates.
Type: Unpaid
For more information: Debra Markowitz, Director, Cinema and Television Promotion, c/o Commerce and Industry, 1550 Franklin Avenue, Mineola, New York 11501; (516)571-4160; (516)571-4161 (fax); URL http://www.co.nassau.ny.us/tv.html.

NATIONAL ORGANIZATION FOR WOMEN
Washington, D.C.
Description: Feminist organization.
Open to: High school students.
Type: Unpaid
For more information: Anita Marie Murano, Intern/Volunteer Coordinator, National Organization for Women, 1000 16th Street, NW, Suite 700, Washington, DC 20036; (202)331-0066; E-mail volunteer@now.org; URL http://www.now.org.

NATIONAL SPACE SOCIETY
Washington, D.C.
Description: Organization committed to public education and the promotion of the civilian space program.
Open to: High school students and graduates.
Type: Unpaid
For more information: David Brandt, Program Director, National Space Society, 600 Pennsylvania Avenue, SE, Suite 201, Washington, DC 20003; (202)543-1900; E-mail prospace@aol.com; URL http://www.nss.org.

FOCUS ON...
PRESIDENTIAL CLASSROOM SCHOLARS

High school students are given the opportunity to spend a week in Washington, DC observing the federal government at work. Students go behind the scenes for seminars and discussions with Washington insiders.

In addition to the <u>Presidential Scholars Program</u>, the following programs are available:
- Future World Leaders Summit
- Science, Technology and Public Policy Program
- Business, Labor, and Public
- Policy Program
- College Intern Program

For more information, visit the website or call 1-800-441-6533 for a free video about the program.

URL http://www.presidential classroom.org

NORTH CAROLINA GOVERNOR'S OFFICE OF CITIZEN AFFAIRS
Raleigh, North Carolina
Description: Responsible for responding to citizen's inquiries and encouraging volunteerism.
Open to: High school students and graduates.
Type: Paid and unpaid internships available.
For more information: Judith C. Bell, Executive Director, North Carolina Governor's Office of Citizen Affairs, 116 West Jones Street, Raleigh, North Carolina 27603; (919)733-2391.

PARTNERS FOR LIVABLE COMMUNITIES
Washington, D.C.
Description: Organization promoting social equity, improving the quality of life, and development of communities.
Open to: High school students.

Type: Unpaid
For more information: Penelope Cuff, Senior Program Officer, Partners for Livable Communities, 1429 21st Street, NW, Washington, DC 20036; (202) 887-5990; E-mail plcomms@concentric.net.

STOP TEENAGE ADDICTION TO TOBACCO
Springfield, Massachusetts
Description: Group committed to stopping the use of tobacco products by children and teens.
Open to: High school students and graduates.
Type: Unpaid
For more information: Laura Mullen, Project Coordinator, Stop Teenage Addiction to Tobacco, 511 East Columbus Avenue, Springfield, Massachusetts 01105; (413)732-7828;
E-mail 105624.1434@compuserv.com.

UNITED STATES DEPARTMENT OF COMMERCE

Washington, D.C.
Silver Spring, Maryland
Suitland, Maryland
Gaithersburg, Maryland

Description: Agency of the federal government that is responsible for international trade, technological advancement, and economic growth.

Open to: High school students.

Type: Paid and unpaid internships available.

For more information:

Washington: Office of Personnel Operations, Room 1069, U.S. Department of Commerce, 14th and Constitution Avenue, NW, Washington, DC 20230; (202) 482-2560.

Washington: Personnel Office, Patent and Trademark Office, 201 Crystal Drive, Crystal Park One, Suite 700, Washington, DC 22202; (703)305-8434.

Washington: Personnel Office, Office of Inspector General, Room 7713 HCHB, Washington, DC 20230; (202)482-3006.

Silver Spring: Personnel Office, National Oceanic and Atmospheric Administration, SSMC #2 OA215 Room 01230, Silver Spring, Maryland 20910; (301) 713-0534.

Suitland: Personnel Office, Bureau of the Census, Federal Building 3, Room 3124, Suitland, Maryland, 20233; (301)457-3371.

Gaithersburg: Personnel Office, Administration Building, Room A-123, National Institute of Standards and Technology, Gaithersburg, Maryland 20899; (301)975-3026.

UNITED STATES DEPARTMENT OF DEFENSE

Washington, D.C.

Description: Federal agency responsible for the national security of the U.S.

Open to: High school students.

Type: Paid and unpaid internships available.

For more information:

Employee Career Development & Training: Student Volunteer Program, Employee Career Development and Training Division, Washington Headquarters Services, Personnel and Security Directorate, 1155 Defense Pentagon, Washington, DC 20301-1155.

Summer Employment Program or Stay-in School Program: Staffing Division, Personnel and Security Directorate, 1155 Defense Pentagon, Washington, DC 20301-1155.

Honors Legal Internship Program: Office of General Counsel, U.S. Department of Defense, The Pentagon, Room 3E999, Washington, DC 20301-1600.

UNITED STATES SENATE YOUTH PROGRAM

Washington, D.C.

Description: Program providing the opportunity for two youth from each state to visit Washington, D.C.

Open to: High school juniors and seniors who are elected student officers.

Type: Scholarship, travel, hotel, and meals are paid for by the W.R. Hearst Foundation.

Other information: Selections are made by the state-level Departments of Education. Each State has an early Fall deadline. Dates will vary.

For more information: U.S. Senate Youth Program, William Randolph Hearst Foundation, 90 New Montgomery Street, Suite 1212, San Francisco, California 94105-4504; (800)841-7048.

THE VEGETARIAN RESOURCE GROUP

Baltimore, Maryland

Description: Organization that provides educational programming about vegetarianism including information about ethics, health and the environment.

Open to: High school students and graduates.

Type: Unpaid

For more information: Charles Stahler, The Vegetarian Resource Group, P.O. Box 1463, Baltimore, Maryland 21203; (410)366-8804 (fax); E-mail The vrg@vrg.org; URL http://www.vrg.org.

VIRGINIA OFFICE OF VOLUNTEERISM

Richmond, Virginia

Description: Supports volunteerism by providing information, technical assistance and training.

Open to: High school students, seniors, and graduates.

Type: Unpaid

For more information: Internship Coordinator, Virginia Office of Volunteerism, 730 East Broad Street, Richmond, Virginia 23219-1849; (804)692-1950.

WEST VIRGINIA COMMISSION FOR NATIONAL AND COMMUNITY SERVICE

Charleston, West Virginia

Description: State government agency.

Open to: High school students.

For more information: Jean Ambrose, Executive Director, West Virginia Commission for National and Community Service, 900 Pennsylvania Avenue, Suite 1000, Charleston, West Virginia 25302; (304)340-3621; (304)340-3629 (fax).

WOMEN'S ENTERPRISE DEVELOPMENT

Long Beach, California

Description: Provide business management training for individuals that would like to own a business.

Open to: High school juniors, seniors, and college students.

Positions available: Depends on projects needed.

Type: Unpaid.

For more information: Ms. Torres Waters, Office Manager, Women's Enterprise Development, 235 E. Broadway, Suite 506, Long Beach, California 90802; (562)983-3747; (562)983-3750 (fax); E-mail

WEDCl@aol.com; URL http://www.wedc.org.

WOMEN'S HISTORY RESEARCH CENTER

Berkeley, California

Description: Organization dedicated to documenting the women's movement and acting as a networking center.

Open to: High school students and graduates.

Type: Unpaid

For more information: Laura X, Director, Women's History Research Center, 2325 Oak Street, Berkeley, California 94708; (510)524-1582; URL http://members.aol.com/ncmdr/index.htm.

WOMEN STRIKE FOR PEACE

Washington, D.C.

Description: Women's organization providing educational programming and lobbying Congress on the topics of peace and disarmament.

Open to: High school students and graduates.

Type: Unpaid

For more information: Edith Villastrigo, National Legislative Coordinator, Women Strike for Peace, 110 Maryland Avenue, E, Suite 102, Washington, DC 20002; (202)543-2660.

SCIENCE/RESEARCH

ARTHRITIS FOUNDATION - NORTHERN CALIFORNIA CHAPTER

San Francisco, California

Description: Organization conducting arthritis research.

Open to: High school and undergraduate students, 17 and over, who reside or go to school in 16 counties/bay area.

Type: Paid

For more information: Internship Coordinator, Arthritis Foundation, Northern California Chapter, 657 Mission Street, Suite 603, San Francisco, California 94105; (415)356-1230; (413)336-1240 (fax); URL http:// www.arthritis.org/offices/nca.

CHICAGO ACADEMY OF SCIENCES

Chicago, Illinois

Description: Science museum.

Open to: High school students and graduates.

Type: Unpaid

For more information: Sheila McCaskill, 2060 North Clark Street, Chicago, Illinois 60614; (773)549-0606 Ext. 3080; E-mail cas@chias.org; URL http://www.chias.org.

FARM SANCTUARY

Orland, California

Watkins Glen, New York

Description: Organization encouraging an end to farm animal abuses.

Open to: High school students, 16 years and older.

Type: Unpaid

For more information: Internship Coordinator, Farm Sanctuary

Orland: P.O. Box 1065, Orland, California 95963; (916)865-4617.

Watkins Glen: P.O. Box 150, Watkins Glen, New York 14891; (607)583-2225.

LAWRENCE LIVERMORE NATIONAL LABORATORY

Livermore, California

Description: Laboratory conducting nuclear weapons, environmental and energy technologies, and laser research.

Open to: High school and college students.

Type: Paid

For more information: Summer Employment Program, Recruitment and Employment Division, Lawrence Livermore National Laboratory, P.O. Box 5510, L-725, Livermore, California 94551-0808; (510)423-2797; E-mail plummer1@llnl.gov; URL http://www.llnl.gov.

NATIONAL AERONAUTICS AND SPACE ADMINISTRATION (NASA)

Moffett Field, California

Greenbelt, Maryland

Pasadena, California

Houston, Texas

Kennedy Space Center, Florida

Hampton, Virginia

Cleveland, Ohio

Marshall Space Flight Center, Alabama

Stennis Space Center, Mississippi

Description: Agency overseeing the U.S. Space Program.

Open to: High school students 16 years or older.

Type: Unpaid

For more information:

Moffett Field: NASA Ames Research Center, University Affairs Office, Code 241-3, Moffett Field, California 94035; (415)604-5802.

Greenbelt: NASA Goddard Space Flight Center, University Programs, Mail Stop 160, Greenbelt Road, Greenbelt, Maryland 20771; (301)286-9690.

Pasadena: Jet Propulsion Laboratory 183-900, Educational Affairs Office, 4800 Oak Grove Drive, Pasadena, California 91109-8099; (818)354-8251.

Houston: NASA Johnson Space Center, University Programs, Mail Stop AHU, Houston, Texas 77058; (713)483-4724.

Kennedy Space Center: NASA Kennedy Space Center, University Program Manager, Mail Code HM-CIC, KSC, Florida 32899; (407)867-7952.

Hampton: NASA Langley Research Center, Office of Education, Mail Stop 400, Hampton, Virginia 23681-0001; (804)864-4000.

Cleveland: NASA Lewis Research Center, Educational Programs, Mail Stop 7-4, 21000 Brookpark Road, Cleveland, Ohio 44135; (216)433-2957.

Marshall Space Flight Center: NASA Marshall Space Flight Center, University Affairs, Mail Stop DS01, MSFC, Alabama 35812; (205)544-0997.

Stennis Space Center: NASA Stennis Space Center, Management Operations, University Affairs Office, Mail Code MA00, SSC, Mississippi 39529; (601) 688-3830.

NATIONAL SPACE SOCIETY
Washington, D.C.

Description: Organization encouraging space exploration, travel and colonization.

Open to: High school students.

Type: Unpaid

For more information: Internship Coordinator, National Space Society, 600 Pennsylvania Avenue, SE, Washington, DC 20003; (202)543-1900.

RESEARCH SCIENCE INSTITUTE
McLean, Virginia

Project Location: Massachusetts Institute of Technology (MIT)

Description: Six-week summer program at MIT combining classroom lectures and tutoring with off-campus internships in scientific research.

Open to: Students who have completed the equivalent of three years of high school. Admission is based on high school academic record, recommendations, PSAT scores (approximately 135; and personal essays). The application deadline is February 1.

Cost/Compensation: No cost except transportation to and from the Research Science Institute.

For more information: Please send a self-addressed envelope with .55 postage to: Ms. Maite Ballestero, Director of Programs, Center for Excellence in Education, 7710 Old Springhouse Road, Suite 100, McLean, Virginia 22102; (703)448-9062.

UNITED STATES DEPARTMENT OF ENERGY
Washington, D.C.

Description: Manages nine energy research facilities nationwide.

Open to: High school students and graduates.

Type: Unpaid

For more information: High School Student Research Honors Program, Office of Science Education Programs, Room 5B168, U.S. Department of Energy, 1000 Independence Avenue, SW, Washington, DC 20585; (202)586-8949.

UNIVERSITY RESEARCH EXPEDITIONS PROGRAM
Berkeley, California

Description: Organization that matches individuals with University of California academics on research projects located throughout the world.

Open to: High school students.

Type: Unpaid; Cost of $700-$1,700.

For more information: Program Liaison, University Research Expeditions Program, University of California, 223 Fulton Street, Berkeley, California 94720-7050; (510)642-6586; E-mail urep@uclink.berkeley.edu; URL http://www.mip.berkeley.edu/urep.

INTERNSHIP REFERRAL SERVICES

AFS INTERCULTURAL PROGRAMS
New York, New York

Description: Student-exchange organization.

Open to: High school juniors and seniors.

Type: Unpaid

For more information: Internship Coordinator, AFS Intercultural Programs/USA, 220 East 42nd Street, 3rd Floor, New York, New York 10017; (800)AFS-INFO.

AMERICAN ASSOCIATION OF OVERSEAS STUDIES
New York and London

Description: Placement service for internships in London and New York.

Open to: High school students and graduates.

Positions Available: Internships in communications, film, law, government, food, tourism, business, and fashion.

Type: $995-$3,995

Other Information: Housing and recreation program available.

For more information: Janet Evans, Director, American Association of Overseas Studies, 51 Drayton Gardens, London, England SW10 9RX; 011-44-171-835-2143; 011-44-171-244-6061 (fax); E-mail aaos2000@hotmail.com; URL http://www.worldwide.edu/uk/aaos/.

CENTER FOR MUSEUM STUDIES, SMITHSONIAN INSTITUTION
Washington, D.C.

Description: Central referral service for internships in the Smithsonian.

Open to: High school seniors and graduates.

Type: Unpaid

For more information: Elena Piquer Mayberry, Intern Services Coordinator, Center for Museum Studies, Smithsonian Institution, 900 Jefferson Drive, SW, A and I Building, Suite 2235, Washington, DC 20560-0427; (202)357-3102; E-mail sintern@cms.si.edu;

URL http://www.si.edu.

THE PARTNERSHIP FOR SERVICE-LEARNING
New York, New York
Description: Organization coordinating programs that link academic study to public service in ten different countries.
Open to: High school seniors and graduates.
Type: Unpaid (Fee for participation)
For more information: The Partnership for Service-Learning, 815 Second Avenue, Suite 315, New York, New York 10017; (212)986-0989; E-mail pslny@aol.com; URL http://www.studyabroad.com/psl.

VOLUNTEER CENTER OF THE LEHIGH VALLEY
Bethlehem, Pennsylvania
Description: Organization providing volunteer referrals and placements.
Open to: High school students and graduates.
Type: Unpaid
For more information: Priscilla Schueck, Co-Director, Volunteer Center of the Lehigh Valley, 2121 City Line Road, Bethlehem, Pennsylvania 18017-2168; (610)807-0336.

Y.E.S. TO JOBS
Hollywood, California
Description: Organization placing minority high school students in internships in the entertainment industry.
Open to: High school students, seniors, and graduates.
Type: Paid
For more information: Jaleesa Hazzard, Executive Director, Y.E.S. to Jobs, 1416 North La Brea Avenue, Hollywood, California 90028; (213)469-2411 Ext. 3598.

FOCUS ON...
NATIONAL NETWORK FOR YOUTH

For 22 years, the National Network for Youth has been a leader in addressing the challenges facing America's young people and their families. The National Network works to fulfill its mission to ensure that young people can be safe and grow up to lead healthy and productive lives.

www.nn4youth.org

YouthNet®
This website offers information about such topics as federal legislation, funding availability, job openings, training opportunities, and news from national, federal, state, and community-based agencies.

URL http://www.nn4youth.org

NOTES

PART-TIME/SUMMER JOBS

For many of you, a part-time or summer job will be your first career experience. There are many places to look for this type of work:

- airports
- libraries
- movie theaters
- camps
- hospitals
- stables
- restaurants
- theme/amusement parks
- farms
- hotels/resorts
- grocery stores
- golf courses
- malls
- newspapers

You might also contact the offices of types of businesses that are interesting to you and see if they are hiring. Keep looking until you find a good match. It is possible to find a way to earn a paycheck and enjoy your work; you just have to be persistent and creative.

While you are searching for a part-time or summer job, you might want to visit some of the websites listed below. They provide thousands of opportunities in the United States and around the world.

- http://www.aifs.org/iaifscam.htm - The Camp America site places international students in camps in the U.S.
- http://www.campchannel.com/campnet/docs/bboard.html - This site gives very basic information about camps and then refers you to their individual websites. It also features information about *The Ultimate Camp Counsellor Manual*.
- http://www.campstaff.com - You register with their service, and they link you to interested camps. You can search basic information on camps such as location, sleep/day, gender make-up and camp specialty.
- http://www.cooljobs.com/ - This website lists some very interesting jobs like working for the Cirque du Soleil, serving as a tour guide for the X Tour (for X-files buffs), MTV's model search and participating as a Jeopardy contestant. They may

not all be for teens, but they are very interesting and worth a look.

- http:www.gospelcom.net/cci/ajobs/ - This site enables you to post your profile and be considered for jobs at CCI/USA camps and conferences
- http://www.kidscamps.com - This is a very helpful and easy to use site. There are good listings of U.S. camps, and you can search by state, region or position type.
- http://www.outdoornetwork.com/JobNet/JobNet.html - This website lists interesting outdoor jobs that are available. Most are for college students, but it is worth a look.
- http://www.potsdam.edu/CAREER/summer.html - This site will link you with several summer job websites including one from Peterson's Guide to Summer Jobs, camp listings, overseas jobs and a parks and ski resort listing.
- http://www.resortinternconnection. com/ - The Resort Intern Connections site features jobs in the resort, travel and tourism fields.
- http://www.search.acacamps.org - The American Camping Association website allows you to search and find camps that interest you. You may search by camp type, location, activities, special interests, affiliation or fee category. You will then need to write or call to find out about job openings.
- http://www.summerjobs.com - This website is very diverse and features many jobs at small businesses both U.S. and international. You may search by key word or location.
- http://www.usajobs.opm.gov/a7.htm - This website is a listing of federal summer jobs and internships for students age 16 and over.
- http://www.usfca.edu/usf/career/summer.html - This site will link you with several other summer job sites including the Back Door Guide to Short-Term Adventures, camp listings, a maritime job website and other summer job listings.
- http://www.wm.edu/csrv/career/stualum/;short.html - This site features two camp listings, a summer job directory and links you to the Cool Works site.
- http://www.yahoo.com/text/Business_and_Economy/Companies/Outdoors/Camping/Commercial_and_Summer_Camps/Employment/ - This website will link you with lots of camp listings.
- http://www.youth.gc.ca/jobopps/summer-e.shtml - This site is actually for Canadian students, but their "international" listing includes many jobs for teens in the U.S.

For many teens, your first job will be as a camp counselor. Many camps from around the

United States are listed below. This list is by no means comprehensive, but it does include jobs all over the country and at almost any type of camp you can imagine. Working as a camp counselor requires a great deal of responsibility and maturity. If you are wondering what the job might be like, or if you are already a counselor and are looking for information on improving your skills, you might like to read:

- *The Ultimate Camp Counsellor Manual: How to Survive and Succeed Magnificently at Summer Camp* by Mark S. Richman, a New York City teacher with 24-years of camping experience. The guide covers virtually everything that could ever happen in the camping situation. It is available for $24.95 + $3.00 shipping/handling by writing to: Mark S. Richman, 645 East 14th Street 2H, New York, New York 10009; (212) 673-4135 or order on-line at http://www. campchannel.com.

If you need more assistance finding a camp, you may wish to contact:

- Camping Advisory Service, National Camp Association, 610 Fifth Avenue, P.O. Box 5371, New York, New York 10185; (212)645-0653

National parks also hire summer and part-time employees. They are located throughout the United States and offer just about any work experience you can imagine. For more information, see the listing of National Park Regional Offices at the end of this chapter.

Below you will find a listing of summer and part-time. It would be impossible to list every site, but this list should give you a good overview of what is out there. If you are interested in working at a site that is not listed, contact them directly and inquire about job openings.

Each listing contains a *description* of the organization or business. Information is given regarding the types of students that positions are *open to*. The *positions available* are listed. Information is given about the *cost/compensation*. A contact is given for you to write or call *for more information*.

> "DON'T WAIT UNTIL HIGH SCHOOL IS OVER TO BEGIN PLANNING YOUR FUTURE. LAY THE GROUNDWORK EARLY WHEN YOU ARE ABLE TO TRY THINGS OUT AND EXPLORE DIFFERENT JOB OPTIONS."
>
> -KIDS AND JOBS WEBSITE

ART/CULTURE

DETROIT INSTITUTE OF ARTS
Detroit, Michigan
Description: Art museum.
Open to: High school seniors.
Positions Available: Volunteer work and internships.
Cost/Compensation: Unpaid
For more information: Gina Alexander Granger, Assistant Educator, Detroit Institute of Arts, 5200 Woodward Avenue, Detroit, Michigan 48202; (313)833-1858; (313)833-7355 (fax); E-mail granter@diapo.ci. detroit.mi.us; URL http://www.dia.org.

ELIZABETH DOW LTD.
New York, New York
Description: Paint and design studio.
Open to: High school students, graduates, or anyone interested in experience.
Positions Available: Product production, office management, interoffice communications, and sampling.
Cost/Compensation: Unpaid
Other information: For more information, call for an interview.
For more information: Xavier Santana, Internship Coordinator, Elizabeth Dow Ltd., 155 Avenue of the Americas, 4th Floor, New York, New York 10013; (212)463-0144; (212)463-0824 (fax).

HERE
New York, New York
Description: Arts center, theatres, puppetry, galleries, and café.
Open to: High school juniors, seniors, and graduates.
Positions Available: One-on-one apprenticeships with established theatre and visual artists. Very rewarding opportunity.
Cost/Compensation: Unpaid (possible travel reimbursements).
For more information: Barbara Busackind, HERE, 145 Avenue of the Americas, New York, New York 10013; (212)647-0202; Ext. 307

NEW STAGE THEATRE
Jackson, Mississippi
Description: Professional nonprofit theater.
Open to: High school students and graduates.
Cost/Compensation: Paid and unpaid.
For more information: Education/Internship Coordinator, New Stage Theatre, 1100 Carlisle Street, Jackson, Mississippi 39202; (601)948-3533; (601)948-3538 (fax).

NORTH SHORE MUSIC THEATRE
Beverly, Massachusetts
Description: Musical theatre.

Open to: High school students. Approximately 3-4 positions available.

Positions available: Technical theater interns (local only).

For more information: Assistant Production Manager, North Shore Music Theatre, P.O. Box 62, Beverly, Massachusetts, 01915-0062; (508)922-8500 Ext. 261.

STRAW HAT PLAYERS
Moorhead, Minnesota

Description: Summer stock theater.

Open to: High school students. Approximately 6 positions available.

Positions Available: Acting company members and theater technicians.

For more information: Director of Theater, Straw Hat Players, Moorhead State University, Moorhead, Minnesota 56563; (218)236-4613.

WESTPORT COUNTRY PLAYHOUSE
Westport, Connecticut

Description: Professional summer theater.

Open to: High school students. Approximately 5 positions available.

Positions Available: Technical interns, administrative/press interns, box office staff, and production staff.

For more information: Julie Monahan, General Manager, Westport Country Playhouse, P.O. Box 629, Westport, Connecticut 06881; (203)227-5137.

COMMUNICATIONS

ASIAN AMERICAN JOURNALISTS ASSOCIATION
San Francisco, California

Description: Professional organization for Asian-American journalists.

Open to: High school students and college students.

Cost/Compensation: Dependent on situation — largely unpaid.

Other information: Provide listings of internships and jobs available, mentoring program, and scholarships.

For more information: Karen Jaw, Program Coordinator, Asian American Journalists Association, 1765 Sutter Street, San Francisco, California 94115; (415)346-2051; (415)346-6343 (fax); E-mail national@aaja.org; URL http://www.aaja.org.

KTEH-TV
San Jose, California

Description: Public television station.

Open to: High school and college students.

Positions Available: Camera; production assistant; PR assistant; and outreach assistant.

Cost/Compensation: Unpaid.

For more information: Personnel Manager, KTEH-TV, 1585 Shallenberger Road, San Jose, California 95131; (408)795-5400; (408)995-5446 (fax); URL http://www.kteh.pbs.org.

HUMAN SERVICES

CAMP BUCKSKIN
Ely, Minnesota

Description: Traditional camp activities and some academics for youth with ADD/ADHD, learning disabilities, and similar needs.

Open to: Qualified individuals, 16 or older.

Positions Available: Counselor/activity instructors, office and kitchen assistants.

Cost/Compensation: Competitive salary, room and board, excellent training, and school credit possible.

Other Information: Located on lake in Superior National Forest near Ely, Minnesota.

For more information: Tom Bauer, Director, Camp Buckskin, 8700 West 36th Street, Suite 6W, St. Louis Park, Minnesota 55426-3936; (612)930-3544; (612) 938-6996; E-mail buckskin@spacestar.net; URL http://www.spacestar.net/useus/buckskin.

CAMP COURAGE
Maple Lake, Minnesota

Description: Camp for physically disabled children and adults.

Open to: High school students. Approximately 10 positions available.

Positions Available: Waterfront personnel and counselors.

For more information: Roger Upcraft, Program Manager, Camp Courage, 8046 83rd Street, NW, Maple Lake, Minnesota 55358; (320)963-3698; E-mail camping@mtn.org; URL http://www.lkdlink.net/~courage.

CAMP EASTER SEALS
Milford, Nebraska

Description: Residential camp for children and adults with physical and developmental disabilities.

Open to: High school students. Approximately 11-12 positions available.

> "START BY TAKING A GOOD, KIND LOOK AT YOURSELF. WHAT ARE YOUR INTERESTS? WHAT GETS YOU EXCITED? FOCUS ON YOUR CREATIVITY, COMMUNITY CONCERNS, SKILLS, OR DESIRE TO HELP OTHERS — THINGS THAT MAKE YOU FEEL GOOD — THAT MAY ALSO LEAD TO SATISFYING WORK."
> - KIDS AND WORK WEBSITE

Positions Available: Cabin leaders, program personnel, kitchen assistants, and lifeguard.

For more information: Brian Stirton, Director of Camping, Camp Easter Seals, 2470 Van Dorn Road, Milford, Nebraska 68405; (402)761-2875; (402)330-0707 (fax).

CAMP SKY RANCH
Blowing Rock, North Carolina

Description: Residential camp for mentally disabled children and adults.

Open to: High school students.

Positions Available: Counselors and lifeguards.

For more information: Dan C. Norman, Director, Camp Sky Ranch, 634 Sky Ranch Road, Blowing Rock, North Carolina 28605-9738; (704)264-8600.

FRIENDSHIP VENTURES/CAMP FRIENDSHIP
Annandale, Minnesota

Description: Residential camp for children and adults with developmental disabilities.

Open to: High school students. Approximately 15 positions available.

Positions Available: Laundry/housekeeping staff, counselors, lifeguards, boating specialist, canteen/camp store manager, office staff, junior counselors, dining hall workers, special interest session leader, and camping specialist.

For more information: Joanne Fieldseth, Human Resources Director, Friendship Ventures/Camp Friendship, 10509 108th Street, NW, Annandale, Minnesota 55302; (320)274-8376; E-mail friendl@spacestar.com.

FRIENDSHIP VENTURES/EDEN WOOD CAMP
Eden Prairie, Minnesota

Description: Residential and day camp for children and adults with developmental disabilities.

Open to: High school students. Approximately 6 positions available.

Positions Available: Laundry/housekeeping staff, counselors, lifeguards, travel leaders, office staff, junior counselors, and dining hall staff.

For more information: Joanne Fieldseth, Human Resources Director, Friendship Ventures/Eden Wood Camp, 10509 108th Street, NW, Annandale, Minnesota 55302; (320)274-8376;
E-mail friendl@spacestar.com.

HAPPY HOLLOW CHILDREN'S CAMP, INC.
Nashville, Indiana

Description: Residential camp for diabetic, asthmatic, and inner-city children.

Open to: High school students. Approximately 3-4 positions available.

Positions Available: Counselors, program instructors, and swimming instructors.

For more information: Bernie Schrader, Director, Happy Hollow Children's Camp, Inc. 3049 Happy Hollow Road, Nashville, Indiana 47448: (812)988-4900; E-mail hhcdir@aol.com.

L'ARCHE MOBILE
Mobile, Alabama

Description: Communities where people with mental disability live with those who help them.

Cost/Compensation: Boarding and lodging are provided.

For more information: Marty O'Malley, 152 Mobile, 151 South Ann Street, Mobile, Alabama 36604; (334)438-2094; (334)433-5835 (fax); E-mail larchmob@acan.net; URL http://www2.acan.net/!// archmob/

MISSOURI COMMUNITY SERVICE COMMISSION
Jefferson City, Missouri

Description: State government agency.

Open to: Anyone 17 or over.

Positions Available: Part-time or full-time Americorps member positions.

Cost/Compensation: Living stipend plus $4,725. Full-time education award.

Other information: Opportunities for individuals to provide community service in return for a living allowance, education award, and the satisfaction of "getting things done."

For more information: Krista Bailey, Program Assistant, Missouri Community Service Commission, 3225 W. Truman Boulevard, Suite 101, Jefferson City, Missouri 65109; (573)751-7488 or toll-free at (877)210-7611; (573)526-0463 (fax).

RAMAPO ANCHORAGE CAMP
Rhinebeck, New York

Description: Residential summer camp for children with emotional and learning problems.

Open to: High school students, 16 and over.

Positions available: Summer camp counselors.

Cost/Compensation: Stipend, room and board, and travel reimbursement.

For more information: Michael Kunin, Associate Director, Ramapo Anchorage Camp, P.O. Box 266, Rhinebeck, New York 12572; (914)875-8403; (914)876-8414 (fax); E-mail info@ramapoanchorage.org; URL http://www.ramapoanchorage.org.

SALESIAN BOYS AND GIRLS CLUB
East Boston, Massachusetts

Description: After-school youth care facility.

Open to: High school students ages 16 and up.

Jobs Available: Summer program counselors and volunteers.

Cost/Compensation: $6.50-$10.00/hour

FOCUS ON...
INFOSEEK

*Do you want to check out the latest news and articles relating to teen jobs? Just go to **infoseek.go.com** and search for teen jobs.*

A recent search of this site identified the following articles:

- Teen Jobs: How Much Is Too Much? - *Christian Science Monitor*
- Teenage Job Hunters Beware – *State of Vermont*
- Kids and Jobs: Are You Working Smarter? - *PBS*

For more information: Ft. Michael Conway, SDB, Executive Director, Salesian Boys and Girls Club, 189 Paris Street, East Boston, Massachusetts 02128; (617) 567-0508; (617)567-0418 (fax); E-mail sbgclub@juno.com; URL http://www.eastboston.com/salesi.

SOUTH BAY COMMUNITY SERVICES
Chula Vista, California
Description: Organization providing counseling services and community youth development.
Open to: Youth from South Bay in San Diego 14-24 years of age.
Positions Available: Peer educators, peer outreach, tutors, and mentors.
Cost/Compensation: Paid part-time positions available and volunteer opportunities.
For more information: Perla Bransburg, Associate Director, South Bay Community Services, 315 4th Ave., Ste E, Chula Vista, California 91910; (619)420-3620.

WEST VIRGINIA COMMISSION FOR NATIONAL AND COMMUNITY SERVICE
Charleston, West Virginia
Description: State government agency
Positions Available: Part-time and summer positions.
For more information: Jean Ambrose, Executive Director, West Virginia Commission for National and Community Service, 900 Pennsylvania Avenue, Suitd 1000, Charleston, West Virginia 25302; (304)340-3621; (304)340-3629 (fax).

WOMEN'S ENTERPRISE DEVELOPMENT
Long Beach, California
Description: Provide business management training for individuals that would like to own a business.
Open to: High school juniors, seniors, and college students.
Positions Available: Depends on projects needed.
Cost/Compensation: Unpaid.
For more information: Mr. Torres Waters, Office

Manager, Women's Enterprise Development, 235 East Broadway, Suite 506, Long Beach, California 90802; (562)983-3747; (562)983-3750 (fax); E-mail WEDCI@aol.com; URL http://www.wedc.org.

INTERNATIONAL

THE ALBANY AGENCY
Location: Europe and United Kingdom
Description: Employment agency.
Positions Available: Au Pairs, Au Pair Plus, and Demi Pairs.
For more information: The Albany Agency, 21 Albany Close, Bushey, Herts WD2 3SG; 0181-950-4025.

CARL-HENRICK NIBBING
Location: Sweden
Description: Helper lives with family and has work to do around the residence/farm.
For more information: C.H. Nibbing, Skillinggrand, 9, S-11120, Stockholm, Sweden.

CLUB MED
Location: Worldwide
Description: Full-service resorts.
Open to: Minimum age 17.
Positions Available: Housekeepers, hotel registration clerks, dance instructors, sports instructors or helpers, computer teachers, and basketball referee.
For more information: Club Med, 3 East 54th Street, New York, New York 10022 or Club Med 106-110 Brompton Road, London SW3 1JJ.

EUROYOUTH
Location: Austria, France, Germany, Spain, Turkey, Italy, Greece, and Portugal.
Description: Placement agency.
Positions Available: Accommodations and food are provided in exchange for English conversation.
For more information: Euroyouth, 301 Westborough Road, Westcliff, Southend-on-Sea, Essex SS0 9PT; (send a self-addressed, stamped envelope); 01702-341434.

1ST FOR AU PAIRS
Location: West Sussex
Description: Placement agency.
Positions Available: Childcare and light housework.
For more information: 1st for Au Pairs, 48 Milton Drive, Southwick, West Sussex BN42 4NE; 01273-1887431; E-mail 106056,2476@compuserve.com.

GOLF LINKS HOTEL
Location: Ireland
Description: Hotel and golf course.
Positions Available: Waitress and housemaid jobs are available for workers, age 17 and up.
For more information: Golf Links Hotel, Glengariff Co., Cork, Ireland.

THE HELPING HAND EMPLOYMENT AGENCY
Location: Great Britain, Austria, Italy, Belgium, France, and Germany.
Description: Employment agency.
Positions Available: Au Pair, Au Pair Plus, and Mother's Helper.
For more information: The Helping Hand Employment Agency, 24 Stourvale Gardens, Chandlers Ford, Hampshire S053 3NE, 01703-254-287; E-mail helphand@tcp.co.uk.

MALTA YOUTH HOSTELS ASSOCIATION
Location: Malta
Description: Placement agency for jobs in youth hostels.
Positions Available: Need people working in positions such as building, administration, decorating, and office work.
For more information: Malta Youth Hostels Association, 17 Triq Tal-Borg, Pawla PLA06, Malta; (send 3 international reply coupons); 356-693957; E-mail myha@keyworld.net.

NANNY AND DOMESTIC AGENCY
Location: Europe and United Kingdom
Description: Placement agency.
Open to: Ages 17 and up.
Positions Available: Nannies, chambermaids, AuPair/Plus
For more information: Lucy Holland, Nanny and Domestic Agency, 400 Beacon Rd, Wibsey, Bradford, West Yorkshire, BDG3DJ, England; 01274402822.

NEIGE ET MERVEILLES
Location: France
Description: International workcamps.
Positions Available: Workcamps positions available for youth, ages 15-17.
For more information: Recruitment Department, Neige Et Merveilles, F-06430 St. Dalmas de Tende, France; (mention workcamps in correspondence); 493-04-62-40.

SOUTH EASTERN AU PAIR BUREAU
Location: United Kingdom and Europe.
Description: Placement agency.
Positions Available: Au Pair, Demi Pairs, Au Pair Plus, Mother's Helpers, and Nanny positions.
For more information: South Eastern Au Pair Bureau, 39 Rutland Avenue, Thorpe Bay, Essex, SS1 SXJ;

(enclose a self-addressed envelope or international reply coupon); 01702-601911.

THIRD WORLD OPPORTUNITIES

Location: Tecate and Las Palmas, Mexico.
Description: This is an awareness program with opportunities to become involved in community action (house-building) projects.
Open to: Students age 15 and up with a knowledge of Spanish.
For more information: Coordinator, Third World Opportunities, 1363 Somermont Drive, El Cajon, California 92021; (619)449-9381; E-mail pgray@ucsd.edu; URL http://www.scansd.net/two.

NATURE/RECREATION

ADIRONDACK WOODCRAFT CAMPS

Old Forge, New York
Description: Residential camp and environmental education camp.
Open to: High school students.
Positions Available: Counselors, kitchen assistants, office assistant, wilderness trip leaders and waterfront staff.
For more information: Chris Clemans, Program Director, Adirondack Woodcraft Camps, P.O. Box 219, Old Forge, New York 13420; (315)369-6031.

AMERICAN YOUTH FOUNDATION-CAMP MINI-WANCA

Shelby, Michigan
Description: Camp for developing the leadership capacities of young people.
Open to: High school students. Approximately 20 positions available.
Positions Available: Kitchen personnel, building/grounds personnel, and kitchen/dining hall workers.
For more information: David C. Jones, Site Director, American Youth Foundation-Camp Miniwanca, 8845 West Garfield Road, Shelby, Michigan 49455; (616) 861-2262; E-mail wancadave@oceana.net; URL http://www.ayf.com.

BACHMAN-LAING TENNIS CAMP

Whitefish Bay, Wisconsin
Description: Tennis camp for boys and girls, ages 7-17.
Open to: High school students.
Positions Available: Tennis instructors.
For more information: J. Cary Bachman, Director, Bachman-Laing Tennis Camp 6040 North Lydell Avenue, Milwaukee, Wisconsin 53217; (414)962-3306.

BIRCH TRAIL CAMP FOR GIRLS

Minong, Wisconsin
Description: Residential camp for girls, ages 8-15.
Open to: High school students. Approximately 9 positions available.
Positions Available: Swimming instructors, counselors, kitchen helpers, housekeepers, and caretaker's assistant.
For more information: Richard Chernov, Owner/Director, Birch Trail Camp for Girls, 6570 Regal Manor Drive, Tucson, Arizona 85750; (520)529-9358; E-mail brchtrail@aol.com.

BOYS AND GIRLS CLUB OF TAMPA BAY, INC.

Tampa, Florida
Description: Youth development agency.
Open to: Open to high school students, college students, and graduates.
Positions Available: Program assistants, youth leaders, and interns.
Cost/Compensation: Varies.
For more information: Lizbeth Moore, Director of Services, Boys and Girls Club of Tampa Bay, Inc., 3020 West Laurel Street, Tampa, Florida 33607; (813)875-5771; (813)875-5483 (fax); URL http://www.bcctampa.org.

BROOKWOODS FOR BOYS/DEER RUN FOR GIRLS

Alton, New Hampshire
Description: Residential religious camps.
Open to: High school students. Approximately 10 positions available.
Positions Available: Trip staff, waterfront staff, and counselors.
For more information: Bob Strodel, Executive Director, Brookwoods for Boys/Deer Run for Girls, Chestnut Cove Road, Alton, New Hampshire 03809; (603) 875-3600; E-mail brook@worldpath.net; URL http://www.brookwoods.org.

BURROUGHS & CHAPIN CO., INC.

Myrtle Beach, South Carolina
Description: Myrtle Beach Pavilion Amusement Park, Broadway At The Beach, NASCAR Speedpark, and Myrtle Waves Water Park.
Open to: Positions available from March through September.
Positions Available: Ride attendant, food service, games attendant, go cart attendant, lifeguards, and park maintenance.
Cost/Compensation: Approximately $6.50/hour.
Other information: Many seasonal positions available - four different parks.
For more information: Tara R. Little, HR Generalist, Burroughs & Chapin Co., Inc., 921 N. Kings Highway, Myrtle Beach, South Carolina 29526; (843)626-6623; (843)626-8461 (fax); E-mail tara. little@burroughs-chapin.com.

Focus On...
CampStaff

*Are you interested in working at a summer camp? Visit **www.campstaff.com** to search for jobs available at over 120 camps throughout the U.S.*

Visitors to this website may:

- Search the FREE on-line database for available jobs.
- Register for FREE with CampStaff and have the ability to e-mail your profile to camps you select.
- Once registered, camps can actually search for you using the database.

Working at a summer camp can be one of the most rewarding experiences of your life!

- www.campstaff.com

CALVIN CREST CAMP, RETREAT AND CONFERENCE CENTER
Fremont, Nebraska
Description: Christian (Presbyterian) co-ed residential summer camp. Season from 6/1-8/25.
Open to: Must be 18-years-old. Approximately 1-2 positions available.
Positions Available: Lifeguards, food service staff, housekeeping staff, group counselors, and wranglers.
Cost/Compensation: Room, board, and competitive salary.
For more information: Doug Morton, Administrator, Calvin Crest Camp, Conference and Retreat Center, 2870 County Road 13, Fremont, Nebraska 68025; (402)628-6455; (402)628-8255 (fax); E-mail calvincrest@navix.net; URL http://members.home.net/calvincrest.

CAMP AGAWAM
Crescent Lake, Raymond, Maine

Description: Boys summer camp celebrating 80th season.
Open to: Open to applicants 18 and over. Approximately 8-9 positions available.
Positions Available: Cabin and activity counselors - sports, swimming, windsurfing, sailing, nature trips, dramatics, tennis, ropes, crafts, and photography.
Cost/Compensation: Start at $1,150 plus room, board, and laundry.
Other Information: 125 campers gain real-life experiences like those tomorrows employers will be look for.
For more information: Scott Malm, Program Director, Camp Agawam, 30 Fieldstone Lane, Hanover, Massachusetts 02339; (781)826-5913; (781)829-0208 (fax); E-mail agawam@worldstd.com; URL http://www.campagawam.org.

CAMP ARCHBALD
Kingsley, Pennsylvania
Description: Residential camp for girls, ages 6-17.

Open to: High school students. Approximately 10 positions available.
Positions Available: Unit leaders, waterfront assistants, assistant unit leaders, and kitchen staff.
For more information: Diane E. Bleam, Camp Director, Camp Archbald, 333 Madison Avenue, Scranton, Pennsylvania 18510; (717)344-1224.

CAMP BARNEY MEDINTZ
Cleveland, Georgia
Description: Residential camp for youth ages 8-16.
Open to: High school students. Approximately 56 positions available.
Positions Available: Waterfront staff, nature crafts staff, songleaders, horseback staff, theatre directors, and special-needs staff.
For more information: Mark Balser, Assistant Director, Camp Barney Medintz, 5342 Tilly Mill Road, Atlanta, Georgia 30338-4499; (770)396-3250; E-mail summer@campbarney.org; URL http://www.campbarney.org.

CAMP BERACHAH
Auburn, Washington
Description: Residential and day camps for ages 5-18.
Open to: High school students. Approximately 15 positions available.
Positions Available: Counselors, recreation director, crafts director, lifeguards, horsemanship wrangler/instructor, safari guides, mountain bike guides, kitchen, housekeeping, and maintenance.
For more information: James Richey or Scott Rossiter, Program Director and Program Assistant, Camp Berachah, 19830 Southeast 328th Place, Auburn, Washington 98092; (253)939-0488 or (800)859-CAMP; (253)833-7027 (fax); E-mail berachah@tcmnet.com; URL http://tcmnet.com/~berachah/.

CAMP CHATUGA
Mountain Rest, South Carolina
Description: Residential camp for boys and girls.
Open to: Must be 19 or older. 15- and 16-year-olds may accrue volunteer hours as service campers. Jobs – 45. Volunteers - 9 per session.
Positions Available: Counselors, junior counselors, nanny, and more
For more information: Kelly Moxley, Director/Personnel, Camp Chatuga, 291 Camp Chatuga Road, Mountain Rest, South Carolina 29664; (864)638-3728; (864)638-0898 (fax).

CAMP CHEN-A-WANDA
Thompson, Pennsylvania
Description: Residential camp.
Open to: High school students. Approximately 12 positions available.
Positionss Available: Waterfront specialists, sports specialists (soccer, baseball, basketball, tennis, go cart/quadrunner, gymnastics, hockey, volleyball), arts and crafts specialists, stage management/scenery staff and ropes/rock climbing/rappelling specialists.
For more information: Morey Baldwin, Director, Camp Chen-A-Wanda, 8 Claverton Court, Dix Hills, New York 11747; (516)543-5868.

CAMP CHIPPEWA
Cass Lake, Minnesota
Description: Residential camp for boys.
Open to: High school students. Approximately 2-3 positions available.
Positions Available: Counselors.
For more information: John P. Endres, Director, Camp Chippewa, 11427 North Pinehurst Circle, Mequon, Wisconsin 53092; (414)241-5733.

CAMP DUDLEY
Westport, New York
Description: Christian residential camp for boys, ages 10-16.
Open to: High school students. Approximately 37-38 positions available.
Positions Available: Counselors, drama tech staff, and outdoor/hiking staff.
For more information: Wheaton I. Griffin, Camp Dudley, RR 1, Box 1034, Westport, New York 12993-9711; (518)962-4720.

CAMP ECHOING HILLS
Warsaw, Ohio
Description: Residential camp with Christian emphasis for children and adults with mental or physical disabilities.
Open to: High school students. Approximately 12 positions available.
Positions Available: Counselors and support staff. Competitive salary plus room and board.
For more information: Shaker Samuel, Camp Administrator, Camp Echoing Hills, 36272 County Road 79, Warsaw, Ohio 43844; (740)327-2311;
E-mail campechohl@aol.com.

CAMP ENCORE-CODA
Sweden, Maine
Description: Music and sports camp for campers, ages 8-17.
Open to: Students graduating from high school by June.
Positions Available: Junior counselor. Certified waterfront staff needed (boating, swimming, sailing, etc.) Counselor in Training (CIT) program after grade 10.
Cost/Compensation: $650 for the season.

Other Information: Camper cost of $2,800 for ½ season or $4,900 for full season.
For more information: Ellen Donahue-Saltman, Director, Camp Encore-Coda, 32 Grassmere Road, Brookline, Massachusetts 02467; (617)325-1541; (617)325-7278 (fax); E-mail ellen@encore-coda.com; URL http://www.encore-coda.

CAMP FIRE CAMP WI-TA-WENTIN
Lake Charles, Louisiana
Description: Residential and day camp.
Open to: High school students. Approximately 3-4 positions available.
Positions Available: Lifeguards, counselors, canoeing instructors, and water safety instructors.
For more information: Joe Hill, Director, Camp Fire Camp Wi-Ta-Wentin, 2126 Oak Park Boulevard, Lake Charles, Louisiana 70601; (318)478-6550; E-mail jdhill@iamerica.net.

CAMP FRIENDSHIP
Palmyra, Virginia
Description: Private residential camp.
Open to: Age 17+ counselor-in-training program.
Positions Available: Junior counselors, kitchen staff, store assistants, and laundry staff.
Cost/Compensation: Junior Staff $50-60/week; CIT program cost $1,390 for 5 weeks.
For more information: Linda Grier, Co-Director, Camp Friendship, P.O. Box 145, Palmyra, Virginia 22963; (804)589-8950; (804)589-5880 (fax); E-mail info@campfriendship.com; URL http://www.campfriendship.com.

CAMP HIDDEN FALLS
Dingman's Ferry, Pennsylvania
Description: Residential camp for girls, ages 8-17.
Open to: High school students. Approximately 4-5 positions available.
Positions Available: Lifeguards, program specialists, nature counselor, and counselors.
For more information: Chris Endres, Camp Administrator, Camp Hidden Falls, Girl Scouts of Southeastern Pennsylvania, 100 North 17th Street, 2nd Floor, Philadelphia, Pennsylvania 19103; (215)564-4657.

CAMP INDIAN RUN
Glenmore, Pennsylvania
Description: Residential camp for girls, ages 6-17.
Open to: High school students. Approximately 6 positions available.
Positions Available: Counselors, lifeguards, riding instructors, cooks, and program specialists.
For more information: Chris Endres, Camp Administrator, Camp Indian Run, Girl Scouts of Southeastern Pennsylvania, 100 North 17th Street, 2nd Floor, Philadelphia, Pennsylvania 19103; (215)564-6953.

CAMP JCA SHALOM
Malibu, California
Description: Residential Jewish camp for youth ages 7-17.
Open to: 18 years and older, graduating seniors, and college students.
Positions Available: Counselors, swimming and water safety instructors, rope course leader, drama specialist and more.
Cost/Compensation: Based on experience/age.
For more information: David Kaplan, Administrative Director, Camp JCA Shalom, 34342 Mulholland Highway, Malibu, California 90265, (818)889-5500; (818)889-5132 (fax); E-mail kapper8050@aol.com.

CAMP JEANNE D'ARC
Merrill, New York
Description: Residential camp for girls ages 6-17.
Open to: High school students. Approximately 5 positions available.
Positions Available: Waterskiing instructors, riding instructors, tennis instructors, canoeing instructors, sailing instructor, music/guitar instructor, drama instructor, dance instructor, arts and crafts instructors, swimming instructors, camping instructors, and land sports instructors.
For more information: Brian P. McIntyre, Assistant Director, Camp Jeanne D'Arc, 154 Gadway Road, Merrill, New York 12955; (518)425-3311; E-mail funatcjda@aol.com.

CAMP KANATA
Wake Forest, North Carolina
Description: Residential camp for boys and girls, ages 6-15.
Open to: High school students. Approximately 12-13 positions available.
Positions Available: Counselors.
For more information: Richard R. Hamilton, Director, Camp Kanata, 13524 Camp Kanata Road, Wake Forest, North Carolina 27587; (919)556-2661.

CAMP MADISON
Kingston, New York
Description: Residential camp for boys and girls.
Open to: High school students. Approximately 5 positions available.
Positions Available: Counselors, lifeguards, outdoor educator, computer instructor, and arts and crafts instructor.
For more information: Jack Thomas, Camp Director, Camp Madison, 201 Powder Mill Bridge Road, Kingston, New York 12401; (212)532-5751; E-mail CampMad84@aol.com; URL http://www.madisonsquare.org.

CAMP MANITO-WISH YMCA

Boulder Junction, Wisconsin

Description: Camp featuring wilderness tripping, canoeing, kayaking, and backpacking.

Open to: High school students. Approximately 15 positions available.

Positions Available: Counselors, tripping assistants, and swimming instructors.

For more information: Anne Derber, Assistant Director, Camp Manito-Wish YMCA, N14 W24200 Tower Place 205, Waukesha, Wisconsin 53188; (414)523-1623; E-mail expmwish@ekecpc.com.

CAMP MATOAKA FOR GIRLS

Smithfield, Maine

Description: Residential camp for girls.

Open to: High school students. Approximately 12 positions available.

Positions Available: Swimming instructors, arts and crafts instructors, sewing instructors, tennis instructors, gymnastics instructors, ski instructors, drama/music instructors, ropes course instructors, English equitation instructors, small craft instructors, and pianist/accompanist.

For more information: Michael Nathanson, Director/Owner, Camp Matoaka for Girls, 8751 Horseshoe Lane, Boca Raton, Florida 33496; (800)MATOAKA.

CAMP MERROWVISTA

Ossipee, New Hampshire

Description: Residential camp for boys and girls ages 8-16.

Open to: High school students. Approximately 6 positions available.

Positions Available: Village leaders, waterfront staff, sailing instructor, outcamping equipment coordinator, outcamping food coordinator, arts and crafts coordinator, kitchen staff, and office staff.

For more information: Heather R. Kiley, Director of Camp Programs, Camp Merrowvista, 147 Canaan Road, Ossipee, New Hampshire 03864; (603)539-6607.

CAMP MERRY HEART/EASTER SEALS

Hackettstown, New Jersey

Description: Residential camp for children and adults with disabilities and day camp for children without disabilities.

Open to: High school students. Approximately 5-6 positions available.

For more information: Mary Ellen Ross, Director of Camping, Camp Merry Heart/Easter Seals, 21 O'Brien Road, Hackettstown, New Jersey 07840; (908)852-3896.

CAMP MICHIKAMAU

Bear Mountain, New York

Description: Residential camp for boys and girls.

Open to: High school students. Approximately 6 positions available.

For more information: Ken Riscinti, Camping Director, Camp Michikamau, 360 Main Street, Hackensack, New Jersey 07601; (201)487-6600.

CAMP MOKULEIA

Waialua, Hawaii

Description: Residential camp for boys and girls, ages 7-15.

Open to: High school students. Approximately 4-5 positions available.

Positions Available: Counselors and aides.

For more information: Verta Betancourt, S.C. Programs Department, Camp Mokuleia, 68-729 Farrington Highway, Waialua, Hawaii 96791; (808)637-6241.

CAMP MONROE

Monroe, New York

Description: Jewish residential camp for boys and girls.

Open to: High school students. Approximately 12 positions available.

Positions Available: Counselors, arts and crafts instructors, swimming instructors, volleyball instructors, gymnastics/aerobics instructors, softball instructors and hockey instructors.

For more information: Stanley Felsinger, Director, Camp Monroe, P.O. Box 475, Monroe, New York 10950; (914)782-8695.

CAMP NEBAGAMON FOR BOYS

Lake Nebagamon, Wisconsin

Description: Residential camp for boys. Individualized program with emphasis on wilderness skills and camping.

Open to: High school students. Approximately 30 positions available.

Positions Available: Cabin counselors with skills in sailing, rowing (crew), riflery, and tennis. Certified (WSI) waterfront instructors.

For more information: Roger and Judy Wallenstein, Directors, Camp Nebagamon for Boys, 5237 North Lakewood, Chicago, Illinois 60640; (800)796-7683; E-mail cnebagamon@aol.com.

CAMP NOCK-A-MIXON

Kintnersville, Pennsylvania

Description: Residential camp for boys and girls.

Open to: High school students. Approximately 12 positions available.

Positions Available: Counselors, swimming instructors, tennis counselors, drama directors, crafts director, kitchen staff, maintenance workers, athletic directors, and adventure course instructor.

For more information: Mark Glaser, Director, Camp Nock-A-Mixon, 16 Gum Tree Lane, Lafayette Hill, Pennsylvania 19444; (610)941-1307; E-mail mglaser851@aol.com.

CAMP O'BANNON
Newark, Ohio
Description: Residential camp for boys and girls, ages 9-14.
Open to: High school students. Approximately 4 positions available.
Positions Available: Co-counselors, assistant cook, and maintenance counselor.
For more information: Ted Cobb, Camp Director, Camp O'Bannon, 62 West Locust Street, Newark, Ohio 43055; (614)349-9646.

CAMP PEMBROKE
Pembroke, Massachusetts
Description: Residential Jewish camp for girls.
Open to: High school students. Approximately 15-16 positions available.
Positions Available: Arts and crafts instructors, music instructor, canoeing instructors, sailing instructors, swimming instructors, and archery instructor.
For more information: Leslie Brenner, Director, Camp Pembroke, 42 McAdams Road, Framingham, Massachusetts 01701; (508)788-6968; E-mail cpembrokebren@juno.com.

CAMP PEMIGEWASSETT
Wentworth, New Hampshire
Description: Residential camp for boys, ages 8-15.
Open to: High school students. Approximately 14 positions available.
Positions Available: Assistant counselors and kitchen workers.
For more information: Robert Grabill, Director, Camp Pemigewassett, 25 Rayton Road, Hanover, New Hampshire 03755; (603)643-8055; E-mail robertgraybill@valley.net.

CAMP RED ROCK
Binger, Oklahoma
Description: Residential camp for girl scouts ages 6-17.
Open to: High school students. Approximately 5 positions available.
Positions Available: Counselors, riding staff, specialists in archery, ropes, and arts and crafts, swimming instructor, and assistant cook.
For more information: Linda Marcotte, Program Specialist Red Lands Council of Girl Scouts, Camp Red Rock, 121 Northeast 50th Street, Oklahoma City, Oklahoma 73105; (405)528-3535.

CAMP RIO VISTA FOR BOYS
Ingram, Texas
Description: Residential camp for boys, ages 6-16.
Open to: High school students. Approximately 4-5 positions available.
Positions Available: Activity instructors and counselors, 17-years and older.
For more information: Freddie Hawkins, Director, Camp Rio Vista for Boys, HCR 78, Box 215, Ingram, Texas 78025; (830)367-5353; E-mail fhawkins@ktc.com; URL http://www.vistacamps.com.

CAMP SEVEN HILLS
Holland, New York
Description: Residential Girl Scout camp for girls, ages 6-17.
Open to: High school students. Approximately 6-7 positions available.
Positions Available: Lifeguards, assistant unit leaders, riding instructors, arts and crafts instructors, ropes course specialists, counselor-in-training, junior counselors, kitchen aides, camp aides, and trip counselors.
For more information: Janet M. DePetrillo, Director of Outdoor Program, Camp Seven Hills, 70 Jewett Parkway, Buffalo, New York 14214; (716)837-6400; E-mail janetp@localnet.com; URL http://www.bflogirlscouts.org.

CAMP SHEWAHMEGON
Drummond, Wisconsin
Description: Residential camp for boys, ages 8-14.
Open to: High school students.
Positions Available: Lifeguards, general staff, campout trip leaders, swimming instructors, assistant cook, and dishwashers.
For more information: Bill Will, Director, Camp Shewahmegon, 1208 East Miner Street, Arlington Heights, Illinois 60004; (847)225-9710; E-mail wwill57321@aol.com.

CAMP SIERRA VISTA FOR GIRLS
Ingram, Texas
Description: Residential camp for girls, ages 6-16.
Open to: High school students.
Positions Available: Counselors, office staff, and activity instructors, 17-years and older.
For more information: Freddie Hawkins, Director, Camp Sierra Vista for Girls, HCR 78, Box 215, Ingram, Texas 78025; (830)367-5353; E-mail fhawkins@ktc.com.; URL www.ktc.vistacamps.com

CAMP SKYLINE
Mentone, Alabama
Description: Residential camp for girls located on top of Lookout Mountain

FOCUS ON...

YOUR STATE'S DEPARTMENT OF LABOR

Many states provide assistance to job seekers. Check with your state's Department of Labor and ask what services they have for teenagers.

ALABAMA
Department of Labor
100 N. Union Street, Suite 620
P.O. Box 303500
Montgomery, AL 36130
(334)240-3417 (fax)

Youth Services Department
P.O. Box 66
Mt. Meigs, AL 36057-0001
(334)215-8100; (334)215-3011 (fax)

ALASKA
Department of Labor
1111 W. Eighth Street
P.O. Box 21149
Juneau, AK 99802-1149
(907)465-2700;(907)465-2784 (fax)
http://www.state.ak.us/local/akpages/
LABOR/home.htm

ARIZONA
Department of Labor
Administration Department
State Capitol, West Wing
1700 W. Washington Street, Suite 601
Phoenix, AZ 85007
(602)542-1500; (602)542-2199 (fax)

ARKANSAS
Department of Labor
10421 W. Markham
Little Rock, AR 72205

(501)682-4500; (501)682-4535 (fax)
E-mail doldir@mac.ar.us

CALIFORNIA
Employment Development Department
800 Capital Mall
P.O. Box 826880
MIC 83
Sacramento, CA 94280-0001
(916)653-0707; (916)657-5294 (fax)

COLORADO
Labor and Employment Department
1515 Anapahoe Street
Tower 2, Suite 400
Denver, CO 80202-2117
(303)620-4701; (303)6200-4714 (fax)

CONNECTICUT
Department of Labor
200 Folly Brook Boulevard
Wethersfield, CT 06109-1114
(860)566-5160; (860)566-1520 (fax)

DELAWARE
Department of Labor
4425 Market Street
Wilmington, DE 19802
(302)761-8000; (302)761-6621 (fax)

FLORIDA
Labor and Employment Security Department

303 Hartman Building
2012 Capital Circle, SE
Tallahassee, FL 32399-2152
(850)488-4398; (850)488-8930 (fax)
http://www.state.fl.us/dles

GEORGIA
Department of Labor
148 International Boulevard, NE
Atlanta, GA 30303-1751
(404)656-3015; (404)657-9996 (fax)

HAWAII
Labor and Industrial Relations Dept.
830 Punchbowl Street
Honolulu, HI 96813
(808)586-8842; (808)586-9099 (fax)
E-mail edpso@aloha.net

IDAHO
Department of Labor
317 Main Street
Boise, ID 83735-0001
(208)334-6100; (208)334-6430 (fax)
http:/www.labor.state.id.us

ILLINOIS
Department of Labor
160 N. LaSalle Street, Suite C-1300
Chicago, IL 60601
(312)793-2800; (312)793-5257

INDIANA
Department of Labor

Find your state's Department of Labor

Indiana Government Center South
402 W. Washington Street
Room W-195
Indianapolis, IN 46204
(317)233-3790; (317)233-3790 (fax)

IOWA
Commerce Department
300 Maple Street
Des Moines, IA 50319
(515)281-5705; (515)281-3059 (fax)
http://www.state.ia.us/government/
com/

KANSAS
Human Resources Department
401 SW Topeka Boulevard
Topeka, KA 66603-3182
(785)296-5000; (785)296-0179 (fax)

KENTUCKY
Labor Cabinet
1047 U.S. Highway 127 South
Suite 4
Frankfort, KY 40601
(502)564-5387 (fax)
http://www.state.ky.us./agencies/
laborhome.htm

LOUISIANA
Department of Labor
P.O. Box 94094
Baton Rouge, LA 70804-9094
(225)342-3111; (225)342-3778 (fax)
E-mail webmaster@ldol.state.la.us

MAINE
Department of Labor
20 Union Street
P.O. Box 309
Augusta, ME 04332-0309
(207)287-5292

MARYLAND
Labor, Licensing, and Regulation
Department
500 N. Calvert Street
Baltimore, MD 21202
(410)230-6000; (410)333-0853 (fax)
E-mail dllr@dllr.state.md.us

MASSACHUSETTS
Labor and Workforce Development
Department
One Ashburton Place, Room 1402
Boston, AM 02108

(617)727-1090

MICHIGAN
Jobs Commission
Victor Office Center, 4th Floor
201 N. Washington Square
Lansing, MI 48913
(517)373-9808; (517)373-0314 (fax)
E-mail customer-assistance@state.mi.
us; or http://www.state.mi.us/mjc

MINNESOTA
Labor and Industry Department
443 Lafayette Road, N.
St. Paul, MN 55155
(651)296-6107; (651)297-1329 (fax)
E-mail dli.commissioner@state.mn.us

MISSISSIPPI
Employment Security Commission
1520 W. Capitol
P.O. Box 1699
Jackson, MS 39215-1699
(601)354-8711; (601)961-7405 (fax)
E-mail webmaster@mesc.state.ms.us;
or http://www.mesc.state.ms.us

Agriculture and Commerce Dept.
P.O. Box 1609
Jackson, MS 39215-1609
(601)395-1100; (601)354-6209 (fax)

MISSOURI
Labor and Industrial Relations Dept.
3315 W. Truman Boulevard
P.O. Box 504
Jefferson City, MO 65102-0504
(573)751-4091; (573)751-4135 (fax)

MONTANA
Labor and Industry Department
P.O. Box 1728
Helena, MT 59624-1728
(406)444-3555; (406)444-1394 (fax)
http://jsd.dli.mt.gov/dli_home/dli.htm

NEBRASKA
Department of Labor
P.O. Box 94600
Lincoln, NE 68509-4600
(402)471-9000; (402)471-2318 (fax)

NEVADA
Business and Industry Department
Labor Commission
Grant Sawyer Building, Suite 4900

555 E. Washington Avenue
Las Vegas, NV 89101
(702)486-2750; (702)486-2660 (fax)
E-mail bliinfo@govmail.state.nv.us;
or http://www.state.nv.us/b&I

NEW HAMPSHIRE
Department of Labor
State Office Park South
95 Pleasant Street
Concord, NH 03301
(603)271-3176; (603)271-6149 (fax)

NEW JERSEY
Department of Labor
John Fitch Plaza
P.O. Box 110
Trenton, NJ 08625-0110
(609)292-2323; (609)633-9271 (fax)
E-mail constituentrelations@dol.
state.nj.us; or http://www.state.nj.us/
labor; or http://www.wnjpin.state.nj.
us.

NEW MEXICO
Department of Labor
P.O. Box 1928
Albequerque, NM 87103
(505)841-8518; (505)841-8491 (fax)

NEW YORK
Department of Labor
State Office Building #12
W.A. Harriman Campus
Albany, NY 12240
(518)457-9000; (518)457-0620 (fax)
E-mail nysdol@ajb.dni.us; or http://
www.labor.state.ny.us.

NORTH CAROLINA
Labor Building
4 W. Edenton Street
Raleigh, NC 27601
(919)733-7166; (919)733-6197 (fax)
http://www.dol.state.nc.us/dol

NORTH DAKOTA
Department of Labor
State Capitol, 13th Floor
600 E. Boulevard Avenue
Bismarck, ND 58505-0340
(800)366-6888; (701)328-2031 (fax)
E-mail labor@pioneer.state.nd.us; or
http://www.state.nd.us/labor

Find your state's Department of Labor

OHIO
Department of Labor
Employment Services Bureau
145 S. Front Street
Columbus, OH 43215
(614)466-4636; (614)466-5025 (fax)

OKLAHOMA
Department of Labor
4001 N. Lincoln Boulevard
Oklahoma City, OK 73105
(405)528-1500; (405)528-5751 (fax)
http://www.state.ok.us/-okdol/

OREGON
Employment Department
875 Union Street, NE
Salem, OR 97311
(503)947-1394; (503)947-1472 (fax)

PENNSYLVANIA
Labor and Industry Department
Seventh & Forster Streets
Harrisburg, PA 17120
(717)787-5279; (717)783-5225 (fax)

RHODE ISLAND
Labor and Training Department
101 Friendship Street
Providence, RI 02903-3740
(401)222-3600; (401)222-3654 (fax)
E-mail jcozine@dlt.state.ri.us; or
http://www.dlt.state.ri.us

SOUTH CAROLINA
Labor, Licensing, and Regulation
Department
P.O. Box 11329
Columbia, SC 29211-1329
(803)896-4300; (803)896-4393 (fax)
http://www.llr.sc.edu

SOUTH DAKOTA
Department of Labor
Kneip Building
700 Governors Drive
Pierre, SD 57501-2291
(605)773-3101; (605)773-4211 (fax)
E-mail labor@dol-pr.state.sd.us

TENNESSEE
Department of Labor
710 James Robertson Parkway
Nashville, TN 37243-0655
(615)741-2582; (615)741-5078 (fax)

TEXAS
Workforce Commission
Texas Labor Commission
T.P.Mahoney
(512)463-2829; (512)463-2222 (fax)
http://www.twc.state.tx.us

UTAH
Labor Commission
160 E. 300 South, 3rd Floor
P.O. Box 146600
Salt Lake City, UT 84114-6600
(801)530-6800; (801)530-6390 (fax)
E-mail icmain.bgerow@email.state.
ut.us

Workforce Services Department
140 E. 300 South
Salt Lake City, UT 84111
(801)526-9675; (801)526-9211 (fax)
http://dwsa.state.ut.us

VERMONT
Labor and Industry Department
National Life Building
Drawer 20
Montpelier, VT 05620-3401
(802)828-2288; (802)828-2195 (fax)

Employment and Training Admini-
stration Department
Five Green Mountain Drive
P.O. Box 488
Montpelier, VT 05601-0488
(802)828-4000; (802)828-4022 (fax)

VIRGINIA
Labor and Industry Department
Powers-Taylor Building
13 South 13th Street
Richmond, VA 23219-4101
(804)371-2327; (804)371-6524 (fax)
http://www.dli.state.va.us

WASHINGTON
Labor and Industries Department
P.O. Box 44000
Olympia, WA 98504-4000
(360)902-5889
http://www.wa.gov/Ini/

Workforce Training and Education
Coordinating Board
Building 17
Airdustrial Park
P.O. Box 43105

Olympia, WA 98504-3105
(360)753-5662; (360)586-5862 (fax)
E-mail wtecb@wtb.wa.gov

WASHINGTON DC
Employment Services Department
500 C Street, NW
Suite 600
Washington, DC 20001
(202)724-7500; 9202)724-7112 (fax)
E-mail des27@erols.com

WEST VIRGINIA
Commerce Bureau
State Capitol Complex, Building 17
2101 Washington Street, East
Charleston, WV 25305-0312
(304)588-2200; (304)558-2956 (fax)
http://www.state.wv.us/tourism

Labor Division
State Capitol Complex
Building 3, Room 319
1900 Kanawha Boulevard, East
Charleston, WV 25305
(304)558-3797 (fax)

WISCONSIN
Workforce Development
Department of Labor
P.O. Box 7946
Madison, WI 53707
(608)266-7552; (608)266-1784 (fax)
http://www.dwd.state.wi.us/

Workforce Excellence Division
Job Seekers Services Bureau
P.O. Box 7946
Madison, WI 53707
(608)266-8212; (608)267-2392 (fax)

WYOMING
Employment Department
Herschler Building, 2nd Floor, East
122 W. 25th Street
Cheyenne, WY 82002
(307)777-7672; (307)777-5805 (fax)

FOCUS ON...

U.S. FISH AND WILDLIFE SERVICE

From Alaska to Florida, the Service manages more than 90 million acres of lands and waters and the wildlife resources found within them.

Summer jobs and volunteer positions are available. Applications for summer employment are usually accepted between January and April. Contact the nearest regional office for opportunities available in your area.

PACIFIC REGION
(CA, HI, ID, NV, OR, WA, Pacific Islands)
911 NE 11th Avenue
Eastside Federal Complex
Portland, OR 97232-4181
(503)231-2018 (Job Information Line)
(503)231-6136 (Personnel Office)

SOUTHWEST REGION
(AZ, NM, OK, TX)
500 Gold Avenue, SW
P.O. Box 1306
Albuquerque, NM 87103
(505)766-2033

GREAT LAKES-BIG RIVERS REGION
(IA, IL, IN, MI, MN, MO, OH, WI)
Federal Building
Fort Snelling
Twin Cities, MN 55111-4056
(612)725-3585

SOUTHEAST REGION
(AL, AR, FL, GA, KY, LA, MS, NC, PR, SC, TN, VI)
1875 Century Center Boulevard, NE
Atlanta, GA 30345
(404)679-4014

NORTHEAST REGION
(CT, DE, MA, MD, ME, NH, NJ, NY, PA, RI, VA, VT, WV)
300 Westgate Center Drive
Hadley, MA 01035-9589
(413)253-8200 (Job Information Line)

MOUNTAIN-PRAIRIE REGION
(CO, K, MT, NE, ND, SD, UT, WY)
P.O. Box 25486
Denver Federal Center
Denver, CO 80225
(303)236-4733 (Job Information Line)

ALASKA REGION
(AK)
1011 East Tudor Road
Anchorage, AK 99503
(907)786-3301

SERVICE HEADQUARTERS
(Metro. Washington, DC area including PG County, MD)

U.S. Fish and Wildlife Service
Department of the Interior
1849 C Street, NW
Washington, DC 20240
(703)358-2120

POLLUTION. DEFORESTATION. THE CONTINUED LOSS OF WETLANDS AND OTHER VITAL WILDLIFE HABITAT WORLDWIDE. THESE ARE THE CHALLENGES AMERICANS FACE EACH DAY. AND, THESE ARE THE CHALLENGES THAT MAKE WORKING FOR THE U.S. FISH AND WILDLIFE SERVICE MORE THAN A CAREER.

Visit the website:http://www.fws.gov.

Open to: Approximately 10 high school students.

Positions Available: Instructors for sports, swimming, fine and performing arts, computer, ropes course, canoeing, cheerleading, flag twirling, baton and Christian leadership. Also employ lifeguards and nature specialists.

For more information: Personnel Director, Camp Skyline, P.O. Box 287, Mentone, Alabama 35984; (205) 634-4001

CAMP TEL NOAR
Hampstead, New Hampshire

Description: Jewish residential camp.

Open to: High school students. Approximately 15-16 positions available.

Positions Available: Arts and crafts instructors, kitchen staff, windsurf instructor, canoe instructors, sailing instructors, swimming instructors, maintenance workers, and archery instructor.

For more information: Marty Wiadro, Director, Camp Tel Noar, 131 Victoria Road, Sudbury, Massachusetts 01776; (508)443-3655; E-mail ctn.wiadro@juno.com.

CAMP TEVYA
Brookline, New Hampshire

Description: Jewish camp for boys and girls.

Open to: High school students. Approximately 19-20 positions available.

Positions Available: Arts and crafts staff, canoe instructors, music instructor, sailing instructors, swimming instructors, athletics instructor, waterskiing instructor, archery instructor, photography instructor, and drama instructor.

For more information: Pearl Lourie, Executive Director, Camp Tevya, 30 Main Street, Ashland, Massachusetts 01701; (508)881-1002.

CAMP THUNDERBIRD
Lake Wylie, South Carolina

Description: Residential camp for boys and girls, ages 7-16.

Open to: High school students. Approximately 32-33 positions available.

Positions Available: Outpost instructors, waterskiing instructors, outdoor living skills personnel, challenge course instructors, English-style riding instructors, riflery instructors, archery instructors, swimming instructors, canoeing/sailing instructors, golf instructors, gymnastics instructors, dance instructors, cheerleading/ in-line skating instructors, athletics instructors, and roller hockey instructors.

For more information: Sloane Frantz, Associate Camp Director, Camp Thunderbird, 1 Thunderbird Lane, Lake Wylie, South Carolina 29710-8811; (803)831-2121; URL http://campthunderbird.com.

CAMP THUNDERBIRD FOR BOYS/CAMP THUNDERBIRD FOR GIRLS
Bemidji, Minnesota

Description: Separate residential camps for boys and girls.

Open to: High school students. Approximately 24 positions available.

Positions Available: Counselors and kitchen personnel.

For more information: Carol A. Sigoloff, Camp Thunderbird for Boys/Camp Thunderbird for Girls, 967 Gardenview Office Parkway, St. Louis, Missouri 63141; (314)567-3167.

CAMP TIMBERLANE FOR BOYS
Woodruff, Wisconsin

Description: Residential camp for boys.

Open to: High school students. Approximately 17-18 positions available.

Positions Available: Counselors, swimming instructors, scuba diving instructors, sailing instructors, tennis instructors, photography instructor, pottery instructor, horseback riding instructors, guitar instructors, golf instructors, trip leaders, assistant cook, and maintenance person.

For more information: Mike Cohen, Director, Camp Timberlane for Boys, 6202 N. Camino Almonte, Tucson, Arizona 85718-3732; (520)544-7801.

CAMP TOKHOMEUPOG
East Madison, New Hampshire

Description: Residential camp for boys ages 6-16.

Open to: High school students. Approximately 3-4 positions available.

Positions Available: Counselors, rock climbing instructor, waterfront staff, kitchen helper, and mountain bike instructor.

For more information: Ted Hoyt, Director, Camp Tokhomeupog, HC 63, Bos 40, East Madison, New Hampshire, 03849; (603)367-8896.

CAMP WASHINGTON
Lakeside, Connecticut

Description: Residential and day camp for children ages 5-18.

Open to: High school students. Approximately 12 positions available.

Positions Available: Counselors in Training (16/17), general cabin counselors, program staff, lifeguards, office, and kitchen help.

Cost/Compensation: Room and board, salary (except CIT program - fee is $200).

Other information: Episcopal diocesan camp offering traditional program plus many specialized programs such as theater, choir, community service, family, mini-, camping skills, and wilderness tripping programs. Also offers an intensive Counselor in Train-

ing program for eight weeks of the summer season.
For more information: Elia Vecchitto, Camp Director, Camp Washington, 190 Kenyon Road, Lakeside, Connecticut 06758; (860) 567-9623; (860)567-3037 (fax); E-mail elia_v@hotmail.com.

CAMP WENDY
Wallkill, New York
Description: Residential camp and day camp for girls.
Open to: High school students.
Positions Available: Counselors, waterfront staff, and kitchen helpers.
For more information: Fran Gallagher, Camp Director, Camp Wendy, 65 St. James Street, P.O. Box 3039, Kingston, New York 12402; (914)3388-5367.

CAMP WESTMINSTER
Roscommon, Michigan
Description: Residential camp.
Open to: High school students. Approximately 8-9 positions available.
Positions Available: Lifeguards, counselors, ropes course facilitators, and kitchen staff.
For more information: Suzanne Getz Bates, Executive Director, Camp Westminster, 17567 Hubbell Avenue, Detroit, Michigan 49235; (313)341-2697; E-mail suzanne_bates@pcusa.org.

CAMP WOODMEN OF THE WORLD
Murray, Kentucky
Description: Residential camp for Woodmen of the World members, ages 8-15.
Open to: High school students. Approximately 7-8 positions available.
For more information: Colleen Anderson, Camp Director, Camp Woodmen of the World, 401-A Maple Street, Murray, Kentucky 42071; (502)753-5382; E-mail campwow@idd.net.

CAMP OF THE WOODS
Speculator, New York
Description: Christian family camp and girls camp.
Open to: High school students. Approximately 112-113 positions available.
Positions Available: Counselors, recreation leaders, waterfront staff, musical performance staff, food service staff, operations staff, and office personnel.
For more information: Scott Sonju, Personnel Director, Camp of the Woods, Route 30, Speculator, New York 12164; (518)548-4311; URL http://www.camp-of-the-woods.org.

CAPITAL CAMPS
Waynesboro, Pennsylvania
Description: Jewish residential community camp. Also sponsor leadership trip to Israel.
Open to: CITS (age 17); staff (18+).

Positions Available: Counselors, specialists, and counselors-in-training.
Cost/Compensation: CITS ($700); staff ($800-$1,500).
For more information: Faye Bousel, Executive Director, Capital Camps, 133 Rollins Avenue, Unit 4, Rockville, Maryland 20852; (301)468-2267; (301) 468-1719 (fax); E-mail staff@capitalcamps.com; URL http://www.capitalcamps.com.

CAT'S CAP - ST. CATHERINE'S CREATIVE ARTS PROGRAM
Richmond, Virginia
Description: Creative arts day camp for grades 2-8. Also, preschool ages 3½-7 years.
Open to: High school students. Approximately 32-33 positions available.
Positions Available: Volunteers (14+ years), junior counselors (high school), and senior counselors (college). Six week summer camp program.
Cost/Compensation: $0-$7.00/hour.
For more information: Jan Holland, Director, Cat's CAP - St. Catherine's Creative Arts Program, 6001 Grove Avenue, Richmond, Virginia 23226; (804)288-2804 Ext.45; E-mail jholland@st.catherines.org; URL http://www.st.catherines.org.

CEDAR POINT
Sandusky, Ohio
Description: Amusement park.
Open to: High school students. Approximately 800 positions available.
Positions Available: Food service staff, housekeeping staff, ride operators, arcade staff, and gift shop cashiers.
For more information: Amanda Rose, Assistant Director of Human Resources, Cedar Point, P.O. Box 5006, Sandusky, Ohio 44870; (800)668-JOBS.

CLEARWATER
Poughkeepsie, New York
Description: The sloop, *Clearwater,* is a nonprofit, environmental education program offering a traditional sailing opportunity.
Positions Available: Sailing apprentices (1 month) and education assistants (2 months) for ages 16 and up. Volunteers also needed age 12 and up.
Cost/Compensation: $25-50/week (compensation).
For more information: Captain, Clearwater, 112 Market Street, Poughkeepsie, New York 12601-4095; (914)454-7673; (914)454-7953 (fax); E-mail captain@clearwater.org; URL http://www.clearwater.org.

COLLEGE SETTLEMENT OF PHILADELPHIA
Horsham, Pennsylvania
Description: Residential and day for youth, ages 7-14 from metropolitan Philadelphia.

Open to: High school students.
Positions Available: Counselors, unit leaders, trip leaders, environmentalists, swimming instructors and kitchen helpers.
For more information: Wally Grummun, Director of Resident Programs, College Settlement of Philadelphia, 600 Witmer Road, Horsham, Pennsylvania 19044; (215)542-7974; E-mail camps2@aol.com.

CRYSTALAIRE CAMP
Frankfort, Michigan
Description: Residential camp.
Open to: High school students. Approximately 4-5 positions available.
Positions Available: Stable helper and junior counselors.
For more information: David B. Reid, Director, Crystalaire Camp, 2768 South Shore Road East, Frankfort, Michigan 49635; (616)352-7589;
E-mail xtalaire@benzie.com.

CYO BOYS CAMP
Port Sanilac, Michigan
Description: Summer camp for boys, ages 7-16.
Open to: Boys, 16 years and older.
Positions Available: Group counselors and counselors-in-training.
Cost/Compensation: $800-$1,000
For more information: Ebony Padgett, Administrative Assistant, CYO Boys Camp, 305 Michigan Avenue, Detroit, Michigan 48266; (313)963-7172 Ext. 145; (313)963-7179 (fax); E-mail steve@cyocamps.org; URL http://www.cyocamps.org.

CYO GIRLS CAMP
Port Sanilac, Michigan
Description: Summer camp for girls, ages 7-16.
Open to: Girls, 17 years and older.
Positions Available: Group counselors and counselor-in-training.
Cost/Compensation: $800-$1,000.
For more information: Ebony Padgett, Administrative Assistant, CYO Girls Camp, 305 Michigan Avenue, Detroit, Michigan 48226; (313)963-7172 Ext. 145; (313)963-7179; E-mail steve@cyocamps.org; URL http://cyocamps.org.

DEEP PORTAGE CONSERVATION RESERVE
Hackensack, Minnesota
Description: Environmental education and resource management demonstration facility.
Open to: High school students. Approximately 1-2 positions available.
For more information: Mr. Dale Yerger, Camp Director, Deep Portage Conservation Reserve, Rt. 1, Box 129, Hackensack, Minnesota 56452; (218)682-2325;

E-mail portage@uslink.net; URL http://www.deep-portage.org.

ECHO HILL CAMP
Worton, Maryland
Description: Private, co-ed summer camp for children, ages 7-16.
Open to: Must be 18-years old. Approximately 4-5 positions available.
Positions Available: Counselors.
Cost/Compensation: Varies.
Other Information: Located on Maryland's eastern shore of Chesapeake Bay.
For more information: Peter Rice, Director, Echo Hill Camp, 13655 Bloomingneck Road, Worton, Maryland 21678; (410)348-5303; (410)348-2010 (fax); E-mail EchoHillCamp@Hotmail.com; URL http://www.echohillcamp.com.

EMANDAL-A FARM ON A RIVER
Willits, California
Description: Residential camp for boys and girls ages 6-16 and a family vacation camp for part of the summer.
Open to: Approximately 3 high school jobs.
Positions Available: Camp counselors, family camp workers, and gardeners.
For more information: Tamara Adams, Director, Emandal-A Farm on a River, 16500 Hearst Road, Willits, California 95490; (707)459-5439; E-mail emandal@pacific.net, URL http://wwwpacific.net:80/~emandal/.

FAIRVIEW LAKE YMCA CAMPS
Newton, New Jersey
Description: Residential camp for boys and girls ages 6-16.
Open to: Must be at least 17 years old. Approximately 9-10 positions available.
Positions Available: Junior counselors, counselors, waterfront, and specialty staff.
For more information: Matt Block, Summer Camp Director, Fairview Lake YMCA Camps, 1035 Fairview Lake Road, Newton, New Jersey 07860; (973)383-9282; (973)383-6386 (fax);
E-mail mattblock@worldnet.att.net..

4-H FARLEY OUTDOOR EDUCATION CENTER
Mashpee, Massachusetts
Description: Residential and day camp for boys and girls ages 7-14.
Open to: High school students. Approximately 9-10 positions available.
Positions Available: Lifeguards, counselors, and kitchen staff.
For more information: Michael Campbell, Executive Director, 4-H Farley Outdoor Education Center, 615

Route 130, Mashpee, Massachusetts 02649; (508) 447-0181.

FRONTIER CITY AND WHITEWATER BAY
Oklahoma City, Oklahoma
Description: Amusement park.
Open to: High school students. Approximately 875 positions available.
Positions Available: Lifeguards, ride operators, games attendants, and retail and food service members.
For more information: Steve Ball, Human Resource Manager, Frontier City and Whitewater Bay, 11501 NE Expressway, Oklahoma City, Oklahoma 73131; (405)478-2140.

FROST VALLEY YMCA CAMPS
Claryville, New York
Description: Residential camp.
Open to: High school students. Approximately 30 positions available.
Positions Available: Counselors, waterfront staff, riding staff, trip leaders, art instructors, and sports staff.
For more information: Rob Lehman, Director of Camping, Frost Valley YMCA Camps, 2000 Frost Valley Road, Claryville, New York 12725; (914)985-2291; E-mail camp4me@aol.com; URL http://frostvalley.org.

FUNLAND
Rehoboth Beach, Delaware
Description: Amusement park.
Open to: High school students. Approximately 20 position available.
Positions Available: Ride and game attendants.
For more information: Steve Henricks, Vice President/Personnel Manager, Funland, 6 Delaware Avenue, Rehoboth Beach, Delaware 19971; (302) 227-2785.

GEAUGA LAKE
Aurora, Ohio
Description: Amusement park.
Open to: High school students. Approximately 980 positions available.
Positions Available: Administrative assistants, gift shop personnel, food service staff, and lifeguards.
For more information: Employment Coordinator, Geauga Lake, 1060 North Aurora Road, Aurora, Ohio 44202; (216)562-8303.

HARVESTING TIMBER IN ALASKA
Alaska
Description: Work in the timber industry at locations throughout Alaska.
Open to: If you are under the age of 18, you need written permission from a parent or guardian.

Positions Available: Road-building crewman, cook, bunkhouse flunky, dishwasher, kitchen helper, mechanics helper, oiler, or general maintenance laborer.
For more information: Alaska Loggers Association, Crazy Horse Drive, Juneau, Alaska 99801. For information about logging in the U.S. write to: "Log Rules and Other Useful Information", Northeastern Logger's Association, P.O. Box 69, Old Forge, New York 13420.

HIDDEN HOLLOW CAMP
Bellville, Ohio
Description: Residential camp for boys and girls ages 7-15.
Positions Available: Counselors.
For more information: Thelda J. Dillon, Director, Hidden Hollow Camp, 380 North Mulberry Street, Mansfield, Ohio 44902; (419)522-0521.

HOLIDAY WORLD AND SPLASHIN' SAFARI
Santa Claus, Indiana
Description: Theme park, water park, golf course, and camp ground.
Open to: High school students. Approximately 375 positions available.
Positions Available: Ride operators, food service staff, lifeguards, games staff, facilities maintenance staff, entertainment staff, admissions staff, office and security staff and gift shop clerks.
For more information: Natalie Koch, Human Resources, Holiday World and Splashin' Safari, P.O. Box 179, Santa Claus, Indiana 47579; (812)937-4401, Ext. 292; E-mail nkoch@holidayworld.com; URL http://www.holidayworld.com.

HONEY ROCK CAMP
Three Lakes, Wisconsin
Description: North campus of Wheaton College providing leadership training and wilderness experiences.
Open to: High school students. Approximately 30 positions available.
Positions Available: Waterfront staff, barn staff, kitchen staff, activity area staff and operational staff.
For more information: Shannon Crowder, Office Manager, Honey Rock Camp, Wheaton College, Wheaton, Illinois 60187; (630)752-5124.

HOWE MILITARY SCHOOL SUMMER CAMP
Howe, Indiana
Description: Howe Military School camp. Some military activities, but lots of typical camp activities.
Open to: Counselors, ages 19-20; waterfront staff, ages 18-20.
Positions Available: Cabin counselors and lifeguards. (Male only.)
Cost/Compensation: Counselors $1,800/six weeks;

waterfront/lifeguard $1,500/six weeks.

For more information: Duane Van Orden, Director, Howe Military School Summer Camp, 1 Academy Place, Howe, Indiana 46746; (219)562-2131; E-mail howemil@aol.com.

JUMONVILLE
Hopwood, Pennsylvania
Description: Residential Christian camp.
Open to: High school students.
Positions Available: Adventure staff, office assistant, lifeguards, snack shop workers, dining room staff, kitchen helper, cookout staff, audio/visual specialist, maintenance/housekeeping assistants, multipurpose floater, and arts and crafts instructor.
For more information: Larry Beatty, President, Jumonville, 887 Jumonville Road, Hopwood, Pennsylvania 15445; (724)439-4912; E-mail LRBeatty@aol.com; URL http://www.jumonville.org.

KEN SLEIGHT PACK TRIPS
Moab, Utah
Description: Wrangling a horse pack trip or trail ride.
Open to: Minimum age 17.
Positions Available: Setting up camp, preparing meals, clean-up and packing everything onto horses.
For more information: Ken Sleight Pack Trips, Pack Creek Ranch, P.O. Box 1270, Moab, Utah 84532.

LIMBERLOST GIRL SCOUT COUNCIL
Fort Wayne, Indiana
Description: Residential camp for girls, ages 7-17.
Open to: Must be 18-years-old.
Positions Available: Unit leaders, assistant unit leaders, lifeguards, waterfront director, and C.I.T. director.
For more information: Jane Straight, Camp Director, Limberlost Girl Scout Council, 2135 Spy Run Avenue, Fort Wayne, Indiana 46816; (219)422-3417; E-mail mschneider@ctlnet.com.

LOCHEARN CAMP FOR GIRLS
Post Mills, Vermont
Description: Residential camp for girls, ages 7-16.
Open to: High school students.
Jobs Available: Field sports instructors, gymnastics instructors, tennis instructors, studio arts instructors, performing arts instructors, sailing instructors, leadership trainers, swimming instructors, canoeing instructors, diving instructor, English-style riding instructors, waterskiing instructors/boat drivers, and kitchen assistants.
For more information: Rich Maxson, Owner/Director, Lochearn Camp for Girls, Camp Lochearn on Lake Fairlee, Post Mills, Vermont 05058; (800)235-6659.

McGAW YMCA CAMP ECHO AND THE OUTDOOR DISCOVERY CENTER
Fremont, Michigan
Description: Residential camp for boys and girls.
Open to: High school students. Approximately 18-19 positions available.
Positions Available: Arts and crafts director, office manager, adventure trip leaders, wilderness site leaders, assistant wrangler, van driver, sailing/canoeing/waterskiing directors, and outdoor education staff.
For more information: Robert Guy, Director, McGaw YMCA Camp Echo and the Outdoor Discovery Center, 1000 Grove Street, Evanston, Illinois 60201; (847)475-7400.

MENOMINEE FOR THE BOYS
Eagle River, Wisconsin
Description: Residential camp for boys.
Open to: High school students.
Positions Available: Team sports instructors, golf instructors, tennis instructors, waterskiing instructors, swimming instructors, soccer instructors, and sailing instructors.
For more information: Glenn Klein, Owner/Director, Menominee for the Boys, 805 Centerbrook Drive, Brandon, Florida 33511; (800)236-2267; E-mail menominee@theramp.net; URL http://www.campchannel.com/menominee.

MOHAWK DAY CAMP
White Plains, New York
Description: Day camp.
Positions Available: Counselors, swimming instructor, ropes instructor, and tennis instructor.
For more information: Mohawk Day Camp, Old Tarrytown Road, White Plains, New York 10603; (914) 949-2635; E-mail mohawk@mhr.net.

NEW JERSEY 4-H CAMPS
Sussex, New Jersey
Description: Residential camp focused on environmental education.
Open to: High school students. Approximately 10-11 positions available.
Positions Available: Counselor, lifeguards, instructors, and kitchen staff.
Open to: Positions available from June to August.
Cost/Compensation: Salary plus room/board and incentive pay.
For more information: Donna MacNeir, Assistant Director, New Jersey 4-H Camps, 100A Struble Road, Branchville, NJ 07826; (973)948-3550; (973) 948-0735 (fax); E-mail 4hcamp@aesop.rutgers.edu; URL http://www.rce.edu.

NEW JERSEY YMHA-YWHA CAMPS
Fairfield, New Jersey

Description: Five Jewish residential camps.

Open to: High school students. Approximately 50 positions available.

Positions Available: Counselors, waterfront, boating and pool staff, athletics staff and specialists in radio, computers, art, photography, cooking, and nature.

For more information: Anne Tursky, Assistant Director, New Jersey YMHA-YWHA Camps, 21 Plymouth Street, Fairfield, New Jersey 07004; (973)575-3333; E-mail njw@njycamps.org.

NORTH BEACH OUTFITTERS, INC.
Duck, North Carolina

Description: Provides adventure-travel, clothes, gear and kayaks.

Open to: Must be 18 or older.

Positions Available: Sales associate. Opportunity to learn business practices, marketing techniques, and display. Must be people-oriented and show initiative in work behavior.

Cost/Compensation: $5.50/hour until trained, then $6.00/hour. Bonus for staying until end of contract. Staff housing available; rent taken from paycheck. Store is located on the sound side and beach is two blocks away.

For more information: Sandra or George Keefe, Owners, North Beach Outfitters, Inc., 1240 Duck Road, Suite 10, Duck, North Carolina 27949; (252) 261-6262; (252)261-7012; E-mail nboduck@pinn. net.

NORTH CAROLINA STATE PARKS AND RECREATION, MOUNT MITCHELL STATE PARK
Burnsville, North Carolina

Description: State park.

Open to: High school students eligible for park attendant or refreshment stand clerk position. Prefer graduate with experience for refreshment stand manager and naturalist positions.

Positions Available: Park attendant, refreshment stand manager, refreshment stand clerk, and naturalist.

Cost/Compensation: Park attendant and refreshment stand clerk ($6.00/hr); refreshment stand manager and naturalist ($7.25/hr).

For more information: Jonathan Griffith, Park Ranger, Mount Mitchell State Park, Route 5, Box 700, Burnsville, North Carolina 28714; (828)675-4611; (828)675-9655 (fax); Email momi@yancy. main.nc.us.

NORTHWEST YOUTH CORPS
Eugene, Oregon

Description: This is a special summer experience that is an educational job training program. Week-long teams often work in remote areas of the wilderness.

Open to: Students, ages 14-19.

Positions Available: Corpsmembers. Sessions are 4-6 weeks long.

For more information: Rachel Graham, Recruitment Coordinator, Northwest Youth Corps, 2621 Augusta Street, Eugene, Oregon 97403; (541)349-5055; E-mail nyc@nwyouthcorps.org; URL http://www. nwyouthcorps.ng.

OREGON MUSEUM OF SCIENCE & INDUSTRY
Redmond, Oregon

Description: Nature, science, and residential camps.

Open to: High school juniors, seniors, and college students.

Positions Available: Camp counselors.

Cost/Compensation: $10-$25/day; room and board (compensation).

Other information: 1-2 week programs for 7-18 year olds in astronomy, marine biology, arid lands ecology, paleontology, and wilderness skills. Counselors supervise campers in camp and in the field.

For more information: Connie Hofferber Jones, Science Camps Administrative Assistant, Oregon Museum of Science and Industry, 7171 SW Quarry Avenue, Redmond, Oregon 97756; (541)548-5473; (541)504-8365 (fax); E-mail omsicamp@transport.com; URL http://www.omsi.edu.

PALISADES INTERSTATE PARK COMMISSION
Alpine, New Jersey

Description: State park.

Open to: High school students. Approximately 10 positions available.

Positions Available: Assistant boat basin stewards, fee collectors/parking attendants, concession stand operators, historic site attendants, and maintenance workers.

For more information: Jennifer A. March, Supervisor of Visitor Services, Palisades Interstate Park Commission, P.O. Box 155, Alpine, New Jersey 07620; (201) 768-0379.

PENN LAUREL GIRL SCOUT COUNCIL
York, PA and Denver, PA

Description: Girls organization.

Open to: High school seniors and graduates.

Positions Available: Counselors, lifeguards, riding instructors, and sailing instructors.

Cost/Compensation: Paid

For more information: Vicky Miley, Camp Administrator, Penn Laurel Girl Scout Council, Inc., 1600 Mt. Zion Road, P.O. Box 20159, York, Pennsylvania 17402-0140; (717)757-3561; (717)755-1550 (fax); E-mail gsinfo@pennlaurel.org; URL http://www. pennlaurel.org.

PINE TREE CAMPS AT LYNN UNIVERSITY
Boca Raton, Florida

Description: Day camp for children ages 3-15.

Open to: High school students. Approximately 25 positions available.
Positions Available: Counselors, computer instructors, and swim instructors.
For more information: Diane DiCerbo, Director, Pine Tree Camps at Lynn University, 3601 North Military Terrace, Boca Raton, Florida 33431; (561)994-2267.

POULTER COLORADO CAMPS
Steamboat Springs, Colorado
Description: Co-ed residential camp and wilderness adventures for youth ages 8-18.
Open to: Approximately 4-5 positions available. Age 16+ for counselors in training (CIT). Age 17+ for all others.
Positions Available: Wranglers, cooks, arts and crafts counselor, CIT, and assistant counselors.
Cost/Compensation: Varies.
For more information: Lisa Nutkin, Director, Poulter Colorado Camps, P.O. Box 772947-T, Steamboat Springs, Colorado, 80477; (888)879-4816; (970)879-1307 (fax); E-mail poulter@poultercamps.com.

RIVERSIDE PARK
Agawam, Massachusetts
Description: Theme park.
Open to: High school students. Approximately 375 positions available.
Positions Available: Ride operators, security staff, food service attendants, games attendants, merchandise sales staff, first aid staff, and cash control staff.
For more information: Jason Freeman, Director of Operations, Riverside Park, P.O. Box 307, Agawam, Massachusetts 01001; (413)786-9300.

ROCKY MOUNTAIN VILLAGE
Empire, Colorado
Description: Residential camp for physically and developmentally disabled children and adults.
Open to: High school students. Approximately 9 positions available.
Positions Available: Nature specialist, assistant cook, athletics specialist, girl's and boy's counselors, maintenance helpers, kitchen helpers, and a secretary.
For more information: Christine Newell, Director, Rocky Mountain village, P.O. Box 115, Empire, Colorado 80438; (303)892-6063; E-mail campinfo@cess.org.

ROLLING HILLS GIRL SCOUT COUNCIL/HIDDEN VALLEY RESIDENTIAL CAMP
Equinunk, Pennsylvania
Description: Residential Girl Scout camp for girls, ages 7-17.
Open to: High school students. Approximately 9 positions available.

Positions Available: Unit assistants, waterfront assistants, assistant cook, kitchen aides, counselors, wranglers, assistant riding director, program directors, boating experience (canoes, sailboats), and lifeguards.
For more information: Lois Klimsey, Director of Camping, Hidden Valley Camp, 1171 Highway 28, North Branch, New Jersey 08876; (908)725-1226; (908)723-4933 (fax); E-mail rhgsc@mail.eclipse.net

SALVATION ARMY OF LOWER BUCKS
Levittown, Pennsylvania
Description: Day camp for children, ages 6-12.
Open to: High school students.
Positions Available: Counselors.
For more information: Maureen C. Carson, Community Programs Coordinator, Salvation Army of Lower Bucks, Appletree Drive and Autumn Lane, Levittown, Pennsylvania 19055; (215)945-0718.

SEA WORLD OF FLORIDA
Orlando, Florida
Description: Marine life theme park.
Positions Available: Food service staff, warehouse personnel, gift shop personnel, operations personnel, landscape personnel, ticket sellers, and tour guides.
For more information: Human Resources Department, Sea World of Florida, 7007 Sea World Drive, Orlando, Florida 32821; (407)351-3600.

SHADYBROOK CAMP AND LEARNING CENTER
Moodus, Connecticut
Description: Residential, coeducational camp for special-needs youth.
Open to: High school students. Approximately 16 positions available.
Positions Available: Waterfront supervisor, recreation specialist, arts and media specialist, special events coordinator, and dining hall supervisors.
For more information: Kirk Zellers, Director, Shadybrook Camp and Learning Center, P.O. Box 365, Moodus, Connecticut 06469; (860)873-8800; URL http://www.shadybrook.com/learningcenter.

SHELLY RIDGE DAY CAMP
Miquon, Pennsylvania
Description: Day camp for girls.
Open to: High school students. Approximately 6 positions available.
Positions Available: Counselors, lifeguards/swim instructors, and nature specialist.
For more information: Chris Endres, Camp Administrator, Shelly Ridge Day Camp, Girl Scouts of Southeastern Pennsylvania, 100 North 17th Street, 2nd Floor, Philadelphia, Pennsylvania 19103; (215)564-4657.

SINGING HILLS GIRL SCOUT CAMP AND CANNON VALLEY DAY CAMPS
Waterville, Minnesota
Description: Residential camp for girls, grades 4-12 and day camp for girls, grades 2-5.
Open to: High school students. Approximately 2-3 positions available.
Positions Available: Counselors and waterfront assistants.
For more information: Tracy D. Christeson, Program Director, Cannon Valley Girl Scouts, Singing Hills Girl Scout Camp and Cannon Valley Day Camps, P. O. Box 61, Northfield, Minnesota 55057-0061; (507) 645-6603.

SIX FLAGS-ST. LOUIS
Eureka, Missouri
Description: Theme park.
Open to: Anyone 15 or over.
Positions Available: Food service, operations, admissions, merchandise, retail, security, entertainment, and cash control staff.
For more information: Karen Wood, Human Resources Recruiting Supervisor, Six Flags-St. Louis, P. O. Box 60, Eureka, Missouri 63025; (314)938-5300; (314)938-4964; E-mail kwood@sftp.com; URL http://www.sixflags.com.

SJ RANCH, INC.
Ellington, Connecticut
Description: Residential camp for girls ages 7-15 with extensive riding and horse care.
Open to: High school students. Approximately 1-2 positions available.
Positions Available: Crafts, kitchen, general and sports staff members and swimming instructors.
For more information: Pat Haines, Director, SJ Ranch, Inc., 130 Sandy Beach Road, Ellington, Connecticut 06029; (860)872-4742; E-mail sjranch@erols.com; URL http://www.kidscamps.com/specialty/sports/sjranch/.

SOUTH SHORE YMCA CAMPS
Cape Cod, Massachusetts
Description: Summer residential camp, adventure trip, and travel.
Open to: 15, 16, and 17 year olds.
Positions Available: Counselor in Training (CIT), Junior Counselor (JC), and campers.
Cost/Compensation: CIT cost $900, JC pays $90/week, and trips cost $900.
For more information: Carol Sharman, Camp Director, South Shore YMCA Camps, 75 Stowe Road, Sandwich, Massachusetts 02563; (508)428-2571; (508)420-3545;
E-mail ssymca@capecod.net; URL http://www.oncapecod.net/ssymca.

ST. ALBANS SUMMER PROGRAMS
Washington, DC
Description: Classes, sports camps and a day camp at a private school.
Open to: High school students. Approximately 20 positions available.
Positions Available: Sports counselors, tutors, day camp workers, and counselors.
For more information: Ms. Kim Lau, St. Albans Summer Programs, Washington, DC 20016-5095; (202) 537-6450.

STONY BROOK-MILLSTONE WATERSHEDS
Pennington, New Jersey
Description: Environmental education day camp.
Open to: High school students.
Positions Available: Camp group leaders, camp naturalists, and camp interns.
For more information: Jeff Hoagland, Education Director, Stony Brook-Millstone Watersheds, Environment Education Day Camp, 31 Titus Mill Road, Pennington, New Jersey 08534; (609)737-7592.

STREAMSIDE CAMP AND CONFERENCE CENTER
Stroudsburg, Pennsylvania
Description: Residential Christian camp.
Open to: High school students. Approximately 16-17 positions available.
Positions Available: Counselors, water safety instructor, dining room worker, maintenance worker, and lifeguard.
For more information: Scott Widman, Streamside Program Director, Streamside Camp and Conference Center, RR #3, Box 3307, Stroudsburg, Pennsylvania 18360; (717)629-1902 Ext. 23; E-mail streamside-camp@juno.com.

STUDENT CONSERVATION ASSOCIATION
Charlestown, New Hampshire
Description: Non-profit conservation organization.
Open to: High school students. Approximately 560 positions available.
Positions Available: Resource assistants, high school trail crew, and high school crew leaders.
For more information: Mel Tuck, Recruitment Director, Student Conservation Association (SCA), P.O. Box 550, Charlestown, New Hampshire 03603; (603) 543-1700 Ext. 157; E-mail hs-program@sca-inc.org; URL http://www.sca-inc.org.

STUDENT ENVIRONMENTAL ACTION COALITION (SEAC)
Philadelphia, Pennsylvania
Description: SEAC is a network of high school and college environmental groups dedicated to building the capacity of students to organize for environmental jus-

Focus On...
Jobs with the Federal Government

There are four federal job programs for high school students:
- *FEDERAL JUNIOR FELLOWSHIP PROGRAM - Students selected work for agencies part-time or during the summer.*
- *STAY IN SCHOOL PROGRAM – A financial need program designed so students can work part time during school and full-time during vacations.*
- *SUMMER EMPLOYMENT PROGRAM – Training and work opportunities for students during the summer.*
- *STUDENT VOLUNTEER SERVICES – Students can volunteer to work with government agencies*

Contact the nearest Federal Job Information Center for more information about these programs:

ALABAMA
Building 600, Suite 341
3322 Memorial Parkway South
Huntsville, AL 35801-5311
(205)544-5803

ALASKA
222 W. 7th Avenue, Box 22
Anchorage, AK 99513
(907)271-5821

ARIZONA
Century Plaza Building, Room 1415
3225 N. Central Avenue
Phoenix, AZ 85012
(602)640-5800

ARKANSAS
See Texas

CALIFORNIA
9650 Flair Drive, Suite 100A
El Monte, CA 91731
(818)575-6510

COLORADO
P.O. Box 25167
Denver, CO 80225
(303)969-7050

CONNECTICUT
See Massachusetts

DELAWARE
See Philadelphia, Pennsylvania

DISTRICT OF COLUMBIA
1900 E Street, NW, Room 1416
Washington, DC 20415
(202)606-2700

FLORIDA
3444 McCrory Place, Suite 125
Orlando, FL 32803-3701
(407)648-6148

GEORGIA
Richard B. Russell Federal Building
Room 940A
75 Spring Street, SW
Atlanta, GA 30303
(404)331-4315

HAWAII
Federal Building, Room 5316
300 Ala Moana Boulevard
Honolulu, HI 96850
(808)541-2791

IDAHO
See Washington

ILLINOIS
175 W. Jackson, Room 530
Chicago, IL 60604
(313)353-6192

INDIANA
Minton-Capehart Federal Building
575 N. Pennsylvania Street
Indianapolis, IN 56204
(317)226-7161

IOWA
See Kansas City, Missouri

KANSAS
One-Twenty Building, Room 101
120 S. Market Street
Wichita, KA 67202
(316)269-0552

KENTUCKY
See Ohio

LOUISIANA
1515 Poydras Street, Suite 608
New Orleans, LA 70112
(504)589-2764

MAINE
See Massachusetts

MARYLAND
Room 101, 300 West Pratt Street
Baltimore, MD 21201
(410)962-3822

Find work with the Federal Government

MASSACHUSETTS
Thos. P. O'Neill Federal Building
10 Causeway Street
Boston, MA 02222-1031
(671-565-5900

MICHIGAN
477 Michigan Avenue, Room 565
Detroit, MI 48226
(313)226-6950

MINNESOTA
1 Federal Drive, Room 501
Bishop Henry Whipple Federal Bldg.
Ft. Snelling
Twin Cities, MN 55111
(612)725-3430

MISSISSIPPI
See Alabama

MISSOURI
Federal Building, Room 134
601 E. 12th Street
Kansas City, MO 64106
(816)426-5702

400 Old Post Office Building
Room 815
Olive Street
St. Louis, MO 63101
(314)539-2285

MONTANA
See Colorado

NEBRASKA
See Kansas

NEVADA
See Sacramento or Los Angeles, CA

NEW HAMPSHIRE
See Massachusetts

NEW JERSEY
See New York City or Philadelphia.

NEW MEXICO
Federal Building
505 Marquette Avenue, Suite 910
Albuquerque, NM 87102
(505)766-2906

NEW YORK
Jacob B. Javits Federal Building

26 Federal Plaza
New York, NY 10278
(212)264-0422

P.O. Box 7267
James M. Hanley Federal Building
100 S. Clinton Street
Syracuse, NY 13260
(315)423-5660

NORTH CAROLINA
4407 Bland Road, Suite 202
Raleigh, NC 27609-6296
(919)790-2822

NORTH DAKOTA
See Minnesota

OHIO
Federal Building, 200 W. 2nd Street
Room 506
Dayton, OH 45402
(513)225-2720

OKLAHOMA
See San Antonio, Texas

OREGON
Federal Building
1220 SW 3rd Avenue, Room 376
Portland, OR 97204
(503)326-4141

PENNSYLVANIA
Federal Building, Room 168
P.O. 761
Harrisburg, PA 17108
(717)782-4494

William J. Green Jr. Federal Bldg.
600 Arch Street, Room 1416
Philadelphia, PA 19106
(215)597-7440

Federal Building
1000 Liberty Avenue, Room 119
Pittsburg, PA 15222
(Walk-in only. For mail or telephone
see Philadelphia)

RHODE ISLAND
See Massachusetts

SOUTH CAROLINA
See Raleigh, North Carolina

SOUTH DAKOTA
See Minnesota

TENNESSEE
200 Jefferson Avenue, Suite 1312
Memphis, TN 38103
(Walk-in only. For mail or telephone,
see Alabama)

TEXAS
6B10
1100 Commerce Street
Dallas, TX 75242
(214)767-8035

8610 Broadway, Room 305
San Antonio 78217
(210)229-6611

UTAH
See Colorado

VERMONT
See Massachusetts

VIRGINIA
Federal Building, Room 220
Granby Mall
Norfolk, VA 23510-1886
(804)441-3355

WASHINGTON
Federal Building
915 Second Avenue, Room 110
Seattle, WA 98174
(206)220-6400

WEST VIRGINIA
See Ohio

WISCONSIN
See Minnesota or if close to Milwaukee, call (312)353-6189.

WYOMING
See Colorado

tice.

Positions Available: Internships in Philadelphia and volunteer and coordination opportunities nationwide.

For more information: SEAC National Office, Student Environmental Action Coalition (SEAC), National Office, P.O. Box 31909, Philadelphia, Pennsylvania 19104-0609; (215)222-4711; (215)222-2896 (fax); E-mail seac@seac.org; URL http://www.seac.org.

SUNSET CRATER VOLCANO NATIONAL MONUMENT
Flagstaff, Arizona

Description: The site includes a volcano with cliff dwelling around it.

Open to: High school students.

Positions Available: Assistance at the visitor's center, educational programming for children and interpretive programs.

For more information: Volunteer Coordinator, Sunset Crater Volcano National Monument, Rte. 3, Box 149, Flagstaff, Arizona 86004; (520)526-0502; E-mail SuZan Meiners@nps.gov

TETON VALLEY RANCH CAMP
Kelly, Wyoming

Description: Residential camp featuring horseback riding and backpacking.

Open to: High school students.

Positions Available: Counselors, kitchen staff, laundry staff, maintenance staff, wranglers, and dishwashers.

For more information: Director of Personnel, Teton Valley Ranch Camp, P.O. Box 8, Kelly, Wyoming 83011; (307)733-2958.

TEXAS STAR RANCH
Grandview, Texas

Description: Residential camp.

Positions Available: Lifeguards.

For more information: Texas Star Ranch, 8000 CR 305, Grandview, Texas 76050; (817)866-4857; E-mail texasstarranch@texasstarranch.com.

THUMB FUN PARK
Fish Creek, Wisconsin

Description: Outdoor fun park.

Open to: High school students.

Positions Available: Lifeguards, ride operators, games operators, haunted mansion actors, food service staff and maintenance staff.

For more information: Peg Butchart, General Manager, Thumb Fun Park, P.O. Box 128, Fish Creek, Wisconsin 54212; (414)868-3418.

TOM AND WOODS' MOOSE LAKE WILDERNESS CANOE TRIPS
Ely, Minnesota

Description: Wilderness canoe/fishing outfitter.

Positions Available: General staff members.

For more information: Lyle Williams, Tom & Woods' Moose Lake Wilderness Canoe Trips, P.O. Box 358, Ely, Minnesota 55731; (218)365-5837.

TUMBLEWEED DAY CAMP
Brentwood, California

Description: Day camp for 400 children.

Open to: High school students. Approximately 15 jobs.

Positions Available: Swim instructors, lifeguards, horseback riding instructors, and horseback riding wranglers.

For more information: Teri Naftulin, Executive Director, Tumbleweed Day Camp, P.O. Box 49291, Los Angeles, California, 90049; (310)472-7474.

UNITED METHODIST CAMPS
Raleigh, North Carolina

Description: Three residential Christian camps.

Open to: High school students. Approximately 15 positions available.

Positions Available: Counselors, lifeguards, sailing/canoeing instructors, naturalists, and arts and crafts instructors.

For more information: Sue Ellen Nicholson, Director, Camping Ministries, United Methodist Camps, P.O. Box 10955, Raleigh, North Carolina, 27605; (919) 832-9560.

UNIVERSITY OF RHODE ISLAND SUMMER PROGRAMS
West Greenwich, Rhode Island

Description: Residential camp.

Open to: High school students.

Positions Available: Lifeguards, counselors, expedition leaders, and day camp teachers. Junior counselor positions available for high school students.

For more information: John Jacques, Manager, Environmental Education Center, University of Rhode Island Summer Programs, 401 Victory Highway, West Greenwich, Rhode Island 02817; (401)397-3304 Ext. 6043; E-mail urieec@uriacc.uri.edu; URL http://www.uri.edu/ajc.

VOLUNTEERS FOR OUTDOOR COLORADO
Denver, Colorado

Description: This organization has a list of hundreds of opportunities for volunteers and interns around Colorado. A free catalog is available.

For more information: Jennifer Burstein, Clearinghouse Coordinator, Volunteers for Outdoor Colorado, 600 S. Marion Parkway, Denver, Colorado 80209-2597; (303)715-1010 or (800)925-2220; (303)715-1212 (fax); E-mail voc@voc.org; http://www.voc.org.

WEST RIVER UNITED METHODIST CENTER
Churchton, Maryland
Description: United Methodist summer camp.
Open to: Resident positions open to persons 18 years and older. Approximately 1-2 positions available.
Positions Available: Food service, program counselors, lifeguards, and sailing instructors.
Cost/Compensation: $175/week and up.
For more information: Andrew Thornton, Manager, West River United Methodist Center, P.O. Box 429, Churchton, Maryland, 20733; (410)867-0991; (410) 867-3741; E-mail westrivercenter@juno.com.

WILDERNESS EXPERIENCES UNLIMITED
Westfield, Massachusetts
Description: Residential program for campers, ages 8-17.
Open to: High school students. Approximately 5 positions available.
Positions Available: Counselors and trip leaders.
For more information: T. Scott Cook, Executive Director, Wilderness Experiences Unlimited, 499 Loomis, Street, Westfield, Massachusetts 01085; (413) 562-7431; URL http://www.weu.com.

WORLDS OF FUN/OCEANS OF FUN
Kansas City, Missouri
Description: Amusement park.
Open to: High school students. Approximately 2,100 positions available.
Positions Available: Food operations staff, ride operations staff, merchandise staff, games staff, lifeguards, ticket sellers, and grounds personnel. Internships available.
For more information: Human Resources Department, Worlds of Fun/Oceans of Fun, 4545 WOF Avenue, Kansas City, Missouri 64161; (816)454-4545.

YMCA CAMP CHEERIO
Glade Valley, North Carolina
Description: Residential camp.
Open to: High school students. Approximately 36 positions available.
Positions Available: Junior counselors.
For more information: Michaux Crocker, Executive Director, YMCA Camp Cheeriio, P.O. Box 6258, High Point, North Carolina 27262; (910)869-0195; E-mail ymcaheerio@aol.com.

YMCA CAMP CHINGACHGOOK
Kattskill Bay, New York
Description: Residential camp for boys and girls.
Open to: High school students. Approximately 20 positions available.
Positions Available: Counselors, general camp staff, and adventure trip leaders.

For more information: Matthew Kerchner, Summer Camp Director, YMCA Camp Chingachgook, Kattskill Bay, New York 12844; (518)656-9462; E-mail chingachgook@aol.com.

YMCA CAMP FITCH
North Springfield, Pennsylvania
Description: Residential camp.
Open to: High school students. Approximately 35 positions available.
Positions Available: Counselors, special population counselor, and kitchen steward.
For more information: Bill Lyder, Executive Camp Director, YMCA Camp Fitch, 17 North Champion Street, Youngstown, Ohio 44501-1287; (330)744-8411.

YMCA CAMP FULLER
Wakefield, Rhode Island
Description: Residential camp for boys and girls, ages 7-16.
Open to: High school students. Approximately 14 positions available.
Positions Available: Counselors.
For more information: Jerry Huncosky, Executive Director, YMCA Camp Fuller, 619 Camp Fuller Road, Wakefield, Rhode Island 02879; (401)521-1470.

YMCA CAMP ICAGHOWAN
Amery, Wisconsin
Description: Residential camp for boys and girls.
Positions Available: Counselors.
For more information: Nancy Hoppe, Executive Director, YMCA Camp Icaghowan, 4 West Rustic Lodge Avenue, Minneapolis, Minnesota 55409; (612)823-5283.

YMCA CAMP IHDUHPI
Loretto, Minnesota
Description: Residential camp for boys and girls.
Open to: High school students. Approximately 18 positions available.
Positions Available: Program director, unit director, waterfront director, riding director, experienced ropes course director, nature director, arts and crafts director, and trip director, and counselors.
For more information: Anna Raske, Camp Director, YMCA Camp Ihduhpi, Box 37, Loretto, Minnesota 55357; (612)479-1146; E-mail ymca-ihd@mtn.org.

YMCA CAMP LETTS
Edgewater, Maryland
Description: Residential camp for boys and girls, ages 8-16.
Open to: High school students. Approximately 10 positions available.

Positions Available: Assistant counselors.

For more information: Scott Peckins, Executive Director, YMCA Camp Letts, P.O. Box 208, Edgewater, Maryland 21037; (301)261-4286.

YMCA CAMP LYNDON
Sandwich, Massachusetts
Description: Day camp.

Open to: High school students. Approximately 35 positions available.

Positions Available: Counselors, archery instructors, and boating instructors.

For more information: Doreen Murphy, Youth and Camping Services Director, YMCA Camp Lyndon, 117 Stowe Road, Sandwich, Massachusetts 02563; (508)428-9251.

YMCA CAMP SEYMOUR
Gig Harbor, Washington
Description: Residential camp.

Open to: High school students.

Positions Available: Cabin leaders, trip leaders arts and crafts specialist, outdoor specialist, outpost coordinators, and unit leaders.

For more information: Dan Martin, Director of Camping and Conference Services, YMCA Camp Seymour, 1002 South Pearl Street, Tacoma, Washington 98465; (206)564-9622.

YMCA CAMP SURF
Imperial Beach, California
Description: Residential oceanfront camp.

Open to: High school students. Approximately 4 positions.

Positions Available: Camp counselors and lifeguards.

Cost/Compensation: $25-$38/day with room and board.

For more information: Mark Thompson, Camp Director, YMCA Camp Surf, 106 Carnation Avenue, Imperial Beach, California 91932; (619)423-5850; (619) 423-4141; E-mail campsurf@ymca.org; URL http://www.ymca.org/camp/.

YOSEMITE CONCESSION SERVICES CORP.
Yosemite National Park, California
Description: Primary concession group in Yosemite National Park.

Open to: Open to high school students. Must be 18.

Positions Available: Housekeeping, varied sports activities, and food service.

For more information: Employee Relations Manager, Yosemite Concession Services Corporation, Human Resources Department, P.O. Box 578, Yosemite National Park, California 95389; (209)372-1236; E-mail hr@ycsc.com; URL http://www.coolworks.com/showme/yosemite.

YWCA OF ST. PAUL
St. Paul, Minnesota
Description: Organization committed to serving women and families.

Open to: Open to high school students and graduates.

Positions Available: Teen counselors and summer positions.

Cost/Compensation: Paid — hourly wage.

For more information: Elizabeth Ellis, Volunteer Coordinator, YWCA of St. Paul, 198 Western Avenue, North, St. Paul, Minnesota 55102-1790; (651)222-3741; (651)222-6307 (fax); E-mail eellisywcaofstpaul.org.

Y.O. ADVENTURE CAMP
Mountain Home, Texas
Description: Residential camp for boys and girls.

Open to: High school students.

Positions Available: Counselors, assistant wrangler, and corral assistant.

For more information: Dan W. Reynolds, Director, Y.O. Adventure Camp, HC 01, Box 555, Mountain Home, Texas 78058-9705; (210)640-3220; E-mail dreynold@ktc.com; URL http://www.kidscamps.com/raditional/yo-adventure.

RESORT/HOSPITALITY

ABSAROKA MOUNTAIN LODGE
Wapiti, Wyoming
Description: Guest ranch.

Open to: High school students.

Positions Available: Waiters/waitresses, cabin staff, maintenance person, front desk person, and wranglers.

For more information: Bob Kudelski, Owner, Absaroka Mountain Lodge, 1231 East Yellowstone Highway, Wapiti, Wyoming 82450; (307)587-3963; E-mail bkudelsk@wyoming.com.

AMERICAN PRESIDENTS RESORT
Custer, South Dakota
Description: Family-oriented facility with cabins, campground, and resort.

Open to: Positions available for the summer season — Memorial Day to Labor Day.

Positions Available: Need desk clerks, housekeeping staff, and laundry workers.

Cost/Compensation: Hourly wage. Housing available.

For more information: Ione Fejfar, General Manager, American Presidents Resort, P.O. Box 446, Custer, South Dakota 57730; (605)673-3373; (605)673-3449 (fax); E-mail APResort@gwtc.net; URL http://www.presidentsresort.com.

AMRAC PARKS & RESORTS, MOUNT RUSHMORE NATIONAL MEMORIAL
Keystone, North Dakota
Description: Provide guest services at Mount Rushmore National Memorial.
Open to: Until October 15.
Positions Available: Food attendant, gift shop attendant, accounting audit, and maintenance.
Cost/Compensation: $5.50 (minimum).
For more information: Russ Jobman, Director Human Resources, Operations, AmFac Parks & Resorts, Mt. Rushmore National Memorial, P.O. Box 178, Keystone, South Dakota 57751-0178; (605)574-2515; (605)574-2495 (fax); E-mail fharvey@mtrushmoregiftshop.com; URL http://www.coolworks.com/showme/rushmore.

BAR NI RANCH
Weston, Colorado
Description: Private guest ranch.
Open to: High school students. Approximately 2-3 positions.
Positions Available: Wranglers, mechanics, cook's helper, waiters, child care, and lawn care assistants.
For more information: Tom and Linda Perry, Ranch Managers, Bar NI Ranch, 6614 Highway 12, Weston, Colorado, 81091; (719)868-3331; E-mail barniranch@aol.com.

BOOTHBAY HARBOR YACHT CLUB
West Boothbay Harbor, Maine
Description: Yacht club with a junior activities program.
Open to: High school students. Approximately 2-3 positions available.
Positions Available: Sailing instructors and tennis instructors.
For more information: Marianne Reynolds, Boothbay Harbor Yacht Club, 34 Pin Oak Road, Skillman, New Jersey 08558; (609)466-0894; E-mail reynoldm.mccc.edu..

BRIDGES RESORT AND RACQUET CLUB
Warren, Vermont
Description: Tennis and condominium facility.
Open to: High school students.
Positions Available: Tennis desk/front desk staff, tennis staff, and swimming instructors.
For more information: Holly Hodgkins, General Manager, Bridges Resort and Racquet Club, Sugarbush Access Road, Warren, Vermont 05674; (802) 583-2922; E-mail bridges@madriver.com; URL http://www.bridgesresort.com.

CUSTER STATE PARK RESORT COMPANY
Custer, South Dakota
Description: Four resorts.

Open to: High school students. Approximately 30 positions available.
Positions Available: Waiters/waitresses, cook's assistants, kitchen/food preparation personnel, housekeeping personnel, front desk/reservations personnel/ hosts/ hostesses, maintenance personnel, and dishwashers/ buspersons.
For more information: Phil Lampert, President, Custer State Park Resort Company, HC 83, Box 74, Custer, South Dakota 57730; (605)255-4541 or (800)658-3530; URL http://www.coolworks.com/showme/custer/ or www.custerresorts.com.

DROWSY WATER RANCH
Granby, Colorado
Description: Mountain dude ranch.
Open to: High school students. Approximately 3-4 positions.
Jobs Available: Wranglers, guides, maintenance staff, assistant cooks, dishwashers, housekeepers, waiters, and office worker.
For more information: Randy Sue Fosha, Owner, Drowsy Water Ranch, P.O. Box 147 J, Granby, Colorado, 80446; (970)725-3456; E-mail dwrken@aol.com, URL http://www.duderanch.com/drowsy_water.html.

EL RANCHO STEVENS
Gaylord, Michigan
Description: Family resort.
Open to: High school students. Approximately 2-3 positions available.
Positions Available: Waiters/waitresses, housekeepers, waterskiing instructor/boat driver, riding instructors/ trail guides, office personnel, and children's counselors.
For more information: Personnel Department, El Rancho Stevens, P.O. Box 495, Gaylord, Michigan 49735; (517)732-5090.

GLORIETA BAPTIST CONFERENCE CENTER
Glorieta, New Mexico
Description: Conference facility.
Open to: High school students. Approximately 60 positions available.
Positions Available: Front desk staff, sound and lighting technicians, preschool workers, day-camp workers, chuckwagon workers, housekeeping staff, food service staff, residence hall/campus ministry staff, conference service staff, and maintenance workers.
For more information: Billie L. Koller, Administrative Coordinator, Glorieta Baptist Conference Center, P.O. Box 8, Glorieta, New Mexico 87535; (505)757-6161.

GRAND TARGHEE SKI AND SUMMER RESORT
Alta, Wyoming

Description: This is a small resort on the west side of Teton Mountain range.

Open to: High school students.

Positions Available: Guest services, accounting/administrative, maintenance, lodging, food and beverage, retail, and rental.

For more information: Personnel, Grand Targhee Ski and Summer Resort, Ski Hill Road, Box SKI, Alta, Wyoming 83422; (307)353-2300 or (800)827-4433.

GRAND VIEW LODGE GOLF AND TENNIS CLUB
Nisswa, Minnesota

Description: Full-service resort located on beautiful Gull Lake.

Open to: High school students. Approximately 60 positions available.

Positions Available: Dining room personnel, beach staff, and housekeeping staff.

For more information: Paul Welch, Operations Manager, Grand View Lodge Golf and Tennis Club, South 134 Nokomis Avenue, Nisswa, Minnesota 56468; (218)963-2234; (218)963-2269 (fax); E-mail vacation@grandviewlodge.com; URL http://www.grandviewlodge.com.

HATCHETT MOTEL AND RESTAURANT
Moran, Wyoming

Description: Motel and restaurant.

Positions Available: Gas station attendants, desk attendants, kitchen helpers, housekeeping staff, waiters/waitresses, yard maintenance person, and relief position person.

For more information: Stan and Carlene Barthel, Managers, Hatchet Motel and Restaurant, P.O. Box 316, Moran, Wyoming 83013; (208)787-2166.

IDLEASE AND SHORELANDS GUEST RESORT
Kennebunk, Maine

Description: Resort serving visitors to Kennebunkport.

Open to: High school students. 1-2 positions available.

Positions Available: Housekeeping associates.

For more information: Sonja Haag-Ducharme, Owner, Idlease and Shorelands Guest Resort, P.O. Box 3035, Kennebunk, Maine 04043; (207)985-4460; E-mail idlease@mail.vrmedia.com; URL http://www.vrmedia.com/idlease/.

THE INN OF THE SEVENTH MOUNTAIN
Bend, Oregon

Description: Resort.

Open to: High school students. Approximately 15 positions available.

Positions Available: Housekeepers, waiter/waitresses, recreation leaders, front desk staff, host/cashier and dishwasher.

For more information: Carol Garrison, Human Resources Director, The Inn of the Seventh Mountain, 18575 SW Century Drive, Bend, Oregon 97702; (541) 382-8711; E-mail executiveoffice@7thmtn.com

KIAWAH ISLAND RESORT
Kiawah, South Carolina

Description: Golf course and resort.

Open to: High school students. Approximately 80 positions available.

Positions Available: Waiters/waitresses, guest service agents, camp counselors, tennis/golf shop attendants, pool and bike shop attendants, and housekeeping staff.

For more information: Human Resources Department, Kiawah Island Resort, 12 Kiawah Beach Drive, Kiawah Island, South Carolina 29455; (803)768-6000; URL http://www.coolworks.com.

LAKE GENEVA CAMPUS, GEORGE WILLIAMS COLLEGE EDUCATION CENTERS
Williams Bay, Wisconsin

Description: Conference center.

Open to: High school students. Approximately 37-38 positions available.

Positions Available: Lifeguards, housekeepers, food service staff, grounds crew, front desk staff, preschool/day care staff, arts and crafts staff, golf course staff, conference center set-up staff, and snack shop workers.

For more information: Richard Miller, Director of Personnel, Lake Geneva Campus, George Williams College Education Centers, P.O. Box 210, Williams Bay, Wisconsin 53191-0210; (414)245-8508.

LAZY HILLS GUEST RANCH
Ingram, Texas

Description: Resort ranch.

Open to: High school students.

Positions Available: Activities director, waiters/waitresses, wranglers, and office worker.

For more information: Mindy Ferguson, Office Manager, Lazy Hills Guest Ranch, Box G, Ingram, Texas 78025; (210)367-5600.

LAZY K BAR RANCH
Big Timber, Montana

Description: Cattle and horse ranch.

Open to: High school students. Approximately 8-9 positions available.

Positions Available: Waiters/waitresses, housekeepers, laundry worker, split-shift worker, storekeeper, choreperson, children's wrangler, and dishwasher.

For more information: Lazy K Bar Ranch, P.O. Box 1181, Big Timber, Montana 59011; (406)537-4404.

MICHILLINDA BEACH LODGE
Whitehall, Michigan
Description: Vacation resort.
Open to: High school students. Approximately 17-18 positions available.
Positions Available: Housekeeping staff, kitchen staff, grounds maintenance staff, and dining room staff.
For more information: Don Eilers, Manager, Michillinda Beach Lodge, 5207 Scenic Drive, Whitehall, Michigan 49461; (616)893-1895.

PALMER GULCH RESORT/MT. RUSHMORE KOA
Hill City, South Dakota
Description: Full-service resort providing camping, cabin, and motel accommodations.
Open to: U.S. students, 16 years or older.
Positions Available: Registration, retail sales, maintenance, housekeeping, and waterslide.
Cost/Compensation: 1997 - $5.30/hr. plus season end bonus.
For more information: Sharon Nilson, Assistant Manager, Palmer Gulch Resort/Mt. Rushmore KOA, Box 295, Hill City, South Dakota 57745; (605)574-2525; (605)574-2574 (fax); E-mail palmerkoa@aol.com.

THE PEAKS AT TELLURIDE RESORT
Telluride, Colorado
Description: Luxury resort and spa.
Open to: High school students. Approximately 7-8 positions.
Positions Available: Kids spa counselors, bell staff, food/beverage staff, kitchen staff, housekeeping staff, and spa staff.
For more information: Human Resources, The Peaks at Telluride Resort, P.O. Box 2702, Telluride, Colorado, 81435; (970)728-6800.

SUNRISE RESORT
Moodus, Connecticut
Description: Summer resort for families, day outing groups, weddings, and music festivals.
Open to: High school students. Approximately 60 jobs available. Must be 19 years old to live on grounds.
Positions Available: Lifeguards, waitstaff, swimming instructors, office personnel and tennis instructor.
For more information: Jim Johnson, Director, Sunrise Resort, P.O. Box 415, Moodus, Connecticut 06469; (860)873-8681.

TOPNOTCH AT STOWE
Stowe, Vermont
Description: Resort.
Open to: High school students.
Positions Available: Housekeeping staff, waiters/waitresses, bell staff/door staff, and locker room attendants.
For more information: Judy Ruggles, Human Resources Director, Topnotch at Stowe, P.O. Box 1458, Stowe, Vermont 05672; (802)253-8585.

WOODSIDE RANCH RESORT
Mauston, Wisconsin
Description: Dude ranch.
Open to: High school students. Approximately 15 positions available.
Positions Available: Food service staff, horse-trail guides, country store clerks, yard and pool maintenance staff, and housekeepers.
For more information: Rick Feldman, Woodside Ranch Resort, W4015 Highway 82, Mauston, Wisconsin 53948; (608)847-4275.

WORLD HOST BRYCE VALLEY INN
Tropic, Utah
Description: Resort.
Open to: High school students. Approximately 8 positions available.
Positions Available: Hosts/hostesses, housekeeping staff, waiters/waitresses, prep cooks, dishwashers, and gift shop sales staff.
For more information: Joe Becker, Operations Manager, World Host Bryce Valley Inn, P.O. Box A, Tropic, Utah 84776; (801)679-8811.

"DON'T DISCOUNT ANY TYPE OF WORK EXPERIENCE. TRY A WIDE-VARIETY OF JOBS NOW — WHILE YOU ARE STILL IN HIGH SCHOOL. IT WILL HELP YOU TO DETERMINE YOUR STRENGTHS, WEAKNESSES, INTERESTS, AND ABILITIES. EVEN A JOB THAT YOU HATE WILL TEACH YOU SOMETHING ABOUT FUTURE CAREER CHOICES."

-ALICE N. CULBREATH
AUTHOR, "TESTING THE WATERS"

Focus On...
Kids and Jobs Website

www.pbs.org/jobs/

Developed by the Public Television Outreach Alliance, the Kids and Jobs website is for teens, parents, and educators.

What will you find at this website?:

- Teens can visit the Teen Career Center for fun exercises on planning and training for careers, visit specific job websites, or chat about careers.
- Parents and educators can find career guidance tools.

FOCUS ON...

NATIONAL PARKS

National parks represent an excellent source of summer and part-time jobs. The sites are extremely interesting and varied. There is literally something for everyone. So if you are interested, contact your regional office and see what openings are available.

ALASKA REGION
National Park Service, 2525 Gambell Street, Anchorage, Alaska 99503; (907)257-2526.

INTERMOUNTAIN REGION (COLORADO/ROCKY MOUNTAINS)
National Park Service, P.O. Box 25287, 12795 West Alameda Parkway, Denver, Colorado, 80225-0286; (303)969-2020.

MIDWEST REGION (GREAT LAKES, GREAT PLAINS)
National Park Service, 1709 Jackson Street, Omaha, Nebraska 68102; (402)221-3456.

NATIONAL CAPITAL FIELD AREA
National Park Service, 1100 Ohio Drive, SW, Washington, DC 20242; (202)619-7256.

NORTHEAST REGION (ALLEGHENY AND CHESAPEAKE AREA)
National Park Service, U.S. Custom House, 200 Chestnut Street, Philadelphia, Pennsylvania 19106; (215)597-4971.

NORTHEAST REGION (NEW ENGLAND)
National Park Service, 15 State Street, Boston, Massachusetts 02109; (617)223-5101.

PACIFIC WEST REGION (COLUMBIA CASCADES)
National Park Service, 909 First Avenue, Seattle, Washington 98104-1060; (206)220-4066.

PACIFIC WEST REGION (PACIFIC GREAT BASIN)
National Park Service, 600 Harrison Street, Suite 600, San Francisco, California 94107; (415)427-1300, option 2.

PACIFIC WEST REGION (PACIFIC ISLANDS)
National Park Service, 300 Ala Moana Boulevard, Suite 6305, P.O. Box 50165, Honolulu, Hawaii 96850; (808)541-2693.

SOUTHEAST FIELD AREA (APPALACHIAN, ATLANTIC COAST AND GULF COAST)
National Park Service, Atlanta Federal Center, 1924 Building, 100 Alabama Street, SW, Atlanta, Georgia 30303; (404)562-3296.
For more information, you might also like to visit the following website or guide:

- **http://www.gorp.com/gorp/resources/US_National_Park/main.htm** - This site will provide you with a wide-variety of information about our national parks. It will also provide you with information on ordering the following publication.

- *National Parks Employment Data* by Ben Benton. A directory of over 130 national parks, preserves, monuments and seashores representing over 750 employers. It will guide you through the process of finding and getting a job. The guide is available for $19.95 + $2.50 shipping/handling and can be ordered online at www.gorp.com/gorp/resources/US_National_Park/main.htm; by writing to Ben Benton, National Parks Employment Data, 124 North San Francisco Street, Suite 100, P.O. Box 1392, Flagstaff, Arizona 86001; (888)261-3136; or E-mail bbenton@infomagic.com.

Focus On...

Your State's Park Service

Your State's Park Service is likely to offer both job and volunteer opportunities. Check with your state's office to see what positions are available for teenagers.

ALABAMA
Alabama Department of Conservation
and Natural Resources
Division of State Parks
64 North Union Street
Mongtomery, AL 36130
(800)252-7257; (205)242-2137 (fax)

ALASKA
National Park Service
2525 Gambell Street
Anchorage, AK 99503
(907)271-2737; (907)271-2510 (fax)

ARIZONA
Arizona State Parks
1300 W. Washington, Suite 104
Phoenix, AZ 85007
(602)542-4174; (602)542-4188 (fax)

ARKANSAS
Arkansas Department of Parks and
Tourism
One Capitol Mall
Little Rock, AR 72201
(501)682-1191; (501)682-1364 (fax)

CALIFORNIA
California Department of Parks and
Recreation
Office of Public Relations
P.O. Box 942896
Sacramento, CA 94296
(916)653-6995; (916)654-8928 (fax)

COLORADO
Colorado State Parks
1313 Sherman Street, Room 618
Denver, CO 80203
(303)866-3437; (303)866-3206 (fax)

CONNECTICUT
Connecticut Department of Environmental Protection
State Parks Division
70 Elm Street, P.O. Box 5066
Hartford, CT 06102
(203)566-2305; (203)566-7921 (fax)

DELAWARE
Delaware Department of National
Resources & Environmental Control
Division of Parks & Recreation
89 Kings Highway, P.O. Box 1401
Dover, DE 19903
(302)739-4702; (303)739-3817 (fax)

FLORIDA
Florida Department of Natural Re-
sources
Division of Recreation and Parks
Marjorie Stoneman Douglas Bldg.
3900 Commonwealth Boulevard
Tallahassee, FL 32399
(850)891-5340 ext. 3866; (904)487-
3947 (fax)
Summer Youth Dept. (850)891-8218

GEORGIA
Georgia Parks, Recreation and His-
toric Sites Division
Department of Natural Resources
Floyd Tower E., Suite 1352
205 Butler Street, SE
Atlanta, GA 30334
(404)656-3530; (404)651-5871 (fax)

HAWAII
Hawaii Department of Land and
Natural Resources
Division of State Parks
P.O. Box 621
Honolulu, HI 96809
(808)587-0300; (808)587-0311

IDAHO
Idaho Department of Parks and
Recreation
Statehouse Mail
Boise, ID 83720
(208)327-7444; (208)327-7406 (fax)

ILLINOIS
Illinois Department of Conservation
Lincoln Tower Plaza
524 South Second Street
Springfield, IL 62701
(800)624-3077; (217)782-9552 (fax)

INDIANA
Indiana Department of Natural Resources

Find your state's Department of Parks & Recreation

Division of State Parks
402 West Washington, Room W298
Indianapolis, IN 46204
(317)232-4124; (317)232-4132 (fax)

IOWA
Department of Natural Resources
Wallace State Office Building
Des Moine, IA 50319
(515)281-5145; (515)281-6794 (fax)

KANSAS
Department of Wildlife & Parks
512 SE 25th Avenue
Pratt, KS 67124
(316)672-5911; (316)672-6020 (fax)

KENTUCKY
Department of Parks
500 Mero Street, 11th Floor
Frankfort, KY 40601
(502)564-8110; (502)564-6100

LOUISIANA
Department of Culture, Recreation,
and Tourism
Office of State Parks
P.O. Box 44426
Baton Rouge, LA 70804
(504)342-8111; (504)342-8107 (fax)

MAINE
Bureau of Parks & Recreation
Department of Conservation
State House Station 22
Augusta, ME 04333
(207)287-3821; (207)287-3823 (fax)

MARYLAND
Department of Natural Resources
State Forest and Park Service
Tawes State Office Building
Annapolis, MD 21401
(410)974-3771; (410)974-3158 (fax)

MASSACHUSETTS
Dept. of Environmental Management
Division of Forests and Parks
100 Cambridge St., 19th Floor
Boston, MA 02202
(617)727-3180; (617)727-9402 (fax)

MICHIGAN
Department of Natural Resources
Parks Division
Box 30257

Lansing, MI 48909
(517)373-1270; (517)373-4625 (fax)

MINNESOTA
Department of Natural Resources
Division of Parks & Recreation
500 Lafayette Road
St. Paul, MN 55155
(612)297-7979; (612)297-1157 (fax)

MISSISSIPPI
Department of Wildlife, Fisheries,
and Parks
Office of Parks
P.O. Box 23093
Jackson, MS 39225
(800)467-2757; (601)364-2008 (fax)

MISSOURI
Department of Natural Resources
Division of State Parks
P.O. Box 176
Jefferson City, MO 65102
(800)334-6946; (314)751-8656 (fax)

MONTANA
Department of Fish, Wildlife & Parks
Park Division
1420 E. 6th Avenue, P.O Box 200701
Helena, MT 59620
(406)444-3750; (406)444-4952 (fax)

NEBRASKA
Game and Park Commission
2200 N. 33rd Street
P.O. Box 30370
Lincoln, NE 68503
(402)471-0641; (402)471-5528 (fax)

NEVADA
Department of Conservation and
Natural Resources
Division of State Parks
123 West Nye Lane
Carson City, NV 89710
(702)687-4370; (702)687-4117 (fax)

NEW HAMPSHIRE
Division of Parks & Recreation
172 Pembroke Road, P.O. Box 1856
Concord, NH 03302
(603)271-3556; (603)271-2629 (fax)

NEW JERSEY
Department of Environmental
Protection

Division of Parks and Forestry
State Park Service
CN 404
Trenton, NJ 08625
(800)843-6420; (609)984-0503 (fax)

NEW MEXICO
Natural Resources Department
State Parks & Recreation Division
P.O. Box 1147
Santa Fe, NM 87504
(505)827-7465; (505)827-4001 (fax)

NEW YORK
Office of Parks, Recreation, and
Historic Preservation
Empire State Plaza
Albany, NY 12238
(518)474-0456; (518)486-1805 (fax)

NORTH CAROLINA
Department of Environment, Health,
and Natural Resources
Division of Parks and Recreation
P.O. Box 27687
Raleigh, NC 27611
(919)733-4181; (919)715-3086 (fax)

NORTH DAKOTA
Parks and Recreation Department
1835 East Bismark Expressway
Bismark, ND 58501
(701)221-6300; (701)221-6352 (fax)

OHIO
Department of Natural Resources
Division of Parks and Recreation
1952 Belcher Drive, Building C3
Columbus, OH 43224
(614)265-6561; (614)261-8407 (fax)

OKLAHOMA
Division of State Parks
500 Will Rogers Building
State Capitol
Oklahoma City, OK 73105
(405)521-3411; (405)521-2428 (fax)

OREGON
Oregon State Parks
1115 Commercial Street, NE
Salem, OR 97310
(503)378-6305; (503)378-6447 (fax)

PENNSYLVANIA
Department of Environmental

Find your state's Department of Parks & Recreation

Resources
Bureau of State Parks
P.O. Box 8551
Harrisburg, PA 17105
(717)787-8800; (717)787-8817 (fax)

RHODE ISLAND
Department of Environmental Management
Division of Parks and Recreation
2321 Hartford Avenue
Johnston, RI 02919
(401)277-2635; (401)934-0610 (fax)

SOUTH CAROLINA
South Carolina State Parks
1205 Pendleton Street
Columbia, SC 29201
(803)734-0156; (803)734-1017 (fax)

SOUTH DAKOTA
Department of Game, Fish and Parks
Division of Parks and Recreation
Joe Foss Building
523 East Capitol Avenue
Pierre, SD 57501
(605)773-3391; (605)773-6245 (fax)

TENNESSEE
Bureau of State Parks
Department of Environment and
Conservation
401 Church Street

Nashville, TN 37243
(615)532-0001; (615)532-0046 (fax)

TEXAS
Parks and Wildlife Department
4200 Smith School Park
Austin, TX 78744
(512)389-4890; (512)389-4436 (fax)

UTAH
Division of Parks and Recreation
Administrative Office
1636 West North Temple Suite 116
Salt Lake City, UT 84116
(801)538-7220; (801)538-7055 (fax)

VERMONT
Vermont Agency of Natural
Resources
Department of Forests, Parks and
Recreation
103 South Main Street – 10 South
Waterbury, VT 05671
(802)241-3655; (802)244-1481 (fax)

VIRGINIA
Department of Conservation and
Recreation
Division of State Parks
203 Governor Street, Suite 302
Richmond, VA 23219
(804)786-1712; (804)371-2072 (fax)

WASHINGTON
State Parks and Recreation
Commission
7150 Clearwater Lane
P.O. Box 42650
Olympia, WA 98504
(206)753-2027; (206)753-1594 (fax)

WEST VIRGINIA
Division of Tourism and Parks
Parks and Recreation
State Capitol Complex
1900 Kanawha Boulevard East
Building 6, Room 451
Charleston, WV 25305
(304)558-2764; (304)558-0077 (fax)

WISCONSIN
Department of Natural Resources
Bureau of Parks and Recreation
Box 7921
Madison, WI 53707
(608)266-2181; (608)265-7474 (fax)

WYOMING
Department of Commerce
Parks and Cultural Resources
2301 Central Avenue, 3rd Floor
Barrett State Office Building
Cheyenne, WY 82002
(307)777-7695; (307)777-6005 (fax)

Do you love to work outdoors? Are you interested in biology? Are you passionate about protecting the environment?
Call your state's Department of Parks and Recreation to inquire about jobs, internships, and volunteer positions available in your area.

NOTES

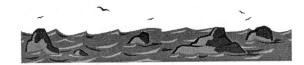

RESOURCES

BOOKS/MAGAZINES/GAMES

GENERAL

After High School, Then What? *How to Determine Career Interests, Set Goals and Get the Job You Want: For Teens and Parents* by Robert T. Pavich.
ISBN 1574810006   softcover   80 pages
$5.99   1997

Career Coaching Your Kids: *Guiding Your Child Through the Process of Career Discovery* by David H. Montross, Theresa E. Kane, and Robert J. Ginn, Jr. Presenting an overview of key events in the lives of children, adolescents, and young adults that may impact their career decisions. Filled with hands-on tools, tips and practical exercises for helping children explore career options.
ISBN 0892061002   softcover   200 pages
$16.95   1997

Career Exploration on the Internet: A Student's Guide to More Than 300 Web Sites! By Elizabeth H. Oakes (editor).
ISBN 0894342401   softcover   208 pages
$15.95   1998

The College Board Guide to Jobs and Career Planning by Joyce Slayton Mitchell. A guide to over 100 occupations and how to prepare for them in high school and college.
ISBN 0874473543   softcover   306 pages
$12.95   1990

Earth Work: *Resource Guide to Nationwide Green Jobs* published by Harper Collins West, SCA. Outlines necessary steps of job search to find jobs in the environmental field.
ISBN 0062585312   softcover
$14.00 + $4.00 S&H
Special ordering instructions: Attn: Earth Work Resource Guide, P.O. Box 550, Charleston, New Hampshire 03603.

Good Works: A Guide to Careers in Social Change. Presents alternatives to traditional employment. Includes aims and projects of over 100 organizations across the United States with contact information, starting salaries, benefits, internships and more.
$24.00 + $2.50 S&H
Special ordering instructions: Good Works, P.O. Box 19405, Washington, DC 20036.

Home School, High School and Beyond: *A Time Management, Career Exploration, Organizational, and Study Skills Course* by Beverly L. Adams-Gordon.
ISBN 1888827157   softcover
$17.95   1996

How to Help Your Child Choose a Career by Luther B. Otto, Ph.D. This book is designed to help parents match their child's choice of school with career orientation, work with lifestyle preference, career with changing economic conditions, and career with long-term demographic trends. Includes a career exploration workbook.
ISBN 0871314347   softcover   329 pages
$11.95   1984

How to Help Your Child Land the Right Job *(Without Being a Pain in the Neck)* by Nella Barkley. A how-to guide for parents about how to navigate the difficult job of helping their job seeker without being intrusive.
ISBN 1563055120   hardcover   350 pages
$19.95   1993

MTV's Now What: A Guide to Jobs, Money and the Real World by J.D. Heiman. A hip, to-the-point, and comprehensive guide to getting a job, life on the job, managing money, and living on your own.
ISBN 0671002023   softcover   239 pages
$12.00   1996

Outdoor Careers: *Exploring Occupations in Outdoor Fields* by Ellen Shenk. Explores outdoor-related fields providing job descriptions and information about salaries, employment outlook, and entry-level requirements. Covers careers in agriculture, food production, biological sciences, engineering, marine careers, recreation, and outdoor careers with indoor twists.
ISBN 0811725421   softcover   272 pages
$14.25   1992
Special ordering instructions: Sagamore Publishing, P.O. Box 647, Champaign, Illinois 61824-0647; (800)327-5557.

What Color is Your Parachute? 1999: *A Practical Guide for Job-Hunters & Career-Changers* by Richard Nelson Bolles. Updated annually, this is a classic on the subject of career exploration. It contains quiz-

zes, exercises, and guidance about finding the perfect career for you.
ISBN 1580080081   softcover   351 pages
$16.95   1999

Working Days: *Short Stories About Teenagers at Work* by Anne Mazer. Fifteen stories explore what it's like to be young and employed.
ISBN 0892552247   softcover   192 pages
$7.95   1997

Your Kids – Their Future: *Every Parent's Guide to Helping Your Child Become Employable* by Gary R. Morrison.
ISBN 0966265106   softcover   219 pages
$19.95   1999

PART-TIME/SUMMER JOBS

National Parks Employment Data by Ben Benton. Provides information about 130 national parks, preserves, monuments, and seashores. Includes information about how and where to apply.
$19.95 + $2.50 S&H
Special ordering instructions: Write to Ben Benton, National Parks Employment Data, 124 North San Francisco Street, Suite 100, P.O. Box 1392, Flagstaff, Arizona 86001; call 888/261-3136 or e-mail bbenton@infomagic.com.

Opportunities in Part-time and Summer Jobs by Adrian A. Paradis.
Provides information about choosing and finding a part-time or summer job or starting a business.
ISBN 0844223158   hardcover   160 pages
$14.95   1997

Overseas Summer Jobs 1999 by Peterson's. Up-to-date complete information on more than 30,000 summer jobs worldwide.
ISBN 1854582208   softcover   256 pages
$16.95   1999

Summer Jobs for Students 1999: *Where the Jobs are and How to Get Them* by Peterson's. Listing of over 25,000 jobs in national parks, business offices, non-profit organizations, camps, resorts, conference centers, dude ranches, theaters, restaurants, hotels, and amusement parks. 47th edition.
ISBN 076890045X   softcover   376 pages
$16.95   1999

The Ultimate Camp Counsellor Manual: *How to Survive and Succeed Magnificently at Summer Camp* by Mark S. Richman. The author is a New York City

teacher with 24 years of experience with camping. This guide for camp counselors covers virtually everything that could ever happen in the camping situation.
$24.95 + $3.00 S&H
Special ordering information: Write to Mark S. Richman, 645 East 14th Street, 2H, New York, NY 10009; call 212/673-4135 or see http://www.campchannel.com.

INTERNSHIPS

America's Top Internships 1999 by Mark Oldham, Samer Hamadeh, and the Princeton Review. Detailed profiles of top 107 internships.
ISBN 0375751696   softcover   405 pages
$21.00   1999

The Internship Bible: 1999 by Mark Oldham, Samer Hamadeh, and the Princeton Review. Includes more than 100,000 opportunities in more than 100 career fields.
ISBN 037575170X   softcover   704 pages
$25.00   1999

Internships in Recreation & Leisure Services: *A Practical Guide for Students* by Edward E. Seagle, Ralph W. Smith and Lola M. Dalton. How to search for an internship, write a cover letter, build a resume, interview, and follow-up.
ISBN 091025155X   softcover   160 pages
$19.95   1992
Special ordering instructions: Venture Publishing, Inc., 1999 Cato Avenue, State College, Pennsylvania 16801-3238; (814)234-4561.

Internship Success: *Real-World, Step-by-Step Advice on Getting the Most Out of Internships* by Marianne Ehrlich Green.
ISBN 0844244961   softcover   192 pages
$12.95   1998

Internships 1997: *The Hotlist for Job Hunters* by Sara Dulaney Gilbert. Lists and describes more than 25,000 internship opportunities in business, government, social services, the arts, and other fields; detailing eligibility requirements, application procedures, and more.
ISBN 0028612256   softcover   432 pages
$19.95   1997

Internships 1999: *More Than 50,000 Opportunities to Get an Edge in Today's Competitive Job Market* by Peterson's. A comprehensive directory of internships across the United States and abroad with tens of thousands of short-term positions available in 28 career areas.

ISBN 0768900441   softcover   647 pages
$24.95   1999

Internships: The Largest Source of Internships Available.
ISBN 0768900441   softcover   648 pages
$24.95   1998

The National Directory of Internships 1998-99 by Gita Gulati (editor).
ISBN 0536011230   softcover
$29.99   1999

National Directory of Arts Internships 1997/98 by Diane Robinson (editor).
ISBN 0945941080   softcover
$75.00   1998

New Jersey Internships by Melissa McKarel, Rebecca C. Smith, and Jeanne Graves.
ISBN 1883216125   softcover
$24.95   1997

The Yale Daily News Guide to Internships 1999 by Kaplan and the Yale Daily News. Insiders guide to internships that pay off.
ISBN 0684852543   softcover   480 pages
$25.00   1999

ENTREPRENEURSHIP

50 Great Businesses for Teens by Sarah L. Riehm. A practical guide shows teenagers how they can earn their own money by setting up businesses, including auto detailing, house sitting, party helper, and tutoring. Includes a step-by-step guide to getting started.
ISBN 0028613376   softcover   256 pages
$14.95   1997

50 Money Making Ideas for Kids by Larry Burkett, Lauree Burkett, Mark Herron and Marnie Wooding.
ISBN 0849940451   softcover   144 pages
$9.99   1997

77 No Talent No Experience and (Almost) No Cost Businesses You Can Start Today by Kelly Reno. Shows how anyone can start a successful business at home with the most basic of equipment and very little cost.
ISBN 0761502467   softcover
$12.95   1996

101 Best Home-Based Businesses for Women by Priscilla Y. Huff. While not written specifically for teenagers, this guide provides information about over a hundred home-based business. It includes information such as start-up costs, pricing guidelines, marketing and advertising tips, equipment needed, income potential, target customers and where to go for more information.
ISBN 1559587032   softcover   362 pages
$12.95   1995

101 Marvelous Money-Making Ideas for Kids by Heather Wood. Discover a way to use your talents to earn money and start your own business. Tips on advertising, marketing, budgeting, pricing, time commitment and purchasing materials.
ISBN 0812520602   softcover
$3.99   1995

An Income of Her Own (Game). Experience being an entrepreneur.
$38.00 + $8.00 S&H
Special ordering instructions: Write to Independent Means, P.O. Box 987, Santa Barbara, California 93102 or call 800/350-1816.

Better Than a Lemonade Stand: Small Business Ideas for Kids by Daryl Bernstein and Rob Husberg. Suggests a variety of small business ideas, including being a birthday party planner, dog walker, and photographer.
ISBN 0941831752   softcover   170 pages
$9.95   1992

Bizz Buzz Activity Card Set. Introduces principles, language, and key concepts of business.
$25.00 + $3.00 S&H
Special ordering instructions: Write to Independent Means, P.O. Box 987, Santa Barbara, California 93102 or call 800/350-1816.

Fast Cash for Kids by Bonnie and Noel Drew. Includes dozens of money-making activities for kids and includes a step-by-step business plan. 2nd edition.
ISBN 1564141543   softcover   256 pages
$13.99   1995

Hers: The Wise Woman's Guide to Starting a Business on $2,000 or Less by Carol Milano. This guide provides step-by-step information about starting and growing a money-making business with less than $2,000.
ISBN 096071172   softcover   207 pages
$12.95   1991

Homemade Business: A Woman's Step-By-Step Guide to Earning Money at Home by Donna Partow. Provides practical strategies for everything from setting up a home business to finding paying customers.

ISBN 1561790435   softcover   176 pages
$9.99   1992

How to Become a Teenage Entrepreneur A video and software package providing information about how to choose a business, how to get customers, and how to make more money.
$29.95 + $4.00 S&H
Special ordering information: Write to Entrepreneurial America, Inc., 22500 Orchard Lake Road, Farmington, Michigan 48336 or call 800/528-8525.

The Lemonade Stand: *A Guide to Encouraging the Entrepreneur in Your Child* by Emanuel Modu. A very thorough guide to entrepreneurship for youth. It provides detailed information about how to run a business as well as extensive information about the philosophy and psychology of entrepreneurship.
ISBN 1887646035   softcover   348 pages
$19.95   1996

No More Frogs to Kiss: *99 Ways to Give Economic Power to Girls* by Joline Godfrey.
$12.00 + $3.00 S&H
Special ordering instructions: Write to Independent Means, P.O. Box 987, Santa Barbara, California 93102 or call 800/350-1816.

Our Wildest Dreams: *Women Entrepreneurs Making Money, Having Fun, and Doing Good* by Joline Godfrey.
$13.00 + $3.00 S&H
Special ordering instructions: Write to Independent Means, P.O. Box 987, Santa Barbara, California 93102 or call 800/350-1816.

Product in a Box Activity Kit. Imagine and invent a new product and business.
$18.00 + $3.00 S&H
Special ordering instructions: Write to Independent Means, P.O. Box 987, Santa Barbara, California 93102 or call 800/350-1816.

A Teen's Guide to Business: *The Secrets to a Successful Enterprise* by Linda Menzies. Oren S. Kenkins, Rickell R. Fisher, Owen S. Jenkins. Offers advice on how to find the right job, create a better product or service, develop a business plan, and deal with money matters.
ISBN 0942361504   softcover
$7.95   1992

The Totally Awesome Business Book for Kids by Adrian G. Berg and Arthur Berg Bochner. This fun-filled guide includes all the information you need to know about starting up a business, how much money

you can make, and the steps to actually do the work — in a very easy-to-understand format.
ISBN 1557042268   softcover   159 pages
$10.95   1995

"Turned on Business"
A magazine edited by teen women. Each issue is full of hints on how to make money, have fun, and do well. Published six times annually.
Special ordering instructions: Write to Independent Means, P.O. Box 987, Santa Barbara, California 93102 or call 800/350-1816.

Working From Home: *Everything You Need to Know About Living and Working Under the Same Roof* by Sarah and Paul Edwards. The definitive guide on working from home. This manual provides advice on every aspect of home business management while focusing on maintaining sanity in your home life.
ISBN 087477764X   softcover   551 pages
$15.95   1994

The Young Entrepreneur's Guide to Starting and Running a Business by Steve Mariotti, Tony Towle, and Debra Desalvo. The founder of the National Foundation for Teaching Entrepreneurship describes how to start and run a business with tips on costs, investment, market research, negotiation and more.
ISBN 0812926277   softcover
$15.00   1996

VOLUNTEERISM

Alternatives to the Peace Corp: *A Directory of Third World and U.S. Volunteer Opportunities* by Filomena Geise.
ISBN 0935028757   softcover   100 pages
$9.95   1999

160 Ways to Help the World: *Community Service Projects for Young People* by Linda Leeb Duper.
ISBN 0816033242   hardcover   136 pages
$19.95   1997

Community Service for Teens: *Caring for Animals* by Bernard Ryan.
ISBN 0894342274   hardcover
$15.95   1998

Community Service for Teens: *Opportunities to Volunteer/ With Teacher's Guide.* by Bernard Ryan.
ISBN 0894342355   hardcover
$114.95   1998

"The Gazette"

A magazine focusing on volunteerism.
Special ordering instructions: Call 800/899-0089 or e-mail voa@voa.org.

Global Work: Volunteer Opportunities. A guide for finding volunteer work. Includes 68 organizations from 120 countries.
$10.00 + $4.00 s/h
Special ordering instructions: Write to Publications Department, InterAction, 1717 Massachusetts, NW, Suite 801, Washington, D.C. 20036, call 202/667-8227 or e-mail at publications@interaction.org.

Helping the Ill, the Poor, and the Elderly: Community Service for Teens by Bernard Ryan.
ISBN 0894342290   hardcover
$15.95   1998

How Can You Help? Creative Volunteer Projects for Kids Who Care by Linda Schwartz and Beverly Armstrong. The ideal resource for kids who want to make a difference through family activities, classroom projects, community service, or youth group programs.
ISBN 0881602132   softcover   160 pages
$9.95   1994

Increasing Neighborhood Service: Opportunities to Volunteer (Community Service for Teens) by Bernard Ryan.
ISBN 0894342339   hardcover
$15.95   1998

International Directory of Voluntary Work edited by Victoria Pybus. Over 600 organizations that need short- and long-term volunteers with varied skills.
ISBN 1854581643   softcover   272 pages
$15.95   1997

The Kid's Guide to Service Projects: Over 500 Service Ideas for Young People Who Want to make a Difference by Barbara A. Lewis and Pamela Espeland. Describes a variety of opportunities for youngsters to participate in successful community service.
ISBN 0915793822   softcover   184 pages
$10.95   1995

Participation in Government: Opportunities to Volunteer (Community Service for Teens) by Bernard Ryan.
ISBN 0894342304   hardcover
$15.95   1998

Promoting the Arts and Sciences: Opportunities to Volunteer (Community Service for Teens) by Bernard Ryan.
ISBN 0894342347   hardcover
$15.95   1998

Protecting the Environment: Opportunities to Volunteer (Community Service for Teens) by Bernard Ryan.
ISBN 0894342282   hardcover
$15.95   1998

"Spirit Magazine"
A magazine focusing on volunteerism.
Special ordering instructions: Call 800/899-0089 or e-mail voa@voa.org.

A Student's Guide to Volunteering by Theresa Foy Digeronimo.
ISBN 1564141705   softcover   192 pages
$10.99   1995

Volunteer Vacations: Short-Term Adventures That Will Benefit You and Others by Bill McMullon. This classic adventure travel guide profiles more than 250 charitable organizations and 2,000 projects worldwide that need volunteers. 6th edition.
ISBN 1556523149   softcover   480 pages
$16.95   1997

TRAVEL & ADVENTURES

The Back Door Guide to Short Term Job Adventures: Internships, Extraordinary Experiences, Seasonal Jobs, Volunteering, Work Abroad by Michael Landes. A guide designed to lead the reader to a lifetime of rich and adventurous work, learn and travel experiences. Thousands of opportunities await you.
ISBN 0898159547   softcover   486 pages
$19.95   1997

Free (And Almost Free) Adventures for Teenagers by Gail L. Grand. Descriptions of more than 200 summer and school-year educational enrichment programs available free or for under $200 for fourth through twelfth graders.
ISBN 0471113514   softcover   270 pages
$14.94   1995

The High School Student's Guide to Study Travel and Adventure Abroad by the Council on International Educational Exchange. More than 200 educational and travel programs for students ages 12-18. Includes work/volunteer opportunities, tours, language courses and more.
ISBN 0312118228   softcover   308 pages
$13.95   1995

Peterson's Study Abroad 1998: Over 1,600 Semester and Year Abroad Programs by Ellen Beal.
ISBN 1560798610   softcover   1008 pages
$29.95   1997

Summer Adventures by Curtis Casewit. Descriptions of hundreds of exciting and interesting learning, earning, and travel adventures. Includes information about how to apply, how much (if anything) you will be paid, the facilities available, and contact information.

ISBN 0020793316   softcover   306 pages
$13.00   1994

MONEY MANAGEMENT

Dr. Tightwad's Money Smart Kids by Janet Bodnar. Shows parents how to guide kids to be super savers, savvy shoppers, and cautious users of credit.

ISBN 081292889X   softcover   280 pages
$15.00   1997

The Kid's Guide to Money: Earning It, Saving It, Spending It, Growing It, Sharing It by Steve Olfinoski. Covers almost every area of finance management. Section on operating your own business. Interesting chapter on teen philanthropy.

ISBN 0590538535   softcover   128 pages
$4.95   1996

Money Doesn't Grow on Trees: A Parent's Guide to Raising Financially Responsible Children by Neale S. Godfrey and Carolina Edwards. For ages three to teenagers, this book teaches children how to earn, save, and spend wisely while helping parents communicate family values about money.

ISBN 0671798057   softcover   175 pages
$11.00   1994

A Penny Saved: Teaching Your Children the Values and Life Skills They Need to Live in the Real World by Neale S. Godfrey and Tad Richards. How to teach children money management: goal setting, budgeting, saving, and ethical behavior.

ISBN 0684824809   softcover
$12.00   1996

Raising Money-Smart Kids: How to Teach Your Children the Secrets of Earning, Saving, Investing and Spending Wisely by Ron Blue and Judy Blue.

ISBN 0840731957   softcover   203 pages
$10.99   1992

ONLINE RESOURCES

The Lemonade Stand Game

The object of the game is to see if you can make your business profitable. To test your skills see http://www.education.world.com.

Youth in Action Network

A free interactive online service for youth, educators, organization members and classrooms wanting to learn more about participating in social action and service projects. Write to Mighty Media, 400 1st Avenue, N, Suite 626, Minneapolis, Minnesota 55401; call 612/399-1969 or 800/644-4898; or see http://www.mightymedia.com/youth/.

WEBSITES

PART-TIME/SUMMER JOBS

http://search.acacamps.org/search.html - The American Camping Association website allows you to search and find camps that interest you. You may search by camp type, location, activities, special interests, affiliation, or fee category. You will then need to write or call to find out about job openings.

http://www.aifs.org/iaifscam.htm - The Camp America site places international students in camps in the U.S.

http://www.campchannel.com/campnet/docs/bboard.html - This site gives very basic information about camps and then refers you to their individual websites. It also features information about the *Ultimate Camp Counsellor Manual.*

http://www.campstaff.com - Register with their service and be linked to interested camps. You can search basic information on camps such as location, sleep/day, gender make-up, and camp specialty.

http://www.cooljobs.com/ - This website lists some very interesting jobs like working for the Cirque du Soleil, serving as a tour guide for the X Tour (for X-files buffs), MTV's model search, and participating as a Jeopardy contestant. They may not all be for teens, but they are very interesting and worth a look.

http://www.gospelcom.net/cci/ajobs/ - This site enables you to post your profile and be considered for jobs at CCI/USA camps and conferences.

http://www.kidscamps.com - This is a very helpful and easy to use site. There are good listings of U.S. camps and you can search by state, region or position .

http://www.outdoornetwork.com/JobNet/JobNet.html - This website lists interesting outdoor jobs that are available. Most are for college students, but it is worth a look.

http://www.potsdam.edu/CAREER/summer.html - This site will link you with several summer job websites including one from Peterson's Guide to Summer Jobs, camp listings, overseas jobs, and a parks and ski resort listing.

http://www.resortinternconnection.com/ - This site features jobs in the resort, travel, and tourism fields.

http://www.summerjobs.com - This website is very diverse and features many jobs at small businesses both U.S. and international. You may search by key word or location.

http://www.usajobs.opm.gov/a7.htm - This website is a listing of federal summer jobs and internships for students, age 16 and over.

http://www.usfca.edu/usf/career/summer.html - This site will link you with several other summer job sites including the Back Door Guide to Short-Term Adventures, camp listings, a maritime job website, and other summer job listings.

http://www.wm.edu/csrv/career/stualum/;short.html - This site features two camp listings, a summer job directory, and links you to the Cool Works site.

http://www. parks.yahoo.com/ - This website will link you with lots of camp listings.

http://www.youth.gc.ca/jobopps/summer-e.shtml - This site is actually for Canadian students, but their "international" listing includes many jobs for teens in the United States.

INTERNSHIPS

http://www.aaja.org – Asian American Journalists Association website. Internship and scholarship information available.

http://www.cie.uci.edu/internsh.html - A listing of internships overseas.

http://www.collegeboard.org/features/home/html/involved.html - Links to several internship sites.

http://www.fbla-pbl.org - The Future Business Leaders of America has a link to internship sites.

http://www.feminist.org/911/internship/internship.html - The Feminist Foundation Majority Internships Directory provides a listing of internships for young women.

http://rsinternships.com - Rising Star Internships site.

http://www.tripod.com/explore/jobs_career/ - The Lifelong-Learning Internships site.

http://www.vicon.net/~internnet - The Intern-Net site.

http://www.worldwide.edu/ - The World Wide Classroom has a directory of over 10,000 schools with international programs worldwide — some of these programs are internships.

VOLUNTEERISM

http://www.ala.org/teenhoopla/activism.html - Provides links to other websites regarding teen activism.

http://www.americaspromise.com/ - America's Promise website includes information, updates and tips for starting your own volunteer project and participating in this nationwide volunteer movement.

http://americorps.org – Americorps website.
http://www.amnesty.org/ - Amnesty International.

http://www.aspca.org - ASPCA.

http://www.bygpub.com - An free online book, *20 Ways for Teenagers to Help Other People by Volunteering.*

http://www.campronal.org/ - Camp Ronald McDonald.

http://www.cancer.org - American Cancer Society.

http://www.citykids.com - CityKids Foundation.

http://www.collegeboard.org/features/home/html/involved.html - Provides links to other websites providing teen volunteer opportunities.

http://www.conservationfund.org/conservation/ - The Conservation Fund.

http://www.earthsystems.org/ways/ - An online book, *54 Ways to Help the Homeless.*

http://www.4h-usa.org - National 4-H Council.

http://www.gospelcom.net/cci/ajobs/volunteer. shtml - This site provides information on volunteering at Christian camps and conferences.

http://www.greenpeace.org/ - Greenpeace.

http://www.habitat.org/ - Habitat for Humanity.

http://www.idealist.org - This is a great webside that matches volunteers with 14,000 nonprofit organizations around the world. You just choose the category, country, city, state, zip, age, skills, language, gender, and when you would like to volunteer. The search then provides you with a listing of agencies that match.

http://www.impactonline.org/ - This is a free service that matches volunteers to organizations. You enter your zip code, how far you are willing to drive, when you can start, and the category that you are interested in, and it will provide a listing of agencies.

http://www.interaction.org - This site provides information about a guide for finding volunteer work. It also provides a link to the Global Work site.

http://www.jsa.org - The Junior State of America.

http://www.mightymedia.com/youth/ - The Youth in Action Network is a free interactive online service for youth, educators, organization members, and clasrooms wanting to learn more about, and participate in, social action and service projects.

http://www.ncpc.org - Youth Crime Watch.

http://www.ngws.org/service/groups/aeowd.htm – Amazing Environmental Organization Web Directory. Includes links to sites in over 100 countries.

http://www.opendoor.com/hfh/ - Homes for the Homeless.

http://www.oprah.com/angelnet/angels6.html - Updates and information about taking part in Oprah's nationwide volunteer initiative - the Angel Network.

http://project.org/ - The Project America site lists organizations needing volunteers, provides information on how you can organize a volunteer project in your community, and provides resources for community service.

http://www.ran.org/ran/ - Rainforest Action Network.

http://www.redcross.org - American Red Cross.

http://www.rif.org - Reading is Fundamental.

http://www.specialolympics.org/ - Special Olympics International.

http://www.talkcity.com/theinsite/ - A website providing links to other websites featuring organizations that help the environment.

http://www.unitedway.org - United Way.

http://www.voa.org/pubs/ - The Volunteers of America website features a variety of information on volunteerism as well as information about their two magazines, *Spirit* and *The Gazette*.

http://www.volunteermatch.org – Search thousands of volunteer opportunities by zip, category, and date.

http://www.wilderness.org – Environmental website with lots of information for youth and ways to get involved.

http://www.ywam.org – Website of Youth with a Mission. Publish the *Go Manual* with international Christian mission opportunities.

ENTREPRENEURSHIP

http://www.anincomeofherown.com/ - The Independent Means Website is for women under twenty and provides information about starting a business, making, saving, and growing money, using money to make a better world, and networking with mentors. Includes an excellent resource directory and ability to order books, magazines, and games.

http://www.aspira.org – ASPIRA is dedicated to education and leadership development of Puerto Rican and Latino youth. Programs encourage youth entrepreneurship.

http://www.bedrock.com/tedi/tedi.htm - This site has been helping young entrepreneurs recognize their dreams since 1991.

http://www.blackenterprise.com – Entrepreneurial information for African-American youth.

http://www.entamerica.com - This is a website sponsored by Entrepreneurial America. It will provide you with information on how you can order *How to Become a Teenage Entrepreneur*, a video and software package.

http://www.EntreWorld.org – Extensive site providing resources for entrepreneurs.

http://www.fbla-pbl.org - The Future Business Leaders of America site.

http://www.girlsinc.org/ - Girls Incorporated is dedicated to "inspiring all girls to be strong, smart and bold."

http://www.ja.org/index.htma - Junior Achievement is the world's largest nonprofit economic education program.

http://www.servenet.org/ - Information about National Youth Service Day and the President's Student Service Awards. Also a volunteer matching program.

http://www.yeo.org - The Young Entrepreneurs' Organization website.

EDUCATIONAL PROGRAMS, TRAVEL AND ADVENTURE

http://www.aave.com - AAVE Teen Adventures provides summer wilderness travel for teens in Hawaii, Alaska and Europe.

http://www.afs.org - The AFS site allows students to search for student exchange programs in the country of their choice.

http://www.apadventures.com/ - Adventure Pursuits provides wilderness adventure programs for young adults in the Western U.S., Canada, and Alaska.

http://www.bctravel.net/adv-experts/calendar.htm - Kootenay Adventure Experts provides adventures for teens in British Columbia.

http://www.csum.edu - Provides information about the High School Foreign Exchange and Language Study Program.

http://www.fieldstudies.org/ - Environmental problem-solving summer programs for teens located around the world.

http://www.gmu.edu/departments/hemlock/summercamp/ta.htm - Teen Adventure is for teens, ages 14-17, and combines outdoor adventure with activities in conservation education in the Blue Ridge Mountains of Virginia.

http://www.gorp.com/arkansasriver - Arkansas River Tours provide whitewater adventures and teen whitewater camps.

http://www.gorp.com/broadreach/ - Broadreach provides summer adventure programs for teens in the Caribbean, Costa Rica, Ecuador, Amazon, Galapagos, Egypt, Red Sea, and Israel.

http://www.gorp.com/cobs/ - Colorado Outward Bound provides wilderness-based schools for teens in Colorado, Utah, Arizona, New Mexico, Alaska, Nepal, and Baja, California.

http://www.gorp.com/dragons/ - Dragons provides small-group teen travel to China, Thailand, Vietnam, India, Mongolia, the Himalayas, Nepal, Tibet and Pakistan.

http://www.gorp.com/gorp/trips/spi_YUT.htm - Provides links to other websites featuring teen adventures.

http://www.his.com/~council/howto2.html - The Council of American Ambassadors provides a link to websites for student exchanges.

http://www.inmex.com/inmex/programs.html - Listing of summer semester of full-year programs for teens.

http://www.natrails.com - North American Trails site includes information for students, ages 13-16.

http://www.sni.net/trips - Adventure Tour Directory.

http://www.yfu.org/ - The Youth for Understanding website allows students to search for student exchange programs worldwide.

CAMPS/ORGANIZATIONS

American Institute of Small Business
Publisher of materials on the subject of small business start-up and operation and entrepreneurship. Publications include: *Business Plan Example, How to Set Up Your Own Small Business,* and *How to Write a Business Plan.* Videos are also available. For more information, write to the American Institute of Small Business, 7515 Wayzata Boulevard, Suite 201, Minneapolis, Minnesota 55426-1604;(612)545-7001; e-mail max@aisbofmn.com; website at http://www.aisbofmn.com.

Association of Small Business Development
Small Business Development Centers are located

throughout the United States. The centers can provide you with information about starting a small business or helping an existing business grow. To find the center located near you, contact the Association of Small Business Development, 3108 Columbia Pike, Suite 300, Arlington, Virginia; (703)271-8700; e-mail info@asbdc-us.org; website http://www.asbdc.us.org.

Camp Advisory Service

Provides information on all types of summer camps. For information, write to Camp Advisory Service, National Camp Association, 610 Fifth Avenue, P.O. Box 5371, New York, NY 10185 or call 212/645-0653.

Camp Start-Up

Camp for teen women, ages 13-18. Work with teens from across the United States, meet successful women business owners, and return home feeling fit, confident, and filled with entrepreneurial ideas. For more information, contact Barbara Dowd at 508/463-0259 or AIOHO at 800/350-2978. Write to Independent Means, P.O. Box 987, Santa Barbara, California 93102; (800)350-1816; website http://www. anincomeofherown.com.

CCI/USA's Volunteer Service Corps

If you are interested in volunteering at Christian camps or conferences contact, CCI/USA's Volunteer Service Corps, Lay Christian Association, 2509 Poinsett Highway, Greenville, S.C. 29609; (864)242-5580; e-mail carolynric@aol.com.

Center on Education and Training for Employment

Provides a catalog which features a diverse array of resources to support and complement formal instruction. Focus is on the areas of workforce education and development. Interesting variety of "school to work" publications. For more information, write to the Center on Education and Training for Employment, College of Education, The Ohio State University, 1900 Kenny Road, Columbus, Ohio 43210-1090.

Creative Education Foundation

The mission of the foundation is to promote and develop creativity and innovation. Offers youth training programs in Creative Problem Solving. The foundation also publishes "The Creativity Catalog" which includes workbooks and exercises for teens. For more information, contact the Creative Education Foundation, 1050 Union Road #4, Buffalo, New York 14224; (716)675-3181; (800)447-2774; e-mail cefhq@cef-cpsi.org.

EDTEC (Education, Training and Enterprise Center)

The New Youth Entrepreneur is an experience-based curriculum for teaching youth about entrepreneurship. Their newest publication is Making Money the Old Fashioned Way: A Story of Black Entrepreneurship. For more information, write to EDTEC, 313 Market Street, Camden, New Jersey 08102; (609)342-8277; (800)963-9361; website http://www.edtecinc.com.

First Nations Development Institute

The Institute was founded to help Indian tribes build sound, sustainable reservation economies. Publisher of "Business Alert" newsletter. For more information, write to the First Nations Development Institute, The Store Building, 11917 Main Street, Fredericksburg, Virginia 22408; (540)371-5615.

Hugh O'Brian Youth Leadership (HOBY)

Each Spring, HOBY conducts (90) Leadership Training Workshops for 10th graders chosen to represent their schools and communities in each of the fifty states, Canada, and Mexico. A select group of students is selected to attend the World Leadership Congress. In addition, HOBY offers a number of other interactive programs to bridge the gap between the leaders of today and tomorrow. For information, write to Hugh O'Brian Youth Leadership, 10880 Wilshire Boulevard, Suite 410, Los Angeles, California 90024; (310)474-4370; website http://www.hoby.org.

Independent Means

Organization offering programs that prepare participants to deliver a variety of entrepreneurial and economic literacy programs for teen women. The organization also offers materials related to mentoring. IM is the sponsor of the National Business Plan Competition. The website features an entrepreneurial game, a question and answer forum, web pages designed by teens, information about Camp $tart-Up, and an online boutique. IM also offers a selection of books, games, and other resources. For information, write to Independent Means, 126 Powers Avenue, Santa Barbara, California 93103; (805)965-0475; (800)350-1816; website http://www.anincomeofherown.com.

Kauffman Center for Entrepreneurial Leadership

Part of the mission of the center is to introduce young people to the excitement and opportunity of entrepreneurship. The center sponsors **EntrePrep**, a unique institute for high school juniors, designed to provide students with the fundamental skills to start a business and become an entrepreneur. The center sponsors **MADE-IT**, a program for seventh-grade girls and their mothers, which provides each mother/daughter team with the knowledge and skills to develop a business feasibility plan and launch a business. **YESS!/Mini-Society** curriculum, for children, ages 8-12, is designed to teach entrepreneurship in ways children understand. The **Entrepreneur Invention Society** is a program in which participants invent products and develop viable businesses based on their inventions. The Kauffman Center is a developer in cooperation with the Center for Entrepreneurial Leadership and EDTEC of the **New Youth Entrepreneur** curriculum. For more information about any of these programs, write to the Kauffman Center for Entrepreneurial Leadership, Ewing Marion Kauffman Foundation, 4900 Oak Street, Kansas City, Missouri 64112-2776; (816)932-1000; websites http://www.entreworld.org or http://www.emkf.org.

MIDAS TOUCH Program

This volunteer program was developed for students from lower economic backgrounds. Rather than focus on theoretical classroom businesses, MIDAS helps students become actual entrepreneurs. For more information, contact Volunteers of America, 3600 Wilshire Boulevard, Suite 1500, Los Angeles, California 90010-2619; (213)389-1500.

M&M Associates

This organization has developed a complete library of books that are helpful to inventors and entrepreneurs, the Inventors & Entrepreneurs Bookshop. They market a teaching game for inventing, a manual for teachers designed to teach and encourage inventing, and a manual about creating your own Invention Convention. For more information, write to M&M Associates, P.O. Box 1020, Fort Jones, California 96032; (916)468-2282; (800)339-3127.

National Center for American Indian Development

The Center's mission is to develop and expand an American Indian private sector by establishing business relationships between Indian enterprises and private industry. For more information, write to the National Center for American Indian Enterprise Development, 953 East Juanita Avenue, Mesa, Arizona 85204; (800)462-2433.

National Center for Financial Education

Publish the *Money-Book Store Catalog* which features a large selection of books, games, and videos for students from preschool through college. For more information, write to the Naitonal Center for Financial Education, P.O. Box 34070, San Diego, California 92163-4070; website http://www.ncfe.org.

National Education Center for Women in Business

The center's mission is to enable the economic self-sufficiency of women through advocacy and educational initiatives in entrepreneurship. **Camp Entrepreneur** is a week-long youth entrepreneurship program for women, ages 12-17. For more information,

contact Seton Hall College's National Education Center for Women in Business, Seton Hill Drive, Greensburg, Pennsylvania 15601; (724)830-4625; (800)NECWB-4-U; e-mail info@necwb.setonhill.edu; website http://www.necwb.setonhill.edu.

The National Mentoring Partnership

This organization is dedicated exclusively to making all kinds of mentoring work for all kinds of kids. Information is available about becoming a mentor or finding a mentor. For more information, write to the National Mentoring Partnership, 2801 M Street, NW, Washington, DC 20007; (202)338-3844.

National Schools Committee for Economic Education, Inc.

This organization provides a catalog of supplementary resources for teaching children simplified economics. For more information, write to National Schools Committee for Economic Education, Inc., 86 Valley Road, P.O. Box 285, Cos Cob, Connecticut 06807-0295.

North Carolina REAL Enterprises

The program uses trained instructors to teach entrepreneurship and small management courses to high school and post-secondary students with help from local REAL "Community Support Teams" composed of entrepreneurs and small business assistance providers. Students assess their interests and abilities, analyze the local community, and research and write a business plan for an enterprise they may open and operate. For more information, write to REAL Enterprises, Inc., 115 Market Street, Suite 320, Durham, North Carolina 27701-3221; (919)688-7325; e-mail ricklarson@mindspring.com.

Project XL

The U.S. Patent and Trademark Office sponsors an education outreach program, Project XL. The program's goal is to add a "T" for thinking to the traditional three "R's." Student inventions and creative works are encouraged. It is recommended for students at all grade levels, educators, and parents. A video about the program is available. For more information, write to the U.S. Department of Commerce, Patent and Trademark Office, Washington, DC 20231; website http://www.uspto.gov/.

Securities Industry Foundation for Economic Education

Creator of **The Stock Market Game** available at the Foundation's website. The Foundation also offers a *Learning from the Market* curriculum guide and *Virtual Economics 2.0*. For more information, contact the Securities Industry Foundation for Economic Education, 120 Broadway, 35th Floor, New York, New

York 10271; (212)618-0519; website http://www.
smg2000.org.

Trickle-Up Program, Inc.
Trickle-Up is a program designed to help economically disadvantaged young women, young people, and
those displaced by war or natural disaster to start their
own business. The organization provides technical
assistance as well as seed capital. In the past nineteen
years, over 66,000 businesses have been started. For
more information, contact the Trickle-Up Program,
121 West 27th Street, Suite 504, New York, New
York 10001; (212)362-7958; e-mail trickleup@vita.
org; website http://www.vita.org/trickle/trickle.html.

Young Entrepreneurs' Organization
For more information, write to 1321 Duke Street,
Suite 300, Alexandria, Virginia   22314 or call
703/519-6700.

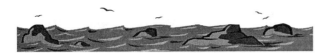

LOCATION INDEX

MIDWEST STATES

Illinois, Indiana, Iowa, Kansas, Michigan, Minnesota, Missouri, Nebraska, Ohio, Wisconsin

NORTH ATLANTIC STATES
Connecticut, Maine, Massachusetts, New Hampshire, New Jersey, New York, Rhode Island, Vermont

PACIFIC NORTHWEST STATES
Idaho, Oregon, Washington, Alaska

ROCKY MOUNTAIN STATES
Colorado, Montana, North Dakota, South Dakota, Utah, Wyoming

SOUTHEASTERN STATES
Alabama, Florida, Georgia, Kentucky, Mississippi, North Carolina, South Carolina, Tennessee, Puerto Rico, Virgin Islands

SOUTHWEST STATES

Arkansas, Louisiana, New Mexico, Oklahoma, Texas

WESTERN STATES
Arizona, California, Nevada, Hawaii

CANADA

CENTRAL AMERICA

SOUTH AMERICA

EUROPE

AFRICA

ASIA

AUSTRALIA

ANTARCTICA

NOTES

AREA OF INTEREST INDEX

BUSINESS/TECHNOLOGY

COMMUNICATIONS

FOREIGN LANGUAGE

HEALTH

HOSPITALITY

HOME/GARDEN

HUMAN SERVICES/EDUCATION

INTERNATIONAL

NATURE/ENVIRONMENT/ RECREATION

PUBLIC AFFAIRS

REFERRAL/PLACEMENT AGENCIES

Science/Math/Research

Tours

COST/COMPENSATION INDEX

PAID

UNPAID

COST OF $0-$249

COST OF $250-$999

NOTES

ALPHABETICAL INDEX

H

I

J

K

L

M

N

O

P

T

U

Z

LET US HEAR FROM YOU

Please write to us with your comments or suggestions for our next edition. Just complete this form (attach additional sheets if necessary) and return to the address below.

Name:_____

Address: _____

Phone: (   ) _____

Comments/Suggestions: _____

_____

_____

_____

Are you a: ☐ student   ☐ parent   ☐ guidance counselor
               ☐ teacher   ☐ librarian   ☐ youth worker   ☐ other

Have you (or has a teen you know) used this book for career exploration? ☐ yes   ☐ no

How would you rate this guide?

☐ excellent   ☐ good   ☐ average   ☐ fair   ☐ poor

Tell us about your career exploration experiences: _____

_____

_____

_____

_____

_____

Return to: **JRC Consulting**
                  PMB-428
                  6671 West Indiantown Road
                  Jupiter, Florida 33458
                  561/748-9430 (fax)
                  e-mail: jrcbook@aol.com

LET US HEAR FROM YOU

Please write to us with your comments or suggestions for our next edition. Just complete this form (attach additional sheets if necessary) and return to the address below.

Name:_____

Address: _____

Phone: (   ) _____

Comments/Suggestions: _____

_____

_____

_____

Are you a: □ student   □ parent   □ guidance counselor
                □ teacher   □ librarian   □ youth worker   □ other

Have you (or has a teen you know) used this book for career exploration? □ yes   □ no

How would you rate this guide?

□ excellent   □ good   □ average   □ fair   □ poor

Tell us about your career exploration experiences: _____

_____

_____

_____

_____

_____

Return to: **JRC Consulting**
                  PMB-428
                  6671 West Indiantown Road
                  Jupiter, Florida 33458
                  561/748-9430 (fax)
                  e-mail: jrcbook@aol.com

ORDER FORM

Postal orders: JRC Consulting, PMB-428, 6671 West Indiantown Road, Jupiter, FL 33458, USA

Fax orders: (561) 748-9430 (*purchase orders only, please)

For more information, or to request a catalog, e-mail: jrcbook@aol.com

Please send the following:

QTY	Title:	Price	Total
____	**Testing the Waters:** *A Teen's Guide to Career Exploration*	24.95	____

Shipping & Handling:
(Add $3 for first item +$1 for each additional item up to $15 maximum.
***No charge on pre-paid orders)*   ____

Sales Tax
(For orders shipped to Florida address, add applicable county sales tax)   ____

Total   ____

UNCONDITIONAL GUARANTEE

You may return any books for a full refund — for any reason, no questions asked.

Company Name: _____

Name: _____

Address: _____

City _____ State:_____ Zip: _____

Telephone (   ) _____

Sales tax:
Please add appropriate sales tax for books shipped to Florida addresses.

Shipping:
$3.00 for the first book and $1.00 for each additional book. Shipping on pre-paid orders is FREE!

Payment:
☐ Check
☐ Money Order
☐ Purchase Order

Order your copy today!

ORDER FORM

📧 Postal orders: JRC Consulting, PMB-428, 6671 West Indiantown Road, Jupiter, FL 33458, USA

📠 Fax orders: (561) 748-9430 (*purchase orders only, please)

🖥 For more information, or to request a catalog, e-mail: jrcbook@aol.com

Please send the following:

QTY	Title:	Price	Total
_____	**Testing the Waters:** *A Teen's Guide to Career Exploration*	24.95	_____

Shipping & Handling: _____
(Add $3 for first item +$1 for each additional item up to $15 maximum.
****No charge on pre-paid orders)*

Sales Tax   _____
(For orders shipped to Florida address, add applicable county sales tax)

Total   _____

UNCONDITIONAL GUARANTEE

You may return any books for a full refund — for any reason, no questions asked.

Company Name: _____

Name: _____

Address: _____

City _____ State: _____ Zip: _____

Telephone (   ) _____

Sales tax:
Please add appropriate sales tax for books shipped to Florida addresses.

Shipping:
$3.00 for the first book and $1.00 for each additional book. Shipping on pre-paid orders is FREE!

Payment:
❏ Check
❏ Money Order
❏ Purchase Order

Order your copy today!

ORDER FORM

Postal orders: JRC Consulting, PMB-428, 6671 West Indiantown Road, Jupiter, FL 33458, USA

Fax orders: (561) 748-9430 (*purchase orders only, please)

For more information, or to request a catalog, e-mail: jrcbook@aol.com

Please send the following:

QTY	Title:	Price	Total
____	**Testing the Waters:** *A Teen's Guide to Career Exploration*	24.95	____

Shipping & Handling: ____
(Add $3 for first item +$1 for each additional item up to $15 maximum.
***No charge on pre-paid orders)*

Sales Tax ____
(For orders shipped to Florida address, add applicable county sales tax)

Total ____

UNCONDITIONAL GUARANTEE

You may return any books for a full refund — for any reason, no questions asked.

Company Name: _____

Name: _____

Address: _____

City _____ State:_____ Zip: _____

Telephone (   ) _____

Sales tax:
Please add appropriate sales tax for books shipped to Florida addresses.

Shipping:
$3.00 for the first book and $1.00 for each additional book. Shipping on pre-paid orders is FREE!

Payment:
❏ Check
❏ Money Order
❏ Purchase Order

Order your copy today!

ORDER FORM

📝 Postal orders: JRC Consulting, PMB-428, 6671 West Indiantown Road, Jupiter, FL 33458, USA

📠 Fax orders: (561) 748-9430 (*purchase orders only, please)

💻 For more information, or to request a catalog, e-mail: jrcbook@aol.com

Please send the following:

QTY	Title:	Price	Total
____	**Testing the Waters:** *A Teen's Guide to Career Exploration*	24.95	____

Shipping & Handling: ____
*(Add $3 for first item +$1 for each additional item up to $15 maximum. ***No charge on pre-paid orders)*

Sales Tax ____
(For orders shipped to Florida address, add applicable county sales tax)

Total ____

UNCONDITIONAL GUARANTEE

You may return any books for a full refund — for any reason, no questions asked.

Company Name: _____

Name: _____

Address: _____

City _____ State:_____ Zip: _____

Telephone ( ) _____

Sales tax:
Please add appropriate sales tax for books shipped to Florida addresses.

Shipping:
$3.00 for the first book and $1.00 for each additional book. Shipping on pre-paid orders is FREE!

Payment:
❑ Check
❑ Money Order
❑ Purchase Order

Order your copy today!